Massimo Pallottino

The Etruscans

Revised and Enlarged

Translated by J. Cremona

Edited by David Ridgway

ALLEN LANE

Etruscologia first published by Ulrico Hoepli, Milan, 1942

First English edition published as *The Etruscans* by Penguin Books, 1955
This revised and enlarged hardcover edition, based on the sixth
Italian edition (1968, 1973), published 1974

Allen Lane
A Division of Penguin Books Ltd
17 Grosvenor Gardens, London SW1W 0BD
ISBN 0 7139 0218 3

Printed by Richard Clay (The Chaucer Press) Ltd,
Bungay, Suffolk

Contents

List of Plates 9

List of Figures in the Text 16

Foreword to the sixth Italian edition (1968) 17

Editor's Preface to the second English edition (1974) 19

A Short History of Etruscan Studies 23

Part 1
The Etruscans and their Place in the History of Italy and the Mediterranean

1. Italy at the Dawn of History 37
   Modern theories 37
   Later prehistory and the cultures of the Italian Iron Age 41
   The languages of primitive Italy 49
   The formation of historical peoples 57

2. The Problem of Etruscan Origins 64
   The present state of the question 64
   The theory of eastern provenance 69
   The theories of northern provenance and of
      autochthony 75
   Towards a solution of the problem 78

3. The Etruscans and the Sea 82
   The Etruscan 'thalassocracy' 82
   The causes and development of Etruscan naval supremacy 83
   Naval clashes between Greeks and Etruscans 89

4. The Etruscans and Italy 91
   The territorial extension of Etruria 91
   The Etruscan domination of southern and northern
      Italy 94
   The spread of Etruscan culture in Italy 99

5

Part 2
Aspects of the Civilization of Etruria

5. Cities and Cemeteries of Etruria   105
   The resurrection of Etruria   105
   Cities of southern Etruria   107
   Cities of central and northern Etruria   116
   Cities of Campania and the Po valley   121

6. The Political and Social Organization of Etruria   124
   Etruscan public institutions   124
   Etruria and its 'peoples'   125
   The primitive monarchy   128
   The republican states   131
   Etruscan society   134

7. The Etruscan Religion   138
   Problems and documents   138
   The Etruscan conception of the divine   140
   Life after death   147
   Forms of worship   150

8. Literature and the Arts   153
   Literature   153
   Music and dancing   155
   Architectural monuments   157
   Figured works of art   162
   The problem of Etruscan art   166

9. Life and Customs   172
   Monuments as a source of information   172
   The setting: the Etruscan town and house   173
   Aspects of Etruscan life   178
   Economic and technical achievements   180
   Weapons and dress   182

Part 3
The Etruscan Language

10. The Problem of Etruscan   189
    The interpretation of Etruscan   189
    Developments in research   192

11. The Sources and the Method   197
    Present means and future prospects   197

Direct and indirect sources   198
Methods of research   204
Variations in time and space   207

12. The Results   209
The alphabet   209
Phonetics   212
Grammar   213
Interpretation of the texts   217
The vocabulary   225

Supplementary Note to the 1973 reprint
   of the sixth Italian edition   235

Notes on the Text   239

Notes on the Plates   273

Notes on Further Reading   294

Indexes
1. Historical and geographical subjects   301
2. Ancient authors   310
3. Modern authors   311

List of Plates

1. A tomb at Tarquinia in the eighteenth century (from Byres, *Hypogaei*)

2. Villanovan trench-graves (*tombe a fossa*) at Veii. (Photo: British School at Rome)

3. Villanovan biconical ossuary from Veii. (Photo: British School at Rome)

4. Villanovan bronzes from Vulci. (Rome: Museo Nazionale di Villa Giulia; photo: Soprintendenza alle Antichità dell'Etruria Meridionale)

5. Villanovan animal-bird askos from Bologna. (Bologna: Museo Civico; photo: Soprintendenza alle Antichità dell'Emilia e Romagna)

6. Cypro-Phoenician gilded silver bowl from Palestrina. (Rome: Museo Nazionale di Villa Giulia; photo: Soprintendenza alle Antichità dell'Etruria Meridionale)

7. Gold pectoral from the Regolini-Galassi tomb at Cerveteri. (Vatican: Museo Etrusco Gregoriano; museum photo)

8. Silver-plated bronze urn from Vetulonia. (Florence: Museo Archeologico; photo: Soprintendenza alle Antichità dell'Etruria)

9. Inscribed funerary stele from Kaminia, Lemnos. (Athens: National Museum; photo: Rome University, Istituto di Etruscologia e Antichità Italiche)

10. Naval battle on a sixth-century Etruscan vase from Cerveteri. (Paris: Musée du Louvre; museum photo)

11. Cippus with late-sixth-century Greek inscription from Gravisca. (Photo: Soprintendenza alle Antichità dell'Etruria Meridionale)

9

12–14. *Three inscribed gold tablets from the Etruscan sanctuary at Pyrgi*
12. The longer Etruscan inscription.
13. The Punic inscription.
14. The shorter Etruscan inscription. (Rome: Museo Nazionale di Villa Giulia; photos: Soprintendenza alle Antichità dell'Etruria Meridionale)

15. *Elogium* of Imperial date from Tarquinia. (Tarquinia: Museo Nazionale; photo: Soprintendenza alle Antichità dell'Etruria Meridionale)

16. Etruscan bronze helmet with Greek inscription from Olympia. (London: British Museum; museum photo)

17–19. *Inscriptions on pottery from Rome*
17. Bucchero plate with Etruscan inscription, from the Capitol.
18. Impasto sherd with Etruscan inscription, from Sant'Omobono.
19. Bucchero sherd with Latin inscription, from Sant' Omobono. (Rome: Musei Capitolini; museum photos)

20. Battle scene in the François Tomb at Vulci. (Rome: Torlonia collection; photo: Rome University, Istituto di Etruscologia e Antichità Italiche)

21. Funerary stele from Bologna. (Bologna: Museo Civico; photo: Soprintendenza alle Antichità dell'Emilia e Romagna)

22. The 'Hypogeum of the Volumni' at Perugia. (Photo: Anderson-Mansell Collection)

23. Pottery from a tomb-group at San Martino in Gattara (prov. Ravenna). (Bologna: Museo Civico; photo: Soprintendenza alle Antichità dell'Emilia e Romagna)

24–7. *'Aerial photographs' of relief-models of Etruscan cities*
24. Veii.
25. Cerveteri.
26. Tarquinia.
27. Vulci. (Rome University: Museo di Etruscologia; photos: Rome University, Istituto di Etruscologia e Antichità Italiche)

28. Veii: the Vignacce valley. (Photo: British School at Rome)

29. Norchia: typical architectural façades. (Photo: Soprintendenza alle Antichità dell'Etruria Meridionale)

30. Inscribed funerary stele of Avle Feluske from Vetulonia. (Florence: Museo Archeologico)

31. Iron *fasces* from Vetulonia. (Florence: Museo Archeologico; photo: Soprintendenza alle Antichità dell'Etruria)

32. Three Etruscan 'peoples' personified in an Imperial marble relief. (Rome: Museo Lateranense; photo: Musei e Gallerie Pontificie)

33. Lady with a pomegranate: bronze statuette. (Harvard University: Fogg Art Museum; museum photo)

34. Divinities and mythological characters on a mirror from Vulci. (Paris: Bibliothèque Nationale; photo: Rome University, Istituto di Etruscologia e Antichità Italiche)

35. A war-god, probably Maris: bronze statuette. (Florence: Museo Archeologico; photo: Soprintendenza alle Antichità dell'Etruria)

36. Uni suckling Hercle on a mirror from Volterra. (Florence: Museo Archeologico)

37. A lesson in divination on a mirror from Tuscania. (Florence: Museo Archeologico)

38. Bronze model of a sheep's liver, from Gossolengo near Piacenza. (Piacenza: Museo Civico; photo: Soprintendenza alle Antichità dell'Emilia e Romagna)

39. Augur (*haruspex*): bronze statuette. (Vatican: Museo Etrusco Gregoriano; photo: Musei e Gallerie Pontificie)

40. 'Canopic' urn from Chiusi. (Arezzo: Museo Archeologico; photo: Alinari)

41. Hermes with soul on a bronze candelabrum from Spina. (Ferrara: Museo Archeologico; photo: Soprintendenza alle Antichità dell'Emilia e Romagna)

42. Archaic gravestone from Chiusi. (Munich: Museum antiker Kleinkunst; photo: Rome University, Istituto di Etruscologia e Antichità Italiche)

43. Lid of a terracotta urn of the Hellenistic period. (Volterra: Museo Guarnacci; photo: Soprintendenza alle Antichità dell'Etruria)

44. Tuchulcha: detail from the Tomba dell'Orco at Tarquinia. (Photo: Soprintendenza alle Antichità dell'Etruria Meridionale)

45. Terracotta daemon's mask from Orvieto. (Orvieto: Museo Faina; photo: Rome University, Istituto di Etruscologia e Antichità Italiche)

46. Painted frieze from the Tomba Cardarelli at Tarquinia. (Photo: Soprintendenza alle Antichità dell'Etruria Meridionale)

47. A stretch of the extant city walls at Volterra. (Photo: Rome University, Istituto di Etruscologia e Antichità Italiche)

48. The Banditaccia cemetery at Cerveteri. (Photo: David Ridgway)

49. Funerary *aedicula* at Populonia. (Photo: Soprintendenza alle Antichità dell'Etruria)

50. The Montagnola tholos tomb at Quinto Fiorentino. (Photo: Soprintendenza alle Antichità dell'Etruria)

51. Ground-plan of the sanctuary at Pyrgi. (Drawing: Soprintendenza alle Antichità dell'Etruria Meridionale)

52. Etrusco-Italic temples. (From M. Pallottino, *Civiltà artistica etrusco-italica*, 1971, p. 75)

53. Decorative details of Etruscan architecture. (From M. Pallottino, *Civiltà artistica etrusco-italica*, 1971, p. 77)

54. Terracotta temple model from Vulci. (Rome: Museo Nazionale di Villa Giulia; photo: Soprintendenza alle Antichità dell'Etruria Meridionale)

55. Castel d'Asso: typical architectural façades. (Photo: Soprintendenza alle Antichità dell'Etruria Meridionale)

56. Terracotta cinerary urn from Chiusi. (Philadelphia: University Museum; museum photo)

57. Stone lion from Ischia di Castro, near Vulci. (Ischia di Castro: Antiquarium Comunale; photo: Soprintendenza alle Antichità dell'Etruria Meridionale)

58. Figured stone slab from Tarquinia. (Tarquinia: Museo Nazionale; photo: Soprintendenza alle Antichità dell'Etruria Meridionale)

59. A Campana slab from Cerveteri. (Paris: Musée du Louvre; museum photo)

60. Painted frieze in the Tomba del Barone at Tarquinia. (Photo: Alinari-Mansell Collection)

61. The Apollo of Veii. (Rome: Museo Nazionale di Villa Giulia; photo: Soprintendenza alle Antichità dell'Etruria Meridionale)

62. Archaic terracotta head of a warrior from Veii. (Rome: Museo Nazionale di Villa Giulia; photo: Soprintendenza alle Antichità dell'Etruria Meridionale)

63. High-relief from the back pediment of Temple A at Pyrgi. (Rome: Museo Nazionale di Villa Giulia; photo: Soprintendenza alle Antichità dell'Etruria Meridionale)

64. Silenus-head antefix from Pyrgi. (Rome: Museo Nazionale di Villa Giulia; photo: Soprintendenza alle Antichità dell'Etruria Meridionale)

65. Lid of a sarcophagus from Chianciano. (Florence: Museo Archeologico; photo: Alinari)

66. The 'Chimaera of Arezzo'. (Florence: Museo Archeologico; photo: Alinari-Mansell Collection)

67. Terracotta votive male head from Veii. (Rome: Museo Nazionale di Villa Giulia; photo: Soprintendenza alle Antichità dell'Etruria Meridionale)

68–71. *Figured terracotta decoration from temples of the Classical and Hellenistic periods*

68. Pair of winged horses from the 'Ara della Regina' temple at Tarquinia. (Tarquinia: Museo Nazionale; photo: Anderson-Mansell Collection)
69. Female head from Temple A at Pyrgi. (Rome: Museo Nazionale di Villa Giulia; photo: Soprintendenza alle Antichità dell'Etruria Meridionale)
70. Head of a youth from the Lo Scasato temple at Falerii. (Rome: Museo Nazionale di Villa Giulia; photo: Soprintendenza alle Antichità dell'Etruria Meridionale)
71. Head of a man from the Belvedere temple at Orvieto. (Orvieto: Museo dell'Opera del Duomo; photo: Rome University, Istituto di Etruscologia e Antichità Italiche)

72. Bronze statuette of a youthful Hercules from Poggio Castiglione. (Florence: Museo Archeologico; photo: Soprintendenza alle Antichità dell'Etruria)

73. Terracotta urn from Vignagrande near Chiusi. (Worcester, Mass.: Art Museum; museum photo)

13

74. Detail of a large bronze krater from Tuscania. (Rome: Museo Nazionale di Villa Giulia; photo: Soprintendenza alle Antichità dell'Etruria Meridionale)

75. The 'Capitoline Brutus'. (Rome: Musei Capitolini; museum photo)

76. The 'Orator': portrait of Avle Meteli. (Florence: Museo Archeologico; photo: Alinari)

77. Terracotta male portrait-head from Tarquinia. (Tarquinia: Museo Nazionale; photo: Soprintendenza alle Antichità dell'Etruria Meridionale)

78. Late Villanovan sheet-bronze hut-urn from Vulci. (Rome: Museo Nazionale di Villa Giulia; photo: Soprintendenza alle Antichità dell'Etruria Meridionale)

79. Hellenistic urn from the territory of Chiusi. (Florence: Museo Archeologico; photo: Soprintendenza alle Antichità dell'Etruria)

80. The Tomba dell'Alcova at Cerveteri. (Photo: Rome University, Istituto di Etruscologia e Antichità Italiche)

81. The Tomba degli Scudi e delle Sedie at Cerveteri. (Photo: Soprintendenza alle Antichità dell'Etruria Meridionale)

82. Detail of the Tomba dei Rilievi at Cerveteri. (Photo: Soprintendenza alle Antichità dell'Etruria Meridionale)

83. Detail of the Tomba dei Caronti at Tarquinia. (Photo: Soprintendenza alle Antichità dell'Etruria Meridionale)

84. Bronze lamp from Cortona. (Cortona: Museo dell'Accademia Etrusca; photo: Alinari)

85. The 'Situla della Pania', from the area of Chiusi. (Florence: Museo Archeologico; photo: Soprintendenza alle Antichità dell'Etruria)

86. Etrusco-Corinthian wine amphora by the 'Bearded Sphinx Painter', from Vulci. (Rome: Museo Nazionale di Villa Giulia; photo: Soprintendenza alle Antichità dell'Etruria Meridionale)

87. Group of bucchero vases from Trevignano Romano. (Rome: Museo Nazionale di Villa Giulia; photo: Soprintendenza alle Antichità dell'Etruria Meridionale)

88. Bronze vase-stand, with vases, from the Vetulonia area. (Florence: Museo Archeologico; photo: Soprintendenza alle Antichità dell'Etruria)

89. Archaic limestone urn from Chiusi. (Chiusi: Museo Civico; photo: Soprintendenza alle Antichità dell'Etruria)

90. Detail of the Tomba degli Auguri at Tarquinia. (Photo: Soprintendenza alle Antichità dell'Etruria Meridionale)

91. Etruscan silver coins from Populonia. (Florence: Museo Archeologico; photo: Soprintendenza alle Antichità dell'Etruria)

92. Bronze situla from the Certosa cemetery at Bologna. (Bologna: Museo Civico; museum photo)

93. Ivory writing tablet from Marsiliana d'Albegna. (Florence: Museo Archeologico: photo: Soprintendenza alle Antichità dell'Etruria)

94. The 'Formello Alphabet' from Veii. (Rome: Museo Nazionale di Villa Giulia; photo: Soprintendenza alle Antichità dell'Etruria Meridionale)

95. Pair of ivory dice from Tuscania. (Paris: Cabinet des Médailles, Bibliothèque Nationale; museum photo, by courtesy of BBC *Chronicle*)

96. The Zagreb mummy. (Zagreb: National Museum; photo: from *Corpus Inscriptionum Etruscarum, Suppl.* I, Plate V)

97. The Capua tile. (Photo: Rome University, Istituto di Etruscologia e Antichità Italiche)

98. The Perugia cippus. (Perugia: Museo Archeologico; photo: Alinari-Mansell Collection)

99. Inscribed Attic red-figure kylix from Tarquinia. (Tarquinia: Museo Nazionale; photo: Soprintendenza alle Antichità dell'Etruria Meridionale)

100. Bilingual (Etruscan-Latin) inscription from Pesaro. (Pesaro: Museo Olivieriano; from R. A. Staccioli, *La lingua degli etruschi*, 1967, Plate 11)

101. Inscription from Santa Marinella. (Rome: Museo Nazionale di Villa Giulia; photo: Soprintendenza alle Antichità dell'Etruria Meridionale)

102. Painted funerary inscriptions in the Tomba degli Anina, Tarquinia. (Photo: Soprintendenza alle Antichità dell'Etruria Meridionale)

List of Figures in the Text

1. Italian cultures of the Iron Age 46

2. The languages of ancient Italy 55

3. The Etruscan expansion over land and sea 88

4. The principal cities of Etruria proper 108

5. The division of the sky according to the Etruscan discipline 145

6. Etruscan alphabets 211

16

Foreword

to the sixth Italian edition (1968)

Twenty-five years have elapsed since the first edition of this book was published. During this period, the progress of studies, ideas and discoveries has led to a very thorough, often revolutionary, reassessment in our knowledge of the civilization of ancient Etruria. Such deep and widespread changes could not but be reflected in the greatly revised and enlarged treatment of the evidence and problems discussed in this book. Yet both the expository criteria and the division of the material into chapters and parts have remained essentially faithful to the original plan.

This may perhaps confirm the validity of the formula on which the book was originally planned. Its aim is to try to satisfy the curiosity of the educated reader who has neither the time nor the means for tracing in the specialist literature the arduous, often highly technical reconstructive processes of science, but who, at the same time, refuses to be satisfied with unsupported statements, axiomatic judgements or simplified surveys. Such a reader rightly expects to be taken to the centre of debate, the heated terrain of scientific controversy, with the help of a guide to direct and inform him. The aim was, therefore, not only to provide an orderly exposition of theories that had already been established, but also and especially to present the critical positions of leading scholars, to bring out the main difficulties and uncertainties, and to point out the directions likely to be taken by research in progress.

These same reasons have given this book the special character which differentiates it from the few good syntheses on the civilization of Etruria that have preceded it (beginning with K. O. Müller and W. Deecke's classic *Die Etrusker*, 1877), as also from the many recent books on the subject published in Italy and elsewhere, the result of the strong reawakening of interest in Etruria and the Etruscans that followed the exhibition of Etruscan art and civilization given in several European cities in 1955 and 1956 – to say nothing of the rapid increase in excavations and discoveries.

It is my hope that the book will usefully continue to function as an introduction and a stimulus, and will still be welcomed by amateurs of archaeology and history, by workers in related fields, and especially

Foreword

– as past experience in the class-room has shown – by university students of the ancient civilizations.

Earlier Italian editions * reflect the progress of Etruscan studies in a series of revisions which were particularly full in the third (1955) and fifth (1963) editions. In the latter, Part I was almost wholly rewritten and the text figures and plates were largely replaced. The present (sixth) edition incorporates and discusses important discoveries that have taken place over the last few years, especially in the field of epigraphy: they have resulted in a considerable reworking of Part III (the section on language), and in numerous other changes or additions made necessary by the general progress of Etruscan and related studies.

M.P.

* And also the translations: *La civilisation étrusque*, Payot, Paris, 1949; *The Etruscans*, Penguin Books, 1955, reprinted 1956; *Etruscología*, Eudeba, Buenos Aires, 1965; *Die Etrusker*, Fischer Bücherei, Frankfurt am Main-Hamburg, 1965; *Etruskowie*, Państwowe Wydawnictwo Naukowe, Warsaw, 1968.

Editor's Preface

to the second English edition (1974)

The first English edition of this book was published as a Pelican in 1955: it has long been out of print, and out of date – which is hardly surprising, since the Italian original has gone through three substantially revised editions in the meantime. This second English edition was originally based on a translation of the sixth (1968) Italian edition made by Dr J. Cremona, who incorporated new material supplied by Professor Pallottino. Further additions were inserted by myself under Professor Pallottino's general direction; they were mainly concerned with new work, but also included a number of references to publications in English – largely because of their obvious accessibility to English as distinct from Italian readers. At a later stage, it became possible to incorporate the Supplementary Note (pp. 235–8) and – at least in bibliographical form – other additional material that appeared in the 1973 reprint of the sixth Italian edition. In general, all these additions affect the apparatus of notes (and the notes on the relevant new plates) rather more than the narrative, and the archaeological chapters more than the others. Any sins of omission or commission should be laid at the editor's and publisher's door rather than at the author's.

In selecting the 102 plates for this edition, and in composing the notes on them, I have endeavoured to strike a balance between old and new friends. This is as difficult with archaeological and art-historical material as it is in real life, and I apologize in advance for any inadvertent offence I may have given. None was intended, and I hope that some regrettable absences may be outweighed, or at least compensated, by the new acquaintances I have enabled English readers to make. I am immensely grateful to all the copyright-holding institutions and individuals, as named, for allowing their photographs to be printed here: and in particular I thank my wife, Dr F. R. Serra Ridgway, for her help in organizing this side of the book.

I have provided a selection of Notes on Further Reading (pp. 294–300). These are designed to help English-speaking students (and perhaps even specialists in related fields) to find their way about the periodical literature and the various monograph series that are currently burgeoning in Italy, where new Etruscan evidence is being acquired, and old evidence is being published (or republished), on a scale and at a pace that combine to defy *aggiornamento*. The latter is a particularly difficult process in Britain: membership of the European Economic Community notwithstanding, the problem of the Italian language remains apparently insuperable. Meanwhile, the name and nature of British archaeology are rapidly becoming identified with rescue excavation at home – to the increasing exclusion of even that sop to the conscience implied by the words 'Continental background'. As well as listing the fundamental Etruscan studies of the past and present, therefore, I have tried to indicate which authors, journals and series are worth watching in future. That it *is* worth keeping up to date with advances in Etruscology must not be doubted for a moment. George Dennis's definition of Etruria as 'the twin-sister of Greece in the work of civilizing Europe' is a telling one, though perhaps in a slightly different sense to that which he intended when he made it. The 1970 Edinburgh Festival exhibition of early Celtic art fastened our attention not on the Early Christian stone crosses of our own Celtic fringe but on the fifth-century B.C. origins in central Europe of 'the first great contribution of the barbarians to European arts' – and on the exotic influences that helped to shape that contribution. Of these exotic influences, in Stuart Piggott's words, 'the most fertile in inspiration seems to have been that of the Classical world, transmitted by the importation from western Greeks and Etruscans of bronze vessels (and, less frequently, painted Greek vases), largely in connection with a wine trade'. Even in our British proto-historical thinking, we simply cannot afford to consign Etruria and the Etruscans to Cloud Cuckoo Land, where 'blue skies archaeology' exists merely as a tourist attraction.

Before trying to keep up with current and future progress in Etruscan studies, however, a careful reading of *this* book is indispensable. *The Etruscans* is a very rare item in the modern literature about the ancient world: it is a text-book. It should not be placed on bookshelves next to the half-baked, half-digested glossy productions of the English-speaking and European 'popular book' industry, which believes in keeping the Etruscans mysterious and therefore presumably profitable – and thereby does a great deal of damage in perpetuating long-exploded myths. The general public *wants* the Etruscans to be mysterious: its archaeological advisers by and large believe in giving the public what it wants. This is why we read with depressing regularity about the death-worshipping Etruscans bringing their indecipherable language from the notoriously mysterious East. Time was when the Etruscans tapped a rich vein of sheer dottiness: one cannot help admiring the breath-taking scope of Sir William Betham's *Etruria-Celtica : Etruscan Literature and Antiquities investigated : or, the language of that ancient and illustrious people compared and identified with the Iberno-Celtic, and both shown to be Phoenician*, published in Dublin in 1842. It is sobering to think of Betham taking time off from his duties as Ulster King of Arms to transliterate the 'Eugubian Tables' into Irish, and to translate the result first into literal, and then into idiomatic, English – only six years before the first appearance of George Dennis's *Cities and Cemeteries of Etruria*. This vein is not entirely worked out even today, as contemporary efforts to identify the Etruscan language with Albanian and Hittite testify. But the general level now is much lower on originality: 'It seems that the earliest Etruscans migrated to Italy from Asia Minor in the late eighth century B.C. and settled in that part of Central Italy which is still known after them as Tuscany' – this sweeping and seriously defective reference to Etruscan origins, printed in 1969, is a fair sample of the sort of statement that one finds flowing effortlessly on to the pages of school books about ancient history and of books about the ancient world for the surprisingly gullible man in the street. And yet what an impressive quantity of fascinating evidence, what a stimulating ebb and flow of archaeological, historical and linguistic hypothesis these well-worn adages conceal! One does not need to be a specialist or even a student to appreciate the masterly way in which Professor Pallottino leads us through the maze of Etruscan origins in Chapter Two of this book. The same is true of the language: Part Three begins by telling us about ourselves: 'Even today, ninety per cent of the educated public firmly believes that Etruscan is totally indecipherable. This belief . . . is over two hundred years out of date'. And then we are shown how very much more complex, and hopeful, the position really is. *Il misterioso popolo etrusco* – that eighteenth-century fossil still preserved in tourist literature – will never be the same again: has never been, in fact, since the first Italian edition of *Etruscologia* cut through the cobwebs in 1942, and since the Pelican edition performed the same essentially hygienic operation for the English-speaking world in 1955.

I alluded above to what can only be called the current boom in the accumulation and publication of hard facts about the Etruscans. Many of the contemporary workers in the wide variety of Etruscan studies were pupils of Professor Pallottino; others have been influenced by him. In other words, an impressive number of Etruscan specialists absorbed this book at a formative stage in their intellectual careers. That is yet another reason why it is 'the basic book' about the Etruscans: it is the text-book written by the one man who, more than any other individual, has contributed by his teaching and his example to the shape and direction of Etruscan studies today.

It is good to have *The* (revised) *Etruscans* in print again, and so to

Editor's Preface

see at first hand how the author, his pupils and his colleagues have made the 1955 edition out of date: long may the process continue with the 1974 edition!

DAVID RIDGWAY
Department of Archaeology
University of Edinburgh
June 1973

A Short History of Etruscan Studies

Various attempts have already been made to outline the development of Etruscan studies from their tentative beginnings in the Renaissance to the intense activity of contemporary scientific research. These surveys have tended to concentrate on results obtained in one of the separate disciplines: archaeological, linguistic or historical[1]; and these retrospective inquiries do not present a point of view broad enough to enable the student to trace out a particular norm, a particular line of development, from the rich and seemingly disparate variety of facts. We feel it is legitimate to seek some such line in the history of the humanities, even if we admit that choice and chance come into play more often here than in other types of research.

Like other disciplines concerned with the history and civilization of ancient peoples, Etruscan studies had an erudite 'prehistory', which lasted until the end of the eighteenth century and the beginning of the nineteenth. There followed a formative phase – formative from the methodological angle – which took up most of the nineteenth century. Finally, the past eighty years or so have witnessed the development of a refined critical approach to historical problems. In purely historical or philological disciplines, scholarly progress has taken place mainly under the impulse of internal movements that determined the gradual and continuous nature of its advance. Etruscan studies, on the other hand, because they rely so much on archaeological evidence, seem more closely dependent upon external contingencies, such as new discoveries or excavations. We may go so far as to say that the rate of progress is determined by the pace of archaeological finds and by the general development of the various branches of classical studies, whether historical, philological or linguistic. Every quickening in the momentum of exploration of Etruscan sites, every step forward in general historical or archaeological methodology has produced a clearly defined phase in Etruscan studies. This, in my opinion, provides the least arbitrary criterion for an attempt to set down in a meaningful order all the facts and ideas that go to make up the history of Etruscan studies.

Etruscan antiquities began to excite interest during the Renaissance, as the result of sporadic discoveries of tombs and inscriptions. They gave rise to the fanciful reconstructions of Annius of Viterbo (1432–1502) and other humanists. Interest shifted later from Roman Tuscia to Tuscany proper, quickening during the eighteenth century in the wake of discoveries and excavations made at Volterra, Cortona, Siena, etc., to develop into that lively branch of antiquarian studies known in Italy by the name *Etruscheria*. Enthusiastic local amateurs, inclined to exaggerate the ancient glories of their Tuscan birthplaces, helped to spread the fame of Etruscan monuments and to encourage an all too often uncritical exaltation of the Etruscans over the other peoples of antiquity. Just as the sixteenth was the century of the rediscovery of Rome, and the nineteenth that of the discovery of Greece, so the eighteenth may certainly be called the century of the discovery of Etruria. It is true that the first attempt at a synthesis of Etruscan references left by ancient authors had been made in the seventeenth century, by a Scot, T. Dempster, whose *De Etruria regali*, written between 1616 and 1625, is a diligent and powerful work, though marred by apocryphal erudition and much fantasy. But Dempster's work was not published or appreciated till well into the first half of the eighteenth century. It gave rise to the work of F. Buonarroti, whose additions and comments on it were published with the original text in 1723–4; to G. B. Passeri's *Paralipomeni* to Dempster (1767) and *Picturae Etruscorum in vasculis* (1767–75); S. Maffei's *Ragionamento sopra gl'Itali primitivi* ('Discourse on the primitive inhabitants of Italy'; 1727) and *Osservazioni letterarie* ('Literary observations', I–VI; 1737–40); A. F. Gori's *Museum Etruscum* (1737–43), *Musei Guarnacci antiqua monumenta* (1744), and *Museum Cortonense* (1750); and M. Guarnacci's *Origini italiche* ('Italic origins'; 1767–72). The year 1726 saw the foundation of an Etruscan Academy at Cortona: it became the focus of scholarly activity in Etruscan studies and published a series of *Dissertazioni* between 1738 and 1795. Outside Italy, a tribute should be paid to the work of the great French antiquarian, A. C. Ph. de Caylus, *Recueil d'antiquités égyptiennes, étrusques, romaines et gauloises* (1752–62). The eighteenth-century passion for things Etruscan was remarkable, despite the often arbitrary or fanciful conjectures and conclusions which it produced and the faults of its critical method. The diligence with which it searched for and collected archaeological material has meant that, when documents have since been lost, its records still retain some measure of value.

Eighteenth-century Etruscological activities reached their climax with the publication of L. Lanzi's *Saggio di lingua etrusca e di altre d'Italia* ('Essay on the Etruscan and other languages of Italy'; 1789, followed by a posthumous second edition in 1824). The work is a small *summa* of current knowledge of Etruria, not just its epigraphy and language, but also its history, archaeology and art. Lanzi was on the threshold of a new phase in Etruscan studies, for he was able to rely on greater knowledge and more accurate methods. This is shown by many of his statements on the language and by his reaction to the claims of eighteenth-century *Etruscheria*, illustrated by his correct attribution to Greece of painted vases which until then had been labelled Etruscan (*De' vasi antichi dipinti volgarmente chiamati etruschi*: 'On ancient painted vases popularly called Etruscan'; 1806). The school of nine-teenth-century Italian epigraphists – G. B. Vermiglioli, F. Orioli, M. A. Migliarini and even A. Fabretti – may be traced back to Lanzi. On the other hand, the spirit of eighteenth-century notions and methods survived in the work of a number of scholars during the first half of the nineteenth century: e.g. G. Micali's *L'Italia avanti il dominio dei Romani* ('Italy before the Roman conquest'; 1810 and 1822), and *Monumenti inediti a illustrazione della storia degli antichi popoli italiani* ('Unpublished documents for the history of the ancient Italian peoples'; 1844); and F. Inghirami's *Monumenti etruschi* (1820–26). These works, however, cannot help reflecting contemporary archaeological discoveries and the general progress in scientific method and knowledge.

The new century did in fact open with the intensive exploration of the cemeteries of southern Etruria, resulting in a whole series of decisive finds at Tarquinia, Vulci, Cerveteri, Perugia, Chiusi and other sites. The first small eighteenth-century collections gathered at Cortona and Volterra were now joined by the growing accumulation of Etruscan material at the Museo Granducale in Florence (the nucleus of today's Museo Archeologico), the Museo Etrusco Gregoriano in Rome and the Museo Etrusco-Romano in Perugia. Excavations resulted also in the formation of the large private collections of Lucien Bonaparte, Prince of Canino, and of the banker G. P. Campana; for the most part this material was later taken out of Italy to form the nucleus of the Etruscan collections at the Louvre, the British Museum and other great Euro-pean museums. Meanwhile, in the late eighteenth and early nineteenth centuries the general study of classical antiquities had undergone a major revolution, the result of the direct contact of the west with the actual monuments of Greece, a movement initiated by J. J. Winckel-mann and continued by E. Q. Visconti, C. Fea, L. Canina, K. O. Müller and B. G. Niebuhr. This period also witnessed the growth of general comparative linguistics out of the mists of pre-scientific scholar-ship; the work of F. Schlegel and F. Bopp defined and demonstrated the original unity of all Indo-European languages.

Following these discoveries and in the footsteps of the general development of scholarship, the study of Etruscan antiquities moved on into the nineteenth century proper, to a stage characterized by historical, archaeological and philological method. An important contributory factor was the foundation of the Istituto di Corrispondenza Archeologica, formed in Rome in 1829 by E. Gerhard and a group of north European professional and amateur scholars known as the 'Hyperboreans'; for many decades Etruscan research and its discoveries were to be recorded in the *Bullettino*, *Annali* and *Monumenti* published by the Institute. Research on topography and on the monuments developed in a series of studies and publications by travellers, archaeologists and architects such as L. Canina (*Antica Etruria marittima*, 1846–51), W. Gell (*The Topography of Rome and its Vicinity*, 1846), G. Dennis (*The Cities and Cemeteries of Etruria*, 1848, with subsequent editions down to 1883), A. Noël des Vergers (*L'Étrurie et les étrusques*, 1862–4). Dennis's work was particularly successful in disseminating knowledge of ancient Etruria among cultivated laymen.

The publication of systematic collections of monuments, works of art and excavation finds was steadily pursued. The works of Micali and Inghirami (see p. 25) were supplemented by the catalogue of the Museo Etrusco Gregoriano (*Musei Etrusci quod Gregorius XVI constituit monimenta*, 1842; a later edition incorporated a few variants). At the same time specialized collections, true *corpora*, of single classes of objects began to appear: vases (E. Gerhard, *Auserlesene Vasenbilder*, 1840–58), mirrors (E. Gerhard, *Etruskische Spiegel*, 1839–67; continued by G. Körte, 1897) and, later, urns (H. Brunn and G. Körte, *I rilievi delle urne etrusche*, 1870–1916). There are also a number of valuable reports on excavations, diligently conducted with a measure of critical method. Essays on art history also make their appearance during this period: but the first attempt at a general synthesis did not appear till 1889, with J. Martha's *L'Art étrusque*.

This period was particularly fruitful in epigraphic studies. The activity of Italian scholars, the followers of L. Lanzi, culminated in the publication of a monumental *Corpus Inscriptionum Italicarum* (*C.I.I.*), with a *Glossarium Italicum*, edited by A. Fabretti (1867), followed by three supplements and an appendix by F. Gamurrini (1880). In the last three decades of the century the study of the Etruscan language took a decisive critical direction. Scholars working in this field (principally W. Corssen, W. Deecke, C. Pauli, S. Bugge, G. Herbig and E. Lattes) were concerned mainly with methods of interpretation and with the relationship of Etruscan and the Indo-European languages. At much the same time, the problem of Etruscan origins first came to be critically formulated: it was no longer debated solely on the evidence of ancient literary sources or linguistic conjectures, but was studied in the light of new discoveries on the early stages of the cultures of Etruria and Emilia (the first cremation tombs at Villanova, near Bologna, came to light in 1856) and of more general advances in the field of Italian prehistory. The chief participants in these debates were W. Helbig, I. Undset, L. Pigorini, E. Brizio and F. v. Duhn. Finally we should mention a synoptic work that has had (and still has) much influence, especially for its collection and re-elaboration of traditional Graeco-Roman data on the Etruscan world: K. O. Müller's *Die Etrusker*, 1828, with the linguistic and archaeological revisions made by W. Deecke in 1877.

The third phase in the history of Etruscan studies came as the result of a general reawakening of interest in Etruria itself: exploratory activity had slowed down considerably during the middle years of the nineteenth century, but it quickened again mainly under the impulse of the new Italian state. The cemeteries of Tarquinia, Vulci, Chiusi, Orvieto, Vetulonia, Saturnia, Narce, and Bologna were excavated first, followed, at the end of the century, by those of Veii, Cerveteri and Spina. Explorations were undertaken on sites and temples at Marzabotto, Capua, Falerii, Orvieto, Veii, Cerveteri, Tarquinia, Volsinii (Bolsena), Vulci, Roselle, Fiesole and Pyrgi. The earliest stages of the civilization of Etruria, the 'Villanovan' and the 'Orientalizing', were revealed, not only at Villanova and Bologna, but at Tarquinia, Veii, Vetulonia, Narce, Bisenzio, Populonia and San Giovenale, to mention only the more important sites. These discoveries were echoed by other, closely related finds in Latium, Campania, Umbria, Picenum and northern Italy. The great museums of Florence, Rome (Villa Giulia), Bologna, Tarquinia and Chiusi were founded, together with smaller local collections at Orvieto, Fiesole, Marzabotto, Siena, Grosseto, etc. European and American museums began to assemble important Etruscan collections (e.g. the Helbig Museum at the Ny Carlsberg Glyptothek, Copenhagen). Systematic explorations were now continuous and general, covering the whole territory of Etruria; and in recent times they have been extended by the development of aerial photography and other modern means of research, particularly in southern Etruria and at Spina. Moreover, this general search was neither restricted to Etruria nor confined within the bounds of its own results: the culture it revealed appeared every decade more closely integrated with the general development of ancient civilizations, both within Italy and in the wider world of Greece and the East. Subtler methods, allied to a broader and more rigorous historical foundation, have refined the scientific basis for the study of the ancient world. Art history has accepted the new principles of contemporary criticism and rejected such preconceived ideas as the imitation of nature or the perfection of Hellenic classicism, opening the way to a better understanding and appreciation of Etruscan works of art. Finally, the discovery of new and longer texts (e.g. the wrapping of the Zagreb mummy, and the Capua tile) and the broadening and deepening of linguistic knowledge (especially on the pre-Indo-European Mediterranean linguistic substrata) have provided us with a new springboard for the study of the Etruscan language.

The publication of general repertories and of inventories of single classes of finds continued apace. Materials belonging to the earlier periods are contained in the illustrated *La civilisation primitive en Italie* (1896–1904) by O. Montelius; tomb paintings at Tarquinia and Chiusi in the fascicules of *Monumenti della pittura antica in Italia* (1937–55); architectural terracottas in A. Andrén's *Architectural Terracottas from Etrusco-Italic Temples* (1939–40); sarcophagi in R. Herbig's *corpus*, *Die Jüngeretruskischen Steinsarkophagen* (1952); painted pottery in J. D. Beazley's *Etruscan Vase-Painting* (1947). Especially characteristic of this later period are a number of monographs on Etruscan centres considered in their various historical and archaeological aspects: one thinks of those published for Bologna (A. Grenier, P. Ducati), Populonia (A. Minto), Cortona (A. Neppi Módona), Chiusi (R. Bianchi Bandinelli), Marsiliana d'Albegna (A. Minto), Saturnia (A. Minto), Sovana (R. Bianchi Bandinelli), Statonia (G. Matteucig), Vulci (S. Gsell, F. Messerschmidt), Tarquinia (M. Pallottino), Blera (H. Koch, E. v. Mercklin, C. Weickert), Capua (J. Heurgon) and Cerveteri (R. Vighi, G. Ricci, M. Moretti). After the Etruscan section of H. Nissen's *Italische Landeskunde* (1883–1902), the most important topographical survey is A. Solari's *Topografia storica dell'Etruria* (1915–20). Illustrated accounts of Etruscan sites and museums have been published more recently by M. Santangelo (*Musei e monumenti etruschi*, 1960) and L. Banti (*Il mondo degli Etruschi*, 1960). Etruscan pre- and proto-historic problems have been studied by, among others, F. v. Duhn, G. Säflund, D. Randall MacIver, J. Sundwall, N. Åberg, F. Messerschmidt, H. Hencken and the present author. The discussion of problems presented by Etruscan and Italic art which began in 1916 as a result of the sensational discovery of the Apollo of Veii has been particularly important. The question of the originality of Etruscan art, first outlined by H. Brunn, J. Martha and J. Wickhoff, has been critically propounded or opposed along different lines of argument by, among others, A. Della Seta, C. Anti, R. Bianchi Bandinelli, D. Levi, G. Kaschnitz-Weinberg, G. M. A. Hanfmann, M. Pallottino, R. Bloch, C. C. van Essen and T. Dohrn. General interest in the art of Etruria led to the publication of special studies of Etruscan painting (F. Weege, F. Messerschmidt, M. Pallottino), sculpture (P. J. Riis, G. M. A. Hanfmann,

A. Hus) and the minor art forms (G. A. Mansuelli, Y. Huls, etc.), and to the appearance of illustrated manuals and albums, among which we should mention the monumental works of P. Ducati (*Storia dell'arte etrusca*, 1927) and G. Q. Giglioli (*L'arte etrusca*, 1935), which, though superseded to some extent, have lost little of their original usefulness.

A large new inventory of Etruscan inscriptions, based upon more up-to-date criteria and on data incomparably richer than Fabretti's *Corpus*, is being published (since 1893) under the title *Corpus Inscriptionum Etruscarum* (*C.I.E.*). Meanwhile the Italian epigraphic school has concentrated its activities on the collection and publication of texts: G. Buonamici, *Epigrafia etrusca*, 1934; M. Pallottino, *Testimonia Linguae Etruscae*, 1954, 1968[2]; the sections on epigraphy ('Rivista di epigrafia etrusca') in the volumes of *Studi Etruschi*. At the same time great strides were made in research on the structure of the language and the interpretation of the texts; during the twentieth century the main workers in this field have been A. Torp, A. Trombetti, S. P. Cortsen, E. Fiesel, E. Vetter, K. Olzscha, F. Slotty, H. Rix and the present writer.

The problem of Etruscan origins was taken up in monographic studies (by L. Pareti, F. Schachermeyer, P. Ducati, M. Pallottino, F. Altheim) and in a very large number of articles. A growing interest in problems concerning ancient Etruscan history and institutions may be seen in the ever-increasing number of publications by writers on Roman political and legal history (G. De Sanctis, J. Beloch, L. Homo, F. Altheim, L. Pareti, S. Mazzarino, P. De Francisci, A. Alföldi, U. Coli, J. Heurgon, etc.). Life and customs have been studied in detail by A. Solari (*La vita pubblica e privata degli Etruschi*, 1928) and J. Heurgon (*La vie quotidienne chez les Étrusques*, 1961, translated into English under the title *Daily Life of the Etruscans*, 1964). Finally, we should mention a number of attempts at a synthesis of the various known aspects of the Etruscan civilization: K. O. Müller and W. Deecke's *Die Etrusker* (1877; 1965[2]), P. Ducati's *L'Etruria antica* (1927), B. Nogara's *Gli Etruschi e la loro civiltà* (1933) and M. Renard's *Initiation à l'étruscologie* (1941); the present outline, first published in 1942, falls into this category. Many other manuals, essays and informative works for the layman have appeared with increasing frequency during the last few years, often translated into many languages. They are not always very reliable; the best include those by R. Bloch, A. Hus, O. W. v. Vacano, L. Banti and G. A. Mansuelli. A number of important miscellanies should also be mentioned: *Historia*, VI, 1957; *Tyrrhenica*, 1957; *Études Étrusco-italiques*, 1963.

Over the past few decades, Florence has developed into the principal centre of Etruscan studies. A Museum of Etruscan Topography had already been founded within the Museo Archeologico by L. A. Milani; there followed the institution of a Permanent Committee for Etruria (1927), the holding of the First International Congress of Etruscan Studies (1928) and the foundation, in 1932, of the Istituto di Studi Etruschi (now the Istituto di Studi Etruschi ed Italici) which A. Minto created and directed for many years. The Institute's journal, *Studi Etruschi*, has appeared in yearly volumes since 1927. The growth in importance of Etruscan studies in Italy resulted in the creation of university chairs (first Rome, in 1926, then Florence and now Bologna and Pisa) and specialized university courses in the subject. Development is also borne out by the subdivision of the territory of Etruria proper into two regions, each under the control of a Soprintendenza alle Antichità, the first in Florence, the second in Rome with jurisdiction over southern Etruria since 1939; the Soprintendenza of Emilia and Romagna is also actively involved. This activity has been supplemented by the interest that the various foreign Schools and Institutes at Rome have devoted to the exploration of Etruscan territory and by the development of Etruscan studies abroad, notably in Germany, France, Belgium and Sweden. Recent national and international congresses and exhibitions – ranging from the exhibition of Etruscan art and civilization that visited a number of European capitals in 1955–6, to the Vienna and Stockholm exhibitions of recent Etruscan discoveries in 1966 – have also greatly contributed to the spread of knowledge about the various aspects and problems of the Etruscan world over widening circles of the contemporary world.

These activities, whether individual or collective, are now wholly and decisively directed towards an integrated vision of Etruscan history and culture. The establishment of Etruscan studies as a unitary historical discipline has taken place only during the last few decades. Until then, scholars working on Etruscan problems pursued their different specializations and methods in their different fields, the historians working on questions of Etruscan origins or institutions, the archaeologists on Etruscan monuments and art history, the philologists on problems of language. This situation arose mainly from the fact that Etruscan studies had developed out of the study of classical antiquity, where, for obvious reasons, the vast accumulation of documents and data does not allow any one scholar to work easily in all its branches: as a result, classical history, archaeology and philology have been autonomous disciplines since the earliest days of modern research. The historians of the Graeco-Roman world, the classical archaeologists and the Indo-European philologists were, in practice, those very same scholars who engaged in Etruscan research, some of them only occasionally, and, for the most part, without any interdisciplinary contacts. There is no doubt that this state of affairs has been a negative factor and may be found at the root of the many uncertainties and unsatisfactory formulations of the problems involved. For the field of Etruscan antiquities, in contrast with that of Greek or Roman antiquities, is relatively limited: the fragmentary documentation makes the convergence and the utilization of all sources and methods seem possible, and indeed indispensable for understanding individual classes of evidence and for attempting a valid historical reconstruction. It is in this sense that we are able to say that the study of the Etruscan civilization has lacked that integrated and coherent outlook which has characterized research on other civilizations of the ancient world, like the Egyptian or the Mesopotamian. The greater spread, both in time and in place, and the greater quantity of their materials have led to the establishment of Egyptology and Assyriology as clearly defined historical disciplines. The need to compare and collate evidence from a variety of sources was certainly often felt during the nineteenth century and the beginning of the twentieth by historians (K. O. Müller, L. Pareti), philologists (W. Deecke, F. Ribezzo) and archaeologists (P. Ducati, A. Minto). But it was only in the work of a scholar of the calibre of B. Nogara that the archaeological and the philological methods came to be fused organically into a single interpretative process. Nogara may in fact be considered the first real 'Etruscologist' in the full sense of the word. The collaboration of scholars centred round the Istituto di Studi Etruschi ed Italici, though still largely specialists working within their own specialties, has contributed much to the establishment of a community of aims in Etruscan studies, conceived as an inevitable necessity by A. Minto, critically formulated by B. Nogara, and firmly professed by the present author, in research as well as in teaching.

Such, very briefly, is the history of Etruscan studies. But we cannot leave the subject without some reference to one other aspect of the interest modern culture has shown for the world of ancient Etruria. Ever since the eighteenth century, as we have seen, this remote world, difficult of access owing to the lack of direct historical documentation and the singularity of its epigraphic remains, had exercised on scholars an attraction quite disproportionate to its importance, especially within the limitations of contemporary knowledge. The echoes of eighteenth-century Etruscomania had also spread well beyond the scholarly circle: witness its influence on English ceramic art (beginning with Josiah Wedgwood's 'Etruria' factory, founded in 1769) and several other marginal traits of the neo-classical applied arts of the period. But it was above all the reports of discoveries made at the beginning of the nineteenth century – the painted tombs, the rich hoards of vases and jewel-

31

lery unearthed from the scrubland and hills of the southern Maremma – that helped to create around Etruria a peculiar aura of romantic suggestion, which the books of Dennis and Noël des Vergers helped to spread, never to disappear again. Scholarly uncertainties and polemics on the interpretation of Etruscan inscriptions, on the classification of the language, on the problem of Etruscan origins, gave birth to the notion of an 'Etruscan mystery'; and this notion, rather than describing, more or less aptly, a scientific situation, developed into a sort of irrational belief, a truly aprioristic sentimental position deeply rooted in modern culture, a commonplace handed down over the generations, regardless of what progress was in fact being made in Etruscan studies. The 'Etruscan' theme has, for instance, inspired some lively passages in contemporary literature, particularly in England: e.g. in D. H. Lawrence's *Etruscan Places* (1932) or Aldous Huxley's novels *Those Barren Leaves* and *Point Counter Point*. Here, the ancient civilization of Etruria is symbolically transfigured into the myth of a 'lost world', of a spontaneously natural human society, festive and sensuous, contrasting with the rational and moral orders of Graeco-Roman and Christian cultures.[2] It is obvious that such suggestive literary fantasies have rested on the often unclear and uncertain picture of Etruscan civilization provided by archaeological and historical research – that is, by the positive data of science – which have contributed to keep prejudices and aberrations alive. The emotional attitude of modern people towards the Etruscans is also shown in the lively curiosity and constantly renewed interest of an ever-growing public, illustrated by the great success of books and exhibitions, the mania for collections, and even by elements of Etruscan inspiration in the figurative and decorative arts and in fashion.

To all this we should add a phenomenon of direct relevance to the scholar, even if it is only marginal and negative. We are referring to the many pseudo-scientific publications on Etruscan origins, on the Etruscan civilization, above all on the Etruscan language, which have appeared with extraordinary frequency during the last few decades. These attempts share the presupposition that all the results and experience accumulated over centuries of historical research are, when it comes to searching for the truth, no more than secondary or of no value at all when compared to the intuition of one gifted individual. They ignore the first principles of critical method, transforming hypotheses into statements, and forgetting all about the need for substantiation. They reach the most bizarre conclusions, whose inconsistency shows up in the way one radically contradicts another. Such an approach to the historical and linguistic problems brings to mind the ingenuities and quirks of seventeenth- and eighteenth-century scholars, and it may be seen as a kind of latter-day Etruscomania. The phenomenon has its place in the suggestive atmosphere of the 'Etruscan mystery', for it is an attempt to unveil it by the working of a miracle: this explains the tendency to improvisation (a tendency that has even afflicted a number of trained scholars), and the deep impression that certain loud pseudo-scientific statements have made on the general public. In the linguistic field especially, the belief – still very widespread – that Etruscan is totally undecipherable has its counterpart in the regular announcements of the discovery of a 'key', eagerly taken up by the popular (and not so popular) press and just as rapidly forgotten. There is no doubt that this state of affairs persistently misleads the general public on these matters, making it harder for the specialist to write for the non-specialist, but all the more necessary.[3]

Part 1

The Etruscans and their Place in the History of Italy and the Mediterranean

CHAPTER I

Italy at the Dawn
of History

Modern theories

When dealing with the legends of antiquity about the foundations of
Rome, Theodore Mommsen, the father of historical philology, wrote:
'History must first make a clean sweep of these fables which, though
purporting to be history, are nothing more than somewhat simple improvisations'.[1] Little did he dream that, in attempting to explain the
origin of the Italic peoples, the cumbersome archaeological and linguistic elaborations of modern scholarship were soon to build up a
whole series of reconstructions and hypotheses no less fabulous or
fantastic than those originating in the pious traditions of antiquity,
even though they were buttressed by an alleged excellence of method
and the authority of undisputed scholars.

This same modern scholarship, which had derided the myths of the
Aborigines or the Pelasgians, in its turn attributed an arbitrary ethnic
significance to certain cultural phenomena on the basis of the often
precarious and provisional evidence of archaeology. It gave body to its
own theories and invented peoples which it called 'Terramara folk',
'Apennine folk', 'Protovillanovans', 'Villanovans', and so on. In
addition the formation of the Italic dialects was explained by the oversimplified concept of an imaginary 'common Italic', of Indo-European
origin, which was supposed to have given rise to the Latin, Umbrian
and Oscan languages. All cultural change or progress was said to have
been caused by foreign invaders. These theories, however naïve and
mistaken they may appear in the light of the latest advances in modern
studies and especially when compared with the most recent archaeological discoveries, have nevertheless been current for many decades:
and they have been characterized by a dogmatism that has often
smacked of intolerance. They have left so deep a mark on research that
even today, when bringing forward new concepts to replace the old, we
unconsciously tend to use the terms and expressions which they created.

But perhaps we should not be too hard on nineteenth-century
scholarship for substituting its own 'myths' for the myths of antiquity.
The youthful ardour of research-workers in a completely new field,
where the last mists of eighteenth-century baroque learning were fast
melting away; the possession of a new weapon – method – believed to

be infallible; the faith in progress and the contempt for the intellectual activities of the past – all these causes explain, even if they cannot excuse, the innate complacency felt for the results obtained and the conviction that they should be regarded as definitive.

Classical tradition had generally conceived the origin of the individual historical peoples and towns of Italy in terms of some external event, whether instantaneous or miraculous: the arrival of a hero from abroad, a foundation-story, or a divine revelation. When a clean sweep had been made of these complicated legends, the historians and archaeologists of the late nineteenth century were in their turn unable to shake off the idea of a precisely dated 'beginning', of a single, determining event from which the first ethnic physiognomy of Italy received its shape. This event was supposed to be a prehistoric invasion on the part of 'Italic' Indo-Europeans, who brought in a new language and a new culture. On the principle that each prehistoric culture must necessarily correspond to a different people (a theory that came to be known as 'Kossinna's Law'), scholars tried to find an automatic identification of linguistic evidence with that provided by archaeology.

It is worth recalling that, according to the view most widely held at the time, the concept of Indo-European linguistic unity, in itself a triumph of nineteenth-century scholarship, implied an original close relationship between groups that were later dispersed, such as the Celtic, Germanic, Italic, Greek, Slav, Armenian, Iranian and Indian peoples. This in its turn implied an original point of departure and a particular moment of arrival in the various regions they inhabited in historical times. The appearance of a language could only signify the arrival of a people. Hence the idea of vast prehistoric migrations on the lines of the barbarian migrations at the time of the decline of the Roman Empire. But the analogy was not a valid one, for the Germanic peoples that spread over Europe and the Mediterranean world imposed their language only on the fringes of the old Romanized territories. From these notions, however, grew the theory of an 'Italic' invasion of prehistoric Italy from continental Europe.

Meanwhile, and mainly as a result of discoveries being made north of the Alps, a new picture was gradually being drawn of successive prehistoric periods and cultures. The beginning of the Bronze Age, following the Neolithic and Copper Ages, was regarded as a revolutionary event whose origin in Italy was identified with the appearance in the Po valley of the so-called *terremare*, prehistoric settlements built on piles and surrounded by a bank and ditch as a protection against floods. A connection was seen between the *terremare* and a few rather poor burials that showed evidence of cremation as a funeral rite. The fact that the *terremare* were an isolated phenomenon, limited to northern Italy, with pile-dwellings related structurally to the 'lake-dwellings' of western Switzerland; the early appearance and the wide distribution of the cremation rite in countries north of the Alps towards the end of the Bronze Age; and, more generally, the affinities between the *terremare* and the cultures of the central European Bronze Age – all these arguments were used to prove that a bronze-using culture had been brought over the Alps into Italy. This was hailed as a new fact of fundamental importance in the understanding of Italian prehistory. It seemed obvious to scholars such as G. Chierici, W. Helbig and L. Pigorini that it pointed to the arrival in the peninsula of the Indo-Europeans: or, in other words, of the 'Italic' peoples.[2]

The 'Pigorini hypothesis', so called after its keenest and most famous exponent, was for a long time the keystone in the interpretation of the linguistic and archaeological data of prehistoric Italy. Its adherents held that Italy's cultural development was affected at an early stage by a decisive ethnic impulse of transalpine origin. Whether this change was held to be solely due to the Terramara wave or whether it was thought that other invasions from the Danube basin followed (thus giving rise to the succeeding Iron Age cultures of Italy, as others believed), the civilizing wave always seemed to proceed from north to south. Traces of the people who had built the *terremare* were seen in several other places, even as far south as Scoglio del Tonno near Taranto, in the form of objects similar to those found in north Italy. Some even linked the origins of Rome itself to the same people: '*Roma quadrata*', the Roman grid-system of streets aligned on the cardinal points, and the very name 'Palatine' combined to suggest that it was the descendants of the Terramara folk who had founded the Eternal City.[3] Thus the myth of the 'Terramara folk' was substituted, in the name of scholarship, for the myth of Romulus and Remus!

During the first years of the present century, the 'Pigorini hypothesis' was opposed with increasing vigour by a growing number of scholars working in a variety of fields. To a greater or lesser degree, they all tended to reaffirm the importance of the earliest prehistoric peoples and cultures in the Italian peninsula, as opposed to that of the presumed northern invaders. Among these scholars we find the anthropologist G. Sergi, who postulated the existence of a Mediterranean race, and the prehistoric archaeologist G. Patroni.[4] The discoveries of P. Orsi in Sicily and of G. A. Colini and U. Rellini in central and southern Italy were gradually showing that the development of Bronze Age culture in the Italian peninsula and islands did not, in fact, constitute a break in continuity with the earlier Neolithic and Copper Age cultures. They also tended to show that the progressive elements from outside were largely of Mediterranean origin, influenced by the Minoan and

The Etruscans

Mycenaean civilizations flourishing in the Aegean world in the second millennium B.C.; in other words, cultural movements were now thought to proceed from south to north, and the *terremare* were seen as a local phenomenon of limited importance – and in any case comparatively late. Pigorini's formulation of the problem was thus reversed. The typical Bronze Age culture of the peninsula, defined and studied mainly by Rellini, received at first the tendentious name of 'extra-terramara culture'; but this was later changed to 'Apennine culture', a name which is universally accepted today.

The Bronze Age Apennine culture was revealed as such an important and widespread phenomenon that it almost appeared to be the first manifestation of Italian unity. Rellini equated it with the Italic people.[5] However, the linguistic difficulty still remained. The fact that the Italic dialects belonged to the Indo-European family indicated an origin in Europe north of the Alps. The establishment of the theory of linguistic substrata, which owed much to the work of G. I. Ascoli, had meanwhile shown and stressed the presence of a large number of pre-Indo-European Mediterranean elements in the vocabulary of the Italic dialects and especially in Latin.[6] It followed that the primitive inhabitants of Italy had not been completely submerged by the invaders and that they must have contributed to the formation of an Italic *ethnos*. Scholars even went so far as to deny or minimize the invasions, and attributed the establishment of Indo-European languages to the infiltration of small groups or to political or commercial contacts, without a change in population in the full sense. These notions were expressed by Patroni's term 'linguistic ferments'.[7] Thus, from a theory which regarded northern invasions and influences as the determining factors in the development of an Italic *ethnos*, scholars passed to the theory that the Italic peoples were a relatively autochthonous element in the framework of earlier Mediterranean culture.

Both theories were defended with arguments that were extreme, passionately controversial or greatly oversimplified. Although the most recent archaeological discoveries and studies are naturally incomplete and subject to constant revision, they nevertheless reflect a situation that is a good deal more complex than anything the supporters of either theory could have imagined – a situation which can only with difficulty be made to fit preconceived models. The first question arising out of the archaeological evidence is the origin and diffusion of cremation, a burial rite which marks the transition from the Bronze Age to the Iron Age in Italy no less than in Greece and continental Europe. The very breadth of the diffusion of the cremation rite, over territories culturally and racially very different, should warn us against attributing this phenomenon to the arrival of new peoples, especially if the concept is oversimplified to that of a single massive invasion. Nevertheless, one must not reject *a priori* the hypothesis that the gradual adoption of new religious ideas and ritual habits might be related, individually and over a limited range, to population movements. Even Patroni, the principal supporter of the autochthonous theory, was willing to attribute the first cremation cemeteries in the peninsula (which he called 'Protovilla- novan') to small groups who had left the Danube basin and the Balkans to cross the Adriatic Sea. On the other hand, scholars from other disciplines (historians like L. Pareti and linguists like G. Devoto) have maintained that a close relationship existed between cremating peoples and Italic peoples, although they admitted that it was limited to the later waves of the latter. Even comparatively recent studies on the subject are still very ready to accept the hypothesis of continental in- vasions, coming mainly from the Balkan and Danubian regions; and a new aspect has been added to the question by the establishment of the theory of a great proto-historic expansion of the Illyrians by H. Pokorny, R. Pittioni and others. They have seen this expansion as determining not only the origin of the Italic peoples in the Adriatic area (Veneti, Apuli), but the very constitution of an over-all Italic *ethnos*.[8]

This intricate problem, bedevilled as it is by the interplay of opinions and hypotheses, is further complicated by the problem of the origin of the Etruscans, which appears to be indissolubly linked to that of the origin of the Italic peoples, especially as regards the interpretation of archaeological evidence. But this is the subject of the next chapter.

Later prehistory and the cultures of the Italian Iron Age

From the period of the first extant written documents and the evidence of historical tradition down to the unification of the peninsula by Rome, the history and civilization of the Etruscan people form part of an Italy which has all the appearance of being divided into a number of ethnic, linguistic and cultural groups, more or less clearly differentiated, and varying in size and in degree of development. In this sense, the history of pre-Roman Italy contrasts sharply with that of Greece, which is that of a single people with only minor differentiations of an ethnic or linguistic character. The ancient Italian native groups displayed characteristics, developments and traditions that were independent from one another. These differences were so marked that they remained fixed in the division of Roman Italy by Augustus, and are still reflected to some extent in the several regions of modern Italy.[9]

Our main concern here is to attempt an outline of ancient Italy in its formative stage, a picture delineated by the archaeological and linguistic evidence available to us. We have already mentioned the principal modern theories about the origin of the Italic peoples; let us now look objectively at the various pieces of evidence in the light of the latest research.

A complete and precise account of the distribution and succession of Italian prehistoric cultures from the Neolithic onwards is still far from being established. Nevertheless, the excavations of L. Bernabò Brea in the Arene Candide cave in Liguria and in the Aeolian Islands to the north-east of Sicily make it possible to recognize the main phases of development in terms of reliable stratigraphical evidence. We can distinguish the following phases. (1) *The Early Neolithic period* characterized by the widespread survival of stone tools in the Mesolithic tradition and by the appearance of the earliest examples of Impressed Ware. (2) *The Middle Neolithic period* which, in the south, witnessed the flourishing of evolved cultures characterized by the presence of painted and incised pottery influenced from the Aegean and the Balkans; the north, on the other hand, saw the spread of Danubian characteristics such as square-mouthed vases and terracotta figurines. (3) *The Late Neolithic period* characterized by the general diffusion of undecorated pottery (the Diana and Lagozza styles). (4) *The Copper Age and the Early Bronze Age*, not always easily distinguishable, with a variety of local cultural trends: in Sicily (Serraferlicchio, Castelluccio, etc.), we find cultures with painted pottery exhibiting clear influence from the Aegean and Anatolia; on the mainland (Rinaldone, Gaudo), there are cultures with globular jars and battle-axes derived from eastern Europe; in Sardinia, west Sicily, west and north Italy (Remedello), we find influence from the Bell-Beaker cultures of western Europe; and, finally, the initial stages of the Apennine culture itself can be seen (Conelle di Arcevia, Gioia del Colle). Typical of this whole period is the rite of inhumation, with crouched burials in rock-cut tombs and trench graves. (5) *The full Bronze Age*, corresponding to the Aegean Late Bronze Age, accompanied by the spread of Mycenaean pottery in Apulia, Sicily, and the Aeolian Islands. In the peninsula, this was contemporary with the Apennine culture and its pottery, characterized by incised spirals and meander-patterns. And in northern Italy, this was the period of the early *terremare* and of the typical lake-dwellings (lasting from the Polada culture, which perhaps began earlier, down to that of Peschiera). (6) *The Late Bronze Age, and the Final Bronze Age*, of which the latter represents the transition to the Iron Age, although the evidence is not yet amenable to definitive classification. Late Mycenaean and Sub-Mycenaean influences linger on in the coastal sites of southern Italy (Apulia, the Pantalica North culture in Sicily), a 'Sub-Apennine' culture developed in the peninsula and spread to the Aeolian Islands (Ausonian Period I), and the *terremare* flourished in northern Italy. During this period, and especially during its last phases, we find the spread of cremation cemeteries containing cinerary urns of pottery. These have been found in northern Italy, further south (Torre Castelluccia, Timmari, Pianello, the Tolfa hills, etc.), and in the islands (Milazzo in Sicily, Lipari, Ausonian Period II): this new cultural phenomenon is called 'Protovillanovan'. (7) *The beginning of the Iron Age* in the full sense of the term, a development immediately preceded and accompanied by the first Greek colonization of southern Italy and Sicily and the first appearance of the great historical centres of Campania, Latium and Etruria.[10]

The dating of these cultural periods, and especially of the more recent ones, is of great importance for the assessment of their historical meaning. It has given rise to specialized research and to heated arguments among interested scholars. In practical terms, we were for long forced to rely solely upon indirect evidence in attempting to reconstruct an absolute chronology: the presence of objects imported from the Near East, from lands with older civilizations (e.g. Egypt) or from cultural areas with a more clearly defined chronology (e.g. the Aegean). It is only in comparatively recent times that we have been able to use a direct method of dating based on the rate of radioactive breakdown of a carbon isotope present in organic matter ('C-14' dating).[11] For our purposes, it seems safe to assume that the Italian Bronze Age proper (i.e. the period spanning its Middle and Late phases) coincided with Mycenaean IIIA and B, from about 1400 to 1200 B.C. On the other hand, the first certain dates marking the beginning of historical times can be deduced from the first Greek settlements at Ischia, Cumae and in Sicily; these coincide with a fairly advanced phase of the Iron Age cultures of Etruria (Villanovan), Campania and Sicily – from about the middle of the eighth century. For all the intermediate periods dating is still uncertain: we oscillate between a so-called 'high chronology', which would put the beginning of the Iron Age as early as the end of the second millennium B.C., i.e. around the year 1000 (O. Montelius, N. Åberg, G. v. Merhart), and a so-called 'low chronology', which would bring the end of the Bronze Age down to about the year 800 B.C., thus shortening the length of the first phases of the Iron Age (G. Karo, J. Sundwall, etc.). Some of the scholars who have opted for a 'low chronology' have even suggested that Protovillanovan features should be regarded as contemporary with the earliest Villanovan phases (G. Säflund); others have gone so far as to bring the date of the beginning of the Villanovan period down to the late eighth century (Å. Åkerström). These divergences appear to have diminished in importance during the last few years. The passage from the transitional cultures to the Iron Age is placed either in the tenth century (G. Kossack, H. Müller-Karpe, H. Hencken) or in the ninth (in the opinion of the author). The problem is complicated by the diversity of opinions on the relationship between the evidence provided by Italy and that provided by central Europe and the Danube basin. The German school, with G. v. Merhart as its main exponent, has insisted on the priority of the so-called 'Urnfield' (*Urnenfelder*) cultures to the north and east of the Alps as the determining factor in the passage from the Bronze to the Iron Age during the last centuries of the second millennium B.C. In contrast, others have considered these cultures in the main to be late and marginal reflexes of the development of Italian Iron Age cultures.[12]

The difficulties in attempting to classify and date the cultural evidence for the Bronze Age–Iron Age transition in Italy are due partly to its scarcity, but mainly perhaps to the very nature of the period itself, which must have been dominated alternately by conservative survivals and vigorous innovating trends. After the collapse of Mycenaean sea-power from the twelfth century B.C. onwards, and during the Sub-Mycenaean, Protogeometric and Geometric periods, contacts between Italy and the Aegean appear to have been much weakened, if not completely absent. In southern Italy, in the coastal sites of Apulia and Sicily, strong Mycenaean Bronze Age traditions together with occasional sea contacts with the East Mediterranean characterize the slow development of local cultures until they take on the Geometric aspect typical of the Iron Age. The inhumation cemeteries of eastern Sicily enable us to follow this evolution through a number of phases which have been called Pantalica North, Cassibile-Dessueri and Pantalica South; the latter lasts until the beginning of Greek colonization in historical times. In peninsular Italy too, the cultural heritage and customs of the later Bronze Age seem to have persisted as the basic features of life in most communities, or at least in the most conservative ones. They take the forms usually labelled Sub-Apennine or Ausonian: in central Italy, for example, the late features of the settlement sites at Monte Cetona and in the region around Orvieto are typical; the same can be said for the last phases of the Terramara culture. At the same time, however, we find the first appearance and spread of cinerary urns in cremation cemeteries, of varying density and reminiscent of the urn-fields of continental Europe. These are not limited to the Alpine regions and northern Italy (Canegrate, Monza, Casinalbo, Crespellano, Reggio, Bovolone, etc.); they are also found in the peninsula and in the islands. This precocious phenomenon is attested in a number of cases by the shape of the urns and by new grave-goods: the presence, for instance, of the characteristic Late Mycenaean type of violin-bow fibula. The cemetery of Torre Castelluccia in Apulia must certainly still belong to the end of the Bronze Age.

The establishment of the rite of cremation seems to have been accompanied by new cultural features, for it coincides with the spread of certain vase forms (especially the biconical ossuary), of a number of new decorative motifs on pottery, and of some bronze types also found in isolated hoards and settlement sites. As a result we can now talk in terms of a true archaeological culture, perhaps even of a chronological phase, called 'Protovillanovan'. We can now be certain – and this is of fundamental importance – that the Protovillanovan phenomenon spread over the whole of the Italian area, from Apulia (Timmari) and Sicily (Milazzo, Lipari) to the west coast of the peninsula (Sasso and Allumiere in the Tolfa hills, Palombara Sabina, Ponte San Pietro near Vulci, Monte Argentario, Sticciano north of Grosseto, etc.), to the Adriatic coast (Pianello della Genga in the Marche) and to the north (Bismantova, Fontanella Mantovana – where, however, the phenomenon is somewhat different from the cremation cemeteries mentioned above). What characterizes the Protovillanovan is the singular uniformity of its manifestations in places far distant from each other, a probable indication that there were close and rapid communications. Within the Etruscan area, Protovillanovan communities seem to have lasted until the beginning of the Iron Age and to have been, in a sense, absorbed by the Villanovan civilization of the great coastal centres that in turn were to become the cities of historical times. Elsewhere, in Latium (Rome, the Alban hills), in Umbria (Terni) and in the Po valley (Este), the local versions of the Iron Age spring directly from types of culture that are Protovillanovan in character; these may be usefully labelled 'Proto-Latial', 'Proto-Umbrian', 'Proto-Atestine' and 'Proto-Golaseccan'.[13]

A clear differentiation into regional cultural groups becomes apparent only with the beginning of the Iron Age proper. This can be recognized by the spread of the use of the new metal and the general adoption of linear decorative styles, coinciding with the flourishing of the Geometric style in the Greek world, from about the ninth century B.C. (see Figure 1, p. 46). The following regional groups may be distinguished: the cultures of Sicily; the southern cultures of Calabria and Campania; the Adriatic cultures of Apulia, and of the Samnite and Picene areas; that of Latium; the Villanovan cultures of Etruria and Emilia (with related groups in southern and Adriatic Italy); the northern cultures of Este (the Veneto), Golasecca (Lombardy, Piedmont) and Liguria.[14] These groups can be divided roughly into two large areas according to the use of inhumation or cremation as a burial rite. The inhuming area comprises southern Italy and the lands bordering on the Adriatic; the cremating area covers Latium, Tuscany, part of Umbria and the whole of northern Italy. An intermediate band runs from north to south between the two areas, from the Romagna across Umbria, down to

Figure 1. Italian cultures of the Iron Age. Areas left in white are those where inhumation was the exclusive funerary rite; hatched areas are those where cremation prevailed (cross-hatching indicates the extent of Villanovan culture); the dots show the principal proto-Villanovan cemeteries south of the Po valley.

Latium. This geographic separation of burial rites is one more indication that the Iron Age was accompanied by the definition and fixation of traditions which were still fluid in the preceding ages.

The Sicilian Iron Age cultures clearly belong to the indigenous Sicels in the eastern part of the island, and to the Sicans in the west; both antedate, or co-exist with, the Greek colonies. Typical examples of Sicel culture are the cemeteries of Pantalica and Finocchito, representing two successive phases between the ninth and seventh centuries; Sican culture is attested e.g. at Cannatello near Agrigento. In south-western Italy – at Canale near Locri, at Torre Galli in Calabria, and in the cemeteries of the Sarno valley and at prehellenic Cumae in Cam-

46

pania, etc. – the inhuming 'Fossakultur' (Trench-grave culture) is grafted on to the indigenous Bronze Age tradition. Recent studies, however, show the region to be culturally somewhat heterogeneous: around Salerno, for instance, there is the group of 'Villanovan' cremation cemeteries and a good deal of pottery that exhibits obvious Apulian influence, etc. It is therefore far from easy to ascribe a precise archaeological identity to the various local populations associated with the area by ancient tradition: *Siculi* (Sicels), *Itali*, *Morgeti*, *Oenotri*, *Ausonii*, *Opici*, etc. At a comparatively late stage, Apulia developed a civilization of its own on a similar basis (distinguished mainly by painted Geometric ware), which lasted until late in historical times as the heritage of the Apulians (Iapygians) or Apulo-Salentines, also known (running from north to south) as Daunians, Peucetians, and Messapians. In another direction, however, these Apulian cultures are more or less closely connected with other Iron Age manifestations found on the Italian and Illyrian Adriatic coasts. On the Italian side, the earliest, richest and most typical of these are associated with the inhumation cemeteries of the Picene region (Novilara near Pesaro, Numana, Pitino near San Severino, Fabriano, Belmonte Piceno, Ascoli, etc.). Others may be recognized, but not so clearly, on the coast and in the interior of the Samnite territory (Alfedena, Capestrano, etc.) as belonging to Italic peoples of Sabellian stock. The influence of this vast cycle of Adriatic Iron Age cultures penetrates deeply into the heart of the peninsula, reaching as far as Umbria (Terni), the Faliscan and Sabine territories, and Latium (Tivoli). The culture of Latium belonged initially to peoples who rigorously practised the cremation rite – the ancient Latins of the Alban Hills and Rome – but it shares features both with the Villanovan culture north of the Tiber and with the southern Trench-grave culture; its chief characteristic is the use of hut-urns as ossuaries.

In northern Italy, the Atestine culture, represented principally in the Este cemeteries, has obvious connections with the Villanovan culture of Emilia, and on the other hand it is also related to cultures in the Adriatic, Alpine and Danubian regions. Nevertheless, its original features and overall development continued without interruption from the early Iron Age until the Roman conquest: it is the culture of the Veneti. The central and western regions – the Po valley and the Alpine and sub-Alpine area – are archaeologically less self-contained and uniform. Here we find both cremation and inhumation cemeteries with grave-goods that are to some extent comparable with those of the Atestine and Villanovan worlds: the culture in this area has been named after Golasecca, a village near Varese, and is also attested by finds at the Ca' Morta near Como, at Sesto Calende, Castelletto Ticino, etc. A variant is evidenced in coastal Liguria by the recently discovered cremation cemetery at Chiavari.

But the phenomenon most relevant to our study is the so-called Villanovan culture, named after Villanova near Bologna, where the first discoveries were made. This culture appears to have been the most significant manifestation of the Italian Iron Age, owing to its wide diffusion, the diversity of its aspects and the multiplicity of its developments. Although it varies in both time and space, its most specific characteristic is the use of cremation tombs in which the ashes are contained within large biconical urns of dark impasto, with incised linear decoration (e.g. Plate 3). These urns generally have only one handle (sometimes one of two handles has been deliberately broken off) and a cover-bowl (but the cover may be a helmet, whether real or imitation).

The following regional groups may be distinguished. (1) The *Villanovan of Etruria*, spread over the whole of Etruria and attested by large cemeteries corresponding to what were to become the main cities of historical times, particularly near the coast (Veii, Cerveteri, Tarquinia, Vulci, Vetulonia, Populonia). Its manifestations are particularly rich and evolved, and include ossuaries capped by helmets, and huturns like those found in Latium, etc. (2) The *Villanovan of Emilia*, represented mainly by the large cemeteries at Bologna. (3) The *group in the Romagna*, found at Verucchio and San Marino, with helmets used as covers as in Etruria. (4) The *Picene* group, recently discovered at Fermo in the Marche, which cannot yet be related to any other. (5) The *Southern Villanovan*, in Campania and Lucania, with cemeteries at Pontecagnano near Salerno, at Capodifiume near Paestum, and at Sala Consilina in the valley of the Tanagro; traces of this type of culture have also been found in Campania proper, near Capua. The whole of this area is separated from Etruria by the Iron Age cultures of Latium and Campania; it features a number of local developments which do not affect its essential characteristics.

Within Etruria and at Bologna, Villanovan culture developed at a pace which appears to be especially marked along the coast of Etruria. Here it evolved without a break right up to the full development of the Orientalizing phase which marks the beginning of the fullest flowering of the Etruscan people. We are able to trace the following phases. (1) A *typical Villanovan* phase, with cremation as the exclusive burial rite. (2) An *evolved Villanovan* phase, which can be dated to the years between the first half of the eighth century B.C. and the beginning of the seventh. It is marked by the presence of both cremation and inhumation, and characterized by an exuberant development of metallurgy and by the influence of the Greek colonies that were being established in southern Italy at the time: an example of this influence is the appearance of painted pottery in the archaeological record. (3) An *Orientalizing* phase (seventh century), in which inhumation is the predominant rite in southern Etruria, characterized by monumental tombs with abundant and rich grave-goods including imported and imitated oriental products. (4) A *Late Orientalizing* phase (sixth century), contemporary with the spread of Corinthian pottery and marking the transition to the Archaic phase of Etruscan civilization.[15] This sequence appears to be less clearly marked and slower in the non-coastal areas of Etruria. At Bologna, on the other hand, the cremating Villanovan culture lasts through the so-called Sàvena-San Vitale, Benacci I, Benacci II and Arnoaldi periods, roughly contemporary with the four phases in Etruria described above. From about the seventh century, Orientalizing influences are more or less discernible in the Iron Age cultures of northern Italy and of the Adriatic. To the south of Etruria, the typical Etruscan Orientalizing civilization makes its appearance at Palestrina in Latium and may be traced as far as Pontecagnano.

The languages of primitive Italy

The sources at our disposal for the linguistic study of the period are extremely limited: they consist almost exclusively of the few inscriptions in the pre-Latin languages of Italy that have come down to us and a limited number of glosses (translated or explained words) handed down by classical literary tradition. Given these conditions, it is hard enough to attempt even a partial reconstruction of the structure of these languages, or indeed, in some cases, to recognize and distinguish one from another and form some idea of their spread and duration. More arduous and uncertain still is the type of research that attempts to establish their origin, their mutual relationships and influences, and their connections with other linguistic areas: to work out, in other words, the linguistic 'proto-history' and 'prehistory' of Italy from the evidence in our possession. Prehistoric linguistics lacks the direct documentation available to prehistoric archaeology. Even toponymy (i.e. the collection and study of place names), although very rewarding, for place names stubbornly resist the ebb and flow of languages, is of little use as a source of knowledge for the study of prehistoric linguistic conditions and phases except in a vague and limited way, owing to the difficulty of establishing the date of origin of names and, more particularly, their original meaning.

These difficulties have not prevented a number of scholars, principally Italian linguists (F. Ribezzo, A. Trombetti, G. Devoto, V. Bertoldi, G. Alessio), from obtaining certain results over the last few decades in the study of the pre-Indo-European substratum or substrata of Italy. These linguistic layers have come to be known by a generic and conventional term, that of 'Mediterranean' languages, for their features appear to be related to those of a much wider linguistic area, ranging from Asia Minor and the Aegean (where the term 'pre-hellenic' substratum is used) to the confines of western Europe.[16] These researches are based first and foremost upon the study of place names; but scholars also rely on the collection of non-Indo-European words in the vocabulary of Latin and Greek and in that of other Indo-European languages of the Mediterranean area. They are even able to use modern spoken dialects which preserve in their vocabulary the relics of very ancient local languages, especially among names of plants and animals, words applied to the configuration of the landscape, technical terms, etc. They also avail themselves of the results of the comparative study of historical languages, documented in inscriptions, thought to represent, whether wholly or in part, a survival of pre-Indo-European substrata, as in the case of Etruscan. This type of research, directed mainly towards abstract reconstructions and, it must be said, still lacking a method of its own, can only give results that are both vague and provisional. But at least the basic fact that there existed in Italy idioms on which the Indo-European languages imposed themselves can be taken as certain. These earlier languages possessed a totally different structure, and were partially related to the linguistic underlayers of other Mediterranean and European lands. It is much harder to establish whether these languages can in their turn be divided into different groups; whether they overlaid each other and, if so, how; or whether they were distributed in different areas; whether linguistic amalgams arose in the course of time; and, finally, how long they survived the Indo-European overlayer, and what was the nature of their relationship with the Indo-European languages.

The widely accepted concept of 'pre-Indo-European' has been further modified and refined into that of 'proto-Indo-European', which implies a differentiation from Indo-European but still within the circle of an original relationship (Kretschmer); and of 'peri-Indo-European', which designates that marginal ground common to both Mediterranean and Indo-European languages (Devoto).[17] These critical refinements are an attempt to avoid the oversimplification of opposing a 'Mediterranean' to an Indo-European linguistic world. Trombetti had postulated the existence of an earlier linguistic layer, to which he gave the name 'Basco-Caucasian', coined from its peripheral survivals, and a more recent one, which he labelled 'Aegeo-Asianic'. The first, now also known as 'Hispano-Caucasian', does not seem to have left any traces in Italy in historical times, except in Sardinia where, as scholars now agree, a language was spoken before the Roman conquest which appears to have been distantly related to the Basque language in the Pyrenees. There are, of course, no written documents, but the relationship is recognizable through a compact set of place names, still noticeable today in the distinctive nature of Sardinian geographical names.[18] This linguistic layer may justifiably be regarded as pre-Indo-European in the proper sense of the word. The term 'Aegeo-Asianic', on the other hand, denotes in practice that whole complex of facts which characterize the linguistic substratum of the Italian peninsula and some of the languages that survived into historical times (e.g. Etruscan) in relation to the prehellenic substratum of the Aegean area and the languages of Asia Minor. This relationship may take a precise shape, as it did in Ribezzo's theory: that of reflecting a very ancient extension of elements, common to both the Aegean and the Italian areas, of an ancient 'Tyrrhenian' unity (to use Ribezzo's term). Or it may be understood as the penetration into the two areas of a prehistoric linguistic wave from the Danube and Balkan regions, as in Kretschmer's theory, where it received the label 'Pelasgic' or 'Raeto-Tyrrhenian'; or, again, as the result of late prehistoric infiltrations and invasions, as in the theory of a supposed immigration of the Etruscans from Asia Minor. But the evidence characterizing this layer shows it to be more or less connected with the Indo-European languages, although they do not seem to account for all the aspects of Italian linguistic prehistory.

The problem has been tackled in a different way: by attempting, for instance, a classification of languages according to area. A number of areas have been proposed: 'Iberian', 'Libyan', 'Ligurian', 'Tyrrhenian', etc. But these seem rather improbable concepts. All we in fact possess are mere indications of the existence of partial regional connections, as, for instance, between Liguria and Sicily (but not sufficiently strong to postulate a 'Sican-Ligurian' linguistic unit), or between the Raetian area of the eastern Alps and the peninsula (hence the concept of a 'Raeto-Tyrrhenian' group). We also find variations which seem to be distributed in certain directions and in certain areas rather than in others, as in the case of the well-known Mediterranean word *pala*, 'rounded eminence or hollow', widely attested in place names in the Alps and in the peninsula (it entered the vocabulary of Latin under the form *palatum*: cf. the English 'palate'); it alternates on the one hand with *bal-* in Liguria and Sardinia, and on the other with *fal-* in the eastern Alps and in the peninsula, as also in historical Etruscan.

As for the Indo-European languages, the problem of their origin, penetration into Italy and development has been and is still one of the main subjects of research among historical linguists. Heated debates centre upon it, as also on the nature of their reciprocal connections and of their relationship with the substratum languages. Many aspects of these questions are still obscure, and opinions vary a great deal.[19] The final stage of this long process is all that we have to go on: the linguistic map of Italy at the beginning of historical times, i.e. when writing begins to spread throughout the peninsula, between the seventh and fifth centuries B.C. The map may be sketched as follows.[20]

Setting aside the languages of colonization (Greek and Phoenician), in the western half of Sicily, which was inhabited by the Sicans, traditionally thought to be of Iberian or Ligurian origin, and by the Elymi, believed to be of eastern provenance, we find faint traces of languages that are not Indo-European or cannot be clearly recognized as such. In the eastern half of the island, on the other hand, the language of the Sicels is certainly an Indo-European one, fairly closely related to Latin but also sharing features with eastern Italic and Adriatic languages.[21]

The nature of the languages spoken by the indigenous populations of south-west Italy, from what is now Calabria to Campania (the *Itali*, *Siculi* (Sicels), *Oenotri*, *Morgeti*, *Ausonii*, *Opici*, etc. of tradition), is still practically unknown, except for relatively late inscriptions in eastern Italic languages. There has been an attempt, based upon the flimsiest evidence, to demonstrate the existence of a series of ancient Indo-European languages distributed along the Tyrrhenian coast, related to Sicel in the south and to Latin in the north.[22] Latin itself originally extended over a somewhat limited territory, which included, as far as we know, the *Latium vetus* area surrounding the Alban hills, and, west of the Tiber, the Faliscan region. The language of the Faliscans gradually acquired the characteristics of a dialectal variant of Latin, and reveals Umbro-Sabellic and Etruscan influences.[23]

In south-east Italy, the inhabitants of Apulia and the Salentine peninsula spoke a language generally known as Messapic, of Indo-European origin and related to the Italic and Illyrian-Balkan languages.[24] In the centre of the peninsula, over a wide area spread along the backbone of the Apennines from Umbria to Lucania, we find a number of peoples differing in name, history and culture but belonging to a single linguistic group of Indo-European origin, distinct from Latin, known as Osco-Umbrian or Umbro-Sabellic (also 'eastern Italic', or, more simply, 'Italic' – a misleading term owing to the over-restricted use of its meaning). These people spread over a wide area in historical times in the direction of the Tyrrhenian Sea and towards the south of the peninsula. Their dialects became differentiated into Umbrian in the north, the Sabellic group in the centre, and Oscan or Samnite in the south.[25] On the Adriatic side, especially in Picenum, there are traces of a dialect known as 'south Picene' or proto-Sabellic: it too seems to be related to the eastern Italic languages at an early stage of their development. At the northern end of the Marche, in the region of Pesaro, we find another obscure dialect, certainly different from the preceding, known as 'north Picene'.[26]

The western or Tyrrhenian part of central Italy is the wide area where Etruscan was originally spoken and from which it gradually spread, though with varying fortunes, towards northern Italy, Latium and Campania. This language (whose origin and description will be dealt with in Part III) represents the most important historical testimony known in Italy and the central Mediterranean of a linguistic tradition whose origin is basically non-Indo-European, or at least whose structure cannot be described in terms that are typical of the Indo-European languages.

Conversely, very little is known of the local pre-Celtic and pre-Latin dialects of northern Italy and of the Alpine regions. In the west we find the Ligurian dialects, believed to have extended across the Alps into southern France, and especially the 'Lepontic' dialect, known through a group of inscriptions found in the region of the Lombard lakes, and in the Val d'Ossola; the picture here seems to be that of an infiltration of Indo-European elements into a pre-Indo-European linguistic substratum. Further east, in the Raetian Alps and the Adige region, there are traces of a dialect known conventionally by the name 'Raetic', probably pre-Indo-European, exhibiting some affinity with Etruscan and also some Indo-European influences.[27] Finally, at the extreme eastern corner of north Italy, east of the Adige river, we find Venetic, the language of the Veneti, of clear Indo-European origin but basically distinct from Latin and eastern Italic, as also from Messapic.[28] The penetration of Celtic into northern and central Italy took place after the beginning of historical times.

It will be seen that we are faced with a set of facts of great complexity, a mosaic of peoples and languages that have little in common with each other. It is a far cry from the over-simple 'Italic' unity conceived by scholars in the past – all the more so now that we have discarded the 'family-tree' theory, which viewed the several Indo-European Italic languages (Latin, Umbro-Sabellic, Venetic, etc.) as dialectal branches of a hypothetical 'common Italic'. We know now that some of these languages tended, if anything, to come closer together as a consequence of the vicinity and coexistence of the peoples who spoke them in proto-historic and historic times. We are a long way too from the picture presented by Greece at the time, one of fundamental linguistic unity marked only by variations of a dialectal nature.

A basic problem arises from the simultaneous presence of languages whose stock is certainly Indo-European and others that are not Indo-European, or that were only partially influenced by Indo-European elements. This fact seems to prove that, in the main, the indo-europeanization of Italy was still being accomplished in historic times. It came to a close only towards the end of the first millennium B.C., when the Roman conquest imposed the general adoption of Latin. But yet another fact emerges from our picture. The 'non-Indo-European' area lies mainly to the west, comprising the main portions of the islands and of Tyrrhenian and north Italy. Moreover, we may add that the oldest linguistic types, those that may be referred to an original Mediterranean Hispano-Caucasian layer, survived precisely in the westernmost region, i.e. in Sardinia. The Indo-European area, on the other hand, comprises the greater part of the peninsula, eastern Sicily and the eastern limb of north Italy. The boundary separating the two linguistic groups roughly follows an imaginary line, more or less corresponding to the twelfth meridian, running from the lower valley of the Adige to the mouth of the Tiber, and reappearing as if to divide Sicily into two (see Figure 2, opposite). The historical importance of this fact is obvious: for if we suppose (as everything leads us to suppose) that the non-Indo-European linguistic area is older than the Indo-European, the position of the latter shows clearly that the indo-europeanization of the peninsula must have occurred from east to west rather than from north to south.

Within the Indo-European languages themselves, it is possible to establish a relation between classification and geographical distribution which provides us with useful clues in attempting to follow their spread and development within Italy. In practice, these languages can be divided into three large groups: one represented by Latin, one by Umbro-Sabellic, and one by the Adriatic languages, i.e. Messapic and Venetic. The Latin group is generally held to include Sicel and the languages supposed to have been spoken by the peoples of south-west Italy. This hypothetical linguistic unity has been labelled 'Latin-Ausonian' (by Ribezzo) or 'proto-Latin' (by Devoto), but we should perhaps prefer – so as not to prejudge the issue – the term 'western Italic' languages. It is well known that, among the Indo-European languages, Latin shows a number of particularly early features.[29] It may therefore be concluded that it belongs to one of the earliest types of Indo-European to have penetrated into Italy. The Umbro-Sabellic or eastern Italic group appears to be later in spread and formation, owing, among other reasons, to its connections with 'central' Indo-European types, especially with Greek. In the case of Venetic and Messapic, the paths taken by their journey into Italy may, in a sense, be said to be still recognizable through their central-European and Illyrian-Balkan contacts.

When we consider the geographical position of these groups in re-

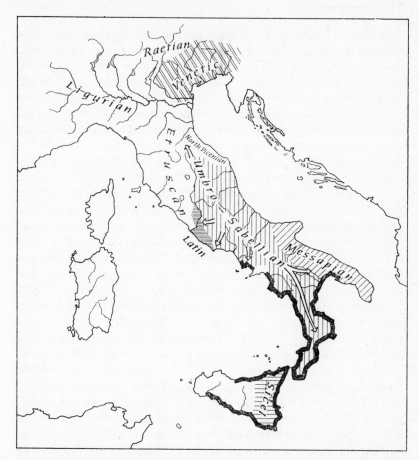

Figure 2. The languages of ancient Italy. Horizontal hatching indicates western Italic languages (Latin and Sicel); vertical hatching, eastern Italic languages (Umbro-Sabellian); oblique hatching, the Adriatic languages (Messapian and Venetic). Areas speaking a non-Indo-European language, or languages whose stock is uncertain, are left white. The black bands round the southern coasts indicate areas of Greek colonization.

lation to each other, it is possible to deduce that a first Indo-European wave, represented by the western Italic languages, may have pushed (or have been pushed) towards the west, where it came into contact with the non-Indo-European linguistic area. It is also possible to deduce that a following wave, the Umbro-Sabellic, established itself in the peninsula by moving across from the Adriatic towards the Tyrrhenian seas, as attested by the spearheads of its advance, in historical times, in the direction of Latium (Sabines, Volsci), Campania, Lucania and Bruttium, modern Calabria (Samnites). A third wave, on the other hand, may be seen in those eastern spearheads, Messapic and Venetic,

55

even though they appear to be independent from each other. The affinities that have been found between Venetic and Latin could perhaps be explained by the position of the former, for, although it is in the eastern, Adriatic area, it is also, like Latin, in direct contact along its western border with the non-Indo-European linguistic area.[30] This confirms the impression that the penetration and diffusion of the various Indo-European languages of Italy travelled mainly from east to west, across the Adriatic and the peninsula, rather than from north to south, across the Alps and northern Italy, as the earlier invasion hypothesis had supposed.

The problem, however, is a good deal more knotty than it appears at first. The historical languages known to us through written documents are only the final outcome of a long and complex process involving the interpenetration and sifting of linguistic tendencies and currents whose nature may in some cases be approximately identified but in others is completely unknown. According to circumstances, some of these tendencies and currents may have developed vigorously; others may have been subjected to a considerable degree of mixing; others still may have completely disappeared, as was the case, in historical times, for some of the lesser languages through the domination first of Umbro-Sabellic and later, this time permanently, of Latin. These obscure formative processes affect the relations of the Indo-European with the pre-Indo-European languages, and of the Indo-European languages with one another. Such processes can more easily be assigned to an age characterized by human communities that were small and unstable than to the urban type of civilization of historical times. This is how we may explain, for instance, the fact that three different linguistic traditions seem to converge in Latin, each represented by a different resolution of the original Indo-European aspirated interdental (d^h), as shown by the types *rutilus*, *rufus* and *ruber* (all adjectives denoting the basic concept 'red'). Devoto ascribes the first to a 'proto-Latin' origin, the second to Osco-Umbrian influence and the third to a linguistic seam which he labelled 'proto-Italic'.[31] It is interesting to note that ancient Indo-European elements appear to have penetrated into historical Etruscan, elements whose phonetic characteristics show them to belong to the first of these three types: e.g. *lautn* ('family') from the Indo-European root *leudh-*. This is confirmed by the ancient distribution of this same word along the Tyrrhenian coast, from Sicily – where it is clearly attested in Sicel – all the way to central Italy. There are, in any case, also strong traces of the interference of eastern Italic languages with Etruscan.

The formation of historical peoples

We have now examined and compared the evidence provided by archaeology and linguistics in the light of present-day knowledge and we have arrived at interpretations rather more subtle and qualified than those of older generations of prehistorians. The conclusion that we must accept is that the origin of the historical national groups of ancient Italy faces us with a problem of extreme complexity which cannot be tackled from only one angle and is not amenable to hasty or axiomatic solutions. Above all we must guard against that instinctive and over-simple way of thinking which has led ancient and modern scholars alike to picture this origin as a single *event*, or as a series of events, identifiable and identified in time. We should stop looking for an external starting-point, for a reality whose shape was somehow already fixed or, at least in embryo, extrapolated back in time. Such attitudes produced, for instance, the notion that the 'Italic peoples' were a fully formed Indo-European group who, on reaching Italy, initiated Italian history. Today we are led to believe the very opposite – we must do so, if only because we cannot close our eyes to the universal evidence of historical analogies – and the modern point of view is rather that the definition of the ethnic and cultural characteristics of ancient Italy is the end point of a long and laborious formative process which is, for the most part, beyond the reach of present-day sources of knowledge.[32]

This process must be considered as being virtually complete by the beginning of the Iron Age. As we have already seen, this was the time when more or less clearly differentiated regional cultures began to appear, and their distribution coincided almost everywhere with those languages soon to be attested by inscriptions and with those peoples whose names have been handed down to us by historical tradition. The reverse is true of the earlier periods, where we find cultural features spread over wide areas and displaying a number of uniform aspects throughout most of Italy, as in the case of the Apennine and Sub-Apennine cultures, or scattered here and there in regions often far distant from each other, as in the case of the characteristic Proto-villanovan cemeteries, which suggests rather the meeting and inter-action of traditional and innovating currents in these areas, without any clear connection with specifically linguistic or ethnic evidence. In fact their situation seems to fit with that fluid stage of interpenetration and gradual elaboration which we postulated for the early history of the Italic dialects. This being the case, we should resist the temptation to give an archaeological identity to the various linguistic seams or, conversely, to seek a name for each of the various cultures which preceded the Iron Age. We should not ask ourselves which prehistoric facts accompany the appearance of the 'proto-Latins' or the ancestors of the Umbro-Sabellians, or, conversely, which language was spoken by the possessors of the Apennine, the Terramara or the Protovillanovan cultures. This is simply because the spread of a particular linguistic type may have occurred without any perceptible changes in culture. And in much the same way, a cultural phenomenon – especially if it is important enough to produce extensive traces in the archaeological record – may have been common to different ethnic groups, linguistically heterogeneous, in the case of populations as yet unstable or of small communities organized along pre-urban lines. We shall seek, therefore, to avoid the use of expressions such as 'Apennine folk', 'Terramara folk', 'Protovillanovans', etc., even as convenient, rough-and-ready labels, for they lead us instinctively to think in terms of ethnic groupings when all we have is a number of shared cultural features.

We are still left, however, with the more general problem of the indo-europeanization of Italy. This is a real and fundamental fact concerning Italian origins and it would be highly desirable to be able to make out, along its main lines at least, when and how it occurred. The internal analysis of the linguistic evidence on its own leads us to deduce that it was not a single event, as was believed at one time. The picture is rather that of a long and complex sequence of inroads, differing from each other in nature and provenance, followed by various local elaborations and versions which were still current in early historical times. The process appears to be projected so far back in time as to suggest that its earliest phases may be ascribed with some degree of certainty to the Neolithic, or, at any rate, to a time many centuries before the appearance of the first written documents. It seems evident, therefore, that this major linguistic innovation, taken as a whole, cannot in any way be related to the cultural innovation involving the introduction into Italy of cremation as a burial rite. The latter is a rather later feature, and should be assigned to a period just before the end of the Bronze Age – although isolated cremating groups may conceivably have played an occasional part in the establishment and spread of individual Indo-European dialects. The old, simple equation which identifies the Italic peoples with the cremating peoples is wholly invalidated by a comparison of the distribution of the cultures and languages of Italy, clearly seen if we bring together the maps on p. 46 and p. 55. *These two maps roughly coincide along a longitudinal line leaving to the east a solidly Indo-European area where inhumation is the predominant burial rite ; to the west of the line is an area inhabited by non-Indo-European, or only partly indo-europeanized, peoples, where cremation prevailed.* This picture is the exact opposite of the one we might have expected if the indo-europeanization of Italy were related to the spread of cremation. We should keep in mind, however, that the facts we have described refer to the Iron Age and the dawn of historical times; they do not necessarily correspond to an earlier state of affairs, though it is difficult to imagine a complete reversal of the situation in the course of a few centuries. On the other hand, the distribution of the earliest evidence of cremation, in both the north and the extreme south of the peninsula, provides no concrete indications of a possible connection between cremation and individual innovating linguistic currents.

Indeed, a number of scholars during the last few decades have noticed a point that is worth stressing, namely a certain parallel between the presumed progression of the Indo-European wave from east to west (i.e. from the Danube and the Balkans across the Adriatic sea into Italy) and the whole series of cultural influences proceeding from the same regions that affected Italy in late prehistoric times. The latter may be traced from the Middle Neolithic period with its square-mouthed vases, through the spread of the painted pottery and incised spirals and meander-patterns of the Neolithic and Bronze Ages, of the globular jars and the battle-axes of Rinaldone, until we reach the connections between the Danubian urnfields and the earliest Italian cremation cemeteries.[33] But it is difficult to be more precise, to define the nature of the currents or exchanges which established these influences on Italian territory. On the other hand, a stream of direct influences so strong as to have suggested a wave of small but actual colonizations reached the peninsula and Sicily from the East Mediterranean, beginning with the painted pottery of the Neolithic cultures and culminating in the Mycenaean wave of the Late Bronze Age.[34] It is quite possible that these phenomena too may be connected with the penetration of Indo-European elements into Italy.

In fact the old invasion theory, modelled as it was on the barbarian invasions of late antiquity, made us accustomed to think that the Indo-European penetration had taken the form of an infiltration by nomadic groups, or even a conquest by war-like tribes, of lands inhabited by a local population who enjoyed perhaps a superior type of civilization, but were less well organized and unable to resist the invaders. Something of this kind may quite possibly have happened in some cases. However, the analogy with historical times has taught us that an invasion such as that of the Celts into Italy did not result in the permanent imposition of a new language; whereas, on the other hand, the latinization of Italy derived from a people possessing an ancient and highly evolved urban civilization and a sophisticated political and military organization. We should therefore consider seriously the possibility that the spread of Indo-European languages in Italy had as its starting point those prehistoric centres of the south that possessed more advanced forms of culture (e.g. those of Apulia) and that it later moved towards the north to cover territories where settlements were fewer and more backward. Such a view would fit the main lines of the picture we have drawn of an east-to-west advance of the Indo-European languages. We would still have to explain the cause and manner of the initial indo-europeanization of the southern centres. But here we are faced with a problem whose solution lies beyond our capacities: we have no reliable evidence, and speculation is therefore pointless. On a purely hypothetical basis we may think in terms of the gradual establishment of small seafaring colonies similar to those which ancient tradition has recorded in the legends of Oenotrius the Arcadian, of Diomedes, of Aeneas, etc.; or even perhaps in terms of pressure and finally settlement by immigrants from the other side of the Adriatic, workers or mercenaries attracted by the more flourishing centres – an analogous process has been proposed to explain the indo-europeanization of parts of the eastern world. These theories do not of course exclude the possibility that other groups of Indo-European speakers, differing in origin and dialect, might in the course of time have established themselves in Italy, arriving from the Balkans or the Danube basin by way of the eastern Alps.

The insistence of classical tradition on the mythical kingdoms of Oenotrius, Ausonius, Italus, Siculus, etc. in the southern half of the peninsula suggests that these regions were witnessing the formation of ethnic and political entities even before the establishment of the Iron Age. And it is not unlikely that the civilizing stimulus of the Mycenaean world may have served to bring about local experiences, perhaps represented archaeologically by the Mycenaean and Sub-Mycenaean influences visible in Apulia and Sicily in the second half of the second millennium B.C. A possible conquest of the Aeolian Islands by peninsular peoples may have left its trace in the legend of Liparus and Aeolus and in the sudden appearance on Lipari of a Sub-Apennine culture labelled in fact 'Ausonian' by Bernabò Brea. Tradition also recalls the conquest of Sicily by the *Siculi* (Sicels) driven on by the Iapygians, and the formation of an 'Aeolian' empire comprising the Aeolian Islands and parts of Sicily and the toe of Italy. On the other hand, the Ausonians are attested in Campania, and the 'Aborigines', descendants of the Oenotrians, appear in their turn as the ancestors of the Latins. When allowance is made for the mythical element and the confusion of these tales, it is still possible to see them as the partial reflection of a primitive history of the Italic peoples, or, to be more precise, the western Italic peoples – Devoto's 'proto-Latins' – at the time of their linguistic and ethnic formation. This phase of their history may be correctly labelled 'proto-Italic' and must have preceded the final definition of the various languages and national groups of history: Latins, Sicels, and other, intermediate peoples (Ausonians, *Itali*, etc.) of whom we know virtually nothing except the name.

With this picture in mind it is difficult to understand, for the moment at least, the significance of the appearance of cremation cemeteries along the coasts of the peninsula and of Sicily. Their extremely early occurrence at the very heart of the most evolved region of Italy (Torre Castelluccia, Lipari, etc.) may perhaps be simply explained as a ritual innovation, possibly the result of eastern influences (in the Near East, e.g. in Hittite Anatolia, cremation was already common during the Late Bronze Age). Alternatively, they may suggest the arrival of small colonies distinguished by this rite. At the same time, the new custom seems to spread along the sea routes between Apulia, north-eastern Sicily (Milazzo, Lipari) and the coasts of west-central Italy (the Tolfa hills, etc.); and along land routes in central and northern Italy between the Adriatic region (Pianello), Etruria, Latium and the Po valley, where it reached the urnfields in and across the Alps. There is no doubt that this phenomenon points to a period of movement and disturbance, also revealed by the large number of small hoards of arms and bronzes, isolated at times, which can be assigned to the same period. It may be that, between the twelfth and ninth centuries B.C., the whole Italian area was affected by the repercussions of the collapse of Mycenaean sea power in the Mediterranean and of its echoes in the Balkans and Danube basin. And it is precisely during this period that we should in all probability place the first consolidation of ethnic clusters destined to become the future national groups of Italy.

A group of western Italic peoples that had adopted the cremation rite, and featured a 'Protovillanovan' type of culture with considerable Mediterranean traits,[35] were responsible, from the ninth century if not earlier, for the development of the Latial culture of the Alban Hills and Rome, and of the Latin *ethnos* with its Faliscan variant across the Tiber. The development of similar communities in southern Italy, such as those of the primitive Campanians, Ausonians or *Opici*, represented by the Iron Age cultures of Cumae and of the Sarno valley, was soon to be arrested by the tide of Greek colonization. As a result they were not able to develop a historically significant physiognomy as the Latins did. Practically the whole of southern Italy was to come under the influence of the Greek world at the beginning of historical times, following a likely and probably early 'proto-Italic' phase at the end of the Bronze Age. The only exception is the extreme south-eastern area, Apulia, where a considerable indigenous local culture developed among Italic peoples, fostered by significant contributions from Illyria. This agrees

with ancient historical tradition, which has given us the names of
Apulians or Iapygians, and also Daunians, Peucetians, Messapians,
etc., of whom we know the language – Messapic – and characteristic
elements of culture: e.g. the Geometric painted pottery that lasted
until the Roman conquest.

Another ethnic and cultural formation, with fairly well-defined
characteristics from the early Iron Age onwards, is that of the Veneti in
north-eastern Italy. It too seems to spring, as in the case of the Latins,
from cremating peoples with a culture related to the 'Protovillanovan'.
But it was soon to assume characteristics of its own in the form of the
Este culture. The other territories of the Adriatic coast and of north
Italy provide a picture which is a good deal less clear. The inhuming
peoples in the northern Marche, attested mainly by the cemetery of
Novilara and speaking what we call 'north Picene', probably constituted a small, embryonic, national group; it is difficult to define and
must have been quickly submerged by the expansion of the Etruscans,
the Umbrians and the Celts. Further south, the flourishing Iron Age
culture of Picenum may be attributed to an Italic or, perhaps, eastern
Italic people on the basis of inscriptions in 'south Picene'. In historical
times it was to be absorbed by the Umbro-Sabellians, though it too was
partly overrun by the Celts in the fourth century. But no name or
precise description of this people has been preserved by ancient tradition, so that the conventional term '*Piceni*', Greek in form, has been
adopted, corresponding to that of the eastern Italic '*Picentes*'. On the
other hand, this area too has traces of the presence of peoples from
across the Adriatic: this is shown by the names of *Iapyges* in Apulia, of
Iapodes in Istria and the mysterious *Iapuzkus* (recorded in the Iguvine
Tablets) referring to a people inhabiting central Italy and bordering on
the territory of the Umbrians, if, as is probable, these names all spring
from the same root. In other words, the very confusion of ancient
ethnographic traditions and the uncertainties of the archaeological and
epigraphical documents combine to indicate clearly that the formative
process of the nations of central Adriatic Italy was still taking place at
the beginning of historical times. The same may be said in a sense of
northern Italy, where the numerous Po valley, Apennine and Alpine
stocks, variously grouped on the basis of the information at our disposal
under the very general labels of Ligurians in the east and Raetians in
the west, were still, at the time of their first contacts with Rome, small
tribal groups or culturally backward rural communities without any
real historical tradition. In the middle and upper Po valley and on the
slopes of the Alps they are archaeologically represented by what we call
the Iron Age Golasecca culture. Etruscan inroads from the south and
Celtic invasions from the north must have deeply affected the charac-

teristics of these peoples (ancient writers mention a Celto-Ligurian people) without however bringing about the formation of more clearly defined ethnic structures.[36]

Finally, we should now consider the only other major Italic people of historical times that was established over the greater part of the peninsula: the Umbro-Sabellians, or rather the peoples variously called Umbrians in the north, Sabines in the north-west, *Volsci* in the west, *Aequi, Marsi, Vestini, Peligni*, etc., in central Italy, and Samnites (and a number of minor related peoples such as the *Lucani* and the *Bruttii*) in the south.[37] They all belong, as we already know, to a well-defined linguistic unit. Their prehistory and proto-history are difficult to re-construct in the light of the archaeological evidence provided by their respective territories. In general terms, it may be supposed that the development and original spread of these peoples occurred within the sphere of the Iron Age cultures of Adriatic type, including their most westerly distribution. In practice we know almost nothing about the early cultures of just those valleys of the Apennines which tradition has regarded as the point of origin of the dispersal of the Sabines and the Umbrians: e.g. the famous lake of Cutilia in the province of Rieti, 'Italy's navel'. On the other hand the Sabines, who had pushed their way into Latium at Tivoli and had reached the fringes of Rome, appear fairly well defined from the eighth century B.C., and this applies to certain aspects of their culture as well. In all probability ethnic group-ings and the formation of a historical tradition were processes which affected the various eastern Italic peoples separately and at different times and which took place earlier in those very groups that had moved westwards and come into contact with the more evolved centres and peoples on the Tyrrhenian coast. Thus Campania was to be the main region to provide (but not before the fifth century) a conscious unity and a literary language (which we call Oscan) for the Samnites. The idea of an 'Italic' nation, distinct from the Latins and from Rome, is a very late concept and became established only at the time of the Roman conquest and dominion of the peninsula.

The survey that we have given so far has not taken account of the interpretation of the Protovillanovan culture of Etruria and of the Villanovan in either Etruria or Emilia, or of the peripheral groups in the Romagna, Picenum and the Salerno region. We have also left out its subsequent Orientalizing phase. The problems concerning their inter-pretation are in fact intimately related to the problem of the origin of the Etruscan people, which is examined in detail in the next chapter.

CHAPTER **2** **The Problem of Etruscan Origins**

The present state of the question

The founder of the 'Etruscan question' – that is, the question of their origins – is Dionysius of Halicarnassus, a Greek historian of the Augustan age, who devoted six chapters (xxv–xxx) of the first book of his *Roman Antiquities* to an examination of the problem. With the critical means at his disposal he refuted the theories that identified the Etruscans with the Pelasgians or with the Lydians, and declared himself in favour of the hypothesis that they were a people 'who had not come from outside, but were indigenous', and whose name was supposed to be Rasenna.

Before Dionysius, opinions about the origin of the Etruscans do not seem to have been based on serious discussion. Like most ancient writings on the origins of peoples and cities of the Greek and Italic world they were on the border-line between history and myth, and at the most sought confirmation in etymological and onomastic similarities. Thus the origins of Rome and of the Latins were traced back to the Trojans by way of Aeneas's wanderings. In the case of the Tyrrhenians (*Tyrsenoi, Tyrrhenoi*), i.e. the Etruscans, there had been talk of an eastern origin – Lydia, in Asia Minor – and of a migration by sea led by Tyrrhenus, the son of King Atys of Lydia, to the Italic territory of the Umbrians (Herodotus, I, 94); they were identified with those mysterious sailors and wanderers the Pelasgians (Hellanicus, quoted by Dionysius, I, 28); and another theory equated the migration of Tyrrhenus with the Pelasgians, who had already colonized the Aegean islands of Lemnos and Imbros (Anticleides, in Strabo, V, 2, 4). The Lydian origin of the Etruscans was accepted without difficulty and became a common motif in classical literature: Virgil makes no distinction between Lydians and Etruscans. Moreover, according to Dionysius of Halicarnassus, there were some authorities who suspected that they were indigenous to Italy. But Dionysius alone gathered the various opinions together, sifted them, and sought to prove his own belief – that the Etruscans were in fact autochthonous – basing his contention on their extreme antiquity and on their cultural and linguistic isolation among the various peoples known to him.

The problem has been taken up again in modern times and has

attracted sharp and vigorous debate, degenerating at times into sterile polemics on preconceived theses. At first only classical texts were used as a basis for discussion; later, archaeological and linguistic evidence was also enlisted.[1] The first stage of the discussion occupied the whole of the eighteenth century and the first half of the nineteenth and was led by N. Fréret, B. G. Niebuhr and K. O. Müller, who supported Dionysius of Halicarnassus's theory and rejected the Asia Minor tradition transmitted by Herodotus. But whereas Dionysius had given positive arguments in support of his theory, these scholars accepted mainly the negative aspect of his criticism and, arguing from the analogy of the name Rasenna (which Dionysius had attributed to the Etruscans) with that of the Alpine Raetians, imagined that the Etruscans had originally descended from the Alps into central Italy. It is significant that from this time onwards the problem of Etruscan origins was considered in terms of *provenance*. This orientation of the problem bore heavily (with a few rare exceptions) on all the later stages of the discussion.

The development of Indo-European comparative linguistics; the discussions on whether Etruscan did or did not belong to the Indo-European group and, more particularly, to its Italic sub-group; the attempts to relate Etruscan to the non-Indo-European languages of the Caucasus and of Asia Minor; the discovery on the island of Lemnos of an inscription written in a dialect apparently close to Etruscan; the identification (based chiefly upon toponymic evidence) of a Mediterranean linguistic substratum over which the Indo-European languages are thought to have spread, leaving scattered islands with earlier linguistic affinities: these were the points at which linguistic research gradually added more weight now to the 'eastern' thesis, now to the 'western', in seeking to explain the origin of the Etruscans.

The same may be said for the evidence of archaeology. At first the discoveries were largely fortuitous, but from the first half of the nineteenth century onwards they were the fruit of excavations conducted with growing regularity in Etruria and neighbouring areas. They revealed the existence of an Etruscan civilization, ethnically defined by inscriptions in the Etruscan language ranging in date from the seventh century B.C. down to the beginning of the Roman Empire. Its area included Etruria itself (northern Latium and Tuscany), Campania, and the eastern part of the Po valley. The earliest (already certainly Etruscan) phase of this civilization, characterized by a strong influx of oriental elements and therefore known as the 'Orientalizing' period, follows immediately upon the 'Villanovan' culture of the Iron Age. We have already described in Chapter One the Italian manifestations of the Iron Age and of the preceding Bronze Age. The burial rite of the pre-

historic period (Copper and Bronze Ages) in Etruria is exclusively inhumation. Cremation appeared with the 'Protovillanovan' cemeteries,
and this rite predominated during the earliest Villanovan phase. The
later Villanovan and the Orientalizing periods witnessed a return of the
predominance of inhumation in southern and coastal Etruria. Subsequent stages of Etruscan civilization saw the co-existence of both rites,
though with a preference for inhumation in the south and for cremation in the north. It is worth recalling that in Republican Rome, too,
both rites existed side by side, strongly linked to family traditions: the
prevalence of cremation at the end of the Republic and during the first
century of the Empire was followed in the second century A.D. by the
general adoption of inhumation, though no ethnic transformation
accompanied the change.

On the basis of the literary evidence, linguistic comparison and the
interpretation of the archaeological record, a great many theories about
Etruscan origins have been put forward since the end of the last century. They may be classified into three main groups: the first takes up
and develops the traditional thesis of antiquity and ascribes an eastern
origin to the Etruscans; the second follows the teachings of Niebuhr
and Müller and believes that the Etruscans came down into Italy from
the north; the third, and most recent, attempts to uphold, though in
less sweeping terms, Dionysius of Halicarnassus's theory on Etruscan
autochthony and seeks the ethnic origin of the Etruscans in the oldest
substratum of those prehistoric peoples of Italy whose existence precedes the diffusion of the Indo-European languages.

Of the three theses, the best known and most widely accepted is undoubtedly the first. It has been especially dear to all those archaeologists
– Italians and foreigners alike – who have studied the antiquities of
proto-historic Italy. These scholars were greatly struck by the coincidence of tradition with the Orientalizing phase of Etruscan civilization, which made its appearance on the Tyrrhenian shores between the
eighth and seventh centuries B.C. as a sudden flowering of civilized life,
in great contrast with the apparently backward manifestations of the
preceding 'Villanovan' Iron Age. Much importance was also attached
to the change-over from cremation to inhumation. Edoardo Brizio in
1885 was the first to put this theory on a scientific footing: he identified
the Etruscan invaders with the bearers of Orientalizing (and later
Hellenizing) civilization into Tuscany and Emilia, and he saw the
Umbrians of Herodotus – i.e. Indo-European Italic peoples – in the
cremating Villanovans. Among the most convinced followers of
Brizio's thesis were O. Montelius, B. Modestov, G. Körte, G. Ghirardini, L. Mariani, A. Della Seta, P. Ducati, G. Patroni,[2] Å. Åkerström,
R. Bloch and A. Piganiol.[3] The oriental thesis has appealed not only to

Etruscologists but also to classical scholars and students of ancient civilizations who are not strictly specialized in Etruscan studies; they are attracted by the authority of tradition, the simple explanation of certain 'oriental' characteristics of Etruscan civilization, the remarkable onomastic similarities between Etruscan and the languages of Asia Minor (expounded by G. Herbig), and by the even clearer linguistic relationships linking Etruscan with the prehellenic language of Lemnos.[4] Brizio's theory has, however, undergone a number of modifications resulting from a closer study of the ancient sources and the archaeological evidence. Thus, for instance, E. Pottier believed that the Etruscans arrived by sea, but by way of the Adriatic, not the Tyrrhenian, following the route which tradition ascribed to the Pelasgians. F. Schachermeyer held that the Etruscan invasion took place in several waves, beginning around the year 1000 B.C.[5] More recently, G. Säflund has attributed the very origin of the 'archaic Tyrrhenian' Iron Age cultures, whether inhuming or cremating (in practice, the Villanovan culture), to an Aegean wave which would bring the ancestors of the Etruscans of history from the islands of Lemnos and Imbros.[6] J. Bérard even went so far as to put the immigration of the 'Tyrrheno-Pelasgians' as far back as the Late Bronze Age.[7] We are told that these prehistoric and proto-historic oriental connections are confirmed by the identification of the Etruscans or Tyrrhenians with the *Trš.w* mentioned in Egyptian hieroglyphs, i.e. with one of the 'Peoples of the Sea' who attempted an invasion of Egypt under the Pharaohs Merneptah and Ramesses III, between the years 1230 and 1170 B.C.[8] Finally, as the concept of the historical formation of the Etruscans from a number of elements gained ground (as we shall see later), the eastern factor was brought forward yet again, but in a limited sense, in the guise of a catalyst provided by the arrival of Near Eastern or Aegean seafaring groups, similar to the Normans in medieval times. Even so, it is still seen as a major determining factor, for it would have imposed the Etruscan language on Italy (H. Hencken,[9] J. B. Ward-Perkins[10]).

The 'northern' theory, though continuing Niebuhr's and Müller's hypothesis, was based principally upon the archaeological discoveries and theories of the last century, especially the 'Pigorini hypothesis' (examined in Chapter One) that the Terramara cremating peoples of north Italy spread down the peninsula, bringing both the Italic and the Etruscan peoples with them – an idea supported by the opinion held by many linguists that Etruscan was an Indo-European Italic language (W. Corssen, E. Lattes). This theory appealed to a few archaeologists, some of whom (F. von Duhn, G. Körte) were later to go over to the 'eastern' theory; but it had most success among specialists in ancient history. Nevertheless, the profound ethnic and linguistic difference between the Etruscan and Italic peoples led G. De Sanctis to reverse the Pigorini hypothesis by identifying the Etruscans with the cremating peoples who had come down from the north, and the Italic peoples with the Bronze Age folk already settled in the peninsula. L. Pareti was inclined to recognize a first Indo-European wave in the Bronze Age peoples (the 'proto-Latin' wave); a second Indo-European wave in the 'Protovillanovan' cremating peoples (the Umbro-Sabellic wave); and, finally, the ethnic nucleus of the Etruscan people in the Iron Age Villanovan culture derived from the *terremare* and the pile-dwellings of north Italy.[11] On the linguistic side, an examination of the 'northern' theory should also take account of P. Kretschmer's hypothesis that the Etruscans belonged to an ethno-linguistic 'Raeto-Tyrrhenic' or 'Raeto-Pelasgic' group supposed to have spread from the Danube and Balkan regions towards Greece and Italy.[12]

The third, or 'autochthonous', theory, first formulated by the historian E. Meyer, was elaborated in the field of archaeology by U. Antonielli and developed mainly by the Italian school of linguists: A. Trombetti, F. Ribezzo, and G. Devoto, who expounded it in detail in the first edition of his book *Gli antichi Italici* (1931). If we consider the links connecting Etruscan with the pre-Indo-European languages of the Mediterranean, the Etruscans do not appear to have reached Italy after the Indo-Europeans, but seem rather to represent a relic of older pre-Indo-European populations – a kind of ethnic island – just as the present-day Basques of the Iberian peninsula represent the last surviving remnants of primitive Hispanic populations in a sea of Romance speakers. And in fact, as we have seen in the preceding chapter, the study of place names seems to demonstrate the existence in the Italian peninsula of a linguistic stratum older than the Italic dialects, somewhat akin to Etruscan and the languages of the prehellenic Aegean and of Asia Minor, a stratum conventionally defined as 'Tyrrhenian' by Ribezzo. The Etruscans would thus represent a western concentration, under the pressure of Italic invaders, of ethnic elements belonging to this primitive layer. They would also naturally have received important racial and linguistic Indo-European contributions. From the archaeological (i.e. cultural) point of view, the earliest ethnic layer would have been that of the Bronze Age inhuming peoples; these would later have been submerged by Italic or proto-Italic cremating peoples (represented in Etruria by the Villanovan culture), giving rise to the Etruscan nation of historical times as a re-affirmation of the original elements of the primitive stock under the cultural influence from the East. This theory, with slight modifications in its formulation, has also been held by 'western' prehistorians such as C. Schuchhardt.

Each of the theories outlined above seeks a satisfactory explanation for the evidence of tradition, of linguistic research and of archaeology in order to reconstruct the sequence of events that led to the establishment and development of the Etruscan people. They are in fact ingenious combinations of the various known elements, but they only partially satisfy the demands that a full, critical evaluation of these elements makes. Each of the three systems and their variants leaves something unexplained or comes up against well-established facts, without however helping in any way the other possible reconstructions. Had this not been the case, the discussion would have ended long ago with a working agreement among scholars, and the debate would not have arrived at a dead end.

The theory of eastern provenance

Let us begin with a critique of the 'eastern' theory. This rests upon the presumed correspondence of the evidence of tradition (which states that the Etruscans came from the Aegean East, whether they be Pelasgians, Lydians, or inhabitants of Lemnos) with archaeological evidence (i.e. the appearance of an Orientalizing cultural phase in central Italy). Moreover, there is the close resemblance of Etruscan with Lemnian, as well as the relationship that is thought to exist between Etruscan and the various languages of Asia Minor (Lycian, Lydian, etc.). Let us first try to establish the actual value of each of these arguments taken separately.

Concerning the migrations and ethnic relations which tradition, in the mouths of Greek poets and logographers, has passed on to us, modern criticism is in general either sceptical or extremely cautious. This is especially the case with the Pelasgians, a people of Thessaly who were thought to have migrated by sea in post-Homeric times to various regions of the Aegean and even to Italy, on the grounds of certain similarities in the form of place names in Thessaly and in the areas where they were thought to have arrived. Thus all zones where the name Laris(s)a appeared – namely Attica, the Argolid, Achaea, Crete, Lesbos, the Troad, Aeolis, and southern Italy – were called Pelasgic, because of Larissa in Thessaly. The same principle has been applied to names resembling that of the Thessalian city of Gyrton, such as Gortyna in Crete, Gortynia in Macedonia, Gortys in Arcadia, Kyrton in Boeotia, Croton in southern Italy, and Cortona in Etruria. That Hellanicus's identification of the Tyrrhenians of Italy, i.e. the Etruscans, with the Pelasgians was largely a learned invention is shown by the facts that when other writers did speak of a Pelasgian occupation of Etruria, it was earlier than, or, at least, distinct from, that of the Tyrrhenians, and that geographers refer to 'Pelasgian' areas in Italy close to the land of the Etruscans or within Etruria itself (in Etruria they mention those cities where there was closest contact between Greeks and Etruscans, e.g. Cerveteri and Spina).[13] This does not exclude the possibility that ancient tradition, recorded by Herodotus himself (I, 57), concerning the presence in Italy (at Cortona?) and in the Aegean (on the shores of the Hellespont) of Pelasgians speaking the same tongue might be based upon the knowledge that very ancient linguistic affinities existed between the prehellenic inhabitants of the two areas in question.[14]

More complex is the problem concerning the migrations of the Tyrrhenians from Asia Minor or from the Aegean islands. It is very probable that, as Pareti pointed out, Herodotus's well-known account (I, 94) of the arrival of Lydians in Italy under the leadership of Tyrrhenus should also be relegated to a place amongst the learned fables of Ionic logographers; Herodotus may have been attracted by the similarity of the name Tyrrhenian (*Tyrrhenoi, Tyrsenoi*) with that of the city of Tyrrha or Torrhebus in Lydia. Tradition knew mainly the Tyrrhenians of Italy, i.e. the Etruscans. References to the existence of eastern Tyrrhenians probably do not go further back than the fifth century B.C.; at any rate they seem to have been unknown to Herodotus and to his sources, since he says that the Lydian migrants acquired their new name only during or after their journey to Italy. It is also possible that the localization of Tyrrhenians on Lemnos, in the Aegean and in Asia Minor (frequent among later writers) was the result of learned elaborations on the part of the Ionian historians, i.e. of the identification of the Tyrrhenians with the Pelasgians (well known as the primitive inhabitants of Lemnos) and with the Lydians.

The question of the *Tr̆š.w*, mentioned in Egyptian writings as invaders from the sea, has often been brought into play by supporters of the 'eastern' theory. The first difficulty arises in reading the word, which in the hieroglyphic inscriptions is literally rendered as *Twrwš'.w* (with the variants *Twrjš'.w*, *Twjrš.w*). The spelling is a syllabic one, adopted for foreign names, where the semi-vowels *w*, *j*, and ' may represent vowel sounds, though it is difficult to be more definite. Among the various assailants of Egypt there is also mention of the *Rk.w* or *Lk.w* (*Lukki*), the *Jqjwš.w*, the *Drdnj.w*, the *Dnn.w*, the *Prst.w* or *Plst.w*, the *Šrdn.w* (*Šerdani, Širdanu*), the *Šqrš.w* or *Šqlš.w*, respectively identified with the Lycians, the Achaeans, the Dardani, the Danai, the Philistines, the Sardinians and the Sicels. Some of these identifications (e.g. the Achaeans and the Philistines) are no longer disputed; others, like the Sardinians and the Sicels, are still uncertain. In equating the *Tr̆š.w* with the Tyrrhenians, scholars had in mind the ancestors of the Etruscans while they were still in the Aegean area or sailing the seas in search of new lands. A comparison of the roots *Trš.w* and *Tyrs-enoi* is less impressive than it seems: the frequency of analogous forms attested in ancient Mediterranean names greatly diminishes the apparent significance. All the same, we cannot definitely exclude the possibility that the *Trš.w* who attacked Egypt were a people who came from the west.[15]

Let us now consider the archaeological aspect of the problem. We should point out straightaway that the existence of an Etruscan Orientalizing phase is not in itself enough to justify the hypothesis of the arrival of a foreign people bringing their own culture with them; it is quite different from the manifestations that accompanied the arrival of Greek colonists in Sicily and southern Italy. During the more evolved phase of the Villanovan culture notable changes began to appear which anticipate the splendour of the subsequent Orientalizing phase: there was the spread of inhumation and the appearance of the first chamber tombs, the use of iron became more general, and decorated bronze objects and precious metals more common; at the same time, there was a greater number of imported objects and decorative motifs (scarabs and amulets of Egyptian type, Greek painted pottery and its imitations, etc.). The passage from Villanovan to Orientalizing was therefore neither radical nor sudden. Many aspects of the Orientalizing phase (the great architectural or pseudo-architectural tombs themselves, black bucchero pottery, ornaments and jewellery) were well within the scope of indigenous culture, though they might well have been stimulated by external influences, both eastern and Greek, and especially by economic prosperity. Individual objects and motifs were imported from Egypt, Syria, Cyprus, Rhodes, and from Greece in general; others came from even more distant lands, Mesopotamia or Armenia (Urartu). A characteristic type of decoration mingled Egyptian, Mesopotamian, Syrian, Aegean and Near Eastern motifs, at times in hybrid compositions; another took over friezes composed of real and fantastic animals as found in luxury articles of Cypro-Phoenician origin (e.g. Plate 6), but re-worked and spread mainly by the Greeks themselves in the course of the seventh century B.C.[16] The main impression gained when considering Etruscan tombs of the Orientalizing period and their sumptuous contents is that the essential forms of the culture they represent had their roots in a local tradition, whereas the spirit and outward appearance of the decorative elements were acquired and may be attributed to eastern 'fashion'. If we ignore for the moment the composite character – indigenous and exotic – of Etruscan Orientalizing, and examine only its imported elements, it becomes clear that they are not confined to Etruria, but are more or less present in many other Mediterranean lands, beginning with

Greece itself, where no Tyrrhenian immigration could possibly be suspected.

After the Orientalizing phase of the seventh and sixth centuries B.C., Etruria received a large measure of cultural and artistic influences from the Greek world (Ionia at first, and later Attica). A much more decisive alteration of the old indigenous culture took place under this influx: it even affected religion and everyday life, as is clearly shown by the Greek gods and myths that penetrated Etruria. No one, of course, would dare put forward the historical absurdity of a sixth-century Greek colonization of Etruria, even though we have convincing proof of the presence of Greek trading communities in Etruscan ports. We cannot therefore see the necessity of explaining the Orientalizing phenomenon by foreign invasion rather than by cultural change.

Nor was there a sudden change in burial rite from cremation, typical of the Villanovan period, to Orientalizing inhumation. In southern Etruria, the earliest Villanovan stages already produced a mixture of trench (*fossa*) graves and cremations in well (*pozzo*) graves. Inhumation gradually established itself during the later Villanovan phases, and this phenomenon took place during the eighth century not only in Etruria but in Latium too, where no Etruscan 'arrival' has been postulated. In addition, it appears to be limited entirely to southern Etruria, while the regions of the interior (e.g. Chiusi) preserved the prevailing rite of cremation during Orientalizing times and for all the successive phases of Etruscan civilization. In southern Etruria itself, the cremation rite was taken up again, though in a limited way, during the sixth century. It is hard to believe in a correlation between such ritual evidence and ethnic factors that was brought about by the substitution of one people for another.

We should now examine the linguistic data. In spite of assertions to the contrary made by Lattes, Pareti and others,[17] a close relationship unites Etruscan with the dialect spoken at Lemnos before the Athenian conquest of the island by Miltiades in the second half of the sixth century B.C.

There are precise agreements in flexional endings (-z, -eiz, -zi, -ai, -aiθ, -ale, -as-ial, etc. in Lemnian, and -s, -eis, -si, -ai, -aiθ, -ale, -as-ial in Etruscan inscriptions); in roots and in words (ναφοθ, ziazi, maraz and marazm, aviz, zivai, zeronai and zeronaiθ, morinail, haralio, arai, etc. in Lemnian, and napti or nefts, zia, mar and maru, avils, zivas, zeri, murinaśie, harc, are and araś in Etruscan inscriptions); and even in whole expressions (holaiezi φokiasiale and larθiale hulχniesi; aviz sialχviz and avils ... śealχls). These resemblances are all the more remarkable in that we have only one Lemnian document of any importance, the funerary stele found at Kaminia (Plate 9).[18] This does not

72

mean, however, that Lemnian and Etruscan were the same language, or even two dialects of the same language. Each has many words and forms with no equivalent in the other. Moreover the meaning of most words in the Lemnian inscription is obscure, so that in order to interpret them recourse is often had to Etruscan, and this leads us into a vicious circle. A comparison is therefore possible only at the formal level. As for Lydian, Lycian and the other known languages of Asia Minor, their relationship with Etruscan appears to be still more problematical: all we have to go on are some uncertain or generic similarities in roots and suffixes, far fewer in number than those shared by Etruscan, Greek and Latin.[19] Further, the onomastic agreements between the Etruscan and eastern languages carry no great weight (as E. Fiesel correctly pointed out) when we consider that they are based upon eastern material collected from languages of great diversity, and that the onomastic agreements linking Etruscan with the Italic languages, for example, do not imply any common relationship between the two. In the case of Lydian, these facts definitely exclude the possibility that the Etruscans, according to the letter of Herodotus's account, were an ethnic group that had split from the main body of the Lydian nation.[20]

Let us now re-examine the arguments in support of the eastern hypothesis, not in isolation, but in the light of their reciprocal geographical and chronological relations. Classical sources agree in placing the original home of the Etruscans within the Aegean or on the Anatolian coast. But those foreign elements that went to make up the Orientalizing phenomenon take us to different points of origin, scattered over the whole of the eastern Mediterranean with, if anything, the highest concentration in the Syrian and Cypriot areas.[21] It seems, therefore, rather as if Phoenician and Greek navigators were the principal vehicle for the Orientalizing wave: they influenced various other regions of the Mediterranean in much the same way. Independent confirmation of this idea may be obtained from an examination of Near Eastern culture of the eighth century B.C. (the period when the migration is said to have taken place), despite the small number of protohistoric excavations made on the Aegean coast of Asia Minor.

The discoveries made in Lemnos, at various coastal points of Ionia and Aeolis in Asia Minor, at Sardis and in the interior of Anatolia have not brought to light any elements common to the civilization of Etruria or to its monuments (if we except those of a rather vague and generic nature, such as tumuli, chamber tombs, rock façades, etc.) for the period termed 'Phrygian' in Asia Minor (ninth to seventh century) and 'Tyrrhenian', but improperly, at Lemnos ('Pelasgian' would be a better term, on the basis of the usual and most authoritative historical tradition).[22] The Geometric pottery of Phrygia, that of Lydia and the characteristic archaic pottery of Lemnos are totally unrelated to Italian indigenous production or to the Greek Geometric pottery found in the west. It is only in the sixth century that we find in the west a few vases of the Lydian type, together with specimens belonging to many other East Greek types. In addition, the grey pottery of the Near East was exported by Phocaean colonists in the Mediterranean, but it is rare in Italy and does not seem to have anything to do with the origin of Etruscan bucchero ware. The typical Near Eastern fibula, so very common over the whole of Anatolia, consisted of a semi-circular bow decorated with bronze rivets with globular heads, or was shaped like a magnet. It does not seem possible that it did not accompany the migrations of an Asian people, and it is conspicuous by its almost total absence in the west. Only one example has so far been found in central Italy – at Riserva del Truglio, in Latium,[23] i.e. outside Etruria proper! The recent discovery of a royal tomb at Gordion, capital of Phrygia, containing large bronze cauldrons with applied decorations similar to those found in the Orientalizing tombs of Etruria and Palestrina, is one more proof of the wide diffusion of Urartian bronzecraft – but it does not prove a direct contact between Phrygia and Etruria.[24] On the other hand, relations between the western centres of Asia Minor and Italy become closer and more direct during the sixth century; this is due to Ionian expeditions to the West and culminates in the preponderant East Greek influence on the arts of Archaic Etruria. But this obviously has nothing to do with the question of Etruscan origins as presented by supporters of the 'eastern' theory.

The identification of the Orientalizing phase with a presumed Etruscan immigration is also placed out of court for chronological reasons. The beginnings of Etruscan Orientalizing cannot be taken further back than the end of the eighth century or, more probably, the beginning of the seventh century B.C., i.e. the period during which Greek colonists were already firmly established on the coasts of Sicily and southern Italy. But Herodotus's account of the Lydian migration should not be detached arbitrarily from his chronological framework which places it during the reign of King Atys of Lydia, i.e. (according to traditional mythical chronology) shortly after the Trojan war, between the thirteenth and twelfth centuries B.C. Such an important event occurring at the dawn of history, side by side with Greek colonization (and competing with it), would not have been passed over silently by ancient historians, nor simply transformed, as in Herodotus, into a mythical event occurring half a millennium earlier. Indeed, the reliable Greek historian Ephorus (quoted by Strabo, VI, 2, 2), when speaking of the founding of Naxos – the earliest Greek colony in

Sicily – stated that before that time (735 B.C. and perhaps earlier) the Greeks would not venture on the western seas for fear of the Tyrrhenians. He therefore implicitly admits the presence of Tyrrhenians around the Italian coasts.[25]

With the breaking of the link that was thought to connect the Orientalizing of Etruria with a possible Etruscan immigration, there remains the possibility that the latter might have occurred at an earlier period – a theory held by Bérard. In this case, however, no firm archaeological evidence has so far been adduced in support, since there are no significant traces of Near Eastern influences in Etruria and only a very few from the Aegean during the Bronze Age and the beginning of the Iron Age.[26]

The linguistic evidence, however, still remains: the similarities between Etruscan and Lemnian are certainly remarkable when considered in the light of the legends that give Lemnos as the original home of the Etruscans. This is the only argument in favour of the eastern theory that carries any weight, though it makes the problem extremely intricate. We cannot exclude the possibility of prehistoric movements or contacts that would have left their mark in the extant relationship between Lemnian and Etruscan. But this relationship could also be explained by postulating a pre-Indo-European 'Aegeo-Tyrrhenian' linguistic unit, as mentioned in the preceding chapter. Etruscan, forced to the extreme west by the Indo-European advance, and Lemnian, relegated to an island, would then represent conservative and marginal relics of such a unit. At any rate, the known Lemnian inscriptions belong to the seventh or sixth century, that is to a period when the Etruscan nation was already formed in Italy. Moreover, to isolate Etruscan from its geographical setting – as the supposition of a late colonization of the coast of Etruria by the Lemnians would lead us to do – would mean going against the evidence of the presence of an ancient 'Tyrrhenian' toponymy in the regions of Italy that were later occupied by Indo-European-speaking peoples, and against the affinities that exist between Etruscan and other very ancient western languages such as 'Raetic'.[27]

The theories of northern provenance and of autochthony

Let us now pass on to a review of the 'northern' theory. The old comparison of the name of Rasenna with that of the Raetians is puerile: the inscriptions found in the region of Trento and the upper valley of the Adige are comparatively late (after the fifth century B.C.) and, even if they reveal ancient ties or later relationships with Etruscan, they prove nothing about an Alpine origin for the Etruscans as a fully constituted people. From the archaeological point of view, the criticism already made of Pigorini's and Helbig's theories seriously invalidates the hypothesis that saw the progress down the peninsula of people from northern Italy. The Etruscan character of the Po valley was the result of a well-defined conquest from the south, as shown by historical sources.[28] Here we may agree with Brizio and Ducati, but with reservations on their chronology of the events, and not accepting that the inhabitants of Villanovan Bologna are to be identified with the Italic Umbrians, whose appearance on the eastern slopes of the Apennines is later still (as made clear in Strabo, V, 1, 10–11).

Linguistics has now definitely discarded the old idea of genetic affinities between Etruscan and the Italic languages, so that, even from this point of view, Pigorini's thesis of a single ancestry for the Etruscan and Italic peoples has lost all substance. This explains De Sanctis's reaction in identifying the Etruscans with cremating peoples and the Italic peoples with the Bronze Age inhuming cultures (or, as we would now say, with the possessors of the Apennine culture). For the purpose of a rough identification of the archaeological and the ethno-linguistic data, such equations would alone be able to explain the correspondence we have already noted between the inhumation and the cremation areas on the one hand and the Indo-European and non-Indo-European linguistic areas on the other.[29]

It has become increasingly clear, however, that we can no longer speak of 'cremating peoples' as a whole, representing a single pre-constituted ethno-linguistic reality. Villanovan culture was not introduced fully-formed from outside: there is no evidence of earlier forms of its development north of the Apennines. On the contrary, its immediate precedents are rather to be sought in peninsular 'Protovillanovan' culture, precisely in Tyrrhenian Etruria, from the Tolfa hills to the region of Grosseto (as far as we can tell at the moment). The early phases of cremating cultures related to the 'Protovillanovan', such as the 'proto-Latial' and 'proto-Atestine', make their appearance at the beginning of the Latial and Atestine Iron Age sequences and belong to historical peoples speaking an Indo-European language but differing from each other in origin, i.e. the Latins and the Veneti. Another casualty is Pareti's opinion that the 'Protovillanovans' are to be identified in origin with the eastern Italic stock – all the less likely since the eastern Italic people of historical times practised mainly inhumation – and that a hypothetical subsequent wave of 'Villanovans' is to be identified with the arrival of the Etruscans. As we have seen, there are no likely critical grounds for the postulation of such theories. In no way can archaeology demonstrate an 'arrival' of the Etruscans from the north.

A further argument against the northern theory is the relationship of Etruscan with the prehellenic languages of the Aegean. This could only be explained by accepting Kretschmer's thesis of a parallel overland immigration into Greece and Italy originating from the Danube basin. We would then still have to explain those elements in the 'Tyrrhenian' toponymy of peninsular Italy which are related to Etruscan and which are, as we have said, both widespread and deep-rooted. These reservations do not, however, exclude the presence in Etruscan of linguistic elements belonging to the north-western branches of the pre-Indo-European substratum (such as 'Ligurian' or 'Raetic'), or even to the Indo-European stock. If anything, their presence points to a widespread mingling in the area of elements of different origins, the result of a complex overlapping of linguistic areas.

The autochthonous theory is also open to justifiable attacks, especially if it is understood in an absolute and schematic way. The linguistic conception of Trombetti, Devoto, Ribezzo, etc., who saw Etruscan as the relic of a greater pre-Indo-European linguistic unit, is, methodologically speaking, perfectly sound. It takes account of the Mediterranean affinities of Etruscan and the presence throughout most of Italy of a 'Tyrrhenian' substratum revealed by the study of place names. In contrast, the archaeological reconstruction attempted by Antonielli and Devoto is open to very serious objections. It presupposes a clear ethnic contrast between indigenous inhuming peoples of the Copper and Bronze Ages and 'Villanovan' cremating peoples who had come down from the north, and identifies the former with the primitive 'Tyrrhenian' stratum, the latter with Italic Indo-European invaders. Once again, however, the almost exact correspondence of the cremation and inhumation areas with non-Indo-European and Indo-European dialects is in sharp contrast with this 'autochthonous' reconstruction. How can Etruria, where cremation (the hall-mark, according to the old Pigorini hypothesis, of the Italic peoples from the north) was most typical and most extensive, and where the preceding Bronze Age cultures were rather secondary and marginal – how can Etruria be the very corner of Italy where the primitive language had preserved its main features down to fully historical times? And how can the Italic languages have triumphed in the east where only sporadic and insignificant traces exist of the passage of the alleged Italic cremating peoples? It is clear that linguistic autochthony cannot be constrained within the absurd limits imposed by archaeological reconstructions in which the mark of the preconceived Pigorini hypothesis is still so very patent. More recently, G. Devoto has tried to understand the equation 'Italic peoples = cremation peoples' in the light of a 'proto-Italic' wave – but without success, for we know nothing definite about Italy's historical ethnography to lead us to such a supposition. At any rate a purely autochthonous origin reveals itself *a priori* as an abstract, unhistoric theory: it clashes with the evidence of cultural developments, which reveal European and eastern influences, and also with the linguistic data, which reveal a clear relationship between Etruria and the Aegean, and the presence of Indo-European elements deep-rooted in the language.

Towards a solution of the problem

None of the three main theories concerning the origin of the Etruscans can thus be convincingly proposed as a solution to our problem. Each contains positive elements revealing its partial validity, and each contains negative elements which prevent its complete acceptance. This state of affairs implies that the formulation of the problem is methodologically unsound, in the sense that all three theories tend to reduce the complexity of a phenomenon as large and many-sided as the origin of an historical nation to schematic and sometimes oversimplified formulas. The Etruscan people have been considered as a unit, a block, right from their inscrutable prehistory; and to explain their appearance in Italy it was necessary to have recourse to the external and oversimple concept of *provenance*: in a positive sense, by accepting the idea of an actual arrival from foreign lands (eastern or northern), thus merely shifting the problem in space without actually solving it; and in a negative sense, by excluding an actual 'arrival' and by identifying the Etruscans with the ancient inhabitants of the peninsula, thus shifting the problem back in time. Even when the idea of a mingling of peoples has been put forward (e.g. a mingling of Tyrrhenians from the East with indigenous Umbrians, or of Mediterranean Bronze Age peoples with Italic cremating peoples), the predominance given to one of the formative elements has had the effect of attributing to it by anticipation the name, the language and the character of the Etruscans.

Now the methodological basis of our discussion must be as follows: we must consider the concept 'Etruscan' as well defined, limited, and attached to a controllable historical reality – that of a nation that flourished in Etruria between the eighth and the first centuries B.C., possessing its own language and its own customs. Various ethnic, linguistic, political and cultural elements contributed to the formation of this historical reality, and this process must have occurred gradually, over a long period of time. We may discuss the origin and provenance of each of these elements; but a more appropriate concept for the overall phenomenon to which they gave rise would be that of *formation*. It may make our meaning clearer to point out that no one would dream of asking where 'the Italians' or 'the French' came from originally; it is the formation of the Italian and French nations that we study. In the case of France, for instance, we tend to speak of its origins by taking into account its palaeo-European, 'Ligurian' and 'Iberian' substrata, the proto-historic Celtic stratum, the Roman conquest and domination, the latinization and christianization of Gaul, the successive Germanic invasions (Franks, Burgundians, Visigoths and Normans), the process of unification effected by the monarchy, and so on. These ethnic and historical factors have all contributed to the formation of the French people. It also becomes clear that in this process an essential factor is the geographical one: the actual territory of a nation is where its formative process has taken place.

The inadequacy of the theories on Etruscan origins is due to the fact that the problem has been considered as one of provenance instead of ethnic formation. Discussion has centred on whether the Etruscans came from the east or the north, or whether they were in Italy all the time: whereas in reality they formed a complex of eastern, continental and indigenous elements which must be isolated, weighed, and compared one with the other. It is, of course, far from easy to reconstruct the conditions and events of later prehistory that determined the birth of historical Etruria. But for the time being we can state quite safely that the formative process of the Etruscans can only have taken place on the territory of Etruria itself; and we can witness the final stages of this process thanks to the rich archaeological documentation we possess for the period from the ninth to the seventh centuries. This point of view, which the present author has been expressing for some years,[30] cannot be confused with an autochthonous theory except in so far as it stresses the conclusion of an historical process rather than its supposed starting-point. A similar point of view has been expressed by the historian F. Altheim, who, though postulating a fusion of eastern immigrants with indigenous peoples, identifies the origin of the Etruscan nation with the formation of a political and cultural κοινή among the inhabitants of Etruria. As we have seen, these notions appear to have been widely accepted even among the most recent supporters of the eastern theory of origin; and they have been reflected in some of the latest discussions of the problem.[31]

The linguistic elements point to eastern affinities within the compass of a pre-Indo-European 'Tyrrhenian' unit. But the distinction between the theories of eastern origin and of autochthony fades if we suppose a Tyrrhenian east-to-west movement in remote prehistoric times (or even later: perhaps during the Bronze Age). Etruscan would in this case have been both the westernmost outpost of such a movement and its last

79

surviving remnant in the Italian peninsula, later to be invaded and then submerged by successive Indo-European waves.

We have already seen how absurd it was to wish to dissociate the cremating peoples of the Villanovan Iron Age from the Etruscan *ethnos*. Their appearance is in fact marked by a remarkable progress in the cultural development of Etruria. With the 'Villanovan' culture we begin to see the growth of considerable centres of population in those very places which were to become the great historical centres of Etruria: Veii, Cerveteri, Tarquinia, Vulci, Vetulonia, Populonia, etc. From the beginning of the Villanovan period down to Roman times, this civilization developed with no breaks or sudden transformations. This cultural horizon clearly represents the first period in the history of the Etruscan people, just as the parallel Iron Age cultures of Latium and Este indisputably represent the beginnings of the history of the Latins and the Veneti. One may debate whether the Villanovan cultures of Emilia or of the Salerno region belong already to the Etruscans. It is certain, however, that there is a surprising coincidence between the area of greatest Etruscan historical expansion (see map on p. 88) and the Villanovan area as we know it from the most recent discoveries (see map on p. 46). If we take this coincidence into account, the Villanovan culture appears to represent an already fully formed and active Etruscan nation, even from the point of view of its expansion in Italy.[32]

But the formation of the Villanovan civilization must itself have been spread over a long period of time. Certain factors (e.g. the cremation rite with ossuaries made of coarse pottery, spherical in shape or with biconical tendencies) should be considered as imported from regions outside our area, perhaps even as the result of more or less substantial immigrations. One may postulate infiltrations from continental Europe by land, a reflection of the spread of the 'urnfields' of central Europe and connected with the cremation cemeteries that make their appearance in northern Italy towards the end of the Late Bronze Age. But infiltrations may also have taken place from the south by coastal or sea routes, if we take account of the fact that the Protovillanovan cemeteries of Etruria and some of the most primitive cremation tombs in the Villanovan cemeteries of the great southern Etruscan cities are closely linked to the Protovillanovan culture of southern Italy (Apulia, Sicily) and of the Adriatic. Finally, there are further elements in common with the Adriatic and Danubian areas, particularly the flourishing production of decorated bronzes during the most evolved phase of Villanovan culture.[33] The Villanovan, considered as a whole, is a new and original phenomenon, locally wrought upon the foundations laid by the Bronze Age Apennine culture, some of the characteristic elements of which it absorbs (e.g. the shape of the large biconical urn

80

of dark impasto with meander-pattern on the neck). It is not necessary, therefore, to postulate a radical ethnic transformation at the beginning of the Villanovan period; but rather an impulse, a determining ferment which brought about the crystallization of 'Tyrrhenian' and Indo-European ethnic elements into what was to become the Etruscan nation as we know it north of the Tiber.

This picture of the formation of the nation is not complete without the inclusion of those elements that accompanied its first historical stages. The intellectual and artistic contacts with the east and with Greece played a preponderant role: they took place via the maritime trade-routes, but probably also through direct contacts, the immigration of individuals or foreign settlements attracted by the mineral resources of the country, the establishment of trading posts, etc.[34] The impression made on the fresh, primitive, malleable, early Etruscan mind by the mature civilizations from across the seas was probably such as to give a definite orientation to the spiritual bent of the nation. It is this that gives the impression of a deep and direct dependence of Etruria on the east, an impression to which the ancients succumbed and which still profoundly affects the minds of modern scholars.

The Etruscan 'thalassocracy'

Discussions on the origin of the Etruscans have generally led scholars to neglect research on more concrete and positive aspects of the subject: the study of the political, social and economic history of the Etruscan world.

It has often been said that it was Carthage that taught the Romans to navigate and be masters of the sea, just as Greece had been their teacher in poetry and the arts. There is some truth in both assertions, in the sense that on the high and universal level of Hellenic culture the influence of both Carthage and Greece played a decisive role in the growth of the civilization and might of Rome. But it would be a serious mistake to imagine that Republican Rome, like the Rome of the kings, was no more than a city of shepherds and semi-barbarous peasants, when in fact she was the neighbour of – and to a large extent participated in – the advanced civilization of Etruria. To the refined generation of Cicero and Augustus, the Roman of one or two centuries before could well have seemed '*ferus victor*', '*arte rudis*'. But when we remember that already between the end of the sixth century and the beginning of the third such superb and mature works of art as the Capitoline she-wolf or the Ficoroni cista were being produced in Rome, we cannot but realize the absurdity of a definition that had almost become a commonplace among ancient writers, and has often been taken at face value by modern scholars.

It was Etruria that first gave the Italic peoples the urge to conquer and dominate the sea. We cannot overlook the unanimous evidence provided by historical tradition: all authorities refer to a Tyrrhenian dominion of the sea ('thalassocracy'). The seafaring activities of the Etruscans had become legendary: they acquired the reputation of fearsome pirates ranging over both the western and the eastern seas. In the Homeric Hymn to Dionysius, for example, the god is kidnapped by Tyrrhenian pirates whom he later succeeds in changing into dolphins. The Tyrrhenians and the Pelasgians were also held responsible for the stealing of Hera's statue on the island of Samos (Athenaeus, XV, 12), for the rape of the women of Brauron in Attica and the conquest and sack of Athens (Plutarch, *De mul. vir.*, 8; *aetia gr.*, 21; Eustathius,

Comm. Dion., 591; Philochorus, *fr.*, 5).[1] The Tyrrhenians were also described as ceaselessly threatening, if not actually controlling, the western seas, especially the Tyrrhenian, the Ionian, and the coasts of Sicily (Palaephatus, *Epist.*, XX; Strabo, VI, 2, 2; etc.). To this list should be added references to an Etruscan colonization of Corsica (Diodorus Siculus, V, 13), Sardinia (Strabo, V, 2, 7), the Balearic Islands and even the coasts of Spain (Stephanus of Byzantium, *s.v. Banaurides*; Ausonius, *Epist.*, XXXI, 326),[2] and the story of the conflict between Etruscans and Carthaginians for the possession of an island in the Atlantic (Diodorus Siculus, V, 19 ff.). Etruscan achievements in naval technique, mentioned by Dionysius (I, 25), are confirmed by the legendary tradition concerning the Tyrrhenian invention of the *rostra* (Pliny, *Nat. Hist.*, VII, 56, 209). Finally, it was the names of the Etruscan people and of a Veneto-Etruscan port, Adria, that were given to the two great Italian seas: the Tyrrhenian and the Adriatic.

Archaeology supports historical tradition about the maritime activities of the ancient Etruscans. Even without taking into consideration the very large – indeed innumerable – number of foreign objects and motifs (eastern, Sardinian, Phoenician, Greek) that have been found in Etruscan tombs (an indication of direct intense maritime activity that cannot be wholly due to Phoenician and Greek shipping) there is no lack of evidence for the spread of Etruscan products along the shores of Italy, Sardinia, Sicily, North Africa, southern France, and Spain no less than in Greece, Asia Minor and Cyprus.[3] This consists mainly of bucchero vases, with some bronzes and even an ivory tablet bearing the effigy of an animal and an inscription in Etruscan, found at Carthage.[4]

The causes and development of Etruscan naval supremacy

When and how did the Etruscan supremacy on the seas become established? How should we interpret the evidence of the classical sources and the archaeological record? It is obvious that such an ample, varied, but in the main unanimous historical documentation as the one referring to Etruscan 'thalassocracy' and piracy cannot have been born from nothing; it must have derived from a widespread feeling of admiration and fear on the part of the Greeks, who were themselves noted for bold seafaring and colonizing ventures. A clear indication of such feelings is the nucleus of the legends about Tyrrhenian piracy, legends unknown to epic literature but which grew up in time to be included in the last stages of the elaboration of Greek myths, between the seventh and fifth centuries B.C. They were obviously embroidered on the nucleus of the frightening tales told in the coastal towns of

Greece and its colonies about these freebooters of antiquity. The historical basis of tradition becomes more evident in those western sea areas that were the scene of the adventures of the Tyrrhenian pirates: we are told of the difficulties the Greeks had to face on the seas around Sicily and of the rivalry between Greeks and Tyrrhenians for the possession of the Aeolian Islands.

This picture of the Tyrrhenians as a ferocious band of privateers fits well with the tendency to oversimplify ethnic characteristics, both good and bad, that was so dear to classical antiquity – even we moderns cannot wholly free ourselves of it. Its origins must obviously be sought in the keen commercial and territorial competition between Etruscan navigators and Greek colonists around the coasts of Italy. Piracy is the most obvious facet of a fierce maritime war, and since we only have the Greek legendary and the historical sources, the bad name given to the Tyrrhenians is understandable. And the great conflict between Greeks and Etruscans in historical times was to be the cause of other preconceived judgements in Greek writings on the moral character of the Etruscans: accusations concerning their luxurious way of life, their sensuality and refined cruelty were far from uncommon.

The fact that, while Homer is silent on the subject of Tyrrhenian piracy, the later Homeric Hymns on the Dionysian myth do refer to it, enables us to place the period of greatest development of Etruscan naval supremacy between the seventh and sixth centuries B.C. Archaeological evidence confirms this, although it is possible to refer it back to an earlier date. If we can trust the passage ascribed to the historian Ephorus (probably derived from one of the Siceliot historians and included in Strabo's *Geography*, VI, 2, 2), we can state that as early as the eighth century, when the Greeks were beginning to establish the first trading outposts on the eastern shores of Sicily, the seas surrounding the island were already being threatened by Etruscan ships. Now the eighth century presents an apparently primitive picture of the cultural development of Etruria, for we know that it was the period of the Villanovan culture. Old mental habits lead us instinctively to associate Villanovan culture (or, more generally, that of Iron Age cremating peoples) with land migrations and ethnic establishments firmly implanted on Italic soil, as opposed to seafaring activities and seaborne influences. But such associations are mainly erroneous, or, at most, only partially true. We have seen in the preceding chapters that it may have been quite possible for small groups of 'Protovillanovan' cremating peoples to have reached the southern coasts of Italy by sea. It is, therefore, all the more permissible to think that those responsible for the origin and spread of Villanovan culture – and it is no longer possible not to recognize in them the Etruscans at the beginning of their historical development – could have sailed and controlled the waters facing their shores, and competed on the sea with the early Greek navigators. It would be difficult to explain in any other way the high density of settlement, attested from the beginning of the Villanovan period, of such great coastal centres as Cerveteri, Tarquinia, Vulci, Vetulonia, Populonia, or the presence of exotic objects in ever-increasing numbers in the graves of the period. Moreover we know today of the existence of Villanovan 'islands', detached from the main territory of Tyrrhenian Etruria, especially that of the Campano-Lucanian area, where historical Etruscan colonies are mentioned by Greek tradition (as we shall see later); this would suggest an early seaborne expansion southwards, giving credit to the tradition of a confrontation with the early Greek colonists as early as the middle of the eighth century.

The coastline of Etruria, jagged and rich in islands, with alternate promontories and flat stretches of coast, must have favoured an early development of coastal navigation for fishing and barter. It is worth noting that facing Etruria lay not only Elba, with its iron deposits, and the other small islands close by, but also the great land masses of Sardinia and Corsica, of which the former already possessed a well-developed culture, particularly remarkable for its architectural forms (the civilization of the *nuraghi*).

When we consider the earliest stages in the development of coastal Etruria we are faced with the problem of the relations between Etruria and Sardinia.[5] The legend concerning the foundation of Populonia by the Corsicans (Servius, *ad Aen.*, X, 172) implies the presence on the coasts of Etruria of inhabitants from the islands facing it. Strabo (V, 2, 7) explicitly mentions Sardinian incursions on the coasts of Tuscany and refers to a possible Tyrrhenian origin of the primitive inhabitants of the island. We have much evidence of commercial relations between the Etruscans of the metal-rich area of north-west Etruria and the Sardinians: some objects, including small bronze boats with animal figurines, found in eighth- (and seventh-) century tombs at Vetulonia are incontestably Sardinian. Here and there we also find elements recalling characteristic types of the culture of the *nuraghi* (Sardinian prehistoric monuments built without mortar in the shape of a truncated cone): e.g. long-necked jugs, whose occurrence at such an early phase seems to be limited to Vetulonia. A Sardinian bronze statuette has been found in a Villanovan tomb at Vulci.[6] There is also the question whether the pseudo-cupolas (*tholoi*) characteristic of the Orientalizing tombs of north Etruria were the result of direct Creto-Mycenaean influence or whether this influence was exerted by way of the Sardinian *nuraghi*, where the same technique is particularly common. There are also apparent traces of Etruscan influence in Sardinia: these may include the name *Aesaronenses* belonging to one of the peoples inhabiting the eastern coast (cf. the Etruscan word *aisar*, 'gods'), the presence of bucchero vases, certain Sardinian bronze statuettes of Etruscan type, and so on. Similarly, some rock-cut tombs (S. Andrea Priu, Fordongianus) share architectural details with the Etruscan sepulchres at Cerveteri.

It is interesting to note that the part of Etruria most closely linked with Sardinia is the northern coast. This is due to geographical reasons: even during the Middle Ages and in modern times sea-traffic between Sardinia and the peninsula still followed the coasts of Corsica and of the Elba archipelago in the direction of Pisa. The mineral resources of the Populonia and Vetulonia regions must also be taken into account: this most important factor closely united the peoples of Etruria and Sardinia in the common skills of mining and working metals. This mineral area is unique in Etruria, or, for that matter, in the whole of Italy. Without wishing to overstress the economic factor in history, we should remember that, apart from the Sardinian mines, the only sizeable iron, copper and argentiferous lead mines in the central Mediterranean were those of Etruria. From the time when they were first worked (during the Iron Age, at the beginning of Etruscan civilization), they must have been the focus of particular attention by the seafaring nations round the Mediterranean.

One of the fundamental facts in the cultural history of Etruria and primitive Italy is the transformation of the Villanovan by the Orientalizing phenomenon, towards the end of the eighth century and the beginning of the seventh. It is so striking that it has been explained, wrongly, as the outward sign of the arrival of a new people. What especially concerns us here is the great display of wealth that accompanied the phenomenon. There was a rapid rise in living standards coupled with a great increase in purchasing power, attested by large quantities of costly articles from far-off lands and of imported precious raw materials such as gold, silver and ivory. The following phase (occupying the sixth century and the beginning of the fifth) also displayed this feature, at least as far as the presence of Greek wares in Etruria is concerned: the cemeteries of the coastal towns of Vulci, Tarquinia, and Cerveteri especially have yielded them by the thousand; as a result, present-day study of Attic pottery is to a large extent based on material from Etruscan sites. It is also clear that, in the commercial exchanges between Etruria and the East, Etruria played on the whole a buyer's role: the quantities of Etruscan articles found in other lands, especially in Greece,[7] cannot be compared with the number of foreign articles found in Etruria. We are thus faced with a new problem: what had Etruria got to give in exchange? Was it wheat? Oil? Wood? It seems unlikely that these goods could represent an adequate exchange for such large-scale international trade with countries that probably produced them too or could import them from elsewhere. Everything suggests that the riches Etruria was able to export were unworked metals from Etruscan mines: copper, lead, iron (we already know that quantities of these metals were sent to Campania: Diodorus Siculus, V, 13) and metal products, especially bronze articles, which have been found as far away as Greece and Cyprus.

These statements appear obvious, and they are in fact admitted by the majority of scholars. They are confirmed by the presence of Greek merchant colonies in the Etruscan ports of Cerveteri and Spina on the Adriatic, in the sixth and fifth centuries: and now by the recent discovery of a Greek sanctuary, founded in the late sixth century, at Gravisca, the port of Tarquinia. The objection might, however, be raised that the growth in wealth, the Orientalizing and the Hellenizing of Etruria appear to be earlier and more marked in the cities of the south than in the actual metal-rich area further north (Vetulonia and Populonia). But such a statement may perhaps be premature: for on the one hand there are traces of ancient and important mineral resources in the south, in the Tolfa hills between Cerveteri and Tarquinia,[8] and on the other hand discoveries at Populonia and more recently at Quinto Fiorentino[9] have revealed in the north too an early and rich Orientalizing movement. The answer might be that, at first, the exploitation of the great natural wealth of Etruria was of most benefit to the centres that specialized in brokerage – centres of early political and cultural attainments in direct contact with the great Mediterranean trade routes, such cities in fact as Cerveteri or Tarquinia – whereas it was only later that the cities that grew up in the neighbourhood of the mining area seized the initiative in the commercial field. This explanation may fit in with the late entry of Populonia into the Etruscan League of twelve cities (Servius, ad Aen., X, 172), and with the fact that at Vetulonia we find a great abundance of bronze objects, whereas imported Greek products such as painted vases are very scarce. It is certain, however, that throughout the centuries the mineral zone represented a constant goal for the Greeks, who sent naval expeditions during the fifth and fourth centuries to attempt the conquest of Elba, though they never succeeded in setting foot on the coast of Etruria. The lasting importance of the southern towns as markets for the exchange of Etruscan raw materials for manufactured articles from abroad is shown by the fact that Dionysius of Syracuse's expedition against the Etruscan mining territory began near Cerveteri, with the capture and sack of the port and sanctuary of Pyrgi (Santa Severa) in 384 B.C.

Not only Greek and Phoenician, but Etruscan seamen too must have

Figure 3. The Etruscan expansion over land and sea. This map refers particularly to the position after the naval battle of the Sardinian sea (540 B.C.). Territories occupied or controlled by the Etruscans are shown by stippling. The black bands round the coasts indicate areas of Greek colonization.

participated, probably from the very beginning, in this great commercial exploitation of the western Mediterranean. Hence the development of Etruscan shipping which culminated in its domination of the Tyrrhenian sea. This is clearly documented by historical sources and confirmed by the frequent Etruscan representations of merchant ships and men-of-war and naval battle scenes between the seventh and fifth centuries B.C.: a definite pointer to the existence of a war fleet, heir to the traditions of the great Bronze Age Mediterranean thalassocracies and a worthy rival to the Hellenic fleets.[10] It is also probable, if we take historical tradition into account, that some Etruscan ships ventured beyond the limits of the Tyrrhenian sea in the direction of the western Mediterranean.

Naval clashes between Greeks and Etruscans

But the Greek colonization of the coasts of south Italy and Sicily presented an obstacle to the free expansion of Etruscan naval and commercial activity. Conflict with the Greeks was inevitable and did, in fact, characterize the final period of the Etruscan thalassocracy, between the sixth and the fifth centuries (see Plate 10); it marked its decline and was echoed in the writings of ancient historians. Naval battles are described as having taken place near Sicily, in the vicinity of the Aeolian Islands (Strabo, VI, 2, 10) or along sea routes within range of the Sicilian bases (Herodotus, VI, 17). There is an explicit reference to a naval expedition against Sicily in the *elogium* to an ancient leader of Tarquinia, Spurinna, preserved in a fragmentary Latin inscription (Plate 15).[11] Other conflicts, as we shall see, are referred instead to the Italian and Corsican coasts, closer to Etruria. This shows that the Etruscan naval sphere of action was gradually becoming restricted.

During this period, Carthage too comes into the picture. By imposing its control on the Phoenician colonies in western Sicily and in Sardinia it gained an entry to the Tyrrhenian sea. The Carthaginians and the Etruscans had anti-Greek interests in common; and for this reason, as well as for positive commercial advantages, perhaps because their economic needs were largely complementary, it was natural that they should work for long-term and wide-ranging co-operation. In his *Politics* (III, 9, 1280*a*, 36), Aristotle speaks of treaties between the two nations and states that their closeness was such that they could be considered as citizens of one and the same state.[12] This series of pacts probably included the first treaty between Rome and Carthage, dated by tradition as having been drawn up towards the end of the sixth century B.C. (Polybius, III, 22). This led, among other things, to actual military alliances against the Greeks, as attested by the account in Herodotus (I, 166) of a naval battle fought by the combined Carthaginians and Etruscans (from Cerveteri) against the Phocaeans in the waters of the Sardinian sea around the year 540 B.C. (a battle which is generally, but improperly, referred to in modern histories as the Battle of Alalia). Greek colonists from the city of Phocaea in Asia Minor had settled on the Ligurian coasts from the beginning of the sixth century and founded Massalia, modern Marseilles. They next settled in east Corsica at Alalia, where they were reinforced by refugees who had been driven from Phocaea by the Persian invasion. The Corsican settlement represented a direct threat to Etruria. After the battle of the Sardinian sea, the Phocaeans of Alalia found refuge in south Italy, where they founded the city of Elea (Velia), whilst the Etruscans took control of Corsica.[13] But this victory could not stop the gradual decline of the Etruscan thalassocracy, for their Carthaginian allies were able to consolidate and extend their political and commercial power (which reached its apogee towards the end of the sixth century) and began to exert pressure on the Etruscans from the south-west just as the Greeks were doing from the south-east. From the Punic and Etruscan inscriptions on the gold tablets found in 1964 in the sanctuary of Pyrgi (Plates 12–14), we know that the 'king' of Cerveteri, Thefarie Velianas, had, at the beginning of the fifth century, dedicated a shrine to the Phoenician goddess Astarte, identified with the Etruscan goddess Uni, in thanksgiving for her protection. The 'king' was probably a tyrant supported or imposed by the Carthaginians on an Etruscan city which was linked to Greece by ancient spiritual and cultural ties, so as to ensure its fidelity to the allied cause.[14]

The decline of Etruscan sea-power became more evident with the beginning of the fifth century, at a time when an economic crisis developed which was to affect the whole of central Italy for several decades, as we can tell from the rapid fall in foreign imports, particularly of Attic vases. On the military plane, the alliance between Etruscans and Carthaginians was weakened by the growing power of Syracuse: soon after the memorable defeat of the Carthaginians at Himera in Sicily, the Etruscans were beaten by the Syracusan fleet near Cumae in 474 B.C. (Diodorus Siculus, XI, 51; Pindar, *Pyth.*, I, 140).[15] From then on, the cities of Tyrrhenian Etruria lost control of the sea and were reduced to modest inland states waiting to be absorbed by the political hegemony of Rome. When in the third century Rome prepared to fight her tremendous naval duel with Carthage, not a trace remained of the Etruscan navy; the Etruscan allies did no more than help to provide materials for the construction of the Roman fleet.[16]

The territorial extension of Etruria

In Tuscorum iure pene omnis Italia fuerat: in the words of Cato (Servius, *ad Aen.*, XI, 567), nearly the whole of Italy had been under Etruscan domination. And Livy (I, 2; V, 33) stresses the power, the wealth and the renown which the Etruscans had acquired on land and sea, from the Alps to the Straits of Messina. These statements are confirmed for the most part by archaeological and epigraphic evidence, which also enables us to specify which areas of the peninsula came directly under Etruscan rule and which were affected only by its influence. In spite of the looseness of the political organization of Etruria, Etruscan expansion, no doubt relying upon the effective union of individual energies, must have been so powerful (especially between the seventh and the fifth centuries B.C.) that it was able to achieve an Etruscan political and linguistic system over the greater part of Tyrrhenian and north Italy. There is no doubt that the cultural mark left by the Etruscans on Italy went far beyond the geographical and temporal boundaries of their national life. Their civilization radiated over the whole of the peninsula and even over northern lands beyond the barrier of the Alps,[1] while at the same time it penetrated deep into the traditions and customs of Rome and survived the death of Etruria as an historical and linguistic entity.

The stretch of land that may be considered as the original territory of the Etruscans lies between the Tyrrhenian sea and the rivers Tiber and Arno: this is Etruria proper or Tyrrhenian Etruria. To it belong the twelve cities which, according to tradition, make up the Etruscan nation; and here, from very early times, Etruscan was written – and therefore spoken. Ancient tradition has been seen by modern scholars as supporting the notion of an Etruscan national territory, corresponding to the Etruria of historical times, where the stock had its roots, the starting-point of sea colonies and land conquests towards Campania and the Po valley. We may well suspect today the validity of such an oversimplified picture; and this for two reasons, or in two distinct senses. On the one hand there is the question whether the whole of historical Etruria was originally uniformly Etruscan in character; on the other the question whether the lands to the north and south of Etruria

91

were in fact later conquests and not part of Etruscan territory from the very start of the formative process of the people.

The hypothesis of a gradual 'etruscanization' of Etruria proper, originally inhabited by peoples of different stock, but unified by a predominant group of Etruscan speakers, was taken up again by F. Altheim.[2] The theory that ascribes an overseas origin to the Etruscans had already regarded the Tyrrhenian colonists as having first settled on the coastal strip, conceived as the starting-point for the gradual occupation of the whole territory. This view seems to be borne out by the difference in the burial rites – mainly inhumation in southern Etruria and cremation in northern Etruria: a sign of the predominance of Tyrrhenian immigrants in those regions nearest their landing points, and of pre-Etruscan (i.e. Umbrian) populations in the interior. The idea of an Italic substratum subjugated by a small number of Etruscan conquerors occasionally re-emerges on the margin of discussions or in the study of certain isolated phenomena: e.g. in the study of the personal names of the Cerveteri inscriptions. These appear to be strongly influenced by Italic elements and, according to R. Mengarelli, the excavator of the cemetery, this proved the original Italic identity of the population.[3] But these are comparatively late inscriptions, mostly belonging to the period of direct Roman domination over the Etruscan city, when it was actually the Etruscan element that was disappearing. The equally fanciful hypothesis of an Italic origin of Veii was thoroughly disproved by the discovery of an abundant crop of archaic Etruscan inscriptions.[4]

We must, however, recognize that within geographically Etruscan territory (i.e. on the right bank of the Tiber) there is evidence of important groups of non-Etruscan speakers: the Faliscans, for instance, who occupied the land within the curve formed by the Tiber between Orte and the territory of Rome. Though politically and culturally dominated by the Etruscans, they always preserved their ethnic and linguistic Latin individuality. It is worth noting that there is no trace of a proper Villanovan culture either in Faliscan or in Latial territories. At the same time, however, we should add that in the very heart of southern Etruria (e.g. on the Tolfa hills and at Bisenzio), local Iron Age cultures too seem to have been, as far as we can tell, substantially unaffected by the characteristic developments of the Villanovan coastal cultures: Protovillanovan traditions seem to have persisted there, closely resembling those of the Latial cultures. This state of affairs seems to point to a transitional ethnic area characterized by an oscillation of proto-Etruscan and 'proto-Latin' elements.[5] Moreover, historical sources record the Umbrian Camertes within inland Etruria, and Chiusi was also known by the name Camars (Livy, IX, 36, 7; X,

25, 11; Cicero, *Pro Sulla*, 19, etc.). The whole of Etruria, not merely Caere, abounds in onomastic and toponymic elements of Italic origin that betray deep and ancient penetrations by peoples with Indo-European tongues. The fact that the growth of population and the urban development occurred earlier in coastal southern Etruria and were more vigorous than in the vast inland areas leads to the conclusion that the formative processes of the Etruscan nation did not take place simultaneously over the whole of Etruria proper. They must have followed a long struggle with Italic elements, especially in the inland areas of southern Etruria, and must have ended in the ethnic assimilation or political conquest of these elements.[6]

The almost complete lack of authentic historical sources prevents us from attempting the reconstruction, even along the broadest of outlines, of the political and military events affecting the various Etruscan cities and their relations one with another. The most vivid aspect of history – the names of kings and rulers, revolutions, wars, alliances, dates; all those things, in fact, that we know with a fair degree of certainty for Archaic and Classical Greece – remains shrouded in darkness for us. Graeco-Roman literary tradition mentions a number of Etruscan heroes, founders of cities and kings: e.g. the name of Arimna or Arimnestus, the first barbarian to dedicate a throne at Olympia (Pausanias, V, 12, 5). Most of these figures have a legendary origin or are the result of the invention and speculation of later mythographers. In a few cases, however, these personages and the events connected with their names seem to possess a certain historical basis. The most reliable information we have from classical authors on the political history of the Etruscan cities, though still vague and indirect, concerns the relations between Etruria and the Greek and Roman worlds. As a result, the very few epigraphic sources that we have on the ancient internal history of Etruria are all the more valuable, for they provide us with direct information. They include Latin inscriptions containing *elogia* of Etruscan historical figures, recovered in fragments at Tarquinia, and the already mentioned gold tablets with inscriptions in Etruscan and Punic found in the sanctuary at Pyrgi.[7]

Very generally, it is possible to make out an organization based upon city states more or less independent of each other, but united (at the time of the Roman conquest at least) in a kind of confederation; and we can glimpse their development from monarchical to republican institutions, a process that will be described in more detail in Chapter Six. We may also presume, on the basis of both archaeological and literary evidence, that the cities of coastal Etruria, and especially Cerveteri, Tarquinia and Vulci, had enjoyed a period of notable power and splendour during the seventh and sixth centuries; but we know nothing precise about their reciprocal relations or the way in which one town may have predominated in turn over the others. An early pre-eminence of Tarquinia is suggested by the antiquity and the importance of traditions concerning its origins.[8] Towards the middle of the sixth century, Vulci too seems to have assumed a position of special import-ance, as we can see from its riches, the scale of its exports and a likely Vulcian intervention in the political battles between southern Etruria and Rome, as we shall have occasion to see.[9] We have already mentioned recently discovered documents that refer to the name of a lord of Cer-veteri, Thefarie Velianas, who ruled at the beginning of the fifth cen-tury. Towards the end of the sixth century, it was probably Chiusi, an inland city, that becomes dominant: this is reflected by the legendary traditions of the deeds of its king, Lars Porsenna, in Latium. This hegemony probably coincided with the beginning of the decadence of the coastal towns. Archaeological evidence in fact indicates that the fifth century witnessed mainly the flourishing of Chiusi, Orvieto and the Etruscan Po valley. As the Etruscan civilization drew on to its close, from the fourth to the second centuries B.C., we note the gradual in-crease in importance of other inland and northern centres such as Volterra, Arezzo, Perugia.

The Etruscan domination of southern and northern Italy

The 'etruscanization' of Italy followed two main directions: to the south, along the Tyrrhenian coast, over Latium and Campania; to the north, across the Apennines and over the lower Po valley. As a result, Etruscan ethnic and political continuity was established from the Gulf of Salerno to the Tridentine Alps. Outside it, to the west, we have western Lombardy, Piedmont and Liguria, all occupied by peoples of Ligurian stock[10]; to the east, the land of the Veneti, the whole of the eastern half of Italy (inhabited by Picenes, Umbrians and Sabellians) and, finally, the southern extremity of the peninsula (see map on p. 88).

We have already noted that the large degree of coincidence between the Villanovan cultural area and that known to have been occupied by the Etruscans in historical times suggests that the Etruscan expansion in Italy was a good deal earlier than had been thought at first. Such a hypothesis agrees fairly well with what we find in the areas of Bologna and Salerno, where there exists a more or less direct archaeological continuity from the Villanovan to the Etruscan periods, as we shall see. We might even relate the Villanovan 'island' of Fermo in Picenum with a statement made by Strabo (V, 4, 2) on the foundation by the Tyrrhenians of Cupra, a city on the Adriatic not far from Fermo, renowned for a sanctuary to Hera. If we can agree on the validity of these correspondences, the presence of Etruscans in southern Italy and beyond the Apennines can be dated back to at least the eighth century. This fits well with what we had to say concerning the beginnings of the Etruscan domination of the sea.[11]

From the historical point of view, the Etruscan domination of Campania, on which some doubt was cast in the past, is no longer problematical except in matters of detail. Our knowledge here derives from the work of J. Beloch[12] and from archaeological and epigraphic discoveries, particularly the long Etruscan inscription on the Capua tile (Plate 97). The settlement of Etruscans on the Campanian coast should almost certainly be related to the full development of their sea-power, directed as we know towards the southern Tyrrhenian sea, Sicily and the Straits of Messina. From the first half of the eighth century, Greek seafarers from Euboea were established on the island of Ischia, from where they founded Cumae, the northernmost Greek colony on the Italian coast. Ancient tradition dwells on the long battle waged by the Etruscans against this city.[13] The Etruscan domination of Campania spread widely both to the north and south of Capua, Acerra, Nola, Nocera, Herculaneum, Pompeii and Sorrento, to which we should add other cities as yet unidentified but known through their coins, such as Uri or Urina (corresponding perhaps to Hyria), Velcha, Velsu, Irnthi.[14] The Campanian dominion had a political structure similar to the mother country: twelve allied city states, probably under the hegemony of Capua. Ancient sources also tell of an Etruscan occupation of the Salerno coast, between Sorrento and the mouth of the Sele, i.e. the ancient *ager picentinum* where the Etruscan colony of Marcina had been founded (Strabo, V, 4, 13; Pliny, III, 70). It is interesting to note that this area has yielded a number of Villanovan and Orientalizing finds at Pontecagnano, and also some with an Archaic Etruscan appearance at Fratte di Salerno; a similar cultural sequence is now attested for the cemetery of Capua itself.[15] Whether the Etruscans ever occupied Pompeii, as stated by Strabo (V, 4, 8), was a long-debated question,[16] which was resolved when A. Maiuri, excavating the temple of Apollo near the Forum at Pompeii,[17] discovered fragments of bucchero vases bearing inscriptions that are certainly in Etruscan.

The existence of an Etruscan phase in the history of Latium and Rome is explicitly stated by historical tradition, particularly in connection with the Etruscan dynasty of the Tarquins who reigned in Rome between the end of the seventh and the last decades of the sixth century B.C. Archaeology has fully confirmed the main lines of this story and its chronological setting.[18] As early as the seventh century the influence of Etruscan art and culture was manifest in Latium: it is attested by the important Orientalizing tombs at Palestrina, very similar to those of Cerveteri and Vetulonia; and it became more strongly marked during the sixth century and at the beginning of the fifth, especially in architecture and in the production of terracotta facings on Archaic temples. During this period Rome itself takes on the character of a fully integrated city, surrounded by a defensive *agger* and possessing a number of monumental buildings. Especially important in this respect is the presence of Etruscan inscriptions (Plates 17–19): besides the two on bucchero vases found on the slopes of the Capitoline hill and at the top of the Palatine, we have a short fragment on an impasto vase which may be dated as early as the end of the seventh century, discovered in the sacred area of S. Omobono in the Forum Boarium.[19] Side by side with the rare archaic Latin inscriptions found in Rome (e.g. the Duenos vase, the famous *Lapis Niger* cippus etc.), these Etruscan inscriptions confirm the importance of the Etruscan element in the population of Rome, and they place the city within the bilingual Etrusco-Latin zone, to which the Faliscan territory is also known to have belonged.

The re-examination of the traditional evidence referring to the Etruscan phase of Roman history should also take into account the legends that relate to the military deeds of two Etruscan brothers, Aulus and Caelius Vibenna from Vulci, and their friend Mastarna, later identified with the king Servius Tullius (Varro, *De ling. lat.*, V, 46; Servius, *ad Aen.*, V, 560; Festus 31/44, s.v. *Caelius mons*; Dionysius of Halicarnassus, II, 36, 2 ff.; Claudius, in *C.I.L.*, XIII, 1668; Tacitus, *Ann.*, IV, 65). In the François Tomb at Vulci, there is a painting of a battle scene (Plate 20): one camp consists of a group of fighters amongst whom we find Aule and Cele Vipinas (the two brothers Vibenna) and Macstrna (Mastarna); the other, of warriors amongst whom is a Cneve Tarchunies Rumach, undoubtedly Gnaeus Tarquinius Romanus, i.e. a member of the Tarquin dynasty. These paintings are accompanied by Etruscan inscriptions, and although they belong to a later period (the Hellenistic age) they undoubtedly represent an ancient Etruscan version of the tradition.[20] Excavations at a sanctuary at Veii have produced a fragment of a bucchero vase which bears an Etruscan votive inscription, the dedicator being one Avile Vipiennas, an archaic Etruscan form of Aulus Vibenna or Aule Vipinas. The inscription has been dated around the middle of the sixth century B.C., at the very period attributed by tradition to the reign of Servius Tullius. It is therefore an original document, contemporary with the historical period referred to by the legend. It is probable that Aulus and Caelius Vibenna were real historical personages, Etruscan *condottieri* who participated in a political struggle whose object was the domination of Rome, and that one of them made a votive offering at the sanctuary at Veii, so very near

Rome.[21] That close relations united Veii and Rome at this time is borne out by the tradition concerning works of art fashioned by Vulca and other Veientine artists for the sanctuary dedicated to Jupiter, Juno and Minerva on the Capitol (Varro in Pliny, *Nat. Hist.*, XXXV, 157; Plutarch, *Public.*, 13).

The Etruscan control of Latium is further confirmed by traditions concerning king Porsenna of Chiusi, whom ancient sources place around the end of the sixth century. By this time, however, it was already threatened by the movement for independence growing in the Latin cities, while at the same time the seafaring activities of the Etruscans enter a period of great economic crisis. The alliance between the Greeks of Cumae and the Latins (Livy, II, 14; Dionysius of Halicarnassus, VII, 5 and 6) accelerated the collapse of Etruscan hegemony over Latium. No doubt it is within this series of events that we should place those traditions concerning the end of the Tarquins, the institution of the Republic and the liberation of Rome from Etruscan rule. We should also add the pressure of east Italic mountain peoples who, like the Volsci, invaded the greater part of Latium down to the sea. For a few decades the Etruscan dominion of Campania survived the territorial separation from the mother country, but it too finally succumbed, around the year 430 B.C., before the descending wave of Italic Samnites (Diodorus Siculus, XII, 31, 1; Livy, IV, 37, 1).[22]

The 'etruscanization' of the Po valley consisted, according to the ancients, of the foundation of twelve cities by the twelve city states in Etruria. Legendary or semi-legendary heroes were said to have taken part in the enterprise, such as Tarchon, the eponymous hero of Tarquinia, and a leader, Aucnus or Ocnus, the son or brother of Aulestes, the king of Perugia, joint founders of Bologna (Felsina), Mantua, etc. (Servius, *ad Aen.*, X, 198, 200). Archaeological finds confirm the presence of Etruscans in territories north of the Apennines: it is therefore permissible to speak of an 'Etruria of the Po valley'.[23] These finds are particularly numerous at Bologna and in its region, which had already in the eighth and seventh centuries seen the flourishing of a Villanovan civilization (see Plate 5) strongly influenced by the Villanovan and Orientalizing of Etruria. From the end of the sixth century, and especially during the fifth and fourth, Etruscan influence became very marked, both in the inscriptions and in its material culture (the 'Certosa culture' of Bologna). In the direction of the Adriatic, the cities of Spina, Adria, Ravenna, and Rimini are mentioned as being Etruscan by classical authors. Spina became an important centre of trade with Greece during the fifth century, as the tombs of its rich cemetery testify. Inland, there were the cities of Parma, Piacenza, Modena and perhaps Melpum, of uncertain location. Near the village of Marzabotto, in the valley of the upper Reno (near Bologna), an inhabited centre has been discovered, whose Etruscan origin is certain, but whose name is unknown. It is important for its well-preserved orthogonal plan; and it must have flourished because of its position on a road across the Apennines and perhaps also because of its mineral resources.

In north Italy, the Etruscan dominion was contained by the Veneti to the east and the Ligurians to the west. Its decline was probably accelerated by the advance of the Umbrians from central Italy, who (according to Strabo, V, 1, 7 and 10–11) occupied Rimini and Ravenna; they had therefore followed and not preceded the Etruscans in the Po valley. The main cause of the Etruscan downfall in the north, however, was the invasion of the Celts from across the Alps (see Plates 21 and 23): the most important tribes, Cenomani, Boii (who gave their name to Bononia, i.e. Bologna), Insubres, Senones, etc., had penetrated into north Italy during the fifth century, if not earlier, had then crossed the Apennines to reach Picenum and Etruria, and succeeded in sacking Rome (in 391 B.C. according to tradition, but more probably around 386).[24] It is likely that a number of Etruscan town-dwellers survived the wave of Celtic invaders – whose warrior tombs are archaeologically distinguished by the presence of objects belonging to the La Tène culture – just as, later, at the same places, the Romans of late Imperial times were to survive the wave of Germanic invasions. We know, for instance, that Mantua prided itself on its Etruscan traditions well into Roman times. It has even been suggested that traces of a dispersion of Etruscan elements in the Alpine valleys are to be seen in some late inscriptions in the Etruscan alphabet that have been found in the Alps. The basis of this theory is the well-known passage in Livy (V, 33): *Alpinis quoque ea gentibus haud dubie origo est, maxime Raetis; quos loca ipsa efferarunt, ne quid ex antiquo, praeter sonum linguae, nec eum incorruptum, retinerent* ('The Alpine peoples too, especially the Raetians, have undoubtedly the same origin [i.e. Etruscan]; but the very nature of their surroundings caused them to grow so wild that the only memory they preserved of their past was the sound of their language, and that not uncorrupted'). A more likely explanation is that these inscriptions belonged to indigenous speakers of a pre-Indo-European dialect possessing only vague affinities with Etruscan.[25]

A final word on the question of Etruscan influence in Liguria. Ancient tradition speaks of Etruscan domination along the Ligurian coast as far as the Val di Magra, and of the founding by the Etruscans of Luni. Archaeology, however, shows that the Ligurian cultural horizon extended as far south as the northern bank of the Arno, and reveals the presence of Etruscan influence at Luni only at a very late period. These regions were probably the object of violent struggles between Etruscans and fierce Ligurian tribes. Etruscan rule seems to have spread mainly along the coastal regions and to have possessed a transitory character, until Rome appeared upon the scene.[26]

The spread of Etruscan culture in Italy

If the political rule and direct colonization of the Etruscans only extended over part of peninsular Italy, their commercial activities and their cultural influence reached much further afield. Situated at the centre of the peninsula, Etruria was in fact the only beacon to radiate its civilization from early times upon generally backward peoples. Its only rivals were the Greek cities of Sicily and southern Italy. Greek culture, however, though more advanced and working upon Etruria itself, did not at first penetrate so deeply as Etruscan culture. As for the influence of Carthage, its cultural importance was only secondary, and limited in range to western Sicily and to Sardinia.

When speaking of a pre-Roman Etrusco-Italic civilization, we are involuntarily led to place upon equal historical and chronological footings the various peoples of ancient Italy (Etruscans, Ligurians, Veneti, Latins, Umbro-Sabellians, etc.), whereas a careful study of the archaeological evidence is sufficient to persuade us that both the predominant role and the absolute chronological priority in the formation of the civilization of ancient Italy belong to Etruria. During the sixth century, the time of the great expansion and the greatest flowering of the Etruscan civilization, the peoples of Emilia, the Veneto and Liguria were still living in a retarded Iron Age. The Picenes and the Umbrians were elaborating ways of life in which primitive and Orientalizing elements were to predominate for a long time – elements which Etruria had discarded long ago – or else they were more or less directly affected by Etruscan influences. Latium and Campania revolved within the orbit of Etruria and Greece. The Samnites showed, and continued to show for many decades, late features of the Adriatic Iron Age culture. All these peripheral regions, with the exception of the extreme south, colonized by the Greeks, possessed what was substantially a survival of the archaic *village* culture. Its definite transformation into an *urban* culture was at first due to the political and cultural predominance of Etruria, and, later, to the unification of the peninsula achieved by Rome, the bearer of civilized forms of life which themselves owed much to Etruria.

That close links united the religion and ritual of Etruria, Umbria and Latium is clearly shown by the texts of the Iguvine Tablets and by the sacred Latin formulas given by Cato in his *De re rustica*. They reveal a close analogy with what we are able to discover of Etruscan ritual literature, e.g. in votive formulas and prayers, the names of deities and liturgical expressions.[27] It is worth recalling that many Etruscan deities are identical with Latin and Italic gods, even to their names: *Uni* – Juno; *Menerva* – Minerva; *Neθun* – Neptune; *Selvan* – Silvanus; *Satre* – Saturn; *Velχan* – Vulcan; *Maris* – Mars; *Vesuna* – Vesona. Even if there were common elements going back to an earlier prehistoric cultural unity, there is little doubt that these close analogies developed chiefly as the result of the cultural and political hegemony of Etruria in central Italy.

The same may be said for personal names. The Etruscans, the Latins and the Umbro-Sabellians shared the characteristic system of a double personal name: the *praenomen*, or personal name, and the name of the *gens*, or family. This system had no parallel among other ancient peoples and probably spread from Etruria.[28] Together with the social system, the Etruscan political system was also adopted in varying degrees by the peoples of Latium and of central Italy. The Roman monarchy, even to its external symbols (the golden crown, the throne, the *fasces*, the *toga palmata*, etc.), was explicitly stated by Latin writers to have been of Etruscan origin. The Umbrians adopted the Etruscan magistrature of the *maru*.[29]

The diffusion of writing is one more important aspect of Etruscan cultural influence on the Italian peninsula. It spread in two directions. To the south, the Greek alphabet adopted by the Etruscans (of a western Greek type, probably originating from Cumae) was also used at an early stage by the Faliscans and the Latins, although it naturally included variants determined by the presence of different sounds, such as *o* and the voiced plosive consonants, foreign to the Etruscan phonetic system. The forms of the written alphabet were still almost identical during the seventh and sixth centuries. Traces of a direct Etruscan influence are common: e.g. the Latin use of the gamma symbol to indicate, as in Etruscan, the unvoiced velar consonant *k* instead of the voiced *g*, or the use of the digraph *vh* to represent the sound *f*. The Umbrians and the Oscans, on the other hand, adopted the Etruscan alphabet directly, though naturally with modifications and additions: these, however, occurred only at a later period, i.e. not earlier than the fifth to fourth centuries B.C. The Etruscan alphabet also spread towards the north: the alphabets of the Veneti, the Raetians, the Lepontians and other Alpine peoples were related to the so-called northern Etruscan alphabet adopted in the Po valley from the end of the sixth century.[30] Today there is a growing tendency to believe that the runic alphabets of central and northern Europe were also derived, at least in part, from the northern Etruscan alphabet.[31]

Let us finally consider the realms of art and culture. Objects found in the Umbrian cities of Todi (Tuder), Bettona (Vettona) and Cagli etc., reveal a very marked Etruscan influence; in some cases we may even speak of articles imported from Etruria. Etruscan Orientalizing elements are also present in Picenum. The whole culture of Latium from the seventh to the sixth century B.C. was closely linked to Etruria: we need only think of the type and shape of the temple, or of its decorations in painted terracotta as seen at Falerii, Rome, Velletri, Satricum and Capua. Painted tombs similar to those of Etruria have been discovered at Rome, Capua, Paestum, and even as far away as Apulia; and they were adopted by the Samnite invaders of Campania, who also took up other Etruscan customs, such as the gladiatorial combats which later spread from Capua to Rome. Similarly, material elements of the Etruscan civilization spread over northern Italy to reach the Veneti, the Alpine valleys and the Golasecca culture, and penetrated, as we have seen, into central Europe.

Thus, despite the persistence of backward and archaic forms right up to the threshold of the Roman conquest, especially in peripheral areas, and despite lingering regional characteristics in some of its cultures, a certain cultural unity was arrived at in Italy well before the unification achieved by Rome. This unity was largely due to the political dominance and cultural prestige of the Etruscans in archaic times. These spiritual and cultural forces were to survive the fifth-century crisis and the declining sea-power of the Tyrrhenian cities, the destruction of the southern and northern Etruscan dominions by the spreading of the Italic peoples and the Celtic invaders, which confined the Etruscan world to Etruria proper, i.e. approximately within the borders of what was to become the seventh region of Augustan Italy – until, very gradually, after a series of wars lasting throughout the fourth century and the first decades of the third, the various Etruscan city states were subdued by Rome and joined the Roman-Italic federal state system, finally to be absorbed into the Roman juridical unity at the beginning of the first century B.C.[32] Even during these last phases of its history Etruria was still evolving, though in a conservative manner, its own ancient rites and institutions. Yet at the same time it was contributing to the formation of the cultural and artistic κοινή of Roman Italy, which, fused with the cultural forces of the Hellenic world, was to form the basis of the civilization of imperial Rome and, ultimately, of the whole of western European civilization.

Part 2

Aspects of the Civilization of Etruria

CHAPTER 5

Cities and Cemeteries of Etruria

The resurrection of Etruria

The history of Etruscan studies is closely linked to the story of the resurrection of the dead cities of Etruria. For more than two centuries now, investigators of all kinds, impelled at first by greed for treasure, simple curiosity or interest in local history and only later by scientific motives, have quarried relentlessly at the remains of the great Etruscan cities and of their cemeteries. Nevertheless, anyone who is familiar with the Etruscan countryside knows that an incalculable amount of evidence needed for the reconstruction of its ancient civilization still lies below ground awaiting excavation.

The story of the rediscovery of Etruria is varied, stimulating, at times even dramatic. At first silence and oblivion lay over the ancient cities: the fresh sap of medieval or modern life and art effectively extinguished all memory of Etruscan monuments in towns, such as Volterra, Arezzo, Cortona, Chiusi and Orvieto, where life has continued uninterrupted since Etruscan days, and the wild Mediterranean scrub concealed the remains of cities that had been abandoned.

> *Ricordi tu le vedove piagge del mar toscano*
> *ove china su 'l nubilo inseminato piano*
> > *la torre feudal*
> *con lunga ombra di tedio dai colli arsicci e foschi*
> *veglia de le rasenie cittadi in mezzo ai boschi*
> > *il sonno sepolcral . . . ?*
> > (Carducci, *Avanti, Avanti!*)

(Do you remember the widowed shores of the Tuscan sea, where the feudal tower bends over the hazy fallow plain with long and dreary shadow and watches from the dark, burnt hills over the sepulchral sleep of the Rasenna cities, buried deep amidst the woods . . . ?)

The very name of many a famous city has been lost. Over the ruins of Tarquinia (once called Corneto), fabulous stories were told of a city called Corythus. The identification of Veii was much disputed during the eighteenth century; in the nineteenth, that of Vetulonia. Today, important centres whose cemeteries were unearthed near Marsiliana d'Albegna and Massa Marittima, and the Etruscan city of Orvieto itself, still remain hidden and nameless to us.

The Etruscans

Little by little, from the darkness of the past, some of the features of the civilization of ancient Etruria began to emerge. At first it was the peasant and the traveller, marvelling at the weapons and jewels the earth had unexpectedly brought forth, or wondering at the strange paintings, the sculptures and the puzzling inscriptions in mysterious underground chambers – finds such as the grottoes that inspired the humanist Lucius Vitellius to describe the 'court at Corythus' in a poem dedicated to Philelphus; or the 'Tomba della Cipollara' near Viterbo, opened in the presence of Pope Alexander VI, with its figured and inscribed sarcophagi which were interpreted by Annius as celebrating the triumphs of the oldest kings of Italy; or the unknown tomb that prompted Michelangelo to draw the head of the king of the Etruscan underworld. Then, at the height of the cinquecento, the golden age of Renaissance sculpture, came the unearthing of superb Etruscan bronzes, now the pride of the Museo Archeologico at Florence: the Chimaera of Arezzo, the 'Orator' of Perugia (Plates 66 and 76). Finally, when interest in ancient Etruria had wakened and reached a climax through the works of Dempster, Buonarroti, Gori and Passeri, there followed in ever-quickening succession the discoveries of tombs at Siena, Tarquinia, Volterra, Cortona. And at last, with the creation of the Etruscan Academy at Cortona, there began the first organized excavations for Etruscan remains.

The most active phase in the resurrection of the dead cities of Etruria began with the nineteenth century. We cannot yet speak of strictly scientific activity, but the greater part of the material we possess came to light during this period of enthusiasm. Excavation and study had begun in the eighteenth century around the centres of northern Etruria; in the nineteenth century attention was mainly concentrated upon the cities of coastal Etruria, especially Cerveteri, Tarquinia and Vulci. For many years the vast cemeteries that surrounded the latter city turned (chiefly through the enterprise of Lucien Bonaparte, Prince of Canino) into an inexhaustible quarry of Greek and Etruscan vases. The interest of local authorities and landowners was joined by that of the newly founded Institute of Archaeological Correspondence and, within the borders of the Papal States, that of the Camerlingate, under whose supervision excavations were undertaken.

The second half of the nineteenth century generally brought a pause in the resurrection of Etruscan cities. The growing interest in prehistory resulted in a series of discoveries that served to illustrate and to locate earlier evidence for human occupation of the Etruscan centres. During this period, the activities of private individuals and local initiative were joined by those of the Italian government, which began to take an active role in the search for and excavation of ancient remains. It was only during the first decades of this century, after the creation of a Direzione Generale delle Antichità e Belle Arti with regional offices in Tuscany, Latium and Emilia, that a new and intensive campaign of exploration began. Town sites and cemeteries were excavated, leading to a better knowledge of the various aspects of the civilization of ancient Etruria and to the enrichment of Italy's national and local museums. Research has gathered momentum in the last thirty years and has been greatly assisted by the use of aerial photography and the development of geophysical techniques of prospecting.[1] New interest has been focused on field work and ancient topography, the study of town sites, of the network of ancient roads and the identification of minor centres, etc.[2] Unfortunately, however, serious research has been and is still plagued by clandestine and uncontrolled excavations whose sole aim is the recovery of readily saleable ancient objects. Such activities, difficult to control in such an archaeologically rich area, are pursued according to the old methods of pre-scientific archaeology, and result in a considerable loss of evidence.[3]

Cities of southern Etruria

Let us now cast a rapid glance at the principal centres of Etruscan life and describe their most obvious characteristics.[4] Geographical and historical factors require a fundamental distinction to be made between southern Etruria on the one hand and central and northern Etruria on the other. The approximate line of demarcation between the two regions is marked by the rivers Fiora, which flows into the Tyrrhenian sea, and Paglia, a tributary of the Tiber; it is substantially the modern frontier between Tuscany and Latium. Southern, or Latian, Etruria consists of volcanic or alluvial terrains and belongs to the volcanic hill and lake system of Latium. Central and northern Etruria, larger in area, lies mainly over the foothills of the Apennines, rich in rivers and vegetation. From the historical and monumental point of view, the two regions are fairly clearly differentiated. The south developed much earlier, with great and early cities built close to the sea or along rivers and lakes, at a relatively short distance from one another: Veii, Cerveteri, Tarquinia, Vulci, Volsinii. Their decadence during the final phase of Etruscan civilization and under the Roman Empire was hastened by the spread of malaria in the Maremma. The limited development of this area in medieval and modern times (it is only quite recently that an agricultural revival has taken place) has done much to preserve its ruins in a wild and primitive landscape. Those cities that stood on the Tyrrhenian shore to the north of the Fiora and Monte Argentario (e.g. Roselle, Vetulonia, Populonia) present much the same characteristics:

107

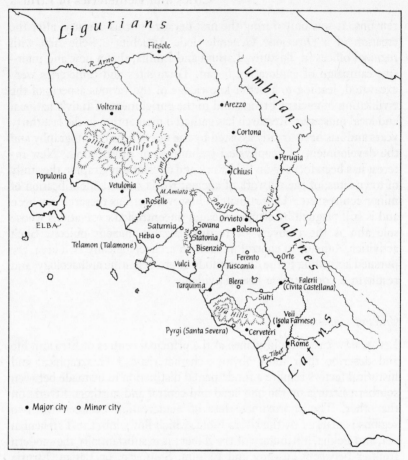

Figure 4. The principal cities of Etruria proper. Modern Italian names, where they differ, are given in brackets.

the same early development followed by the same early decadence, the same Maremman landscape, etc. Altogether different is the case of the centres of inland Etruria: Chiusi, Cortona, Perugia, Arezzo, Fiesole, Volterra. These stood at considerable distances from one another and developed later than the cities of the south: they flourished mainly during the final phase of Etruscan civilization and in Roman times. More significant, however, is the fact that they have continued without a break from antiquity to modern times; we should not think of them as dead cities, and it is here that we can look for links between the ancient Etruscan nation and the flourishing civilization of the Tuscan Renaissance.

An ordered survey of the cities of Etruria should begin with Rome itself, the Etruscan form of whose name was *Ruma-*.[5] There is no doubt

108

that Rome was for a period (in the sixth century B.C.) the centre of an Etruscan monarchy, with monumental buildings, works of art, institutions and a religion all under Etruscan influence. The inhabitants were of Latin and partly of Sabine stock, but recent finds of vases with Etruscan inscriptions testify, as we have already seen, to the presence of Etruscan inhabitants as well. Tradition places these in the Velabrum quarter, surrounding the Vicus Tuscus, close to the Capitoline hill, once the *arx* of the Etruscan kings (Varro, *De ling. lat.*, V, 46; Livy, II, 14, 9; Dionysius of Halicarnassus, V, 36; Festus, 536/355, *s.v. Tuscum vicum*). Naturally, after the expulsion of the Tarquinian dynasty the city became thoroughly Latin, ethnically, linguistically and politically. Important traces of its Etruscan phase survive, however: we can see them in its temples and the terracotta coverings that decorated them; in the Capitoline temple built on the three-celled plan after the Etruscan manner with the help of artists from Veii; and in the sacred site of S. Omobono in the Forum Boarium. We can see them too in some of the older remains of the city walls and in those few areas left of the early cemeteries, particularly on the Esquiline hill, that have escaped the upheavals of nearly three thousand years of constant building activity.

A few miles north-west of Rome, between the two branches of the Cremera, stood the city of Veii on a rocky spur.[6] Veii flourished mainly in Archaic times; its life was stilled or at least much reduced after the Roman conquest at the beginning of the fourth century B.C. The Romans did not totally destroy it, and there are in fact many remains dating back to Republican and Imperial times. Under Augustus, the contrast between its ancient grandeur and contemporary decadence was romantically brought out in the famous lines of Propertius (IV, X, 27):

Heu Veii veteres! et vos tum regna fuistis
et vestro positast aurea sella foro.

Nunc intra muros pastoris bucina lenti
cantat, et in vestris ossibus arva metunt.

(Veii, thou hadst a royal crown of old,
And in thy forum stood a throne of gold!

Thy walls now echo but the shepherd's horn,
And o'er thine ashes waves the summer corn.[7])

This picture still corresponds to the impression received by the modern sightseer as he approaches the site from the hamlet of Isola Farnese, making his way across the picturesque ravine of the Cremera towards the heights of the ancient city, uninhabited and still largely unexplored (Plates 24 and 28). On a level site outside the city walls, at Portonaccio, the excavations of the last few decades, frequently interrupted, have brought to light a sanctuary connected with the cult of the health-giving waters emerging from the hillside. There stood the temple, of which only the tufa foundations remain, built on the Etruscan plan with three cells (or one cell and two wings) and with a wide forecourt. Along one of its sides there is a pool, in whose healing waters the pilgrims probably bathed. In front of the temple a rectangular altar, of later construction, has been found. The whole surrounding area has yielded fragments of painted architectural terracottas from the upper portion of the temple, and also votive objects, fragments of vases with Etruscan inscriptions, etc. The most important find consists of fragments of a series of large terracotta statues, the most famous of which is the Apollo of Veii (Plate 61), unearthed in 1916. These statues were *acroteria* placed on the roof of the rich temple: they reveal the hand of an artist with a most original style working towards the end of the sixth and the beginning of the fifth century B.C. Elsewhere within the city, and especially in the locality known as Campetti, large quantities of votive objects have come to light, particularly terracotta figurines and heads (Plate 67). All this material is generally believed to be earlier than the fourth century B.C., and the same may be said of the objects found in the cemeteries that surround the city, which date back to the Villanovan period (Plates 2 and 3). There are painted tombs too: the 'Tomba delle Anatre', with Geometric decoration of the seventh century, and the 'Tomba Campana' with Orientalizing decoration of the early sixth.

Standing between the sea and the lake of Bracciano, a few miles from the coast, we can see the remains of another great and famous Etruscan metropolis: Cerveteri (i.e. 'old Caere'), well-known to the ancients for its seafaring activities.[8] The original Etruscan form of the name was probably *Chaisre*, whence *Cisra*, and χaire. The modern village of Cerveteri is its impoverished descendant: see Plate 25. The huge area of the ancient city, protected by rocky cliffs or, in more accessible places, by walls of square stone blocks, is surrounded by its cemeteries. These extend down the valley of the Sorbo (where the famous Orientalizing 'Regolini-Galassi' tomb was found in the nineteenth century) and on neighbouring hills (Banditaccia, Monte Abatone). The monumental complex of Banditaccia (Plate 48), excavated and restored during the last fifty years, is one of the most interesting and inspiring archaeological areas not only of Italy, but of the whole Mediterranean world. A whole series of tumuli may be seen there, heaped on rock or stone plinths, varying in size, the largest reaching one hundred feet in diameter. Carved out of the tufa at the base of the tumuli, one or more groups of sepulchres may be found; these imitate the interior of houses and consist of several rooms, with doors, windows, columns and pilasters outlined on the walls, beamed or coffered ceilings, and including furniture, armchairs, funerary couches, etc. (see Plates 80–82). Other monuments have been dug squarely out of the rock, opening out on to the straight 'streets of the dead', which cross at right angles as in the towns of the living. Later tombs are deeper and may take the form of vast hypogea, sculptured in imitation of city architecture and occasionally featuring stuccoes, paintings and inscriptions. Within the city, temples abounding in figured terracotta coverings and votive objects have been found.

The material recovered at Cerveteri stretches without a break from Villanovan down to Roman times. But the overwhelming majority of the excavated tombs and their contents belong to the seventh and sixth centuries B.C. During this period, Caere must have been an exceptionally rich and populous city, perhaps one of the most splendid in the world then known. In addition to bronze and silver Orientalizing objects, fine jewellery and local impasto or bucchero pottery, large quantities of imported Corinthian, Rhodian, Ionian and Attic vases have come to light. It is highly probable that foreign artists or schools settled to work in this promising market, as in the case of the Ionian potters responsible for the production of the well-known 'Caeretan hydriae'. Various styles of Archaic Greek painting meet in Caere, reflected in the characteristic painted terracotta plaques used in panelling and decorating the internal walls of buildings and tombs. A great number of decorative architectural terracottas have also been found, mostly archaic but from later periods too, and numerous votive terracotta figures and heads. Remarkable too are the archaic sarcophagi and pottery urns moulded in the shape of couches with the figures of the dead reclining upon them, alone or in couples.

Cerveteri had a number of ports on the coast: *Alsium* (near Palo), *Pyrgi* (Santa Severa) and *Punicum* (Santa Marinella). Of these, the most famous historically is Pyrgi, where there was a sanctuary to the goddess Leucothea or Eileithyia, who may with certainty be identified with the Etruscan goddess Uni. Pyrgi was sacked by Dionysius of Syracuse in 384 B.C. It later became the site of a Roman military colony: its girdle of walls survives, built of polygonal stone blocks. Current excavations have revealed the foundations of a Greek-type peripteral temple from the end of the sixth century and of another large three-celled temple from the first half of the fifth century, with numerous figured and ornamental decorative terracottas from various periods (Plates 51, 64 and 69). Notable among these is a monumental late Archaic high-relief depicting scenes from the Theban Cycle (Plate 63). Among the finds, the remains of the archives of the first temple include three gold tablets containing a dedication to the Phoenician goddess Astarte, who also came to be identified with Uni: two are inscribed in Etruscan and one in Punic (Plates 12–14).[9]

Between Cerveteri and Tarquinia stand the trachytic hills of Tolfa, tunnelled with many ancient mining shafts. Here numerous traces of 'Protovillanovan' culture have been found: the cemeteries of Sasso di Furbara and Allumiere, various settlements, the hoard of Coste del Marano, etc. There are also the remains of a number of small Etruscan settlements as yet almost wholly unexplored.[10]

A little to the north stands Tarquinia (in Etruscan *Tarχ(u)na-*).[11] Tarquinia lived on through the Middle Ages down to modern times as the town of Corneto (renamed Tarquinia), one of the most sizeable of Latian Tuscia (Plate 26). It rises at one extremity of the height of Monterozzi, whereas the Etruscan and Roman city had occupied the parallel hill of La Civita. On this latter hill, the city walls of squared stone blocks dating back to the fourth century B.C. have come to light. Among the finds, we should single out the foundations of a large temple on a site known as the 'Ara della Regina'; to the decoration of its pediment belonged the terracotta fragment in painted high-relief representing two winged horses shown in Plate 68. In the same area a number of Latin inscriptions were found, commemorating the deeds of Etruscan historical and priestly personages (Plate 15).

Tarquinia, too, had a port on the coast at Gravisca, where current excavations have so far brought to light part of a Greek sanctuary founded around 570 B.C. The finds include a cippus (Plate 11) bearing a Greek inscription in the dialect and alphabet of Aegina: 'I belong to the Aeginetan Apollo; Sostratos had me made . . .' It is worth noting that Herodotus (IV, 152) records that a Sostratos was the most successful of the Greek merchants who traded with Tartessos in southern Spain.[12]

The development of the various proto-historic cultural stages of southern Etruria (ranging from the Villanovan to the late Villanovan and Orientalizing periods) is extraordinarily well documented by an imposing series of *pozzo* (well) and *fossa* (trench) graves, chamber-tombs and tumuli, scattered on the heights that surround the city. From the eighth century down to Roman times, the dead were buried mainly on the Monterozzi hill, where thousands of hypogea were dug out of the rock. Many have painted decorations, and tomb paintings are as characteristic of Tarquinia as imitative architectural carvings are of Cerveteri. Today we have knowledge of some sixty well-preserved painted tombs, more than half of which have been discovered or rediscovered in the past few years. The paintings of some of the most famous (the Tombs of the Chariots, of the Triclinium, of the Funeral Couch) and of some of the most recently discovered (the Tombs of the Olympic Games, of the Ship, of the Black Sow) have been detached from their walls under the supervision of the Istituto Centrale del Restauro.[13] This unique collection of monuments has provided us with the most valuable series of documents in our possession on the ancient painting of the Greek and Italic worlds, from the Archaic to the Hellenistic period. It reveals many unusual aspects of Etruscan figurative taste and provides us with an extraordinarily vivid picture of the life, customs and beliefs of the people. Among the most characteristic art objects found in the Tarquinia cemeteries, we should mention the Archaic stone slabs decorated with friezes and figured scenes in the Orientalizing tradition forming part of the structure of the tombs (see Plate 58); and, from a later period, many stone or terracotta sarcophagi with reclining figures reproduced on the lids and figured reliefs on the sides. There is also a large number of inscriptions painted on tomb walls or carved on sarcophagi; some are of substantial length and important to the study of Etruscan epigraphy.

About twelve miles to the north-west of Tarquinia, on the banks of the Fiora, there stood another great city of southern Etruria: Vulci (in Etruscan, *Velχ*-).[14] The ruins of this city and of its boundless cemeteries stretch along a vast area between the two small towns of Montalto di Castro and Canino, in one of the most picturesque districts in the whole of central Italy (Plate 27). The tumuli and hypogea of Vulci do not differ much from those of Cerveteri or of Tarquinia; among the most remarkable is the François Tomb (named after its discoverer): the paintings on its walls have been detached and are now in the private Torlonia Museum in Rome. They belong to the Hellenistic period, and feature portraits of the dead together with mythical and historical scenes, the latter referring to events that occurred during the earliest phases of Etruscan history (the exploits of the Vipina brothers and of Macstrna).[15] One of the most outstanding monuments at Vulci is a grandiose tumulus consisting of an intricate network of underground chambers and passages, termed 'La Cuccumella'. Vulci was especially important as a centre for the manufacture and marketing of bronze products. This may be seen already in the vases and weapons of the late Villanovan period (Plates 4, 78), but it is in the sixth century particularly that the art reaches its fullest expression with the production of fine objects in the Ionic-Etruscan style: candelabra, statuettes and especially the characteristic rod tripods adorned with applied figures. Imported pottery has been found in such quantities that Vulci, of all the centres in the ancient world, may perhaps be called our richest source of knowledge of Greek vase painting. Local imitations of Corinthian (Plate 86), Ionic and Attic vases also flourished in the city, followed later by a considerable production of red-figured Etruscan ware. Vulci is also distinguished for its funerary sculpture in volcanic stone (cf. Plate 57), a tradition developed in the Archaic

113

period and continued until Hellenistic times; we find statues, reliefs, cippi, sarcophagi and figured architectural decorative elements, such as composite capitals adorned with carved heads. Recently, the systematic exploration of the city area has been started; the base of a temple and numerous votive terracottas of late Hellenistic times have so far come to light.

The great cities of southern coastal Etruria contrast strongly with the inland centres, which are generally smaller and less important historically. Their modest remains have attracted only limited attention from scholars and excavators, so that a number of sites close to the lakes of Bracciano, Vico and Bolsena may be considered as still virtually unexplored.

The extreme eastern end of this territory, between the Monti Sabatini, Monti Cimini and the Tiber, was inhabited, as we know, by Latin-speakers strongly influenced by their vicinity to Etruria. Closer to Rome, the city of Capena survives in a number of sizeable Archaic cemeteries; the sanctuary to the goddess Feronia stood near by. The land of the Falisci extended to the north, with Falerii (now Civita Castellana) as its principal centre and other ancient settlements at Narce, Vignanello, Corchiano, etc.[16] The archaeological and monumental features of this region are very close to those of Etruria and Latium. From the cemeteries that have so far been excavated emerges a picture of a busy and well-settled society, the possessor of a rather original culture during the seventh and sixth centuries B.C. After this period, the traditions of the area appear to have centred on the town of Falerii, which became, in some respects, as important as the major Etruscan cities and Rome itself. On its well-protected and picturesque site, it has preserved within and without its walls important traces of temples richly decorated with figured terracottas: Archaic at Sassi Caduti and Hellenistic at Lo Scasato (Plate 70). During the fourth century it developed a school of vase painting which may be considered among the most important of central Italy. The Romans, who finally subdued the city in 241 B.C., transferred it to another site, a short distance away: Falerii Novi (Santa Maria di Fàlleri), where imposing walls in the Etruscan style still stand.

Among the truly Etruscan centres close to Faliscan territory, we should record Nepi (*Nepet*); Sutri (*Sutrium*, in Etruscan *Suθri-*),[17] a bone of contention between the Etruscans and the Romans during the fourth century, with imposing city walls and rock tombs belonging to a late period; Orte (*Horta*), on a high, dominating site in the valley of the Tiber; Bomarzo (*Polimartium*); Ferento (*Ferentum*) near Viterbo, which flourished in Roman times but was preceded by an Etruscan settlement on the neighbouring height of Acqua Rossa; excavated by the King of Sweden, Ferentum is especially important for the traces of private houses with early terracotta decorations. Viterbo itself is probably also of Etruscan origin (*Surina* ?); its Museo Civico preserves a notable collection of finds made in the surrounding district.[18] But the most characteristic monuments of this area are the rock sepulchres concentrated on a band of territory joining Viterbo to Tarquinia. Their façades are carved out of the tufa and sculptured so as to imitate houses and temples. They are found at San Giuliano near Barbarano, at Blera, Norchia (Plate 29), Castel d'Asso (Plate 55) and, further to the north, in the Vulci hinterland, at Sovana (*Suana*).[19] The development of these rock cemeteries began in Archaic times and reached its peak during the last centuries of Etruscan civilization. At the same time, there are traces of an even earlier development on the more distant sites of inner southern Etruria: e.g. at San Giovenale and at Luni sul Mignone, where Swedish archaeologists have uncovered small settlements dating back to the Bronze Age and revealing a period of close contacts with the Protovillanovan world of the Tolfa district[20]; at Monterano, on the upper Mignone[21]; at Vetralla, further north; at Bisenzio (*Visentium*) near Capodimonte, at the south end of Lake Bolsena, whose cemeteries testify to the richness and comparative originality of its culture between the eighth and sixth centuries B.C.; and especially at the sites that lie clustered around the upper reaches of the river Fiora: Ischia di Castro, Poggio Buco (probably corresponding to *Statonia*),[22] Pitigliano, etc. Many of these small proto-Etruscan towns fell into decline towards the end of the Archaic period, perhaps owing to the growing hegemony of the great coastal cities. There remain, however, important traces of an intense life down to Hellenistic and Roman times, both in the rock sepulchres and in other manifestations reflecting the metropolitan culture of the region, such as the figured stone or terracotta sarcophagi in the Tarquinia and Vulci style – often with local provincial traits – found at Vetralla, Civita Musarna, Tuscania (*Tuscana*), etc.

Within this inner zone of southern Etruria grew up one of the most important Etruscan cities, considered by the ancients to be the very centre of the nation: this is Volsinii (in Etruscan, *Velsna-*, *Velzna-*). In its neighbourhood, in fact, there stood the famous sanctuary of Voltumna (the *Fanum Voltumnae*), where the yearly gathering of the twelve Etruscan 'peoples' took place, accompanied by feasts and celebrations. Roman Volsinii certainly stood close to modern Bolsena, whose name derives from it. Recent excavations in the same area have produced remains of the Etruscan period as well, thus supporting the hypothesis of its identification with the Etruscan city that flourished before the Roman conquest and pillage of 265 B.C.[23] A powerful girdle of city walls, built of squared blocks and double-curtained, crowns the acropolis dominating the lake; upon it, the remains of a small temple of the Hellenistic period have been found. A second sacred site had been discovered earlier at Mercatello, lower down the hill. But no clues survive to help identify the deities worshipped at these sanctuaries, nor have we the means to locate the famous temple of the goddess Nortia, where nails were hammered in to number the passing years (Cincius Alimentus, in Livy, VII, 3, 7). The whereabouts of the *Fanum Voltumnae* itself is still uncertain: it has been variously located at Orvieto, at Montefiascone and so on, but it might well have been within Volsinii itself or in its immediate neighbourhood. On the other hand, there are very few traces of Etruscan cemeteries, particularly of the Archaic period, around Bolsena: and this is remarkable, in view of the historical importance of Etruscan Volsinii.

Altogether different is the case of Orvieto, upon its high pedestal of red tufa watching over the valley of the middle Tiber, about eight miles, as the crow flies, north-east of Bolsena.[24] Its Etruscan origins have been confirmed by an imposing series of discoveries of sacred buildings and deposits, with architectural and votive terracottas, within the city enclosure, and also by the cemeteries that surround it: these include architectural chamber tombs, aligned along regular sepulchral streets (the 'Cannicella' and 'Crocefisso del Tufo' cemeteries), and painted tombs found in the vicinity (Sette Camini, Porano). It seems that this great centre flourished especially between the sixth and fourth centuries B.C. After that period, there are few traces of its existence before late Roman times. Procopius (*De Bello Gothico*, II, 20) refers to the city as *Ourbibentos*, perhaps meaning *Urbs vetus*, whence Orvieto. Obviously the ancient name was lost. If this city is to be identified with Volsinii, as many scholars believe, its name was transferred to the place of Bolsena when the inhabitants were banished by the Romans (Zonaras, *Ann.*, VIII, 7).

Cities of central and northern Etruria

As we follow the Tyrrhenian coast towards northern Etruria, we first come across a series of minor centres clustered around the Argentario promontory and the valley of the Albegna.[25] At Ansedonia, not far from the Orbetello lagoon, and set upon a picturesque height overlooking the sea, stand the imposing polygonal walls and remains of Cosa, long believed to be Etruscan but now known to have been a colony founded by Rome in 273 B.C.[26] The coastal works, which include the well-known 'Etruscan' or 'Queen's cutting', are Roman too. Originally, Cosa belonged to the territory of Vulci. Traces of Roman polygonal walls similar to those at Pyrgi and Cosa can be found at Orbetello, which is certainly of Etruscan origin. On a promontory further along the coast lay Telamon, in Etruscan *Tlamu*, where the remains of a temple with architectural terracottas and a deposit of votive objects have been unearthed: they may be connected with a battle known to have been fought in this area by Romans and Gauls in the year 225 B.C.[27] On the heights near the left bank of the Albegna, in the neighbourhood of Marsiliana d'Albegna, a large early cemetery was discovered and excavated, containing circular tombs and much Orientalizing material: it has been connected with the town of *Caletra*, whose site is unknown.[28] Other Etrusco-Roman centres in the same area include *Heba* (the modern Magliano) and, further upstream, *Saturnia* (or *Aurina*).[29]

Further north, in the valley of the Ombrone, are the ruins of another great historic Etruscan city, Roselle (*Rusellae*), whose position and fortunes have, in a sense, been inherited by Grosseto, a few miles away. Until recently, this centre was among the least known and explored: only in the last decade or two has systematic excavation of the area been undertaken. They brought to light sections of the city wall, stone and unbaked brick buildings extending down to the seventh century B.C., and parts of the town site.[30]

Still within the Grosseto area but nearer to the sea stood Vetulonia, whose Etruscan name was *Vetluna, Vatluna*.[31] The site of this famous city was sought in several places along the Etruscan coastal belt, and until the last few decades was the object of heated arguments between those scholars who placed it at Poggio Colonna and those who identified it with Poggio Castiglione near Massa Marittima. There can no longer be any doubt that the first is the correct site; and remains of city walls and of houses have indeed been found there. But the importance of the city is revealed to us most clearly by the vast cemeteries that surround it. An intensive excavation of the site was conducted towards the end of the last century: the abundant material found there now constitutes a notable part of the collection at the Museo Archeologico in Florence. The most important tombs are marked by stone circles or are in the shape of tumuli, and the funerary furnishings, consisting for the most part of bronze objects (e.g. Plate 8), have been attributed to the period stretching from the eighth to the sixth century B.C. The Pietrera tumulus has provided the first specimens of large stone Etruscan statuary, representing figures of the dead, both male and female. After this period, as far as we can tell from archaeological evidence, the city must have fallen into rapid and complete decline, for there remain no traces of life after the beginning of the Roman period. The presence of other notable centres in the hinterland may be inferred from a necropolis discovered near the lake of L'Accesa, in the neighbourhood of Massa Marittima.[32]

Further to the north stood Populonia (or Populonium, the Etruscan form of which was *Pupluna*, *Fufluna*), on a height dominating the bay of Porto Baratti, north of Piombino.[33] It is the only important Etruscan city built right on the sea shore. Its discovery is comparatively recent. Large-scale excavations have been conducted in its necropolis since the beginning of this century under the direction of the Soprintendenza dell'Etruria based in Florence. The city, almost totally unexplored, still preserves its powerful girdle of walls. The most characteristic funerary monuments of Populonia are great tumuli comprising chambers with false cupolas or vaulted roofs; within these chambers, objects have been found dating from the Villanovan period down to the late sixth century. An important feature of the site is the presence round the city of vast fields of iron slag, the result of the smelting of iron ores extracted from the Elba mines in Etruscan and Roman times: for Populonia was one of the most important iron centres of the ancient world. The earliest tombs were found under the slag: this is now being removed and submitted to a new industrial process of extraction, with excellent results. More traces of Etruscan mining activity may be seen on the slopes of the so-called 'Colline Metallifere'.

Let us now examine the inland cities, which are mainly scattered along the banks of large rivers. Here, we should first mention Chiusi (its Etruscan name was in all probability *Clevsin-*, but it also appears under the name of *Camars*).[34] This city, famous for its part in the history of both Etruria and Rome, never ceased to be a sizeable inhabited centre throughout the Middle Ages and up to modern times. This explains the almost complete disappearance of all Etruscan buildings on the one hand, and, on the other, the early and frequent discoveries made in its vicinity. A characteristic feature of Chiusi and of the surrounding region is the presence of a large number of cemeteries distributed near the city and neighbouring towns (Pania, Poggio Gaiella, Poggio Renzo, Dolciano, Sarteano, Chianciano, Città della Pieve, Montepulciano). These small towns all possessed a substantially similar type of civilization; their presence shows that the territory was thickly scattered with small rural centres under the aegis of the metropolis. The earliest cultural phase of Chiusi (after the first Villanovan period) is characterized by cremation tombs containing the so-called canopic urns, i.e. ossuaries with a lid in the shape of a human head and roughly imitating the human form (Plate 40: cf. Plate 56); funerary statues derive from these canopic urns. Typical objects of the late sixth and the fifth centuries include stone sepulchral cippi and small cinerary urns decorated with reliefs representing banquet scenes, games, funeral ceremonies, etc. A few chamber tombs in the environs of Chiusi have painted scenes from daily life, as at Tarquinia, and largely belong to the fifth century B.C. This artistic production is representative of the most flourishing period in the history of the town, a period that coincides with the beginning of the decadence of the coastal cities. We may remember, in fact, that tradition ascribes to the end of the sixth century the deeds of Lars Porsenna, the attacker and, according to some sources, the conqueror of Rome, indicating that a period of considerable expansion was under way in the history of Chiusi. Later, the end of the fifth century and the beginning of the fourth witnessed the production in and around Clusium of funerary statues, singly or in groups, and sarcophagi, in which we can recognize the beginnings of the individual portrait. The Hellenistic period, on the other hand, gave birth to a rich collection of small cinerary urns, mainly of painted terracotta, with the dead person's portrait on the lid and mythological reliefs on the front (Plate 73).

Perugia represents the typical development of an Etruscan and Roman city into an important urban centre of medieval and modern times. This continuity of life did not erase the ancient structure of the town or its Etruscan monuments; both belong to the most flourishing period in the early life of the city, coinciding with the final phase of the Etruscan civilization, from the fourth to the second centuries B.C.[35] The many remains include long tracts of fine city wall built with large squared blocks of travertine, the imposing arched gateway that came to be named after Augustus, and the handsomely sculptured design of the Porta Marzia, adorned with sculptured deities which, with humanistic acumen, the Renaissance architect Sangallo succeeded in incorporating into one of the bastions of his Rocca Paolina. As the main centre of Etruscan studies during the nineteenth century, Perugia was the subject of intense research on its urban and suburban monuments; occasional discoveries and sporadic excavations led to the creation of the valuable Etruscan collection now in its museum. The territory of Perugia, lying between lake Trasimene and the upper Tiber and opening towards the valleys of Umbria, must have originally included scattered villages varying in size, each with its own cemetery, some of which have yielded a number of valuable Archaic figured bronzes (San Valentino, Castel San Mariano) and sculptures inspired from Chiusi (Sperandio). Even the later family tombs seem to be scattered around the city heights: e.g. the San Manno hypogeum, vaulted and containing a long inscription, or the Volumni Hypogeum, hollowed out of the rock in the Palazzone cemetery and consisting of several chambers containing reliefs and cinerary urns with figured decorations and Etruscan and Latin inscriptions belonging to the second and first centuries B.C. (Plate 22). Typical of Perugia and its surrounding area are the small travertine and terracotta urns decorated in relief. Among the numerous inscriptions which may be seen in the Perugia museum, there is a cippus in-

119

scribed with the longest Etruscan epigraphic text on stone in our possession (Plate 98).

The role of Perugia as a centre of research on ancient Etruria in the nineteenth century had previously been filled during the eighteenth by Cortona (in Etruscan, *Curtun-*).[36] Since then, discoveries and excavations have been made in the neighbourhood of the town. Of the old city there remain important traces of the walls; of the cemeteries surrounding the town, isolated tumuli (locally known as '*meloni*') and a circular mausoleum of later date, known as 'la Tanella di Pitagora' ('Pythagoras's little den'). In the Museo dell'Accademia Etrusca at Cortona is preserved a famous bronze candelabrum with rich figured decorations (Plate 84). We might also mention the fact that the well-known bronze statue of Avle Meteli, known as the 'Orator' (Plate 76), preserved in the Museo Archeologico at Florence, is generally thought to have been found at Sanguineto on the shores of lake Trasimene, south of Cortona; but the interpretation of other historical sources leads us to Pila, near Perugia.[37]

Arezzo was undoubtedly one of the most important cities of northern Etruria, as is shown by the frequent mention of its name in historical sources, especially at the time of its contacts with Rome.[38] But little has survived of its monuments. It stood at the summit of the hill on which the modern town lies and was surrounded by a stone and brick wall, parts of which have been excavated. A section of the Etruscan city level has also been identified. Here, during the sixteenth century, a famous bronze Chimaera was found, now in the Museo Archeologico at Florence (see Plate 66). A number of recently discovered late Archaic terracotta plaques, with frames in figured relief, and fragments of Hellenistic figures, probably part of a pediment, survive from the city's temples. Votive terracottas have also been found in large numbers, but tombs are rare. During the third century B.C., Arezzo was an industrial centre noted for the production of metals; it was to maintain this position until the early years of the Roman empire, when its famous manufactures of red pottery with stamped reliefs (*terra sigillata*) were exported and imitated throughout the ancient world.

In the Florence region there is another great Etruscan centre, sited on the hill of Fiesole, north of the river Arno.[39] The excavation of the city area has brought to light the foundations of a temple with an altar in front of it close to the Roman theatre, together with a fine stretch of city wall. But here too, as in the majority of the north Etruscan cities, monumental remains belong to a late period. The Fiesole acropolis was most likely at the centre of a substantial number of settlements scattered on the heights overlooking the Arno or down in the valley itself. These go back to the Villanovan period, as shown by some tombs found in the very heart of Florence. Florence itself was to grow in importance only during Roman times. The Orientalizing period is now documented by recent finds of rich funerary furnishings in the pseudo-cupola tomb of La Montagnola, between Quinto and Sesto Fiorentino, and in the Comeana tumulus.[40] Over the whole of the Florence region and especially around Fiesole, finds include Archaic stone funerary stelai with sculptured decorations, elongated or in the shape of a horse-shoe, recalling similar monuments found at Populonia on the one hand and the stelai of Bologna on the other. It is in fact likely that the Fiesole region constituted a point of contact with the Etruscan Po valley across the Apennine passes.

Within central Tuscany, between the Ombrone and Arno rivers, the chief Etruscan city was Volterra (in Etruscan *Velaθri*), rising on a high hill overlooking the valley of the Cecina.[41] It too survived the end of the ancient world, but the medieval and modern town is much reduced, both in size and in population, from its original proportions: the area it now occupies is far more restricted than the one indicated by the powerful girdle of Etruscan walls (see Plate 47), enlarged between the fifth and fourth centuries B.C. so as to include the Guerruccia plateau, full of Archaic tombs. Of the old city's monuments, the gate known as the Porta dell'Arco, embellished with sculptured heads of Etruscan deities, is perhaps the most remarkable. The oldest (Villanovan) cemetery has been almost wholly destroyed by the huge picturesque landslide of Le Balze. The most typical monuments of Volterra and of its region consist of Archaic sculptured stelai, fourth- and third-century painted vases, and especially of alabaster cinerary urns with high-relief decoration, of which there is a large collection in the local Museo Civico Guarnacci. The region around Volterra, largely agricultural in character, contained numerous villages and other minor centres. The Val d'Elsa and the Chianti and Siena regions must also have been densely settled with scattered villages. Archaic cupola tombs have been found at Casal Marittimo and Casaglia, and a large tumulus with four tombs was discovered at Castellina, in the Chianti area. Later tombs have yielded small urns such as the one discovered at Asciano. A remarkable site with Archaic buildings and terracotta revetments is coming to light at Poggio Civitate, near Murlo.[42] It was only in Roman times that a new urban settlement came to be formed at Siena (where the Museo Civico exhibits many of the remains that have been recovered in the region).

Cities of Campania and the Po valley

To this review of the principal characteristics of the cities of Etruria proper should be added a mention, however brief, of the Etruscan centres in Campania and the Po valley. The capital of the Etruscan dominion in Campania was Capua (known also as Volturnum), which later became one of the greatest and most populous cities of both the Italic and the Roman worlds. It stood upon the present site of Santa Maria di Capua Vetere. Recent excavations have brought to light sections of the early cemetery (ninth to sixth centuries). The most characteristic archaic remains include architectural terracottas, bronze cinerary urns, votive statuettes and painted vases, now gathered mainly in the local Museo Campano: most of these finds come from the city site (especially the Fondo Patturelli sanctuary) or from the cemetery. The type and style of these monuments are related to those of Latium and Etruria, but they have a character of their own and display direct Greek influence. Etruscan dominion over the city was reliably confirmed by the finding of a tile (now in Berlin) bearing a long Etruscan inscription. Other Etruscan centres in Campania were Suessula, Nola, Acerra, Nocera, Herculaneum, Pompeii, Sorrento and Marcina (close to Salerno, according to ancient sources). But the Etruscan political and cultural hold over these cities, whatever its antiquity or duration, was no more than transitory. A cultural development parallel to the one found in Etruria proper (from the Villanovan to the Orientalizing and the Archaic period of the sixth and fifth centuries) may be recognized, for the moment at least, in the Salerno coastal region. On the other hand, a definite thread of Etruscan or Etrusco-Italic influence (painted tombs, sculpture etc.) appears to have outlived the Samnite conquest in Campania as far south as Paestum.[43]

Northern Etruria had its centre at Bologna (in Etruscan, *Felsina*), a city formed out of Villanovan settlements, with extensive cemeteries; it flourished during the fifth century with the Certosa culture, which is characterized by carved stelai, Etruscan bronzes, Greek vases and Etruscan inscriptions. The abundant material found in its tombs is now in the city's Museo Civico.[44] Among its bronzes is the very fine Certosa situla (Plate 92), with relief decoration, clearly influenced by the Iron Age culture of Este. An interesting Etruscan city in the vicinity of Bologna was discovered in the valley of the Reno, close to the modern village of Marzabotto.[45] It was built on an orthogonal plan, with paved streets and a highly evolved water system; on the acropolis the foundations of a number of sacred buildings can still be seen. Excavations have yielded material dating from the sixth to the fourth centuries B.C. This material was kept in the private museum of the Villa Aria; it was much damaged during the Second World War, and what survived now belongs to the State. The sea town of Spina was another important centre: its cemeteries, rich in splendid Greek vases from the fifth and fourth centuries B.C. and in Etruscan bronzes and gold jewellery, was identified and excavated within the last decades in the reclaimed Valle Trebba and Valle Pega, near Comacchio; the tomb furnishings went to form the archaeological museum at Ferrara.[46] The last few years have seen attempts to identify the extent of the city by means of aerial photography and trial excavations. Outside the regions of Bologna and Spina, it is not possible to speak with certainty of Etruscan centres, except for limited periods of occupation and influence: apart from their mention in historical sources, all that survives are a few Etruscan archaeological and epigraphic traces and some clues given by place names. This is the case with *Caesena* (Cesena; probably cognate with the Etruscan *Keisna*, a family name found at Bologna), *Ariminum* (Rimini; probably from an Etruscan *Arimna*), Ravenna, Adria, *Mantua* (Mantova; in Etruscan *Manθva-?*), *Mutina* (Modena), Parma, and the city which the Romans were later to rechristen *Placentia* (Piacenza).[47]

CHAPTER 6 The Political and Social Organization of Etruria

Etruscan public institutions

Our knowledge of the institutions and political history of Etruria is severely limited by the absence of direct sources or traditions. The only information available on the subject we owe almost exclusively to occasional and summary references in Greek and Latin writers, chiefly relating to events concerning Etruscan contacts with Rome. We know that, in historical times at least, political sovereignty coincided with the city and its surrounding territory, as it did in the Greek πόλις. But it is also possible to glimpse a coalition of the various city states into an alliance of a non-temporary character, a league whose basis was predominantly religious, economic, at times even political, though its existence did not effectively weaken the independence of each individual state. As for institutions within the city, we can recognize a gradual evolution from the monarchy of Archaic times to the republican oligarchy of Hellenistic times. These basic data are naturally accompanied by a good many other elements; but here interpretation becomes far more difficult.[1]

It is only quite recently that answers to some of these questions have been sought in monuments: their structure (as for instance the characteristics of tombs), their figured decorations, their inscriptions, all help to integrate the fragmentary data provided by tradition. Naturally the inscriptions would be of decisive importance to our knowledge of the political institutions if only we were able to interpret them wholly and convincingly. Nevertheless, the present state of our knowledge of the language (an outline is given in the last part of this book) permits the use of inscriptions, and particularly funerary inscriptions, in an important role in research on the magistracies.[2] It is only natural that many difficult problems arise from the study and comparison of literary evidence and monumental sources, and it is to these problems that we shall devote most of the following pages, since they form the most lively part of the subject.

The Political and Social Organization of Etruria

Etruria and its 'peoples'

First and foremost, what do we know and what can we say about the Etruscan 'league'? The term is a modern one: ancient writers speak of the *duodecim populi*, of the *duodecim* (or *quindecim*) *populi Etruriae*, of δώδεκα ἡγεμονίαι (Dionysius, VI, 75), and more simply of *Etruria*, or *omnis Etruria*. The fact that the great cities of Etruria proper were twelve in number (to which corresponded a like number in northern Etruria and in Campania) had, in all probability, a ritual significance: analogous cases recur in the ancient world, and it is a possible, though not a necessary, conclusion that the Etruscan league had as its model the league of the twelve cities of Ionia, on the west coast of Asia Minor, especially in view of the close cultural ties linking Etruria and Ionia.[3] That it was a real and political institution as well as a notional unit may be deduced from a study of the references to the twelve Etruscan states found in ancient authors (especially Livy, IV, 23; V, 1; X, 16; etc.); reference is made, for instance, to consultative meetings held by the Etruscan states and their heads (*principes*) at the *Fanum Voltumnae*. Pareti rightly pointed out that such evidence is not sufficient to prove the continuity or the supreme power of the presumed Etruscan federal union. Having established the existence of annual pan-Etruscan festivals and games at the sanctuary of Voltumna (similar to the Pan-Hellenic games at Ephesus, Olympia, Delphi, and Corinth), one might still suppose that only exceptional political circumstances, such as the threat of Rome, could have induced the representatives of the various Etruscan states to meet in consultation at the national shrine and go so far as to form a political and military coalition.[4]

However, there are also references that seem to point to a certain continuity in this institution and to some dependence on it of the individual states: e.g. a passage in Servius (*ad Aen.*, VIII, 475), which states that Etruria had twelve *lucumones*, or kings, one of whom was head of the others; or Livy's references (I, 8, 2; V, 1) to the election of a king by the twelve peoples, each of which provided a lictor for the *fasces*, and to the election of a *sacerdos* at the *Fanum Voltumnae* on the occasion of the gatherings of the states. Our assessment of the Etruscan league wholly depends upon the reliability of these statements. It is interesting to note that in two of the passages the word 'king' is mentioned; they must therefore refer, as far as we can tell, to a period earlier than the fourth century B.C. The two passages in Livy mention an elected head of the alliance, a personage who by the end of the fifth century (i.e. at the time of the conflict between Veii and Rome) was designated by the title of *sacerdos*, and therefore was invested with mainly religious powers – or powers reduced to the religious sphere alone.

The Etruscans

A few Latin inscriptions of Imperial times (when ancient Etruscan institutions and titles still formally subsisted) give us the title *praetor Etruriae*, accompanied occasionally by the name of a city in the locative case (*Tarquiniis, Pisis*). This title also appears in the form *praetor Etruriae XV populorum*, i.e. of the Etruscan national community, which in Roman times seems to have been increased by three cities.

Among the various offices filled by Etruscan personages and recorded in Etruscan inscriptions, we know the title *zilaθ meχl rasnal* (*C.I.E.* 5360, Tarquinia – cf. also *C.I.E.* 5472: *zilaθ .... rasnas* (Tarquinia), and *C.I.E.* 5093: *meχlum rasneas clevsinsl .... zilaχnve* (Orvieto), where the noun designating the magistracy has been turned into a verb). Thanks to the famous passage in Dionysius (I, 30, 3), where the Etruscans are designated by their national name of *Rasenna*, we know that *rasna* signifies 'Etruscan'. On the other hand, the magistrature designated by the word *zilaθ*, apparently the highest office in the Etruscan republics, corresponds very probably with the praetorship of the Romans. Thus there appears to be an obvious correspondence between the title *zilaθ meχl rasnal* and *praetor Etruriae* (*populorum*). It is doubtful whether this title can be identified with the supreme head of the league. We should also think of it as designating a collegiate magistrature: i.e. the representatives of each state to the federal councils, or the magistrates connected to the league itself, the equivalents, perhaps, of the *principes* and *lictores* recalled in the above-mentioned passages by Livy.

If the accounts of the supremacy of one of the ancient sovereign states over the others are not wholly without foundation, it might just be possible to suppose that an early institutional alliance did in fact exist between southern Etruscans at the beginning of historical times, under the hegemony of one or the other city. The important role played by Tarquinia in the early legends of Etruria may lead us to infer a period of Tarquinian hegemony. Later, this ancient unity would have assumed the character of a religious confederation, with celebrations and national gatherings at the sanctuary of Voltumna, near Volsinii. The election of an annual supreme magistrate is perhaps a survival of the supreme sovereignty of one head over the others. We know from Livy that in the fifth century the future king of Veii was a candidate for the election (which implicitly confirms the importance of the national magistracy), but was defeated.

Whatever the case may be, there is no doubt that at the time of Etruria's contacts with Rome the political structure of the nation rested mainly on a system of small regional states, each having at its head a large city. We do not know what conditions reigned during the Archaic period, but the co-existence of various centres of great importance at short distances from each other (e.g. Veii, Cerveteri, Tarquinia, Vulci), with their own sovereigns, their own characteristics and customs, seems to have been inspired by the city-state system encountered in the contemporary Greek and Punic colonies of the west. This political structure had been adopted by Latium at the time of Etruscan influence and had received in Latin the technical term *populus*, which is probably of Etruscan origin.[5] In a sense, *populus* appears to be a synonym of *civitas* and πόλις. The official names of the *populi* are those of the inhabitants of the city itself: Veientes, Tarquinienses, Caeretani, Clusini, etc. (see Plate 32). It is probable that with the passing of time the various sovereign cities acquired more or less territory and subjugated rival cities, as we can see occurring for Rome at the beginning of its history. But it is also possible that some of the conquered cities retained some partial autonomy or contracted alliances with their conquerors: this might explain the presence of towns of minor importance in the territory of the major cities, especially in southern Etruria – e.g. the presence of Nepi, Sutri, Blera, Tuscania, Statonia, Sovana, etc. within the sphere of influence of Veii, Tarquinia and Vulci. There is also the possibility that colonies may have retained some form of dependence on their city of origin, as in the Etruscan expansion towards Campania and the north. As far as we are aware, however, the principle of autonomy and division must also have prevailed in the political constitutions of the Etruscan dominions in southern and northern Italy.

The great cities whose magnificent remains can still be seen must therefore have been the centres of the political and cultural life of Etruria. Tradition tells us that they were twelve in number (it is not until the days of Rome that we hear of fifteen peoples). Which were these cities? At the time of the Roman conquest the following were certainly counted among them: Cerveteri, Tarquinia, Vulci, Roselle (Rusellae), Vetulonia, Populonia, Volsinii, Chiusi, Perugia, Cortona, Arezzo, Fiesole, Volterra. Veii had been annexed by Rome by the beginning of the fourth century B.C. Some of the minor centres must still have been autonomous during the fourth and third centuries B.C., as the existence of coins bearing the names of Peithesa, Echetia, and other unidentified cities seems to indicate. Centres that flourished in Archaic times, as for instance Bisenzio, Marsiliana d'Albegna (Caletra?) and Vetulonia itself, later fell into decadence, while other cities developed only towards the end of the Etruscan civilization, when Etruria was under Roman domination: e.g. Siena, Pisa, Florence and Luni.

There is no historical evidence to document the stage that preceded the organization into cities, and we are thus unable to ascertain what political system originally existed in the proto-historic settlements of

Etruria. Indirect references in ancient authors and the analogy of the primitive constitution of Rome may lead us to the conclusion that the cities were divided into tribes, probably three in number, which in their turn were each divided into four *curiae* (Servius, *ad Aen.*, X, 202).[6] Apart from these few conjectures we are left in utter darkness as to the organization of the cities and their dependent territories.

The primitive monarchy

The actual conditions reigning in Etruscan cities during the Roman age, on the eve of the great social upheavals that marked the political life of Italy during the first century B.C., have influenced the general interpretation of Etruscan social and political institutions as reflected in the writings of ancient authors. The cities seem to have been governed by aristocratic oligarchies, and these were only sporadically and temporarily replaced by other classes of society. The oligarchies governed through magistrates designated at times by the name of *principes*. This tradition is for the most part confirmed by the existence of large and wealthy family tombs with many depositions, with inscriptions referring to members of a few closely related families, in particular epitaphs listing the titles of various temporary and collegiate offices according to a system known from the constitutions of other city states of the ancient world.

Such a state of affairs cannot, however, have existed in Etruria during the earlier centuries of its history. Many sources refer to the existence of kings in Etruscan cities. The term *lucumo* (Latin *lucumo*, *lucmo*; Greek Λοκόμων, Λουκούμων; Etruscan, probably *lauχume*, *lauχme*, *luχume*) sometimes forms part of the name of Etruscan personages, as in the case of Tarquinius Priscus at Rome; but it is generally used as a common name to designate the Etruscan chiefs. Virgil's commentator, Servius, on one occasion calls *lucumones* the magistrates in charge of the *curiae* of the city of Mantua (*ad Aen.*, X, 202); on other occasions he identifies them explicitly with the kings of the cities (*ad Aen.*, II, 278; VIII, 65, 475). On the basis of the notion of an aristocratic state, K. O. Müller (and others after him) assumed that the *lucumones* were the equivalent of the *principes*, both terms merely denoting the eldest sons of noble families. But it is probable, as we have seen, that the term *principes* indicated the magistracies of the republican state, perhaps even the supreme magistracies, rather than a social rank. In the same way, everything leads us to suppose that the title *lucumo* designated the Etruscan king of the Archaic period, according to the repeated and explicit statement made by Servius on this matter. It thus seems unnecessary to seek, as S. P. Cortsen did, the Etruscan word for 'king' in the root *purθ-* and in the title *pursna*, *purtsna*, *purθne*, taken for a proper name in the case of Porsenna, king of Chiusi.[7] We are probably faced here with a parallel to what occurred in Rome with the word *rex* (*sacrificulus*): the title assumed by the ancient monarchs may not have been abolished when the state changed from a monarchy to an aristo-cratic republic; it was substantially emptied of its political content and preserved, alongside the new republican magistracies, as a religious institution. In an inscription referring to a Tarquinian priest of the second century B.C. (*C.I.E.* 5430), among the verbs denoting the offices filled by the priest we find the verb *lucairce*, whose root is connected with that of the word *lucumo*. In the Zagreb mummy text, mention is made of ceremonies celebrated *lauχumneti*, i.e. 'in the *lauχumna-*', probably the residence of the *lauχume*, the lucumo (compare the Roman *Regia*, the official residence of the *pontifices* in Rome). Finally, the elective head of the *Fanum Voltumnae*, whom Livy designates as a priest, was originally probably no other than the king elected by the twelve peoples and the most powerful lucumo mentioned by Servius, even though the importance of his functions may have been sub-stantially reduced and transformed with the passage of time and changes in political ideas.

What was the nature of the primitive Etruscan monarchy? Un-fortunately our knowledge is insufficient to answer the question, and all we can do is put forward certain suppositions based on the analogy with what little is known with historical certainty of the Roman monarchy. The king must have held supreme judiciary power, which he exercised, according to Macrobius (*Saturn.*, I, 15, 13), once a week in public audiences. He must have been the military and religious head of the state. We are a little better informed on certain ceremonial customs and external symbols relating to the monarchy, for these were inherited by Rome and were considered by ancient writers to have had a specifically Etruscan origin. Amongst these were the golden crown, the sceptre, the *toga palmata*, the throne (*sella curulis*), the *fasces*, and other symbols of power; also perhaps the ceremony of the triumph.[8]

The problem of the origin of the lictor's *fasces* is particularly interest-ing.[9] Writers of the imperial age such as Silius Italicus (*Punica*, VIII, 483 ff.) and Florus (I, 1, 5) believed them to be of Etruscan origin. We have already referred to the passage in Livy mentioning the lictors sent by each Etruscan city to escort the elective head of the union. The earliest representation of a *fascis* without axe occurs in a fifth-century Chiusi relief now in the Palermo Museum. This destroys the hypothesis that the lictors and *fasces* in the escort of the Etruscan magistrates of the federated cities (as shown on sarcophagi from Tarquinia) were imitated from a Roman custom. In 1893, during the excavation of an Archaic tomb in the Vetulonia necropolis, there came to light an object made up of many parts of oxidized iron. This was thought by I. Falchi to be a *fascis* consisting of small hollow rods and a double-bladed axe. The object disintegrated when it was moved, but was put together again in the Museo Archeologico in Florence, where it may still be seen (Plate 31). Some doubts have been expressed as to the original shape of the object and its interpretation as a *fascis*,[10] but Falchi's view is probably correct, even if the find is a model reduced in size for funerary purposes and the axe a double-bladed one. The presence of double-axes at Vetulonia for fighting or ceremonial purposes at a time roughly contemporary with that of the tomb mentioned above (seventh to sixth century B.C.) is attested by a representation of one in the hand of an armed warrior on a funerary stele bearing the name of Avle Feluske (Plate 30). But the strangest coincidence of all is the fact that according to Silius Italicus it was the inhabitants of Vetulonia who invented the *fascis*. If this is so, we have here another fortunate instance of agreement between the literary tradition and the archaeological record. The axe is well known as a political and religious symbol among the civilizations of the East and the Mediterranean world: e.g. in Crete, during the Minoan civilization, and in nuragic Sardinia.[11] Archaic Italy, standing as it did at the confluence of various Mediterranean cultural currents, undoubtedly made use of the axe as a chieftain's weapon, as well as a tool and an instrument of war; this may be seen in the reliefs of the bronze situla of the Certosa at Bologna (see Plate 92), or on the figured stelai of Larth Ninie and Avle Feluske, found respectively at Fiesole and Vetulonia. The Vetulonia example is unusual in that it reproduces a double-axe, which may also in fact have been a symbol of authority. Thus on the one hand there was the axe, the ceremonial weapon of the king, and, on the other, the bundle of wooden rods for corporal punishment carried by the sovereign's escort when the sovereign was acting in his judiciary capacity: it is quite possible that the two became united in a single object symbolizing sovereignty in its fundamental aspects, the judiciary, the military, and perhaps also the religious. It is probable that only one *fascis* was used at first, and that the increase in the number of lictors followed the extension of the sovereign's authority over a larger number of cities.

The material symbol of the *fascis* corresponded to a political and religious authority which the Romans designated by the name of *imperium*. For further confirmation that the axe symbolized sovereign power, there is the fact that only the *imperium maius* and certain special circumstances gave the Roman magistrate the right to hoist the *fascis* with the axe. The *imperium*, distinct from a more general *potestas*, represented full judiciary and military power: it is in fact the sovereignty of the old kings of Rome passed on to the Republican magistrates. The concept of *imperium*, with its religious undertones, was doubtless derived from the Etruscan monarchy.[12] A gloss of the late lexicographer Hesychius even provides us (though in Greek form) with the Etruscan word for the Greek ἀρχή ('power'), probably corresponding to the Latin *imperium*: this is δρούνα, which probably reflects an Etruscan **truna*,* *θruna*, a cognate perhaps of the prehellenic root of τύραννος and of the root of the Etruscan name for Venus, *Turan* ('lady'?, 'mistress'?).

The republican states

When studying the transition from monarchy to republic that took place in Etruria between the sixth and fifth centuries B.C., the widespread occurrence of this political phenomenon should be kept in mind: it is found to have taken place along substantially similar lines in the institutional history of Greeks, Phoenicians, Latins and Etruscans. Analogies such as these clearly demonstrate the profound unity underlying the Mediterranean civilizations, as far as certain important aspects of public life are concerned, even before the spread of Greek and Roman cultural influences. Primitive monarchies on a religious basis gave way to oligarchic states with temporary collegiate and elective magistracies; this process is at times paralleled or followed by the seizure of power on the part of individuals (tyrannies) or by solutions of a democratic nature. In many Greek cities, this transformation was already taking place in proto-historic times, during and after the Mycenaean age, whereas other cities (e.g. Sparta) preserved monarchic institutions, at least in form, till they ceased to exist as historical entities. The new solutions arrived at by the western Greek world seem to have been already largely established by the beginning of the colonization movement. In Rome and in Etruria the change occurred during the sixth century. The Phoenician cities of Syria and Africa too, though with results that varied with time and place, tended to change their monarchies into republican oligarchies from about the eighth to the fourth century B.C.

Once this point is established, the causes of the constitutional changes in Latium and Etruria need no longer be sought in purely local conditions; political mimetic processes brought about a general tendency for the differentiation of society into classes, the consolidation of genealogical and religious traditions in the aristocracy, and the emasculation of primitive monarchical institutions. At most we may ask ourselves whether these early monarchies in Italy ever fulfilled the political needs of local tendencies: they may have merely masked a power limited

131

originally by the authority of heads of families or of assemblies, under the influence of purely external eastern forms. If this were the case, the changes of government we are considering may be no more than a return to original and genuine political institutions. The question should be discussed mainly in conjunction with the question of the primitive Roman *gentes* and their place in the monarchical state: a thorny problem indeed.[13]

The political crisis at the end of the sixth century is in any case the sign of a decisive change of direction in the development of the constitutional system both of Etruria and of the Italic states generally. The many theories put forward to account for the passage from primitive monarchies to republican magistracies[14] tend to explain it either as a continuous and necessary evolution or as a sudden innovation. An innovation of this type might indeed be ascribed to the imitation of foreign institutions, whether Greek, Latin or even Etruscan. It has also been tentatively proposed that a transitional stage should be inserted at the very beginnings of the republican state and before the establishment of collegiate magistracies (e.g. the Roman consulship, involving equality of powers): the magistracy would then have been entrusted to one pre-eminent individual and would possess a prevailingly military character, almost a long-term dictatorship taking over the archaic monarchy. It is in this sense that traditions concerning such Roman titles as *magister populi* or *praetor maximus* have been interpreted. Some have seen a similar type of power in the Etruscan figures of *Mastarna*, whose name (*macstrna*, without a *praenomen* in the François Tomb at Vulci) was believed to be an actual title, derived from Latin *magister*. All the more significant then that some sources identify Mastarna with Servius Tullius in Rome, whose constitutional reforms were thought to underlie the very origin of the republic (Livy, I, 60). A pattern of strong personal power in Etruscan and Latin cities between the end of the sixth century and the beginning of the fifth would thus echo the widespread tyrannies which characterize contemporary western Greek cities (e.g. Aristodemus at Cumae), through a kind of political mimicry. The gold tablets bearing Etruscan and Punic inscriptions recently found at Pyrgi have contributed to the discussion of this problem, since they invest their donor (Thefarie Velianas, described in Punic as 'King of Caere' or 'reigning over Caere', but in Etruscan probably already as '*zilac*', i.e. *praetor*) with all the characteristics of a head of state enjoying unshared personal power.[15]

But even if a period of military dictatorship occurred between the archaic monarchy and the republic of full historical times, the collegiate nature of the supreme office (with equal authority, as in Rome, or unequal, as amongst the Samnites), its temporary nature, and the authority of an aristocratic senate were soon to bring a further change in the direction of an oligarchic republic. In the case of the Etruscan cities, all we have to document this change are a few meagre clues provided by inscriptions and references in historical sources, and the analogy with Rome. From these we may deduce the existence of a senate composed of the heads of the *gentes*; popular assemblies; a supreme, temporary, single or collegiate magistracy; and other collegiate magistracies of a political and religious nature. There was in any case a general tendency to parcel out power, to decrease it and to place it under constant reciprocal control, so as to prevent the rise of a tyrant. This stiffening of oligarchic institutions was accompanied by a hatred for monarchy of which we possess few but eloquent testimonies: we need only think of the opposition of the Etruscan cities to the threatened Veii, owing to the fact that she was governed by a king (Livy, V, 1). Etruria seems to have carried this tendency further than Rome. Differences also appear with regard to the claims for a more active part in government made by the lower classes: in Etruria, unlike Rome, the latter were generally deprived of any possibility of being included in a progressive development of institutions towards plebeian rule. Thus Volsinii, Arezzo, and perhaps Volterra went through short periods of popular anarchy. It was only with the crumbling of traditional Etruscan society and the granting of Roman citizenship (a consequence of the *lex Iulia* at the beginning of the first century B.C.) that the popular classes managed to assert themselves over the impoverished and archaic ruling classes.[16]

The titles of the Etruscan magistracies, in their original forms, are known to us through the *cursus honorum* of the funerary inscriptions, some of which must have been written in the form of actual poetical *elogia* to the dead man, as in the case of the Roman inscriptions of the Scipio family. It is, however, far from easy to establish the nature of the various offices, their inter-relations, the differences between them, and their correspondence with the magistracies of the Latin and Italic worlds.

The most frequent title is one drawn from the root *zil-*, whose origin is still obscure and uncertain (but already encountered at Cerveteri by the beginning of the fifth century), in the forms *zil, zil(a)c* or *zilχ*, and *zilaθ*. To these nominal forms there corresponds a verb *zilχ-* or *zilaχ-* with the meaning 'to be *zilc* or *zilaθ*'. We already know that *zilaθ* corresponds in some cases to the Roman title *praetor*. It is quite certainly a high office, perhaps the highest in the land; but the title is often accompanied by determinants (*zilaθ* or *zilχ parχis; zilaθ eterau* and *zil eteraias; zilc marunuχva; zil ceχaneri*) which may indicate a specialization of functions (cf. the Latin *praetor peregrinus*) or the headship of a particular college (*zilc marunuχva* = head of the college of the *marunu*?). Thus the title may well have possessed both a specific and a generic acceptation, just as in the case of Latin *praetor*.

Another important office, considered by some to be the highest post of a presumed college of *zilaθ*, is designated by the root *purθ-*. Scholars have connected this with the title πρύτανις, of prehellenic origin, known also in the Greek cities of the west and perhaps borrowed from them by the Etruscan cities.[17] It appears under the forms *purθ*, *purθne*, *purtśvana*, *eprθne*, *eprθnevc*, etc. It is also possible that it may correspond to the Latin and Roman title *dictator*.[18]

Yet another title frequently found in inscriptions is *maru*, *marniu*, *marunuχ*: its religious connotations are made evident by its connection with the priestly title *cepen*, and with determinants of the type *maru paχaθuras caθsc* or *marunuχ paχanati*, which contain the names of the gods *Paχa* (Bacchus) and *Caθa*. The title also appears in Umbria, as the college of *marones*. It has been thought to correspond to the Latin *aedilis*. Other administrative or military offices are designated by the terms *camθi*, *macstrevc*, etc.

To indicate the urban character of the magistracies, and, perhaps, to differentiate them from magistracies connected with the league, the terms *spurana*, *spureni*, *spureθi*, etc. are added in inscriptions (from *spur*, 'city'). And although some clues point perhaps to life-magistracies (*svalas*, *svalasi* = 'διὰ βίου'?), in most cases a numeral next to the title indicates the number of times the office was held (as in the Roman *cursus honorum*) and bears witness to its temporary nature.

Etruscan society

The oligarchic state presupposes a social organization based on the family. Only the most obvious characteristics of the latter, as revealed in inscriptions and on monuments, are known to us. The Etruscan personal name system was identical with the Latin and the Italic, and quite distinct from the one in use among other peoples of the ancient world. The Greeks, for instance, had a simple name accompanied by a patronymic (Apollonios of Nestor) or an epithet to indicate descent (Ajax Telamonios), without clearly expressing the idea of family continuity. The formula current in ancient Italy is systematically made up of a double element, the *praenomen* (or personal name proper) plus the *gens* or family name. Thus it is the only personal name system of the ancient world to foreshadow a custom that was to become general, for social, cultural and political reasons, in the civilization of the modern world. Next to the two principal elements, the patronymic and the matronymic were often used, and at times even the names of the grandparents. A third element may later be found added to the name of the *gens*: the Latin *cognomen*, which may have had a personal origin, though it was generally used to designate a particular branch of the *gens*.

The Etruscans probably created the *gens* name system at the beginning of their history, and this would point to a keen feeling for the family unit and its continuity. The most ancient of the two elements is certainly the personal, or individual, as its very brevity clearly shows (*Vel, Laris, Arnθ*, etc.). The *gens* names, on the other hand, are always derivatives and formed by means of adjectival suffixes (e.g. *-na*) attached to personal names (*Velna*), names of divinities (*Velθina*) or place names (*Suθrina*), etc. The number of known *gentes* is very large indeed: an interesting fact, for it excludes the hypothesis of an opposition between a narrow oligarchy composed of members of the *gentes* and a population outside the *gens* system. Here the question becomes particularly delicate and complex, especially when considered in conjunction with the *gens* system of primitive Rome as generally reconstructed by scholars.

Indeed one has the impression that originally the whole Etruscan people (excluding slaves) was included in the framework of the *gens* system: not in a few, very large family groupings, but in numerous separate families, each distinguished by a name, perhaps along lines similar to those of the modern world at the end of the Middle Ages, when family names began to be used and everyone, from the highest to the lowest, ended by adopting a single onomastic system. It is possible of course, although no proof has yet been given, that there existed in Archaic Etruria as in Republican Rome patrician and plebeian *gentes*. But the impression given is that originally there were no great differences in social level. The only real lower class was composed of servants, actors and acrobats, foreigners, etc., who in monuments appear distinguished by a personal name only and were therefore placed outside the *gens* system.

If a society of freemen, sub-divided into numerous small family units, can be reconciled with a monarchical constitution of Archaic type (like the one dominant in Etruria up to the end of the sixth century B.C.), the same would seem more difficult for the later oligarchic state attested in passages in ancient writers. A great many families belonging to this later period are now known to us through inscriptions in each of the cities of Etruria, all apparently equal in social standing. But it is also possible to make out the beginnings of larger family units, with a common *gens* name but branching into numerous ramifications, spreading at times outside the territory of the city of origin. These reveal the formation of the *gens* in the Roman sense of the word, and in many cases a surname (*cognomen*) was added to the name of the *gens* so as to distinguish the various branches of the family. The small Archaic tombs, each of which belonged strictly to one family, were replaced by imposing family hypogea providing for the burial of a much larger number of persons. Marriages between individuals of certain *gentes* became more and more frequent, those very same *gentes* whose members most often held political or priestly office. It is not easy to provide a clear explanation of these data; certain *gentes* may have gradually predominated over others belonging to the same original social system to form the new oligarchy. This phenomenon was especially characteristic of some northern towns of Etruria proper: Volterra, for instance, where the *gens* Ceicna (Cecina) with its numerous ramifications predominated; or Arezzo, where the Cilnii, the ancestors of Maecenas, seem to have ruled for a time.

It is even harder to establish the position of the lesser or plebeian *gentes* within the framework of the oligarchic state or the characteristic features of the proletarian and serving classes.[19] Funerary inscriptions belonging to persons generally designated by the terms *lautni*, *etera*, or *lautneteri* occur fairly frequently, especially in northern Etruria. In other cases, they bear a single personal name (the mark of the servant class) or contain a name of foreign origin. The word *lautni* is derived from *lautn* ('family') and literally stands for 'familiar, of the family', though its use corresponds to that of the Latin *libertus*. As for *etera*, the precise meaning of the word is unknown. Some translate it as 'slave' or identify it with πενέστης (the interpretation of *etera* as 'of noble birth' or 'noble on the mother's side' is wholly unfounded). There were particular magistracies connected with the *etera*: the *zil eteraias*, the *zilaθ eterav* and the *camθi eterau*. A social and political rising of the lower classes took place in Arezzo and Volsinii during the third century B.C.: as historical tradition tells us, it took the form of an actual proletarian revolution, with seizure of power and the temporary abolition of caste differentiations between lower and aristocratic classes (e.g. the abolition of the ban on intermarriage).[20] We still do not know, however, whether such a revolt should be interpreted as a clash between families of higher and lower rank but still within the *gens* system (similar to the struggle between patricians and plebeians in Republican Rome) or as a rising of elements outside the *gentes*. On the other hand, H. Rix has recently shown that, not later than the second century B.C., the northern Etruscan cities witnessed a general and peaceful ascent of individuals from the lower classes; their personal names (Cae, Tite, Vipi) rose to become *gens* names.

As we have been dealing with the family and the personal name system of the Etruscans, we may end with a few words on the so-called Etruscan 'matriarchy'. This is no more than a learned invention, which was born from the comparison of the customs of Etruria with those of Asia Minor, as reported by Herodotus (I, 173), and was supported by references in ancient authors to the freedom of the Etruscan woman. That fact that Lydian children were called by their mother's name instead of their father's was compared to the Etruscan use of the matronymic as revealed by inscriptions. It is the patronymic element, however, that predominates in Etruscan inscriptions, even though many epitaphs bear the name of the *gens* and at times that of the mother.[21] There is no doubt that in Etruria (as, later, in Rome) woman's place in society was remarkably high, and certainly quite different from that of the Greek woman. The fact that women took part with men in banquets, far from being a sign of dissolution – as maliciously stated by many Greek writers, astonished and scandalized at a custom quite foreign to the Greeks of classical times – is a mark of social equality: yet another link between the civilization of ancient Etruria and the customs of the modern western world.[22]

CHAPTER 7 The Etruscan Religion

Problems and documents

Since the aim of this book is not so much to pile detail upon detail on the various aspects of Etruscan civilization but to interpret the evidence and discuss certain fundamental problems as yet unsolved, there would be little point in repeating what has already been said elsewhere on the religion of the Etruscans, whether considered as a whole or in its several aspects: the deities, the forms of worship, the interpretation of divine will, funerary customs, etc. Religion is in fact the best known facet of the Etruscan civilization. This is hardly surprising, because of the relative abundance of references in literary sources and the great quantity of archaeological material which, in one way or another, throws some light upon the subject.[1] This does not mean, however, that everything has been said that can be said, or that the data in our possession have been so thoroughly worked on that no further research or results may be expected. Clemen's work on the subject (*Die Religion der Etrusker*, 1936) is a case in point: here, the various problems have been attacked from the most original angle, with an intelligent and modern critical approach. This book, together with the more recent and no less praiseworthy essays by Giglioli and Grenier,[2] confirms our opinion of the need for a comprehensive survey that would re-examine all useful sources, both literary and archaeological, and give us a wider, deeper understanding of the Etruscan religion.

The Etruscans' reputation for being a most religious race strikes us as one of those frequent literary commonplaces continually to be found in the works of ancient writers. Livy (V, 1, 6) describes them as *gens ante omnes alias eo magis dedita religionibus, quod excelleret arte colendi eas* ('a people who above all others were distinguished by their devotion to religious practices, because they excelled in their knowledge and conduct of them'). Arnobius (*Adv. gentes*, VII, 26) calls Etruria *genetrix et mater superstitionum*. There is even an ingenuous folk-etymology that would derive Tusci from θυσιάζειν, 'to sacrifice' (Isidore, *Etym.*, IX, 2, 86; cf. also Dionysius of Halicarnassus, I, 30, 3). Modern scholars too seem prone to give credence to this striking reputation the Etruscans enjoyed amongst the ancients. In actual fact, the *quantitative* assessment of the religiosity of another people runs the risk of naïveté unless we take into account the historical reasons that prompted it. Etruscan traditions were of very great importance to the Romans of Imperial times, not only because Etruria made the first and most important contribution to the definition of those Italic religious forms among which the religion of Rome developed from its very beginnings, but also because religion was that portion of the Etruscan legacy which Rome acknowledged with the least reserve, and which was the most vigorous in resisting the overwhelming impact of Greek culture. But more important are the *qualitative* differences between the religion of Etruria on the one hand and those of Greece and Rome on the other. Etruscan religion is characterized by a scrupulous attention to ritual, to conformity and to the will of the gods, the continual dread of dark and overwhelming forces, of inexorable time limits. The Etruscans' sense of the nonentity of man before the value of the divine was a feeling unknown to the Greeks, even in the anguish they felt before the all-powerful Fates; and the Romans tended to resolve it in a prevalently juridical concept of the relationship between man and god – a solution both concrete and practical. Thus, in both the religion and the religious art of the Graeco-Roman world, the role of protagonist is still played by man. In Etruria, on the other hand, the deity appears to dominate the stage completely, as if reciting an eternal monologue in which the only role left to man is that of a cautious and timorous commentator. Once this qualitative point of view is accepted, the result of the comparison becomes obvious, and the statements of ancient writers on the deep and exceptional religiosity of the Etruscans are shown to be fully justified.

In attempting to reconstruct a picture of the particular combination of spiritual attitudes, tendencies, rules and practices that constituted the religious world of the Etruscans, the question of sources is of fundamental importance. These are of two kinds: direct, e.g. original Etruscan texts, like the ritual text of the *liber linteus* (linen book) of the Zagreb mummy or that of the Capua tile (both still partly obscure); inscribed objects (e.g. the famous bronze model of a liver found at Piacenza); figured monuments (paintings, sculptures, and especially scenes engraved on the back of mirrors; see Plates 34 and 36); the ruins of temples, tombs, etc.; or indirect, such as the accounts by Latin and Greek authors of Imperial and post-classical times. This second class of documents must naturally be submitted to a thorough critical examination before they can be used, for in matters as delicate as religious beliefs and ritual, many alterations, misunderstandings, and contaminations of the original elements are bound to occur. Owing to the relative similarity of some of the spiritual attitudes of Etruria and Rome, and the correspondence between deities and parallelism of various ritual forms, it is hardly surprising that Etruscan traditions, as transmitted by Roman writers on religious matters, or included in the treatises of Christian apologists (e.g. Arnobius), should have reached us in somewhat distorted versions. Typical in this respect is the tradition referring to the creation of the world: the Etruscans believed, according to the medieval encyclopaedist known as Suidas, that this took six millennia to accomplish – an obvious reminiscence of biblical cosmogony. In this particular case the explanation probably lies in the contamination of Etruscan and Christian elements within literary elaborations of late Roman times.

To conclude, the elements that can be used for a reconstruction of Etruscan beliefs and ritual are both limited and of uncertain interpretation. The loss of original Etruscan religious literature is irreparable: how small our knowledge of the spirit, the dogmas, the rites of Christianity would be if all we had to go by were a few sacred images and liturgical objects, and some ruined churches![3]

The Etruscan conception of the divine

Even if we did possess more evidence, it would not be easy to obtain a true picture of Etruscan religious concepts in their original and most genuine forms. The influence exerted by Greece was too powerful and too ancient in character, especially with regard to mythological and artistic inspiration, not to have left a considerable mark upon Etruscan religious attitudes and manifestations. This is particularly evident in the Etruscan conception of both the individuality and the form of the divine. Clemen has attempted to find in certain aspects of Etruscan religious conceptions survivals of fetishist forms such as the worship of weapons, trees, waters, etc. It is doubtful, however, whether the worship of weapons or trees was ever a genuine manifestation, even among earlier Mediterranean civilizations: it may have constituted a religious symbol whereby the personality of the god, even if not conceived anthropomorphically, was represented by its attribute. Similarly, it is difficult to connect Etruscan animism with animism understood as the worship of ancestors.[4] There is, however, no doubt that in the most genuine forms of Etruscan religious expression – genuine both because they were recorded by the ancients and because they continued to survive despite the contrast they offered with the more widespread and familiar forms belonging to the classical world – their conception of supernatural beings was permeated by a certain vagueness as to number, attributes, sex and appearance. This vagueness seems to point towards an original belief in some divine entity dominating the world through a number of varied, occasional manifestations which later became personified into gods, or groups of gods and spirits. This outlook is perhaps responsible

140

for the concept of the *genius* as a vital and life-giving force which is, or may be, a single divinity or the prototype of a great number of male or female spirits (which include those beings known by the name of *lasa* [5]) mingling with men and gods, and inhabiting the underworld; or which may actually manifest itself in non-anthropomorphic sexual symbols. The Roman *genius*, reflecting and accompanying both human and divine beings, may well have been originally an Etruscan conception.

Thus one is naturally led to the conclusion that the great individual deities were solely due to foreign, or, to be more specific, Greek, influences, playing upon this vague and amorphous religiosity. Such a conclusion is unlikely to be true, however, especially when it is considered that the formation of the Etruscan civilization occurred rather late in the Mediterranean world and was preceded by centuries, not to say millennia, of cultural minglings and elaborations. The concept of a supreme deity, with eminently celestial attributes, manifesting his will by means of the thunderbolt, may in no way be considered to have been a late motif or one imitated from outside. The same may be said about the concept of the goddess of love, Turan (whose name probably meant originally 'the lady'), which certainly crystallized within the compass of the primitive religious elaborations of the Mediterranean world. At most we may speak of a marked archaic or primitive flavour to Etruscan religious conceptions, of lingering themes and beliefs that had already been discarded, or were being discarded, by their Mediterranean neighbours. This will become more apparent in the light of the following pages.

The influence of Greece may, on the other hand, have assisted and favoured the individualization, personalization and humanization of Etruscan deities, multiplying and defining aspects of the major deities, promoting local spirits and heroes to the rank of national gods, fusing groups of beings with analogous characteristics into one. A typical case is that of Veltha or Veltune or Voltumna (*Vertumnus* in its Latin form): a god with strange and contrasting attributes, represented at times as a maleficent monster, at others as a vegetation god of uncertain sex, or even as a mighty war god. By a typical process, this local earth spirit, worshipped in a small part of southern Etruria, is individualized and transformed into a superior divinity, the national god *par excellence*, the *deus Etruriae princeps* (Varro, *De ling. lat.*, V, 46).[6] In the same way, the protecting spirits of war, represented as armed heroes, tend to coalesce into a single deity, the Italic Etrusco-Roman Mars, on the model of the Greek god Ares.

We thus pass to the second consequence of Greek influence on the Etruscan religion: the giving of human forms to (or anthropomorphization of) the various deities, or, to be more precise, the external, formal moulding of divine figures on patterns provided by Greek anthropo-morphism. It is possible that the Etruscans possessed from the very beginning a certain anthropomorphic image of their own for their gods. But we cannot tell how important the distant influence of the mature civilizations of the Near East may have been on such popular repre-sentations. It must certainly have played a part in the case of the war gods mentioned above or in that of the celestial god Tin, which a crude bronze statuette represents as a young man holding a thunderbolt in his right hand.[7] But Greek literature and art soon imposed – from the first half of the sixth century at least – their own representation of the great divinities as they gradually came to be elaborated in the various cities of the Greek world.

As a result of this process a whole series of Etruscan deities came into being, substantially parallel, if not identical, with those of Hellas: *Tin* or *Tinia* (Jupiter), corresponding to Zeus; *Uni* (Juno) to Hera; *Menerva* (Minerva) to Athene; *Sethlans* (Vulcan) to Hephaistos, *Turms* (Mercury) to Hermes, *Turan* (Venus) to Aphrodite (cf. Plate 33), *Maris* (Mars; cf. Plate 35), to Ares, etc. A number of Greek divinities were also introduced directly into Etruria: Herakles, who became the *Hercle* of the Etruscans and the Hercules of the Romans[8]; Apollo, who in Etruria became *Apulu* or *Aplu*; Artemis, known as *Aritimi* or *Artumes*. Characteristic specializations of gods, myths and ritual also gradually came to be modelled upon corresponding Greek forms. At the Pyrgi sanctuary the local goddess Uni was probably recognized by the Greeks as their own Eileithyia or Leucothea, just as she certainly had been assimilated to the Phoenician goddess Astarte. Monuments and texts give evidence of the variety and complex origin of the Etruscan pantheon: the lead tablet found at Magliano, the Capua tile (Plate 97), and the Zagreb mummy text (Plate 96) all mention individual deities, as also the bronze model of a sheep's liver found at Piacenza (Plate 38), perhaps used by *haruspices* to facilitate the reading and interpretation of the liver of sacrificed sheep.[9]

Next to the major deities whose personalities and outer forms came to be fixed under the influence of the Greek Olympian gods, there survived a number of indigenous supernatural beings, colleges of obscure and mysterious divinities, whose number and whose very names were unknown (Varro, in Arnobius, III, 40). Ancient writers, recalling, though often none too clearly, native traditions, speak of *Dii Superiores* or *Involuti* (i.e. enveloped in the shadows of mystery), who advised Jove when to hurl his dreaded thunderbolts (Caecina, in Seneca, *Quaest. natur.*, II, 41); the *Dii Consentes* or *Complices*, also advisers to Jove, pitiless and nameless, generally thought to be twelve in number (Varro and Caecina, in the passages referred to above); the

Penates, divided into four classes: of the heavens, the waters, the earth and the souls of men (Nigidius Figulus, in Arnobius, III, 40); the 'nine gods' (*novensiles*), casters of lightning (Pliny, II, 52, 138; Arnobius, III, 38); the *Favores Opertanei* (Martianus Capella, *De nupt. Merc. et Philol.*, I, 45); the *Lares*, the *Manes*, etc. The relationship between some of these deities is far from clear: Varro, for instance, identifies the *Consentes* with the *Penates*. Indirect references appear to indicate that many should be considered as gods of fate. Etruscan texts, in their frequent mentions of the word 'gods' (*aiser, eiser*), most probably refer to such divine colleges, i.e. to the gods considered as a collective object of worship rather than individual deities (Zagreb mummy, lead tablet of Magliano, various minor inscriptions).

There is also no lack of specific determinants, as in the case of *eiser śi-c śeu-c* (Zagreb mummy), or *aiseraś θuflθicla* or, simply, *θuflθas, θuplθaś*, etc. (in the genitive case)[10]: in the latter word there may be a correspondence with the Latin *consentes, complices*, on the analogy of *tuśurθir = consortes, coniuges*, if we accept the correspondence of the Etruscan root *θu-, tu-* with the numeral 'one' and its consequent equivalence to Latin *una*, 'together'.

Next to colleges of twelve gods and to enneads, the existence of triads has also been conjectured, on the basis of the shape of the three-cell temple and the analogy with the religion of Rome – first and foremost, that of Jupiter, Juno and Minerva, worshipped upon the Capitoline hill in Rome, and generally thought to be of Etruscan origin; but the question is still open to discussion.[11] The existence of dyads, however, is more certain: each is composed of a male deity and an accompanying goddess (e.g. the infernal pairs *Aita* and *Phersipnai*, *Mantus* and *Mania*), or of twins such as the *Dioscurides*, Castor and Pollux (*Tinas clenar*; see Plate 99), or the *θuluter* on a terracotta from Bolsena (*C.I.E.* 5180).

The religiosity of the Etruscans most clearly manifested itself in the so-called 'discipline', that complex of rules regulating relations between men and gods.[12] Its main basis was the scrupulous search for the divine will by all available means; among these the most important and traditional were the reading and interpretation of animal entrails, especially the liver (*haruspicina*), and the interpretation of lightning. Both these sciences may be traced back to the Near East, particularly to Mesopotamia[13]; in Etruria, however, they assumed strikingly national characteristics, so that even when they were adopted by Rome, so thoroughly imbued with Etruscan traditions, they were never assimilated and always retained their foreign flavour. It is interesting to note that the Romans, like the Umbrians before them, preferred a divination based upon the observation of the flight of birds (*auspicium*). But

143

auspicium too probably formed part of the Etruscan discipline, comprised in that branch which dealt with reading the divine signs or prodigies known as the *ostenta*. Other aspects of the Etruscan discipline include detailed rules governing the ritual of ceremonies and sacrifices, the doctrine of fixed time limits for both men and states (a doctrine connected with the religious chronology of the 'centuries'), and beliefs and prescriptions concerning life after death.

Among the many gaps in our knowledge of the Etruscan discipline, there is one question of fundamental importance that is as yet unanswered: what is the significance of this discipline taken in its entirety? To what vision of the world, human and divine, did it give rise? Both worlds were intimately connected, according to a principle of mystical participation and indistinctness that calls to mind the mentality of primitive peoples. As far as we are able to perceive from available sources, many aspects of Etruscan spirituality that seem obscure when appraised by standards belonging to Graeco-Roman thought become clear when seen from the viewpoint provided by different systems of religious conceptions.[14] Heaven and earth, supernatural and natural reality, macrocosm and microcosm appear to echo each other down open or recondite channels within a pre-ordained unitary system in which the orientation and division of space assume fundamental importance. In this connection, the findings of modern scholarship (which are susceptible to further progress) are based upon the comparison of the names of deities written in the various compartments into which the surface of the bronze liver found at Piacenza is divided with the partition of the sky, and its divine inhabitants (Plate 38 and Figure 5), according to Pliny (*Nat. Hist.*, II, 54, 143) and Martianus Capella (*De nupt. Merc. et Philol.*, I, 45 ff.).[15]

The 'sacred' space, orientated and sub-divided, corresponds to a concept which in Latin finds its expression in the word *templum*.[16] It refers to the sky or to a consecrated area on earth (the enclosed space of a sanctuary, city, or acropolis etc.) or to a much smaller surface (e.g. the liver of an animal used in divination), as long as the orientation and partition of the area follow the celestial model. Orientation is determined by the four cardinal points, joined by the two intersecting straight lines of which the north–south line was called *cardo* (a word of pre-Latin origin) and the east–west *decumanus*: both these words belong to Roman town-planning and surveying vocabulary, which we know to have been closely connected with the Etrusco-Italic doctrine. The observer's place is at the cross-point of the two lines, with his back to the north: he will then have behind him the whole space to the north of the *decumanus*; this half of the total space is in fact called the 'posterior part' (*pars postica*). The half placed before him towards

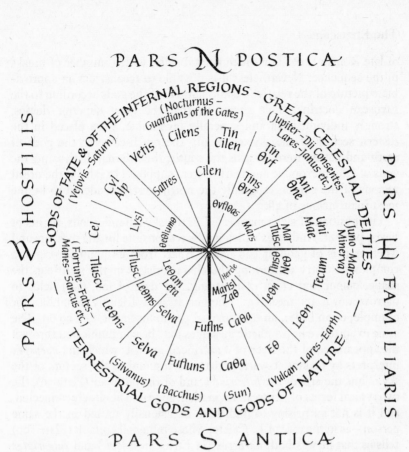

Figure 5. The subdivision of the sky according to the Etruscan discipline. The names on the outer circle are based on Martianus Capella and those within sixteen sectors on the bronze liver from Piacenza.

the south constitutes the 'anterior part' (*pars antica*). A similar partition of space also occurs along the *cardo*: to the left of the observer, the eastern sector, of good omen (*pars sinistra* or *familiaris*); to the right, the western sector, of ill omen (*pars dextra* or *hostilis*).

The vault of heaven, thus quartered and oriented, was further subdivided into sixteen minor sections in which were placed the habitations of many divinities. This plan appears to be reflected in the outer ring of sixteen compartments on the Piacenza liver and in the inner compartments corresponding, though not very clearly, to them. There are unmistakable identities between the gods of the sixteen celestial regions, quoted by Martianus Capella, and the names of the divinities inscribed upon the liver, though the correspondence is by no means absolute: the original Etruscan tradition presumably reached the writer

145

of late Roman times in a much altered state, with a number of breaks in the sequence. Nevertheless it is possible to reconstruct an approximate picture of the relative cosmic stations of the gods according to the Etruscan doctrine. This shows us that the great superior deities, strongly individualized and generally favourable, were placed in the eastern sectors of the sky, especially the north-eastern; the gods of earth and nature were towards the south; the infernal deities and the gods of fate, inexorable and fearful, were supposed to inhabit the dread regions of the sunset, especially the north-west, considered to be the most inauspicious of all.

The position of signs manifested in the sky (thunderbolts, flights of birds, portents) indicates which god is responsible for the message and whether it is of good or bad omen. Apart from its point of origin, a complex casuistry concerning the characteristics of the sign (e.g. the shape, colour and effect of lightning, the date of fall, etc.) helps to narrow down its meaning: whether it is a friendly reminder for example, or an order, an unequivocal pronouncement, and so on. The same exhortative or prophetic messages may be communicated through the appearance of the liver of a sacrificed animal, which the *haruspex* interprets by making its various parts correspond to the sectors of the sky. Thus the arts of the *fulguriator* and of the *haruspex* (Plate 39), the two typical forms of Etruscan divination, appear to be closely connected, and it is not surprising to find them occasionally united in the same person – as in the case of L. Cafate, whose bilingual epitaph (Plate 100) tells us that he was both *haruspex* (in Etruscan *netśvis*) and *fulguriator* (i.e. interpreter of lightning, in Etruscan *trutnvt frontac* or *trutnvt*?).[17] Similar rules must have governed the divinatory observation of the flight of birds, as Umbrian (the Iguvine Tablets) and Latin sources make clear. In this respect special importance was attached to the observation area on land, i.e. to the augural *templum*, with its orientation and partitions, to which is almost certainly connected the lay-out of sacred enclosures and of the temple itself, i.e. the sacred edifice containing the divine image. This generally faces south or south-east in Etruria, with a *pars antica* corresponding to the façade and colonnade and a *pars postica* represented by the cell or cells. Similarly, the sacred rules of orientation were observed (ideally at least) in the lay-out of cities – as shown by Marzabotto in Emilia – and in the partition of fields.

In these conceptions and practices, as in all Etruscan ritual manifestations, one receives an impression of surrender, almost abdication, of all human spiritual activity before the divine will, shown by the two-fold obsession: how to know the will of the gods and how to put it into effect. This led to highly developed divinatory practices on one side and to the rigid observance of the smallest ritual detail on the other. Thus even the fulfilment or violation of divine laws, or the reparations wrought by expiatory rites, appear to be largely formal and devoid of authentic ethical content,[18] an attitude widely diffused in the ancient world but particularly marked, it seems, in the religion of Etruria. It is possible, however, that at least some of the more rigid aspects of this formalism took shape only during the final phase of Etruscan civilization and among those very priestly classes whose ritual and theological elaborations are found expressed in the sacred books. Such tendencies were probably, and perhaps unconsciously, favoured by the desire of the priests themselves to be considered as the sole interpreters of the divine will and thus to gather into their hands the reins controlling the spiritual life of the nation.

Another aspect of this 'primitive' mentality is illustrated by the illogical and mystical interpretation of natural phenomena, which, persisting as it did till a fairly late period, contrasts strikingly with the scientific rationalism of the Greeks. Particularly significant and revealing in this respect is the following passage from Seneca (*Quaest. nat.*, II, 32, 2) on the subject of lightning: *Hoc inter nos et Tuscos ... interest: nos putamus, quia nubes collisae sunt, fulmina emitti; ipsi existimant nubes collidi, ut fulmina emittantur; nam, cum omnia ad deum referant, in ea opinione sunt, tamquam non, quia facta sunt, significent, sed quia significatura sunt, fiant* ('The difference between us [i.e. the Graeco-Roman world] and the Etruscans ... is the following: that whereas we believe lightning to be released as a result of the collision of clouds, they believe that clouds collide so as to release lightning: for as they attribute all to the deity, they are led to believe not that things have a meaning in so far as they occur, but rather that they occur because they must have a meaning').

Life after death

The mystic unity between the heavenly and terrestrial worlds extended, in all likelihood, to the underworld, which, according to later Etruscan doctrines, was the abode of the dead.

Much of our knowledge of the civilization of ancient Etruria comes, of course, from tombs: the very great majority of inscriptions are funerary in character, and we owe our fundamental data on the development of artistic forms and various aspects of everyday life to tomb paintings, sculptures and furnishings. Naturally the tombs also offer us, more or less directly, clues about beliefs concerning the future destiny of man and the customs and rites connected with those beliefs. Nevertheless, we are still far from possessing a clear picture of Etruscan

147

eschatology. Complex and contrasting themes point to different levels of religious attitudes and to heterogeneous influences – a source of many problems as yet unsolved but particularly alluring to the research worker.[19]

The very character of the tombs and their contents, especially during the earliest phases, is an unmistakable pointer to the persistence of primitive beliefs, common to the whole Mediterranean world, according to which the individuality of the dead man, however it was conceived, survived, linked in some way to its mortal remains, wherever these were laid. Hence the necessity for the living to guarantee, protect and prolong this survival in a concrete way, not just as the sentimental tribute of loving piety but as a religious obligation in which the element of fear probably played an important part. This type of belief gave rise to the tendency in Etruria and elsewhere, especially in ancient Egypt, to build the tomb in the shape of a house, to provide it with furniture and household objects, to ornament it, with decorations which must, originally at least, have carried a magical meaning; to surround the corpse with clothes, jewellery or arms, to provide it with food and drink and an entourage of statuettes to represent the servants; and, finally, to reproduce the features of the dead man himself and so provide an incorruptible 'seat' for the soul menaced by the decomposition of the body: whence, probably, the development of the funerary portrait, reflecting the earlier practice of Egypt.

But what was the true and deeper nature of the religious ideas that were reflected in such customs, and how they were able to subsist and evolve by the side of other, contrasting beliefs, are both matters that remain on the whole obscure. For at the beginning of their history, Etruscan cities witness the almost exclusive prevalence of cremation. This rite, wherever it appears and in whichever way it spreads, cannot but reflect beliefs incompatible with the idea of a material link between the body and the soul of the dead man. Indeed cremation appears at times to carry the idea of a 'liberation' of the soul from the shackles of matter towards a celestial sphere.[20] It is all the more odd, therefore, that in Etruscan tombs of the Villanovan and Orientalizing periods the ashes and bones of the cremated dead are sometimes contained in urns in the shape of houses or in vases attempting to reproduce the features of the dead person (the so-called 'canopic urns' of Chiusi). This reveals, from the very earliest formative period of the nation, a mingling of beliefs and perhaps the re-establishment of Mediterranean funerary traditions over cremation.[21]

Nor is it possible to state categorically that belief in man's survival in the tomb excludes all belief in the transmigration of souls to a world beyond the grave. It is certain that in Etruria this belief became progressively more established and definite under the influence of Greek religion and mythology, with the consequent weakening of earlier beliefs. This realm beyond the grave was conceived on the lines of the Homeric Hades and peopled with local divinities, the spirits of ancient heroes and the shades of the dead. Monuments as early as those of the fifth and fourth centuries, but especially those belonging to the Hellenistic period, represent death as a journey to the kingdom of the dead (see Plate 41), the future subterranean abode of the soul: a sad, hopeless sojourn, dominated at times by fear inspired by the presence of monstrous demons or even by tortures inflicted upon the dead. It is, basically, the materialization of the fear of death in an essentially pessimistic eschatology. Two infernal figures are the most symbolic of death: Vanth, the goddess with the great wings, representing, like her Greek counterpart Moira, implacable fate; and Charun the demon, a semi-bestial figure armed with a heavy hammer, who may be considered as a frightening deformation of the Greek Charon, whose name he assumes (Plate 45; cf. Plate 83).[22] Etruscan demonology is both rich and picturesque: it includes a number of other personages, either partly inspired by Greek mythology (e.g. the Erinyes), or completely original, such as the horrific Tuchulcha with the face of a vulture, the ears of a donkey and armed with serpents (Plate 44). Symbols of chthonic animals like the snake and the horse are also frequently represented.[23]

Even for this later period monumental sources are insufficient, because of their fragmentary and external aspects, to provide a reliable and complete picture of contemporary beliefs about the underworld. To judge from tomb paintings and reliefs, the fate of the dead was inexorably sad, and the same for all: the merciless law spared no one, not even the most illustrious dignitary – his superiority is expressed only in the sumptuous clothing, the attributes of office and the retinue that accompanied him on his journey to the underworld. However, a number of references to consoling doctrines of salvation, more or less explicit, exist in literary tradition (Arnobius, II, 62; Servius, *ad Aen.*, III, 168; Martianus Capella, II, 142); these mention the possibility of attaining a state of beatitude or even deification, by means of certain rituals supposed to have been described in the Etruscan *Libri Acherontici*. A precious original document of such a ceremony of suffrage, with prescriptions as to offerings and sacrifices to deities (especially infernal deities), has been preserved in the Etruscan text of the Capua tile, which dates back to at least the fourth century B.C.[24] We do not know how much the development of these new eschatological beliefs is due to the diffusion among the Etruscans of Orphic or, still more, Dionysiac doctrines (the cult of Bacchus is in fact widely attested in Etruria, even in connection with the world of the dead).[25] Nevertheless hopes of

149

salvation appear to be tied to the concept of magico-religious rituals proper to a primitive stage in spiritual development, rather than to the superior ethical principle of reward for the good done during life on earth.

Forms of worship

Monumental sources and documents written in Etruscan (as far as we are able to understand them), together with references in classical literature, provide us with ample data for the reconstruction of Etruscan religious life and forms of worship. Traditional customs in this respect, at least in their material aspects (i.e. sacred places and temples, the organization of the priesthood, sacrifices, prayers, offerings of votive gifts, etc.), do not differ substantially from their counterparts in the Greek, Italic, and, especially, Roman worlds. This may be explained first by taking into account the common spiritual orientation of Graeco-Italic civilization from the Archaic period onwards, and secondly by considering the very strong influence exerted by Etruria on Rome in matters of religion. Etruscan religious antiquities should not therefore be studied in isolation from the much more detailed and complex picture provided by Greece and Rome in the matter of ritual; as a result, it becomes all the more difficult to estimate how far the Etruscans' ritual practices reflected their religious mentality.

In the first place we should attribute to the Etruscans that concrete and almost materialistic adherence to rules established *ab antiquo*, that scrupulous formalism of ritual, and that frequent demand for expiatory sacrifices which can be detected within the body of Roman religious traditions as elements foreign, as it were, to the simple and rustic religiosity of the earliest Latins, pointing to the presence of a collateral factor which it is impossible not to identify with the ceremonial of an ancient and mature civilization, i.e. the civilization of Etruria. This *ars colendi religiones*, to quote the expression used by Livy in a passage to which we have already referred,[26] accords fully with the feeling of the subordination of man to the deity which, as we have seen, was a predominating factor in Etruscan religion, and presupposes faith in the magical virtue of ritual, a faith frequently met in more primitive mentalities.

This concrete quality is shown by precise determinations as to the place, times, persons and formalities in which or by means of which the act of invoking or placating the deity should take place: proceedings which the Romans designated by the term *res divina* and the Etruscans (probably) *ais(u)na* (i.e. 'divine' service, from *ais*, 'god'), which was the source of the Umbrian word *esono*, 'sacrifice'.

These proceedings take place within consecrated ground, the

templum, of which mention has already been made: an enclosure with altars and sacred buildings containing images of the gods. Such buildings were often made to face south or south-east.[27] The concept of consecration of a particular piece of ground or building for worship was perhaps expressed in Etruscan by the word *sacni* (whence the verb *sacniśa*): this status could be extended, as in Greece and Rome, to a complex assemblage of enclosures and temples, as on the acropolis of many cities (e.g. Marzabotto). Characteristics in some ways similar were shown by funerary enclosures, near which or within which sacrifices were offered and gifts deposited.

The regulations pertaining to the timing of feasts and ceremonies must also have been of especial importance in Etruria; these, together with the ceremonial surrounding acts of worship, constituted the subject-matter of the *Libri Rituales* mentioned by tradition. The longest Etruscan ritual text in our possession, the Zagreb mummy text, contains an actual liturgical calendar with indications as to the month and day on which the ceremonies described were to take place.[28] It is probable that other documents were drawn up in the form attested by the sacred calendars of the Romans: i.e. consecutive lists of days countermarked solely by the name of the feast or of the deity to be honoured. The Etruscan calendar may have been similar to the pre-Julian Roman calendar: we know the names of some of its months,[29] and it seems that the name of the 'Ides' (at about the middle of the month) may have been of Etruscan origin; the numbering of the days of the month was, however, consecutive, unlike the Roman system. Each sanctuary and each city must have had, as is to be expected, its own particular feasts, as in the case of the *śacni cilθ* – the sanctuary of a city which remains unidentifiable – referred to in the Zagreb ritual. On the other hand, the annual celebrations at the sanctuary of Voltumna, near Volsinii, were national in character, as we know now from tradition.

We are again obliged to have recourse to comparisons with the Italic and Roman worlds when trying to understand the nature and organization of Etruscan priestly bodies. There are at any rate grounds for believing that they were many and had specialized functions, closely connected with public magistracies and often grouped into colleges. The priestly title *cepen* (with the variant *cipen* found in Campania), particularly frequent in Etruscan texts, is, for example, often followed by an attribute that determines its sphere of action or its specific function: e.g. *cepen θaurχ*, a name that almost certainly indicates a funerary priest (from *θaura*, 'tomb'). Other words connected with priestly office, both general and specific, include *eisnevc* (related to *aisna*, the sacrificial action), *celu*, and, perhaps, *tamera*, *śanti*, *ceχasie*, etc.

There are, moreover, priests with divinatory functions: the *haruspices* (*netśvis*), represented on Etruscan monuments in a characteristic dress consisting of a pointed cylindrical cap and a fringed mantle (see Plate 39), and the interpreters of lightning (*trutnvt?*). The title *maru*, *marun-*, was connected, as we know, with sacred functions, such as, for example, in the cult of Bacchus (*marunuχ paχanati, maru paχaθuras*). The double title *cepen marunuχva* is worthy of note, combining probably a priestly office with the functions pertaining to the *maru*; there is also *zilχ ceχaneri*, which has been understood as something approaching the Roman *curator sacris faciundis*. Collective terms such as *paχaθuras* and *alumnaθuras* probably refer to confraternities or to some other colleges, and should be compared as to their formal structure with such formations as *velθinaθuraś*, i.e. 'members of the *Velθina* family'. At Tarquinia there existed in Roman times an *ordo LX haruspicum* (*C.I.L.*, XI, 3382), probably of ancient origin. One of the priests' attributes was the *lituus*, a stick curved at one end, which is, however, frequently pictured on monuments in connection with profane activities: e.g. in the hands of judges at athletic competitions.[30]

Worship was directed towards interrogating the will of the gods, according to the rules of divination, and invoking their help or pardon by means of an offering. It is probable that both these operations were closely connected, though literary sources distinguish between victims sacrificed for the consultation of their entrails (*hostiae consultatoriae*) and victims destined as true offerings (*hostiae animales*) in place of human sacrifice. The offering of liquids and food appears to be similarly mixed in complex ceremonials with the blood-offerings of animals. These liturgies are minutely described in prescriptive tones and a specialized technical language by the ritual specifications in the Zagreb mummy text and on the Capua tile; unfortunately our knowledge of Etruscan is not sufficient to allow us to establish accurately the meaning of the terms used in the description of the rites, and, consequently, we cannot fully reconstruct the ceremonies. Prayer, music and dance must all have played a large part in them.

Votive gifts offered in sanctuaries for favours requested or received consist mainly of statuettes in bronze, stone or terracotta, representing the divinity, the giver or even animals, in substitution for victims, or parts of the human body; also vases, arms, etc. These objects, kept together in vaults or deposits, often carry dedicatory inscriptions. They vary greatly in aesthetic merit and in value, consisting for the most part of modest moulded terracotta figurines: a sign that round the great centres of worship deep and widespread popular religious feelings flourished.[31]

CHAPTER 8 Literature and the Arts

Literature

In many of its aspects, we are forced to regard and study the civilization of Etruria as if it were a prehistoric civilization although it belongs to full historical times; for we are often almost wholly limited to its external and material manifestations. We have not, in fact, the direct light thrown by a great literary tradition to help us penetrate into the thought, feelings and way of life of its creators as is possible with the other great peoples of the classical world. We owe much, it is true, to indirect information (whether contemporary or not) which Greek and Roman authors have left us, and also to documents written in Etruscan (mostly short inscriptions, often difficult to interpret): we have seen this when dealing with the political and social organization and the religion of Etruria. But neither can make up for the lack of a national literature with poetical, historical and technical works.

We may doubt whether a true literature ever existed among the Etruscans.[1] The fact that it has not reached us, however, is no valid argument against its existence. We possess Greek and Latin literature almost entirely because it was passed down to us uninterruptedly from scribe to scribe, through the centuries of the Middle Ages. Ancient texts on papyrus and epigraphic documents restored to light by archaeology are relatively secondary in importance. If the works of classical writers were copied and handed down to modern times, it was because they were written in a living language and constituted an essential foundation of European civilization. Even so, only a small fraction of the output of Greek and Latin authors is now in our hands. On the other hand, the original texts of the pre-Roman peoples of Italy, including the Etruscans, had ceased to be of any interest from Imperial times: they were couched in languages no longer spoken and presumably incomprehensible to all except perhaps a few scholars. It is obvious that it would occur to no one to transcribe and preserve them for future generations.

A type of Etruscan literary activity, it is true, has been positively, though indirectly, attested by the notice it received in Greek and Roman sources, consisting mainly of fragmentary references to the existence of books with religious content known in translation or in compendia among priestly or scholarly circles in Rome. We know that they were classified into three fundamental groups under the names of *Libri Haruspicini*, *Libri Fulgurales*, and *Libri Rituales*.[2] The first dealt with divination by the examination of animal entrails and the second with divination from objects struck by lightning. As for the *Libri Rituales*, they seem to have dealt with a much vaster and more complex field: the rules of worship, the formalities governing the consecration of sanctuaries, the foundation of cities, the division of fields, civil and military ordinances, etc. Moreover they contained special texts on the division of time and on limits in the life of men and peoples (*Libri Fatales*), on life beyond the grave and rituals of salvation (*Libri Acherontici*) and, finally, on the interpretation of miracles (*Ostentaria*).

Etruscan and Roman tradition tends to attribute to these works an extremely ancient and venerable origin, to the extent that a number of them were actually believed to go back to the teachings of the genius Tages (*Libri Tagetici*, corresponding, as far as we can tell, to the *Libri Haruspicini* and *Acherontici* – see Plate 37) or the teachings of the nymph Vegoia or Begoë, to whom were assigned the *Libri Fulgurales* and the passages on mensuration contained in the *Libri Rituales*. They were, in fact, believed to have been divinely inspired and to have originated in a kind of primordial 'revelation', identified with the very origins of the Etruscan civilization. And it is quite possible that the collection of sacred books known during the last centuries of the Etruscan nation, and translated (in part at least) into Latin, did contain elements of great antiquity. But the essentially normative aspect of the texts appears rather to reflect an evolved and, perhaps, final phase in the spiritual and religious development of Etruscan society. It may be that this final and, as it were, 'canonical' elaboration took place within narrow priestly circles, such as the Order of the Sixty *Haruspices* which still flourished at Tarquinia in Roman times (see p. 152), a world to which doubtless belonged a certain Tarquitius Priscus (or Tuscus?) to whom Roman tradition attributed the composition, vulgarization and translation into Latin of a number of sacred books.[3]

Let us now consider the nature of this religious literature. It was probably varied and heterogeneous, with some sections in verse or at least metrically composed (*carmina*), others minutely ritual and prescriptive. We are able to form an idea of the latter by considering surviving original texts in Etruscan like the Zagreb mummy text or the Capua tile. Some scholars have already pointed to a possible connection between the funerary ritual of the tile and the *Libri Acherontici*. Altogether, the corpus of sacred books must have possessed a fundamentally religious inspiration but also, at the same time, a certain juridical character. It was a treatise of sacred doctrines and, at the same time, a constitution, a collection of laws, including profane ones: e.g. the laws concerning the right of property (*terrae ius Etruriae*).[4]

There remains the question whether the Etruscans did pursue other forms of literary activity, and, if so, to what extent these forms developed independently of sacred literature. The existence of annals or historical documents seems to be confirmed by the report of *Tuscae Historiae* quoted by Varro (Censorinus, *De die nat.*, 17, 6). There is on the other hand a complete lack of references to epic or mythological narrative. Although we cannot exclude the possibility that this genre was cultivated in Etruria, we should point out that the Etruscan mentality does not seem to have been inclined to that mythographic inventiveness which distinguished the Greeks. With rare exceptions, their figurative art merely imitates and re-elaborates the sagas of gods and heroes received from the Greek world.

That convivial poems and Fescennine satires (whose origins used to be traced back to the Faliscan town of Fescennium) had their parallels in Etruria is quite possible, but cannot be definitely proved. There are on the other hand a number of funerary inscriptions longer than average and with, perhaps, a metric or rhythmic structure that may point to the existence of *elogia*, or praises, sung in honour of important deceased personages. Dramatic poetry, as evidenced by the mention of a certain Volnius, author of tragedies in Etruscan (Varro, *De ling. lat.*, V, 55), was probably only a late phenomenon, modelled upon Greek drama.

The presence has often been pointed out in Etruscan texts of regular groupings of words and syllables, repetitions, alliterations, rhymes, etc., which point to a marked disposition for the rhythmic form. But we have no reliable data on the existence of a quantitative metre comparable to that of Greek or Latin verse.[5] It is highly probable at any rate that votive inscriptions, particularly those belonging to the archaic period, and certain funerary inscriptions were in verse form, as was frequently the case among the Greeks and Romans. Sacred hymns and prayers, and perhaps profane songs as well, must also have possessed a metric form.

Music and dancing

Music, whether accompanied by song or not (and especially the latter), must have played a major role in the ceremonies and public and private life of the Etruscans, if we are to judge from the evidence of both literary and monumental sources.[6] The instruments (and, consequently, the rhythms, harmonies, and melodic arrangements) are manifestly the same in Etruria as in the musical world of the Greeks;

155

this identity is not surprising in view of the many debts Etruscan cities owed to the civilization of Greece. Among the string instruments we should mention the zither, the lyre, and the *barbiton*; among the wind instruments, the double pipes (*tybiae*), the straight trumpet (*salpinx*, *tuba*) and the curved trumpet (*cornu*); among the percussion, the castanets played by dancing women. As in Greece, duets consisting of a zither player (or lyre or *barbiton* player) and a double pipe player were a common combination, as can be deduced from the frequency with which they are represented in banqueting and dancing scenes found in tomb paintings.

And yet Etruria must have had its own individual tendencies and traditions in genres and practice against this common musical background. We should not disregard the insistence with which ancient writers speak of the popularity of the double pipes amongst the Etruscans, almost as if it were a national instrument (see Athenaeus, IV, 154a) brought over from Lydia and transmitted by the Etruscans to the Romans: the pipe player was in fact called *subulo* in Rome, a name derived from Etruscan. Indeed the art of pipe playing was widespread in Greece, but attributed originally to the Phrygians and the Lydians: it reflects a taste for the pathetic and the orgiastic in music. In this case too, as with other manifestations of their artistic culture, the Etruscans appear to have adopted those elements of the complex artistic experience of the Greeks that were closest to their own sensibilities,[7] especially in the direction of those forms elaborated by the East Greek cities of Asia Minor. We must logically suppose that Etruscan music preferred the modes defined by Greek theorists as Lydian, Hypo-Lydian, Phrygian, and Hypo-Phrygian, with their respective tonal systems, as against the grave and solemn Dorian music. On the other hand, Greek tradition agrees in attributing the trumpet or *salpinx* to the Etruscans (Aeschylus, *Eumen.*, 567 ff.; Sophocles, *Ajax*, 17; Euripides, *Phoen.*, 1377 ff.; etc.). Though we need not take this to mean that the trumpet was actually invented in Etruria, nevertheless this ancient instrument must have played a characteristic part in Etruscan military and, perhaps, religious ceremonials and must eventually have been made and exported by Etruscan bronze manufacturers. Figured monuments, however, more commonly show a curved trumpet or horn, or a straight trumpet curved at one end like the *lituus*.

At any rate the popularity of wind instruments corresponds to a notable development in the practice of music apart from song. Music (with dancing and mime) not only formed part of the religious celebrations and stage performances of Etruria, but also frequently accompanied, as an exciting rhythmic and melodic commentary, various moments in the ritual and in the public and private life of the Etruscans, e.g. in games, hunting, the preparation of banquets, even the scourging of slaves. The connection of music with gesture rather than with words finds its parallel in forms of stage performance peculiar to Etruria; these, our sources tell us (Livy, VII, 2, 4 ff.), were mimed by masked actor-dancers (*histriones* or *ludiones*), reminiscent at times of both farce and satire. This does not exclude the possible existence of drama with acting and dialogue, which after the fourth century must certainly have been influenced by Greek dramatic forms, as borne out by the many statuettes found in Etruscan tombs representing masked comedy types.

Etruscan dancing is known to us chiefly through the tomb paintings of the sixth and fifth centuries. It generally appears to be performed by professional dancers: solo dancing girls accompanied by a double pipe player; dancers in couples; and above all troops of men and women, which advance in separate lines with individual movements and are led by musicians (*cithara-* or lyre-players and flautists), who perhaps filled the role of dance leaders, for they join in the steps of the dance. Occasionally – as for example in the paintings of the Tomb of the Inscriptions at Tarquinia – members of the *gens* to which the family of the dead man belong may be seen dancing too. The jerky movements of the legs and the emphatic and presumably rapid gestures of the arms and head reveal a type of dance that must have been markedly rhythmical and animated if not actually orgiastic, presumably inspired by the Greek *sikinnis* of Dionysiac origin. But the documents we possess, limited by the time and range of funerary art, are not sufficient to prove that this was the only type of dance practised in Etruria, though it fits the musical 'modes' we have assumed to be dominant.[8]

Architectural monuments

Of a quite different order is the wealth of direct evidence we possess on the architecture and figurative arts of ancient Etruria, for these are the very monuments and materials brought to light by archaeological discovery. In spite of the destruction of so many ancient works of art, both buildings and objects, by time or the superimposition of new civilizations, these documents are sufficient to allow us a broad vision of the artistic activity of ancient Etruria both in its tendencies and in its developments.[9]

The buildings of Etruria cannot of course be studied on the same basis as those of Greece and Rome. Only in fortifications and tombs was stone employed to the exclusion of other materials; in other constructions, i.e. temples or civic buildings, it was used only for the foundations: the remainder of the building was composed of lighter

157

materials like wood, rubble, unbaked bricks or terracotta. This means that all that remains of such edifices is their plan and a few fragments of the decorations. Nevertheless it is possible to reconstruct their original aspect by using rock tombs and urns as models, or the small votive reproductions (e.g. Plate 54) made to imitate them.[10]

Walled structures offer much variety in materials and techniques according to the time, place and type of building. The commonest materials were limestone, travertine, sandstone and tufa, all locally quarried; the absence of marble (so important to Greek architecture) is due to the fact that the exploitation of the Carrara quarries began only in Roman times. The style of masonry varies from large irregular roughly hewn blocks (as shown, for example, by the city walls of Vetulonia) to the fine revetments of small squared blocks found in the walls of southern Etruscan cities and in other (especially funerary) constructions. Generally speaking, no evolution from a rougher and more primitive type of structure to more refined and elaborate styles can be detected: square, regular walls were known and built from the earliest stages of the Etruscan civilization, and differences in technique seem to be due rather to particular conditions such as materials at hand, available craftsmanship, urgency, etc. Contrary to an opinion once current among many archaeologists, the true polygonal style must be considered foreign to the building customs of the Etruscans, and a late introduction on the part of the first Roman colonists in the fortresses of Pyrgi, Cosa, and Saturnia.[11] The partial (if not complete) use of unbaked bricks in domestic architecture or even in military constructions seems to be attested at Roselle from the end of the seventh century,[12] and appears to form part of a tradition that seems to have been very widespread in the Mediterranean under the influence of Greek building. It is probable that the brick city walls of Arezzo were built within the framework of this tradition. Also widely diffused in Etruria was the system of pseudo-vault and pseudo-cupola coverings, formed by the progressive convergence of blocks laid in horizontal courses, a system widely spread throughout the Mediterranean.[13] Later, the technique of the true arch became established, evidenced by city gates (e.g. at Volterra and Perugia) and sepulchral monuments, a prelude to the dominant structures in Roman architecture. In this predilection for vault covering, Etruscan architecture carries over (without inventing), perfects and applies ancient Near Eastern forms which Greek classical architecture rejected as foreign to the rigorous rectilinear motif of its conceptions, based upon the architrave.

Among the more notable examples of military architecture, we should mention the city walls of Tarquinia (and surviving sections of similar constructions at Veii, Cerveteri, Vulci, Sutri, etc.), of Volsinii, Vetu-

Ionia, Chiusi, Cortona, Perugia, Fiesole and Arezzo. These works are generally attributed to between the sixth and fourth centuries, with later additions and rebuilding, since they generally remained serviceable in Roman times and, in one or two cases, even later. In spite of the variety of styles, they are all continuous walls, originally uninterrupted by towers: projections and indentations occur only in connection with gates. These may at first have been spanned by lintels; but the grandiose Porta dell'Arco at Volterra, and Porta Marzia and Porta 'di Augusto' at Perugia feature the true arch together with architectural and figured decorations on their façades. The ancient aspect of city walls, with battlements and arched gateways, is documented on figured urns and sarcophagi.

Funerary architecture is somewhat heterogeneous in character owing to the fact that it represents the occasional complement or development of sepulchral styles of varied origin and inspiration. The great majority of tombs, even those of a monumental type, were in fact hewn out of the living rock, whether they consisted of underground graves (ranging from modest *pozzetti*, primitive pits, to the grandiose and complex hypogea of a later age) or external adaptations in the shape of circular tumuli and quadrilateral constructions covered with earth, or façades sculptured on the cliff face. These works, though not architectural in character, are closely connected with architecture in so far as they often imitate faithfully to the minutest detail the shapes of real buildings in their exterior and interior aspects, their decorative elements and even occasionally their furnishings and fittings. Walled structures, however, are frequently found, sometimes as simple additions to the rock walls and ceilings, sometimes making up the whole of the monument. Sepulchral chambers built during the earliest phase feature false vaults and, occasionally, false cupolas, as in the tomb of Casal Marittimo near Volterra or in the recently discovered tomb near Quinto Fiorentino (Plate 50). In later years, finely constructed barrel-vaulted chambers were built, e.g. the tomb of the Granduca at Chiusi or the San Manno hypogeum near Perugia. The round tumulus (with drum hewn out of the rock as at Cerveteri – see Plate 48 – or built upon it as at Populonia – see Plate 49) became far less frequent after the fifth century, but evolved, owing perhaps to contacts with Hellenistic funerary architecture, towards the great circular Roman mausoleum of Imperial times like that of Augustus or of Hadrian in Rome (e.g. the 'Tanella di Pitagora' at Cortona). There is also no lack of quadrilateral tombs shaped like small temples, e.g. at Populonia. Finally, mention should be made of a type of tomb built on a plinth and surmounted by large cippi shaped like truncated cones or by obelisks; a type known chiefly through the reliefs of sepulchral urns, but directly attested, though outside Etruria, in the so-called Tomb of the Horatii and Curiatii near Albano in Latium. A fine monument of this type, with several obelisks adorned with bells, is mentioned by ancient sources as having existed at Clusium and is identified as the Tomb of King Porsenna.[14] Funerary cippi consist of miniature replicas of these forms.

Domestic and religious architecture have common origins and characteristics. The various forms of the Etruscan house will be described later (see p. 175). The temple was identified at first (as in the early Greek world) with the rectangular house with sloping roof but without portico, as evidenced by votive models (see, for example, Plate 54) and the remains of an edifice discovered on the Veii acropolis. It later assumed more complex forms, parallel in certain aspects to those of the Greek temple. The type attributed to the Etruscans by Vitruvius (*De archit.*, IV, 7; see Plate 52) is characterized by a plan in which the width is slightly less than the length, the front half occupied by a colonnaded portico and the back consisting of three cells, each dedicated to a different deity, or by a single cell flanked by two *alae* or open ambulacra. Monumental remains at Veii, Pyrgi, Orvieto, Fiesole and Marzabotto show that this plan was widely and lastingly used in Etruria from the Archaic to the Hellenistic period; it was used for the Temple of Capitoline Jove in Rome, first built in the days of the Etruscan dynasty of the Tarquins. It seems certain, however, that sacred edifices were also built with a plan more similar to that of the Greek temple: i.e. with a lengthened rectangular base and a columned façade (prostyle) or a continuous colonnade on all four sides (*peripteros*) as in the 'Ara della Regina' at Tarquinia or in the older of the Pyrgi temples. The originality of Etruscan temples does not in any case reside so much in their lay-out as in the materials used for their construction, in the proportions and forms given to the raised part of the building and in the types of decoration. We have already referred to the fact that, apart from the foundations, they were generally built of light materials with a framework made of wood. This meant limited development as to height (as was the case in the measurements of the 'Tuscan' temple, according to Vitruvius), wide intercolumnar spaces and a broad roof with marked lateral projection of the eaves. Wooden beams require the protection of compact but light materials, whence the universal use of polychrome terracotta coverings[15]; these developed colourful geometric and figurative decorative patterns, with longitudinal or terminal facings for the beams and cornices, adorned with antefixes and *acroteria* (see Plate 53). The pediment was originally open, so that the roof timbers could be seen from the front; later, a closed pediment was adopted, decorated with figured compositions as in Greek temples.

These characteristics of the Etruscan temple have undoubted

1. A tomb at Tarquinia in the eighteenth century (from Byres, *Hypogaei*).

2. Villanovan trench-graves (*tombe a fossa*) at Veii.

3. Villanovan biconical ossuary from Veii.

4. Villanovan bronzes from Vulci.

5. Villanovan animal-bird askos from Bologna.

6. Cypro-Phoenician gilded silver bowl from Palestrina.

7. Gold pectoral from the Regolini-Galassi tomb at Cerveteri.

8. Silver-plated bronze urn from Vetulonia.

9. Inscribed funerary stele from Kaminia, Lemnos.

10. Naval battle on a sixth-century Etruscan vase from Cerveteri.

11. Cippus with late-sixth-century Greek inscription from Gravisca.

12–14. *Three inscribed gold tablets from the Etruscan sanctuary at Pyrgi*

12. The longer Etruscan inscription.

13. The Punic inscription.

14. The shorter Etruscan inscription.

15. *Elogium* of Imperial date from Tarquinia.

16. Etruscan bronze helmet with Greek inscription from Olympia.

73. Terracotta urn from Vignagrande near Chiusi.

74. Detail of a large bronze krater from Tuscania.

75. The 'Capitoline Brutus'.

76. The 'Orator': portrait of
Avle Meteli.

77. Terracotta male portrait-head
from Tarquinia.

95. Pair of ivory dice from Tuscania.

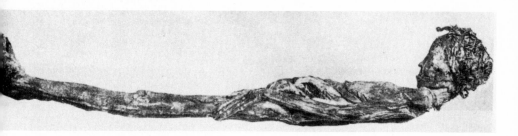

96. The Zagreb mummy.

97. The Capua tile.

98. The Perugia cippus.

99. Inscribed Attic red-figure kylix from Tarquinia.

100. Bilingual (Etruscan-Latin) inscription from Pesaro.

101. Inscription from Santa Marinella.

102. Painted funerary inscriptions in the Tomba degli Anina, Tarquinia.

counterparts in the primitive architecture of Greece and, as has been said, partial parallels with the archaic and classical Greek temple. The difference resides in the fact that the Greek temple tends to develop as early as the seventh century B.C. into an edifice almost entirely built of stone and evolving its own unmistakable architectonic forms, whereas in the Etruscan temple there is no departure from the traditional use of wood as a building material until full Hellenistic times; if anything, the decorative exuberance of the terracotta facings became more marked. These show (especially during the sixth and fifth centuries) many variations in conception and development: the longitudinal facings of the beams, for instance, may form a continuous frieze figured in relief, of East Greek inspiration (the so-called 'first' or 'Ionic' period), or they may simply feature painted ornamentations accompanied by the stressing of the overlying and projecting cornice, as in the fictile decorative systems of Greece proper or of its colonies in southern Italy and Sicily (the 'second' or 'Archaic' period). This latter type of decoration became established from the end of the sixth century and coincided with the most splendid phase in the development of the Etruscan temple, characterized by shell-shaped antefixes, by frontal relief decorations on the plaques terminating the longitudinal beams, and by large figured *acroteria*, as shown by the typical decorations of the temples at Veii and at Pyrgi. This scheme was to remain substantially unchanged during the centuries that followed. The only innovation worthy of note was the introduction of a closed decorated pediment with a single figured terracotta composition in high relief in the Greek style. It may have made its appearance as early as the fifth century, though it is mainly known from the fourth at Tarquinia, Telamon and Luni ('third' or 'Hellenistic' period). When treating of the forms and coverings of the Etruscan temple we should not neglect to mention the historically fundamental fact that these same characteristics and developments are also met in the temples belonging to Faliscan territory, Latium and, though with a number of differences, Campania. We may thus speak of an architectural cultural link uniting all Tyrrhenian Italy north of the area directly affected by Greek colonization.[16] The establishment of a stone temple instead of the traditional wooden structure took place under the influence of Greek models, but with original characteristics, during the course of the fourth century and the subsequent Hellenistic period.[17]

The predominance of elements of Archaic inspiration even in works belonging to a comparatively late period may, for that matter, be observed in all the motifs of Etruscan architectural decoration, whether in stone or in wood and terracotta buildings, and in the innumerable reproductions and imitations for funerary and votive purposes. Vitruvius speaks of a 'Tuscan' order, distinct from the Doric, Ionic and Corinthian orders of Greek architecture. It is characterized by a type of column that is in fact found in Roman monuments and which represents a variant of the Doric column, with the same capital but possessing a smooth shaft and footings. Its Etruscan origin is proved by evidence from as far back as the Archaic period. It was, presumably, the shape of the majority of wooden columns in sacred and civic buildings. In reality it is a survival and an elaboration of the so-called 'proto-Doric' type, with moulded plinth, a noticeably swollen shaft devoid of channellings, and capital with curved cushion. In primitive Greece, it was very quickly replaced by the true Doric column. Together with it, there was in Etruria another widespread type of column and pilaster, with capitals adorned with flowered volutes, both simple and composite, which owe their inspiration to eastern capitals from Syria and Cyprus and to the so-called 'Aeolian' capitals of East Greece,[18] which also disappeared from the Greek world with the establishment of the Ionic capital. Archaic-type mouldings, with dadoes, strings, guttae and ogees, dominate on the bases and copings of buildings, altars, cippi, etc. The frames of doors and windows stress the jambs at each side of the tapered embrasures and jutting architrave, which, at a later date, curves at each end to form characteristic 'ears'. The non-figured ornamentation of cornices, copings and other elements of the superstructure of buildings is dominated by motifs whose inspiration is mainly Ionic: stylized leaves, cable mouldings, lotus leaves and flowers, spirals, meanders, etc. The Doric frieze system, where metopes alternate with triglyphs, seems to spread only after the fourth century and frequently features true pilasters in lieu of the triglyphs.[19]

Figured works of art

The documents we possess on the figurative arts of Etruria come almost exclusively from sanctuaries and tombs. This is not merely due to the circumstances surrounding their preservation and discovery. In this field more than any other, the religious and funerary inspiration of works of art does in fact seem to prevail over the profane. There is at any rate an almost complete lack of evidence of a monumental art aimed at exalting or commemorating historical events or civic occasions as in the Greek and Roman worlds; in this respect, a parallel may be drawn with Etruscan literature and its prevalently religious inspiration. On the other hand, the close ties binding art with religion, and the generally concrete, not to say utilitarian, bent of the Etruscan mind must have obstructed the process, visible more or less clearly in the Greek world, which led to an autonomous conception of the artistic phenomenon as an activity that was not merely practical and ethical but aesthetic as well. This inability to arrive at a conception of art for its own sake, an inability shared by all pre-classical civilizations, explains why Etruscan figured art generally presents the characteristics of the craftsman's art, decorative and applied, and never, or only very exceptionally, reaches the level of what is usually termed 'great' art, i.e. the personal work of an artist aware of his creative capacity and socially appreciated because of it. Only one Etruscan craftsman is known to us through ancient literary tradition (Varro, in Pliny, XXXV, 157): Vulca the modeller, of Veientine origin, who also worked in Rome during the sixth century B.C.

A short review of the categories of surviving monuments according to their techniques may help to clarify these preliminary considerations. The plastic arts[20] are represented by bronzes (other metals are less frequent), terracottas and sculptures in stone: marble is almost wholly absent, for it was not available locally and only very rarely imported. Indirect sources allow us to presume that wood was also very widely used; moreover, small objects feature intaglios in ivory, bone, and amber. Statuary belonging to holy places may be classified as follows: divine images as objects of worship, often mentioned in ancient authors (e.g. the famous painted terracotta statue of Capitoline Jove in Rome, attributed to Vulca) but now generally lost; votive statues and groups representing deities and worshippers, of which we possess copious examples, in particular small bronzes and terracottas from sanctuary deposits; and parts of the architectural decoration of temples, such as the great acroteria to which the famous Apollo of Veii (Plate 61; and cf. Plate 62) belonged. Within the funerary sphere should be mentioned the statuettes found in tombs, the canopic urns from Chiusi, the great portrait-statues and the figures sculptured upon the lids of sarcophagi (e.g. Plates 65 and 73): it is especially with this latter genre that the development of the personal portrait or likeness is connected (see Plate 77). Apart from these sacral or funerary manifestations there may have been a type of statuary of an honorific character such as statues erected to celebrate illustrious men, as was customary in republican Rome (Pliny, *Nat. Hist.*, XXXIV, 26). We should be especially careful, however, in attempting to identify this type of monument: until recently, for example, it was thought that the famous bronze known as the 'Orator' in the Museo Archeologico at Florence was an honorary statue; but the presence in the inscription of words with sacral and funerary connections like *flere* (interpreted as 'god' by K. Olzscha) and *sanśl* seems to point to some religious purpose (see Plate 76).[21]

Full relief is also encountered in the decoration of bronze, ivory and terracotta articles, often of a very high quality: the same bronze workshops must have produced votive statuettes and decorative parts applied to candelabra, vases and other objects.

Among the architectural terracottas, figures in half relief often alternate with others in full relief.[22] In the Archaic *acroteria* and antefixes of southern Etruria and the Faliscan territory, there are figures and groups standing free in space but modelled as if they were reliefs. Conversely, in compositions on pediments, figures in high relief tend to detach themselves from the background as if they were statues. Both characteristics have their counterparts in the great ornamental sculpture decorating Greek temples. True low relief is met in friezes found on beam facings. The mythological repertoire usually provided the craftsmen with their subjects. But reliefs appear to have become especially common in funerary art, as witnessed by, for example, the Tarquinia slabs ornamented with scenes and friezes belonging traditionally to the 'Orientalizing' repertoire (Plate 58); the sepulchral stelai of Volterra, Fiesole and Bologna from the sixth to the beginning of the fourth century and picturing the dead person, his surroundings or his journey to the underworld; the scenes on the cippi and Archaic urns from Chiusi (Plate 42), with realistic subjects such as funerals, banquets, dances and athletic games; the mythological, infernal and decorative compositions sculptured on the walls of tombs, especially on the sides of stone sarcophagi (southern Etruria, Chiusi)[23] and of the alabaster (Volterra), terracotta (Chiusi) and travertine (Perugia) cinerary urns produced between the fourth and first centuries B.C. (Plate 43).[24] Of especial importance is the working of sheet bronze with embossed decorations for the ornamentation of furniture, shields, chariots, vases and candelabra; this began during the Orientalizing period and flourished in the course of the sixth century: the finds at a few rich tombs of the Perugia region are deservedly famous.[25] This same technique was applied on the minutely adorned situla of the Bologna Certosa (see Plate 92), which has been connected with a tradition known as 'Situla Art' belonging to the palaeo-Venetic and Alpine region.[26] A similar technique on objects of smaller proportions is met in precious metal vases and in goldwork. Mention should also be made of intaglios on ivory (e.g. Plate 85),[27] bone, etc., and of the very rich collection of seals in negative relief carved in hard stones. In all these more strictly decorative or 'applied' productions, figures and compositions derived from Greek mythology prevail.

Painting is represented by numerous monuments of conspicuous importance, an exceptional state of affairs for the classical world before late Hellenistic times.[28] These Etruscan documents are of especial importance because the original works of the great painters of Greece are almost all lost. The custom of painting the walls of underground tombs was especially prevalent at Tarquinia, but also occurs, though sporadically or less intensely, at Chiusi, Orvieto, Cerveteri, Vulci, Veii and elsewhere. Many of the paintings that have come to light in the last few centuries have now been lost or are irreparably damaged, but others remain in good condition. A large number of painted tombs have been recently discovered or rediscovered at Tarquinia by means of drillings made by the Lerici Foundation[29]; some of these paintings have been detached so as to preserve them from further deterioration.[30] Besides wall paintings we also possess a number of paintings on terracotta slabs which were originally fitted together to line and decorate the inner walls of sacred buildings (as is almost certainly the case with those found in the Portonaccio sanctuary at Veii) and tombs (such as the Cerveteri groups: see Plate 59). Finally, in a few isolated cases, the sides of sarcophagi and urns feature painted decorations instead of reliefs: the most famous and best-preserved example is the 'Amazon' sarcophagus from Tarquinia, now in the Museo Archeologico at Florence. The subject-matter of these paintings was originally purely decorative (like those of Orientalizing inspiration) or taken from Greek mythological themes. The great Archaic funerary paintings of the sixth and fifth centuries at Tarquinia and Chiusi, however, reproduce funeral scenes, with banquets, dancing and circus games (see Plates 46, 60, and 90), or, more generally, scenes from everyday life (hunting, fishing, etc.). After the fifth century, the prevailing subjects consist of scenes from beyond the grave, journeys to the underworld, infernal banquets, etc., together with mythological compositions (Orvieto, Tarquinia, Vulci); stress was given to the portrayal of the dead person's features.

Etruscan painted pottery[31] appears more or less faithfully to imitate Greek pottery, very popular in Etruria, especially during the Archaic period. East Greek craftsmen probably worked in the cities of Etruria during the sixth century and formed local schools: this occurred in the case of the production of the 'Caeretan hydriae', decorated with lively mythological themes. Ceramic workshops that imitated red-figured Attic pottery were also highly productive during the fourth century, parallel to the workshops that flourished in southern Italy. Draughtsmanship appears to be even more directly inspired by Greek models: it is manifested in engravings on the backs of mirrors (Plates 34, 36, and 37) and on bronze cists, and often exhibits a high degree of workmanship. Owing to their principally antiquarian interest, bronzes, ceramics and jewellery are more fully treated in the chapter dealing with aspects of Etruscan life (pp. 177 ff. and 185 ff.).

The Etruscans

The problem of Etruscan art

Having considered the various categories of artistic monuments, we are now faced with a greater problem, indeed the problem *par excellence*: that of their aesthetic meaning. Many of the works in our possession obviously cannot be considered as original creations: they belong to the products of traditional craftsmanship, and only distantly reflect the main trends in the history of art. There are, however, some monuments or groups of monuments where subjective impressions and objective considerations lead us to detect the hallmark of a more or less distinct artistic personality. The problem lies in determining to what extent this possibility corresponds to reality; that is, whether in these cases we are really faced with original creations, great or small, or whether these are still straightforward imitations of objects now lost; and, in that case, where we could expect to find the originals.

The first fact to come to our notice is that the very great majority of the themes, types and motifs of Etruria's artistic production find their antecedents and inspiration in Greek models. This dependence extended, broadly speaking, to stylistic forms too. As a result, the development of Etruscan art, from the beginnings of the Archaic period down to late Hellenistic times, mainly echoed the various phases of development undergone by Greek art. But there are differences: Etruria ignored certain Greek motifs, while developing others which met with little popularity in Greece or which belonged to styles that had already been discarded. There are also indications of attitudes foreign or even opposed to the figurative conceptions of the Greek world.

We should ask ourselves to what extent Etruscan artists meant to react against the dominant formulas from Greece with original solutions. We should then seek to establish whether, in realizing an individual artistic vision, they created the conditions for the growth of local traditions distinct from those of Greece, and how widely and for how long these traditions were able to impose themselves. On the other hand, if we accept the growth of autonomous trends in Etruscan art, it becomes necessary to decide whether such trends were ephemeral and unrelated or whether a connection existed between them; and whether a hypothetical 'constant' in the tendencies of Etruscan taste down the centuries should be attributed to historical continuity or whether it corresponded to a deep-seated predisposition in the Etruscan mind for ways of expression different from those of the Greeks. All these questions may, in the end, be gathered into one: to what extent and in what sense can one speak of 'Etruscan art'? [32]

Nineteenth-century critics, largely dominated by classical or natural-

166

istic preconceptions, tended on the whole to answer this question in the negative. For them, Etruscan productions were to be regarded as provincial manifestations of Greek art, crude and aesthetically valueless. All finds of any value made in Etruria were at once attributed to Greek artists. But the new directions taken by art history and aesthetic criticism at the beginning of the twentieth century, particularly as a result of the work of A. Riegl, allowed full validity of expression to artistic experiences outside the classical orbit and opened the way to the comprehension of stylistic phenomena of the ancient world that had hitherto been misjudged, as in the case of the artistic production of Etruria. From the analysis of individual works of art recently discovered (e.g. the Apollo of Veii: see Plate 61) or rediscovered in the light of a new aesthetic sensibility (e.g. the 'Capitoline Brutus': see Plate 75), the originality of Etruscan art and its independence from that of Greece were more or less cautiously affirmed, on the grounds of its different, unmistakable vision of form, evident even in imitations of Greek types and motifs. It was even suggested that a peculiar disposition of the Italic peoples (including therefore not only the Etruscans but also, though later, the Romans) led them to conceive reality according to 'illusionistic', 'inorganic', immediate and strongly individualized images, in contrast to the 'naturalistic', 'organic', 'typal' vision of Greek art – a disposition which G. Kaschnitz Weinberg tried to define with his concept of 'structure'. A number of justified criticisms have been made of these points of view. More recently, the statement has even been made (by R. Bianchi Bandinelli) that there are no true works of art in Etruria except those under the direct influence of Greek forms, and that Etrusco-Italic 'originality' was no more than the occasional and ephemeral manifestation of a colourful popular craftsmanship incapable of producing a true artistic tradition.

For the most part, then, the problem remains unsolved. This is perhaps because it has been wrongly formulated, by those who deny the originality of Etruscan art as well as those who uphold it. For Etruscan art has been generally considered as a whole, ignoring the fact that it embraces many types, over a period of at least seven centuries, and that the transformations that took place in the course of such a long span of time (from proto-history to the beginnings of the Roman Empire) do not merely concern Etruria and Greece but have decisive bearings on the whole development of ancient art. It is obvious that perspectives must vary according to the times; it would therefore seem more logical, and closer to the concrete reality of history, to examine the problem of 'Etruscan art' by referring to the situation in each period rather than conducting an abstract search for an all-round solution.

We shall find that at first, during the eighth and seventh centuries,

167

artistic activity in the cities of Etruria developed parallel to that of other Mediterranean countries, including Greece, in a complex interplay of themes of prehistoric origin (particularly evident in the lively realism displayed by the smaller products of the plastic arts) and of oriental influences which characterize that phase in the history of decoration which we call 'Orientalizing'. Clearly for this period it would not be correct to speak of subordination to Greek art. It would be better to say that, parallel with Greece, Etruria participated, from its western peripheral position, in one of the last elaborations of an ancient Mediterranean artistic experience. But with the exception of a few traces of originality in the plastic funerary arts (as in the expressive heads of the Chiusi canopic urns) there is no sign of the burgeoning of local or national artistic traditions. This is in fact where the difference from Greece lies, a difference that was to have far-reaching repercussions, for, at this crucial age, Greece, with its vigorous creative spirit, was to leave the formulas of the old world far behind and open a new chapter in the history of world art.

Unsupported by a tradition of its own, Etruria was fatally destined to be absorbed into the orbit of Greek artistic experience. For the latter's power of attraction did not reside only in the intrinsic superiority of its aesthetic values: it owed much to its widespread implantation in the Greek colonies of Sicily and the Italian mainland. This took place effectively from the beginning of the sixth century, and it is most likely that Archaic Greece influenced the arts of Etruria (and its religion, institutions, music, dress, etc.) not merely through the importation of objects and models, but also through the activity of Greek craftsmen in Etruscan cities. But it is just during this period (from the sixth century to the first decades of the fifth) that the artistic production of Etruria burst into a wonderful, and even, in certain aspects, unsurpassed, flowering, especially in temple architecture, in the plastic arts, in bronzes, in painting and in the 'minor' arts; a very large number of works appear, refined in technique, of high stylistic value and not without a certain peculiar 'character' that makes them often recognizable as Etruscan or of Etruscan inspiration. The original dilemma between dependence or independence now acquires overtones that render it all the more delicate as the facts seem to lead towards contradictory judgements, thus explaining the hesitancies of modern critics: these works of art, though 'Etruscan', do not in fact cease to be 'Greek' – a statement that may at first seem paradoxical, but which clearly is not, once we have freed ourselves of the notion of 'national art', which is not applicable to this particular case.

We should also keep in mind the fact that Greek Archaic art does not represent a rigidly unitary or stylistically coherent phenomenon; it is more the result of the local elaborations of many and varied scattered centres, with changing, lively and multiple currents crossing and re-crossing each other in all directions. This essentially regional frame-work also included territories that were partially hellenized, and even non-Greek but under the influence of the civilization of Greece: e.g. Cyprus, Lycia, Caria, Lydia and Phrygia in the Near East, Macedonia and Thrace in the north, Etruria in the west. These countries were not merely receptive 'provinces' in the elaboration of Archaic art, passively submitting to the stamp of the Greek creative genius; they themselves participated as 'regions' of a vast civilized community, according to their own particular circumstances, requirements and capabilities, and, therefore, they displayed characteristics of their own within the greater compass of a peri-Hellenic unity. In the case of Etruria, an outline of the 'regional' artistic peculiarities of the Archaic period may be traced in the following principal traits: (1) the existence of religious and funerary requirements predisposing the figurative arts to a concrete, immediate and realistic representation of reality[33]; (2) the noticeable persistence of formal patterns, techniques and traditions belonging to the earlier 'Mediterranean' and Orientalizing phase; (3) the direct and very close relations with the artistic experience of the East Greek world, i.e. of the coastal and island centres of Aeolis and Ionia in western Asia Minor, relations that were close enough from the middle of the sixth century to the beginning of the fifth for the figurative arts of Etruria to follow much the same patterns as those of the East Greek world and create what in fact has come to be known as Ionic-Etruscan art; (4) the local appearance of schools and artistic personalities with a high standard of achievement (bronze-casters at Vulci and Perugia, painters like the Master of the Tomb of the Baron at Tarquinia, modellers in terracotta at Veii like the creator of the Apollo and his followers, etc.); it would be difficult to deny these artists an authentic, original and, at times, powerful creative genius.

A radical change occurred during the first half of the fifth century. Greece passed from Archaic to classical art by a process of fundamental importance to the history of human civilization. But the activity of the great Greek masters tended to become more closely knit from a stylistic point of view and to acquire a more 'national' character, concentrating more and more around Athens and the Peloponnesian cities. At the same time, the peripheral regions declined, for reasons of a political and economic order. Etruria was left isolated. The classical spirit, the result of an unrepeatable and inimitable moment, found no echo in Etruria, where, among other things, the favourable historical conditions that encouraged the artistic flowering of Archaic times came to an end, bringing in their wake a long period of depression and decadence.

The Etruscans

Thus, over the whole of the fifth century and well into the fourth, we witness the persistence of patterns and formulas belonging to the Archaic tradition or inspired by Greek art of the 'Severe' style, i.e. of that transient stage between archaism and classicism. The lingering of outmoded styles in marginal areas (as, for example, in the contemporary 'Sub-Archaic' art of Cyprus[34]) became clearly manifest. The penetration of classical influences was tentative and sporadic. In this atmosphere, deprived of a unitary and established tradition such as had existed previously, artistic vitality only broke out in small, ephemeral bursts of expressive originality. The activity of bronze craftsmen, however, continued as vigorously as before.

Contact was re-established between the artistic worlds of Greece and Etruria after the fourth century B.C., and it continued throughout the Hellenistic period, finally merging in the triumphal victory of Hellenism in Roman Italy at the end of the Republic and the beginning of the Empire. But the attitude of Etruscan artists towards the products of Greece no longer appears the same as in Archaic times. We can no longer speak of the original working out of a common inheritance: it is now the imitation of 'foreign' models, more or less faithfully and successfully reproduced. Not only forms and single typological patterns are taken over, but whole compositions for the decoration of buildings and objects, especially in the case of paintings. For this last phase, the concept expressed by certain modern critics, namely that of Etruria as a 'province' of the Greek world – which means the denial of all artistic originality – might seem to be justified.

Account should be taken, however, of another aspect, quite different in order and importance, of the figurative activity of the Etruscans during the Hellenistic age. In single works of art or groups of monuments (especially funerary monuments), there appeared stylistic patterns and solutions that presented a clear contrast with classical taste: compact structures with geometric tendencies, 'unfinished' forms, disproportions, exasperations in the treatment of certain expressive details, etc. We may well ask if and to what extent these manifestations are to be explained as the handing down by craftsmen of remote Archaic formulas, survivals favoured by the static quality of the Etruscan ritual, or as popular improvisations of no consequence, or even as the chance effects of a falling-off in the quality of manual techniques. But it is also possible that they may be the reflections, however indirect, of the activity of artists who, by adopting age-old local conventions and reacting against Greek models according to their temperament, were seeking new forms of expression.

This hypothesis turns to certainty as far as the art of portraiture is concerned. For Etruscan portraiture offers us many authentic and

170

original works of art (large bronzes, paintings, etc.) and innumerable secondary products (sarcophagus lids, terracottas) which witness in their turn the formation of a lasting local tradition centred on the activity of the great masters of the craft. In contrast with the Greek portrait (its original inspiration in the fourth century, and occasionally its model in Hellenistic times), the Etruscan portrait tends to seek a maximum of expressive concreteness for a person's features and, in a sense, for individual 'character', neglecting the organic coherence of natural forms but stressing their essential elements by means of a simple, rough, discontinuous and, at times, violent use of lines and masses. We may well say that a new style was born, a new artistic tradition independent of the Greek world: a tradition which is 'Etruscan', but which is also more generically 'Italic', for its seeds went on being cultivated, after the decline of Etruria as a nation, by the art of Roman Italy and of the Western world under the empire. Such an 'expressionist' view of reality – particularly manifest in the portrait but present in other art forms as well – was to live in the popular art currents of the first centuries of the empire, and spread to the provincial art of Europe to break out impetuously as the great courtly art of the end of the second and the third centuries A.D.; it was destined to become one of the most significant contributions to the artistic inheritance of late Imperial and medieval times.[35]

CHAPTER 9 **Life and Customs**

Monuments as a source of information

However important our knowledge of the cultural life of a people as revealed by the manifestations of its religious feelings, of its thought, of its organizing abilities and artistic attitudes, we shall never really come close to it or understand its psychology unless we are able to visualize and understand the various aspects of its everyday life, to enter its houses, to glimpse it in its familiar surroundings and discover its traditions and customs.[1]

There is no doubt that literature, especially in such forms as comedy, satire, letters, etc., is irreplaceable as a source of information on the private life and habits of ancient peoples. The complete loss of Etruscan literature (if indeed there ever existed a literature with 'homely' or private themes, like the Roman satire or epistle) deprives us of a valuable source for the reconstruction of the family life and customs of ancient Etruria.

But besides literary sources there are also monumental, or archaeological, sources: on the one hand, objects actually preserved in the tombs, as well as the character, the peculiarities, the very arrangement of the tombs, and also the few remains we have from settlement sites; on the other, figured works of art reproducing actual scenes from contemporary life. As far as this type of evidence is concerned, Etruria is in an exceptionally privileged position. We have already referred to the deep-rooted tradition of creating life-like settings around the dead in their tombs, settings as authentic and as sumptuous as possible, with jewellery, weapons, tools, household articles. Thanks to this tradition, excavations of Etruscan cemeteries have provided us with ample and direct sources of information on the personal clothing, the weapons, the articles of everyday life and the objects that furnished the home. Our only limitation in this field, unfortunately of fundamental importance, is the almost total disappearance of objects made of perishable materials such as cloth, leather, wicker or wood. The climate of Italy has prevented the survival of these objects in the great majority of cases: hence the gaps in the 'ethnography' of ancient Etruria. Only exceptionally, as in the case of tombs at Cerveteri, Bisenzio, and Vulci, have we been able to recover wooden tools and pieces of furniture, wicker baskets,

172

pieces of leather ornaments, etc. We have also been able to find a few small pieces of cloth or imprints of cloth on oxidized bronze.[2]

Figured monuments allow us to see the objects that have survived as they were actually used in everyday life, and they complete the picture for us by including those that have perished. Tomb paintings in particular have a documentary value surpassing that normally offered by artistic representations left by the classical world, with the exception of a few 'popular' Roman frescoes and reliefs, which perhaps derive their naïve realism and directness of expression from the tradition of Etrusco-Italic art. In the Greek world, as early as the Archaic period, man played the preponderant or even exclusive role, with a background reduced to a few necessary elements strictly relevant to the human form, frequently rendered symbolically or by simple allusive touches. With the Etruscans, however, as with Oriental peoples, artistic composition had a descriptive and narrative character and indulged in background detail. That is why tomb paintings and sculptures introduce to us, plunge us into the very heart of, a past reality. And though these reproductions appear naïve and stylized in form and technique, they are nevertheless almost photographically faithful to the chosen subject. If one can read them, in spite of the difficulties of their formal language, and knows how to 'translate' them (there is often no need for a translation), one can, thanks to these monuments, witness banquets, dances, games, etc., as they unfolded 2,500 years ago. And their general pictorial accuracy is complemented by a close accuracy to details of furniture and dress.

The archaeological evidence for Etruscan life covers the whole development of its history, from its beginnings to the threshold of imperial Rome. In the case of figured monuments, the richest crop is yielded by the golden age of Etruscan civilization, i.e. the sixth and fifth centuries B.C., to which the greatest number of painted tombs belong. We shall therefore refer principally to this period, during which the Etruscan way of life was formed and defined. But we shall also take into account variations that took place through the centuries, especially where dress is concerned. It should be understood that the evidence supplied by monuments concerns principally the higher or well-to-do strata of society, those classes whose financial means and requirements for prestige or aristocratic pride permitted and imposed the building, decoration and furnishing of imposing and lasting funerary monuments.

The setting: the Etruscan town and house

We should begin the study of the social and private life of the Etruscans by stating that it would be historically inconsistent to imagine its setting as something contrasting with that of the contemporary Greeks or, for that matter, of the other evolved peoples of the Italy of the time, equally imbued with Greek culture. Geographically and historically, the Etruscan experience belonged to this same world, and although it cannot be denied that Etruria had traditions of its own, woven into its own peculiar complex of beliefs and practices, the fundamental structure of its organization, techniques, habits and fashions cannot be detached from that of its neighbours. One of the commonest errors into which hasty amateur historians and even the occasional professional tend to fall is to attribute to the Etruscans an original conception of town-planning or a unique experiment in hydraulics, to speak of 'Etruscan technology' in the working of metals, or of 'Etruscan medicine', 'Etruscan dress', etc. as if these aspects of knowledge and life were in effect exclusive or typical to Etruscan civilization when in fact they formed part of the common inheritance of a much larger world, and were for the most part little more than provincial reflexes of the inventions and conquests of Greek civilization.

As an example, we may look at the problem of the genesis and development of urban centres, basic to the social, political, economic and cultural way of life of the Etruscans. The city may be said to have acquired in Etruria a sacred meaning of its own, and it followed, in theory at least, ritual dictates concerning its foundation, its delimitation and the placing of its gates, streets and sacred buildings.[3] Nevertheless it is obvious that the Etruscan urban system (as against the prehistoric system of scattered dwellings and villages) is derived from Near Eastern and Greek models, and that it developed at the same time as the first Greek colonization of Italy. The town plan with streets crossing at right angles and directed towards definite points of the compass has frequently been attributed to the Etruscans, on the grounds not so much of what ancient sources have to say (they are far from explicit on this point) as of the examples given by Marzabotto, Capua, Pompeii, etc. In fact, such a plan constitutes one of the most typical manifestations of Greek town-planning: it spread westwards as early as the Archaic period and came to be refashioned with new, more rigorous forms during the fifth century, when it became consecrated by tradition and known as 'Hippodamean' architecture.[4] The development of Rome as the result of the fusion of several primitive villages rising on a number of hills (though this too cannot be demonstrated historically with absolute certainty[5]) suggests an analogous progressive growth for the cities of Etruria, via the grouping of single prehistoric or protohistoric hamlets. This process may have occurred in the course of the Villanovan period – during a proto-urban phase, mirrored perhaps at Bologna[6] – or maybe even later, especially in northern Etruria. At the

174

same time, the siting of major cities on clearly delimited heights and the presence of Iron Age cemeteries all round them seems to suggest a unitary structure from their very beginnings, enlarged occasionally by a constellation of minor, suburban agglomerations. At any rate, extensive city walls make their appearance from the Archaic period,[7] and it is possible that the unitary character of Etruscan cities may have been precociously represented by their political, religious and commercial centres (corresponding to the Greek 'agora'), limited largely to the communal aspects of everyday life.[8]

Let us now examine the private house and some of the main questions which it raises. Discussions on the shape and plan of the Etruscan house have been many: all too often it has been considered as an abstract architectural entity, as a type, reproducing substantially a single original plan, as in the case of the so-called 'Pompeian' house.[9] In actual fact, the numerous documents that may be used in the reconstruction of Etruscan private dwellings offer considerable variations, variations that do not merely occur in the evolutionary direction, i.e. along the successive phases of the Etruscan civilization. Direct evidence is provided by the foundations of houses found in many parts of Etruria, and especially at Marzabotto near Bologna (where an entire residential centre may be seen) and at Vetulonia, Tarquinia, Veii, and lately also at Roselle. From the very beginnings of Etruscan civilization, the house with rectilinear plan tended to replace everywhere the ancient round or oval dwellings of Italian prehistory: a relic of the earliest phase of this movement is the 'hut-urn' of the Villanovan culture. The belief that the dead man's life continued in the grave was chiefly responsible for the fact that tombs and urns were made to look like houses; and these were at times imitated down to the smallest detail of architecture and furnishing (Plates 78–83). The rock-cut tombs discovered in the Cerveteri cemetery provide us with valuable evidence of the various types of interior by giving us the lay-out and general arrangement of the rooms, the decoration of doors, windows and ceilings, and even the furniture (round tables or hampers, stools, beds, etc.). Details of the external architecture of the house may be learned from the rock sepulchres of the tombs of inland Etruria, at Blera, Norchia, and Castel d'Asso. As for the house as a whole, especially in its later phases, useful information may be gathered from a number of cinerary urns found at Chiusi (Plate 79).

The house originally consisted of a rectangular building comprising a single room, protected by a double-sloped roof set at a low pitch. This is, in its simplest form, the type of house which seems to have spread via the land route, and which forms the basis of the Mycenaean *megaron* and of the Greek temple. At a very early stage, however, it grows richer

175

and more complex by the addition of external elements with porticoes, or by an increase in the number of rooms. The sixth-century tombs at Cerveteri have in their most usual form a plan that may to some extent be considered the ancestor of the Italic or 'Pompeian' house: an un-roofed entrance hall (corresponding to the corridor in the tomb), a small courtyard (the future atrium?) on to which open two lateral rooms, and, at the back, the main body of the house; this consists of a transverse passage or transept with coffered ceiling or gabled roof, which in its turn gives access to one, two or three rooms covered by a gabled roof. The three-roomed type became the most usual and its resemblance to the Etruscan three-cell temple is significant. The transverse passage may correspond on the one hand to the porticoed forecourt of the temple, on the other to the *alae* of the Pompeian house; the back rooms are thought to be preserved in the three rooms of the typical Pompeian house. It is worth noting that the transverse vestibule occasionally assumed the form of a portico supported by pilasters and columns. There is no lack of variants, which may take the form of circular or semicircular rooms or vestibules roofed with radially set beams.

Ancient sources appear to agree in attributing the invention of the atrium to the Etruscans: the very word *atrium* is said to be of Etruscan origin, and in fact the form *aθre* does occur in an Etruscan text. The atrium does not, however, appear in models of tombs belonging to the Archaic period; it only becomes recognizable in later monuments, as in a rock-cut tomb at Tarquinia (Tomba della Mercareccia; see Plate 1), where the first room has a ceiling shaped like the roof of an atrium, or in a small urn from Chiusi now in the Berlin Museum. More complex and architecturally more evolved types are attested by an urn in the Museo Archeologico at Florence modelled in the shape of a small building with arched doorway and two floors, and an urn from Chiusi featuring on its first floor a veranda supported by columns. It is very doubtful whether the houses at Marzabotto (joined together into *insulae*) ever possessed upper storeys.

We have referred to the furniture, which must have been rather limited, as in all civilizations of the ancient world.[10] Funerary paintings and sculptures depict beds with ornamental legs, cushions and covers painted or embroidered in lively colours and geometric patterns, rectangular or circular tables, throne-shaped chairs, stools, foot-rests, etc. A typical piece is the wicker or wooden chair with a round seat and a wide splayed back found sculptured in a few Cerveteri tombs or reproduced in bronze among objects in grave-groups from Chiusi and Palestrina; it also survives in marble in that curious late monument with Archaic affinities known as the 'Corsini chair'.[11] Its shape lives on to reappear in provincial figured monuments belonging to Roman Imperial times and in European popular craft.

Bronze candelabra too may be included amongst household objects; many have come down to us as actual specimens or reproduced in paintings. Some are elongated in form and surmounted by a statuette and tips in the shape of a bird's beak in which candles or torches were fixed (but see also Plate 88). We also possess many oil candelabra with a small dish at the top, meant to hang from the ceiling, such as the famous figured candelabrum of Cortona (Plate 84).

We ought to mention too the whole series of bronze or terracotta containers, ranging from large archaic *lebetes* (cauldrons), supported on tripods or on circular pedestals, to vases imported from Greece or their Etruscan imitations, such as *amphorae*, kraters (for wine; e.g. Plate 74), *hydriae* (with three handles, for water), jugs, pails, pans, plates, goblets, chalices, glasses, perfume vases in the shape of animals, etc. Vases made of precious metals – gold, silver or silver-gilt – must naturally have been rarer; they occasionally appear reproduced in paintings. Examples in our possession have mostly been found within graves belonging to the Orientalizing period.

The oldest pottery vessels (ninth to sixth century) were made of unpurified clay (impasto) and have a stick-burnished surface: they vary in colour (black, brown, red or yellow) and in shape. They occasionally imitate metal types, and are found ornamented with applied decoration, incisions or painting. From the seventh century onwards, Greek influence helped to spread the use of potter's clay, with figured and Geometric painted decoration: Proto-Corinthian, Corinthian, Ionic, Rhodian, Laconian, Chalcidian and Attic vases were imported in large quantities and imitated locally. During the second half of the sixth century and throughout the whole of the fifth, Attic pottery alone was imported, first black-figured vases and then red-figured. A type of native pottery, bucchero (probably derived from impasto), dominates in Etruria from the end of the seventh century to the beginning of the fifth, with many varied forms. Bucchero pottery is characterized by the polished surface of its black or grey clay (see Plate 87). The fourth century witnessed the spread of red-figured ware in imitation of the vases of Attica and of the Greek cities of southern Italy: the most important local school belongs to the Faliscan territory, but others are known at Vulci, Chiusi, Perugia, Volterra, etc. At a later period there is a predominance of vases that are glazed in black and red, with decorative elements or figures stamped or in relief. From this late type of pottery was developed the great vase industry of Arezzo, which was to flourish at the beginning of the Empire to give rise to the characteristic ware of the Roman world, the so-called *terra sigillata*. Besides these metal and clay vessels, we should also make a passing reference to vases made of ivory, alabaster, glass paste (imported or imitated from the Near East) and wood, though it is only exceptionally that specimens made of wood have survived.

One monument, unique in the ancient world, has provided us with an exceptional picture of all the objects that went to furnish a home: furniture, instruments, everyday objects, etc. This is the 'Tomb of the Stuccoes' or of 'the Reliefs' at Cerveteri (see Plate 82). It consists of a large chamber, shaped to resemble the inside of a house, along the walls of which the dead were arranged in niches furnished with beds. The surface of the walls and pillars is decorated with painted stucco reliefs representing objects that are supposed to be hanging on them. Among these we can recognize weapons (helmets, shields, swords, greaves), vases, flower wreaths, a fan, a pilgrim's bag, a satchel, kitchen knives, spits, tools (axe, tongs, knife), a round table, ropes, wooden trays, sticks, etc.[12] The general effect is very striking. We are filled with wonder at the resemblance, or rather the identity, of some of these objects belonging to the third and second centuries B.C. with those in use today; e.g. the rectangular wooden kitchen trays or the satchel. This picture of everyday life is filled out by the objects found in the graves of many Etruscan cemeteries, both for weapons and for instruments. Bronze fans, similar to the one found reproduced in stucco in the Tomb of the Reliefs or pictured on other Etruscan monuments (as in the paintings of the Bruschi Tomb or in the Tomb of the Shields at Tarquinia) have been discovered in the 'Tumulus of the Fans' at Populonia. Objects belonging to the *mundus*, i.e. to the requirements of feminine toilet, should also be added to this list: *cistae*, bronze mirrors, small wooden boxes in the shape of animals for cosmetics, etc.

Aspects of Etruscan life

The reconstruction of the life led in the houses of the rich does not present great difficulties. We have already referred to the place of woman in the home: how she participated in banquets and feasts on a footing of perfect equality with men. During the Archaic period, men and women feasted stretched out on the same couch: Aristotle is probably referring to this custom when he comments (*Ath. Pol.*, 1, 23, d): 'The Etruscans take their food in the company of their women, lying under the same mantle'. This settlement has also been supposed to refer to a mistaken interpretation of some sarcophagi on which husband and wife appear lying under a mantle, a symbol of marriage. The Etruscan marriage ceremony did in fact include the rite (also found in present-day Jewish custom) of covering the bride and bridegroom with a veil: this is borne out by the relief on a small urn from Chiusi (see Plate 89), whose interpretation cannot be mistaken. But it is possible that a veil may have been used also on the convivial couch. We presume that the Greeks tended to be hostile to the Etruscans and to misunderstand them, probably as a result of ancient political rivalries that made them find cause for scandal in the formal liberty enjoyed by Etruscan women, which was so unlike, at least for the classical period, the segregation that was the lot of the Greek woman. It was easy, almost natural, therefore, to attribute to Etruscan women the character and behaviour of the *hetaerae*, the only women in Greece who took part in banquets with men. Thus, with that ease with which the classical world accepted and transmitted unchecked information (especially on 'barbarian' customs) to be used almost as literary commonplaces, were born and spread those libellous statements on Etruscan licentiousness insisted upon by Athenaeus (IV, 153, d; VII, 517 ff.) and re-echoed even by Plautus (*Cistellaria*, II, 3, 20 ff.). After the fifth or fourth century, women at banquets no longer lay on couches like the men, but were seated, following the custom which was to remain firmly established throughout the Roman world. Paintings of banquets with several beds (generally three: hence the Roman *triclinium*), as found in the Tombs of the Leopards and of the Triclinium, both at Tarquinia, are full of natural and joyful simplicity. There are also a number of banquets in the Greek style, men only being present, culminating at times in abandoned orgies accompanied by dances and abundant libations (Tomb of the Inscriptions, Tarquinia). Solemn banquets, like other festivities and important occasions (e.g. games, funerals, etc.), were regularly accompanied by music and dancing.

A noteworthy series of paintings deals with games and entertainments (Tombs of the Augurs, the Chariots, the Olympic Games, the Funeral Couch and Francesca Giustiniani at Tarquinia, painted and relief tombs at Chiusi).[13] It is evident that Greek influence dominates this aspect of Etruscan life, but the agonistic and professional character of Greek games and matches seems to give way to the spectacular. Nothing is more interesting or suggestive in this respect than the Tomb of the Chariots at Tarquinia, where the artist has pictured a large sports field or circus bisected along its two axes, the long and the short, showing the arena and the wooden stands on which spectators are sitting. In the arena we see charioteers in their chariots, horsemen, wrestlers and boxers, vaulters with and without pole, an armed runner, umpires and various other characters. On the stands, spectators of both sexes take the liveliest interest in the course of the games, shown by the impassioned expressions on their faces. Quite possibly members of the most illustrious families took part in these sports. The Etruscan game of the Truia (*ludus Troiae*) is worth mentioning in this respect: it consisted of a horse race along an intricate course shaped like a maze (as borne out by a graffito on an Archaic Etruscan vase), and we know that it was still performed as an exercise for Roman youths at the beginning of the Empire.[14] Of a more popular character, the various activities of the showman (acrobatics, trick riding, clowning) are expressively portrayed in paintings at the Tomb of the Jugglers at Tarquinia and the Tomb of the Monkey at Chiusi. Lastly we must mention a bloodier kind of sport in which it is possible to recognize a forerunner of the Roman gladiatorial combats; these were in any case believed by ancient tradition to be of Etruscan origin (Athenaeus, IV, 153 f.) and certainly reached Rome by way of Campania, which had early come under the influence of Etruria. They probably owe their origin to a funeral rite, an attenuation of the human sacrifices that in many primitive civilizations accompany the death of princes or the illustrious; for in blood fights the stronger or the abler of the contestants has a chance of survival. A match of this kind is reproduced in the Tomb of the Augurs at Tarquinia (Plate 90): a masked figure, designated by the name of φersu (corresponding to the Latin *persona*, 'masked figure'), with a hood and a ferocious dog on the leash, fights a semi-naked adversary armed with a cudgel but with a sack over his head. The latter is presumably a man condemned to death, fighting an uneven battle; but if he is able to hit his opponent's dog with his cudgel, he will have the other at his mercy.[15]

Economic and technical achievements

It is far from easy to reconstruct the various aspects of the economic life of ancient Etruria, especially as in the majority of cases we only possess documents that are vague or indirect. It is chiefly by comparison with the Greek and Roman worlds that we derive what knowledge we have. It may be supposed that, to begin with, the resources of the inhabitants were predominantly agricultural and pastoral. Soon, at least, in some areas, they must have been transformed by the exploitation of mineral riches and integrated later by the development of a land and sea communication system.

A sufficiently accurate picture of Etruscan production during the last phase of the nation's history is given by the well-known passage in Livy (XXVIII, 45) listing the contributions that the principal annexed or federated Etruscan cities made to Scipio Africanus's oversea expedition during the second Punic war. Here is the list of loans, drawn up according to each district's resources:

Caere (Cerveteri):	corn and other foodstuffs
Tarquinii (Tarquinia):	sail-cloth
Rusellae (Roselle):	corn and timber for ship building
Populonia:	iron
Clusium (Chiusi):	corn and timber
Perusia (Perugia):	corn and timber
Arretium (Arezzo):	corn, weapons and wrought tools
Volaterrae (Volterra):	corn and pitch

We can make out, clearly defined within the central and southern zones, the agricultural districts (Cerveteri, Roselle, Chiusi, Perugia, Arezzo, Volterra), some of which were also exploiting the last remnants of the large forests that once covered the area; Populonia on the other hand appears as an iron-working centre, and Arezzo as an industrial city.

The metal-rich area is mainly situated within the territories of Vetulonia (with its metalliferous hills) and Populonia (which included the island of Elba). To these, we should add the Tolfa massif, where there are traces of abandoned ancient mines. In these areas, the extraction of metals (copper, iron and, to a lesser extent, lead and silver) may have begun as far back as prehistoric times, and was practised systematically from the beginnings of the Iron Age. Its bearing upon the history of Archaic Etruria is very great indeed: in a sense, as we have seen, it has been a determining factor in the growth of the nation. The very development of the coastal cities seems to be connected with the exploitation of mineral resources, and the continuous pressure and menace of the Greeks on the coasts of Etruria is a sign of the importance attached to the possession of the mining districts, to being able to influence them, or simply to being in their neighbourhood. We know nothing of the technical aspects of extraction and the first working of the ores except meagre data provided by archaeological evidence (shafts in certain parts of the metal-bearing hills, tools found in them, slag produced by the smelting of iron around Populonia). A few ancient sources also tell us, for example, that Populonia was the first centre for the smelting of metal extracted from the Elba mines, and for brokerage and distribution, but no further treatment seems to have taken place there.[16] Etruscan production was largely determined by the abundance of mineral ores: the quantities of weapons, tools, and domestic objects in bronze and iron found in graves prove this. Particularly noteworthy is the artistic production of manufactured objects found at Vetulonia, Vulci, Bisenzio, Cortona and the neighbourhood of Perugia. Livy's source, quoted above, mentions also Arezzo, which

181

produced the famous Chimaera (see Plate 66). Etruscan iron and bronze were also worked in Campania, and it is probably from here that both the unworked metal and the finished products reached the Greek world (Diodorus Siculus, V, 13). Etruscan bronze trumpets were renowned in Greece, and a fragment of a tripod of the Vulci type has been found on the Acropolis at Athens.[17] Other aspects of industrial and craft production should not be overlooked: e.g. the textile and leather industries; Etruscan footwear was renowned and exported throughout the Mediterranean (Pollux, VII, 22, 86).

Etruscan technical achievements are also well illustrated by their skill in the search for water and its exploitation and transport. The search was performed by the *aquilices*, or water-diviners. Pliny (*Nat. Hist.*, III, 20, 120) mentions the canals dug by the Etruscans in the lower Po valley; and in fact drainage systems dating back to the pre-Roman era have been found on various sites of southern Etruria. These prove that hydraulic engineering was intensively applied to the reclamation and irrigation of land. Life in the marshy areas of the Maremma and of the lower Po valley cannot be explained unless malarial infection was not yet common during the golden age of Etruscan civilization; but malaria must in fact have helped to hasten the decline of many Etruscan coastal towns in late Hellenistic times.[18]

During the golden age of great international commerce, the bulk of trade consisted of exchanges in kind. But payments were also made in unworked copper (*aes rude*), and in wrought metal objects, Greek coins (struck after the seventh century B.C.) and probably also in silver, which was weighed in units originating from the eastern Mediterranean (called, improperly, the 'Persian foot', and equivalent to about 5·7 grams); these were to remain typical of the Etruscan system of weights. The minting of true silver and gold coinage began, especially at Populonia, from the middle of the fifth century under the influence of the Greek coinage of southern Italy and in accordance with the Etruscan and Chalcidian weight systems (see Plate 91). Bronze coins (either cast – *aes grave* – or struck) began to circulate much later – not earlier than the imposition of Roman hegemony at the end of the fourth century.[19]

Weapons and dress

Whatever its origin, the large bronze situla (a kind of pail) found in the vault of the Certosa of Bologna is a precious document on the life led in the cities of the Po valley, then under Etruscan influence, during the first half of the fifth century B.C. (see Plate 92).[20] Round the top band a remarkable military parade unfolds: horsemen armed with battle-axes, three infantry platoons belonging to different services, as shown by their armament, and a group of pioneers with axes. On the Etruscan art of war, tradition tells us but little. We know, however, that the primitive military organization of the Romans owes much to the Etruscans. At first, battles were fought on chariots, but after the sixth century only cavalry was used. The three infantry services of the Certosa situla remind one of the three Roman orders of the *velites*, the *principes* and the *triarii*.

As offensive weapons, the Etruscans had the heavy lance, whose point and ferrule were of iron or bronze; the light lance or javelin; the long sword, the use of which seems to have ceased as early as the Archaic period, a relic of the armaments of the late Bronze Age; the short sword; the curved sabre (*machaira*) in use from the sixth century onwards; the dagger; the battle-axe, of which the earliest examples were double-axes, and, as already stated, probably belonged to the armament of chiefs. Their defensive weapons were the bronze helmet, the shield, the cuirass and greaves. Primitive helmets have a crest or crown and cheek-pieces; but the use of Corinthian and Attic helmets spread quite early. The classic Etruscan bronze helmet is pear-shaped, sometimes with a crest of plumes; many specimens have been found in tombs: one has appeared as a votive offering in the Greek sanctuary of Olympia, bearing an inscription to Zeus which tells that it was dedicated by the Syracusan tyrant Hiero, as war-booty after the naval battle waged by the Greeks against the Etruscans in the vicinity of Cumae in 474 B.C. (Plate 16).[21] Cuirasses were originally made of cloth with attached discs or squares of sheet metal; later they were made entirely in bronze, either with separate parts or all of a piece, moulded to the muscles of the male torso. Round bronze shields appear in the Archaic period as well as later; the Certosa situla, however, also shows elliptical and squarish shields, probably made of wood or leather. Mention should be made of offensive and defensive cudgels, perhaps a relic of the ancient clubs used by primitive men; Archaic monuments show one or two examples, while a type of stick with a curved end, the *lituus*, tended to become more and more exclusively a mark of priesthood and as such passed on to the Roman world.

We come now to the clothes worn by Etruscan men and women: here again there is no direct evidence, if we except jewellery and other items made of non-perishable materials. But figured monuments provide us with a good number of detailed clues. Naturally, clothes are influenced by climate no less than by local traditions; but Greek prototypes had a determining influence on fashion too. Masculine semi-nudity, a typically Mediterranean custom, was still common in archaic Etruria: indeed the small figurines of the Villanovan period give many examples

183

of complete masculine and feminine nudity, though it is not possible to tell how far this corresponded to the habits of everyday life (in art, it is a good deal less frequent than in Greece). At any rate, in the full civilization of the sixth and fifth centuries men still went naked to the waist, especially in the intimacy of the home, though wearing at the same time elaborate footwear and pointed caps. This traditional usage is reflected in the 'heroic' dress worn by the banqueting dead portrayed on the carved lids of sarcophagi and urns of the Hellenistic period. Only slaves and athletes are shown completely naked, and then not always so. A tight-fitting jacket covering the whole trunk and derived from the bordered loin-cloth became the fashion during the last years of the sixth century. It was then superseded by the tunic, an imitation of the Greek *khiton*.

The second typical item of masculine attire was the mantle, made of a thicker, coloured cloth, which protected the upper part of the body from the cold; its use was already quite widespread during the Archaic period. As the items of masculine dress increased in number and the tradition of Mediterranean semi-nudity became progressively weaker, the mantle acquired an ever-growing importance until, enlarged and enriched with painted or embroidered decorations, it became the Etruscan national dress, the *tèbennos*, the direct ancestor of the Roman toga. Women and old people wore – without substantial variations from Archaic down to later times – a tunic shaped like a shift that reached down to the feet, of light material, pleated or decorated at the edges; over this a painted mantle of heavier cloth was worn. From about the end of the seventh century to the beginning of the fifth, materials with a net pattern that is thought to have been embroidered were used; these may be seen made into tunics (on a statuette from Cerveteri in the Capitoline Museum in Rome and on cinerary urns from Chiusi) or mantles (on the Certosa situla).

From the earliest times one is struck by the very special care and interest which Etruscans devoted to their footwear. The Archaic tombs at Bisenzio have yielded sandals in the shape of jointed wooden clogs with bronze reinforcements. Shoes could be of leather or of embroidered cloth. During the sixth century, the most typical form of shoe was raised behind the calf and curved upwards to a point at the front: these are the so-called *calcei repandi* of East Greek origin, some of whose characteristics still survive today in the *ciocie* of the mountainous regions of Central Italy. At a later period, high ankle-boots were still in use, together with low sandals. All these various forms passed, almost without change, to the Roman world.

For the head, a kind of dome-shaped cap in embroidered cloth was in use during the sixth century; this was worn by both men and women and many variants were common. It is the *tutulus* of Near Eastern, Ionic origin, and it became the typical Etruscan head-dress. Other current forms include a pointed or hooded cap worn by certain personages, priests and deities (as for instance by the above-mentioned *φersu* at the Tomb of the Augurs); a woollen or leather cap with a wide base and cylindrical crown (see Plates 37 and 39), worn by *haruspices* and attested in various monuments,[22] and, finally, a wide-brimmed hat in the Greek style (*pètasos*) that seems to have been particularly popular amongst the lowest classes (cf. the piper in the Tomb of the Monkey at Chiusi) and in the colder north (Certosa situla). Usually, however, both men and women went bare-headed, a custom that after the fifth century became very general.

At first men were bearded and wore their hair long, well over the shoulders; but from the late sixth century, young men were clean-shaven and had their hair cut short, thus following the Greek fashion. The beard disappeared altogether after the third century B.C., and did not again become fashionable in Italy till four hundred years later under the emperor Hadrian. In early times (from the eighth to the sixth century), women wore their hair long, knotted or plaited behind their backs; later they allowed it to fall in ringlets over their shoulders, until finally (in the sixth to fifth century) it was knotted into a crown over the head or gathered in a net or cap. The bleaching of hair was probably practised, for it seems to be attested by paintings in the Tomb of the Leopards at Tarquinia. During the fourth century, the prevalent hair-style allowed the hair to fall in ringlets over the cheeks; later, in the full Hellenistic period, women preferred to wear their hair tied in a knot at the back of the head, in the Greek style.

Jewellery played an important role in the attire of the Etruscans. Towards the end of the Bronze Age, the use of fibulas (safety-pins) spread widely throughout the Mediterranean world: they are amongst the most characteristic objects found in tombs belonging to the Iron Age. Those worn by men differ from those worn by women in that the bow is broken and serpentine in shape. Fibulas were generally made of bronze, though precious metals were also used; they were often richly adorned with paste jewellery or amber. Some specimens belonging to the Orientalizing period, such as the disc-shaped gold fibula of the Regolini-Galassi tomb, are huge and lavishly decorated. The use of fibulas became less popular during the sixth century and practically ceased after the fifth: they are only preserved by traditional costumes such as those worn by *haruspices*. Other types of jewellery include diadems, ear-pendants, necklaces, bracelets and rings (and see Plate 7). During the Orientalizing period, the lavishness with which they were used was almost barbaric; and the same may be said of the Hellenistic

185

age. The only time when jewellery was worn with elegant moderation by Etruscan men and, especially, women was the golden age of the sixth and fifth centuries; and it is to this period that we attribute those magnificent necklaces hung with *bullae* or acorns, and ear-rings wrought by means of the exquisite technique of granulation.[23]

Part 3

The Etruscan Language

CHAPTER 10 **The Problem of Etruscan**

The interpretation of Etruscan

In the preface to my first book on Etruscan (*Elementi di Lingua Etrusca*, 1936), I wrote: 'Though naturally biased in favour of the subject, I cannot help feeling the growing need for a book conceived along the lines of the present work. The quick succession of ephemeral discoveries on the part of amateurs has brought in its wake the natural disorientation of all interested in the language of Etruria, faced at the other extreme by the obstinate scepticism of those who, sweeping aside the good with the bad, look upon the problem of the language as the favourite playground for cranks, a kind of "comic" page in the annals of linguistics. The aim of this book is to provide a better understanding of the difficulties involved and the directions to be followed, to narrow the problem to its true limits and contain it within prudent, methodical but real and accurate statements, as removed from the intransigent certainty of those who claim to have found the "key" as from the un-informed scepticism of Pyrrhonian critics'.

The situation has changed little in the intervening years. Modest but fruitful advances towards a solution of the language problem continue as before, but so does the peculiar prejudice rooted in the public at large on what may be considered the very symbol of the Etruscan 'mystery'. Even today, ninety per cent of the educated public firmly believes that Etruscan is totally indecipherable. This belief is echoed in the press and repeated in the majority of text-books, even though it is over two hundred years out of date. Among scholars too – historians, archaeologists or philologists – only the vaguest notions are entertained on the present state of research in Etruscan linguistics, on the results that have been achieved, whether provisional or established. It seems appropriate, therefore, that this book should expound at some length the present state of our knowledge of the question and the nature of the problems involved in the study of the Etruscan language.[1]

To begin with, there is no problem of 'decipherment', if by decipherment we mean the reading of a set of unknown symbols: as we shall see, the Etruscan alphabet is perfectly legible. As to the meaning of words and texts, the basic question 'are they or are they not clear?' (in other words: 'do we or do we not understand Etruscan?', for this is

189

the form in which it is commonly put) corresponds only very approximatively, not to say crudely, to a correct formulation. A once-for-all answer would be possible only if we possessed a general 'key', some external means of throwing full light on the texts: e.g. a known language so close to Etruscan as to explain its roots and forms automatically, or substantial glossaries and bilingual documents such as have permitted the interpretation of ancient Egyptian, Sumerian, Akkadian or Hittite.[2] In the case of Etruscan, however, there are no documents written in closely related languages. Nor are we able to derive more than very limited use from the few glosses handed down by ancient writers or from the few bilingual inscriptions that have actually reached us. For the most part these consist of very brief funerary inscriptions in Latin and Etruscan, made up almost entirely of proper names. Quite recently they have been added to by the parallel texts of the gold tablets from Pyrgi, one in Etruscan, the other in Punic.[3] Substantial in length and similar in content (a sacred dedication), they may be considered as constituting in effect a bilingual inscription. They have given rise to new hopes and do in fact appear to have opened a new phase in linguistic research, though it is still too early to predict how far it will take us. Even in the case of the Pyrgi tablets, moreover, the non-literal correspondence of the two 'versions' (a common feature of ancient bilingual inscriptions), the difficulties facing the construction of the Etruscan text, and the rather circumscribed nature of the lexical and grammatical data that can be analysed in the light of external information, all seem to exclude the likelihood that the new documents will provide the 'key' that will open once for all the gates to the interpretation of the language.

As a result, the study of Etruscan today rests on a slow striving for results rather than on the expectation of a sudden revelation. The history of the numerous attempts made since the eighteenth century proves that the most solid and universally accepted results have been obtained mainly through a critical internal analysis of the texts, step by step, from the first elementary confirmations (e.g. the identification of personal names on inscriptions) down to the latest extensive and complex grammatical and lexical data summed up in Chapter Twelve. It is also possible that progress will speed up with the increase of material under study and of elements for internal comparison and external checks; we may thus hope to acquire a much vaster body of knowledge than at present, turn hypotheses into certainties, and, to all intents and purposes, reach the goal of a substantial understanding of even the longest and most complex texts.[4]

It becomes obvious from the foregoing that we cannot answer the question whether Etruscan has been interpreted or not by a simple yes or no. Our answer will have to be a partial one, shifting and forward-looking: that we know today a good many things about the language but that many others are obscure, that areas of darkness gradually become more circumscribed or clarified as the result of much hard work. We should also avoid an attitude common to many laymen tending to contrast with almost dialectic neatness the obscurity of Etruscan and the clarity of other idioms of antiquity such as Greek or Latin: an antithesis that rests on the untenable comparison between a language surviving in a few modest archaeological documents and languages known through a vast literature and a great tradition that is still alive. In this context, it may be worth recalling the existence of archaic Latin texts (e.g. the Forum cippus, the Duenos vase and the poem of the Arval Brothers) whose interpretation is no less problematical and controversial than that of many contemporary Etruscan texts. We should not be surprised that many uncertainties surround our knowledge of a number of ancient languages known wholly through inscriptions, even though they belong to well-known linguistic families: e.g. the Umbrian of the Iguvine Tablets. Even in the case of idioms studied the world over, e.g. Egyptian, Hebrew or even Greek, there still persist, despite the advances of modern linguistic and historical research, obstinate dark corners, uncertain technical expressions and ἅπαξ λεγόμενα, i.e. isolated and obscure words scattered about the texts. In the case of Etruscan, linguistically isolated and, as a result, poorly documented, these gaps are greater than elsewhere and, in the more difficult contexts, merge into large patches of obscurity. The progressive reduction in the number of these gaps will provide the opportunity of crossing the line between the 'untranslatable' and the 'translatable'.

A simile drawn from contemporary life may help to convey more concretely the present-day position of our knowledge of Etruscan. Imagine a modern English-speaker attempting to read a magazine or newspaper printed in the Latin alphabet, but written in an unknown language unrelated to any other known to him (say Hungarian or Turkish). A cultured and intelligent person with some linguistic training might make some sense out of the text: his knowledge of the events and news contained in the paper, names of persons and places, technical terms of 'universal' usage, recognizable and translatable quotations from documents or authors actually known to him, and, perhaps, the help of illustrations, these would all enable him to arrive more or less easily at an understanding of the headlines, of some of the shorter items of news and the general meaning of some of the longer articles. Such is the position of modern interpreters confronted with Etruscan texts. This is why difficulties grow in proportion to the length of texts, and why many of the versions that have been put forward have such a

191

hypothetical and provisional character. This state of affairs underlines the merit of scholars who slowly and patiently have wrested and continue to wrest results that are definitely positive.

Developments in research

Until the last quarter of the nineteenth century, attempts to understand Etruscan were based mainly upon etymological comparisons with other languages and language families. The criteria employed had their roots in the amateur researches of seventeenth-century or even Renaissance enthusiasts (e.g. Annius of Viterbo or Pier Francesco Giambullari), the only difference being that attempts at deriving Etruscan words from the Hebrew (it was thought at the time that all languages derived from Hebrew) were slowly replaced, with the general advance in linguistic knowledge, by theories seeking to establish a relationship between Etruscan and the Indo-European languages, chiefly Latin and the Italic dialects (L. Lanzi, A. Fabretti, W. Corssen and E. Lattes) but also Greek and Armenian (S. Bugge), or by hypotheses of a presumed affinity with Basque and Caucasian (V. Thomsen), Ugro-Finnish (J. Martha) or even Dravidian (S. Konow)! Such attempts did not exclude the examination of various intrinsic features of the texts, whether epigraphic, phonetic, morphological or lexical (the beginning, in fact, of the 'combinatory' method); but the chief criterion consisted in deducing semantic and grammatical values from outside sources, from languages in those linguistic groups to which it was thought Etruscan belonged.

The almost wholly negative results of these individual attempts at etymological comparison – which by their very nature had to be accepted or rejected as a whole – and the progress of scientific criticism led inevitably to a reaction. This was prepared by the slow, conscientious, often unrecognized labours of collectors and epigraphists, notably Italian (e.g. L. Lanzi, G. B. Vermiglioli, M. A. Migliarini, G. C. Conestabile, and A. Fabretti), whose attention was mainly directed towards the isolation and direct examination of monuments. Their work culminated in the publication of Fabretti's monumental *Corpus Inscriptionum Italicarum* (*C.I.I.*), completed later by F. Gamurrini's three *Supplements* and *Appendix* (1867–80). It is to these first steps in critical research, some of which go back to the eighteenth century, that we owe a few fundamental discoveries in the interpretation of Etruscan: e.g. the conjunctive value of the enclitic particle *-c* (corresponding to Latin *-que*), the genitive or adjectival function of the endings *-s*, *-sa*, *-al*, the feminine endings *-i*, *-ei*, the pronoun *mi*, the meaning of a number of words such as *ril*, 'aged [*x*] years', *clan*, 'son', *turce*, 'has given', etc., especially in connection with the very frequent onomastic formulas found in funerary inscriptions. It is worth stressing the fact that such results were achieved without recourse to comparisons with other languages; they relied exclusively on the study of epigraphic formulas (more or less consciously referred to similar formulas belonging to the Latin, Italic or Greek world), and on the internal critical analysis of Etruscan texts.

But the insufficiency of the etymological method became apparent only after the publication of a work by the famous latinist W. Corssen, *Über die Sprache der Etrusker* (1874), which stated that Etruscan belonged to the Indo-European family of languages and, in particular, to its Italic branch. Corssen followed this premise (with apparent methodological rigour) with a general attempt at a morphological analysis and an interpretation of the texts. The thirty-nine pages of W. Deecke's *Corssen und die Sprache der Etrusker. Eine Kritik* (1875) were sufficient to bring down, like a house of cards, the imposing structure erected by Corssen.

This significant episode resulted in a change of direction in research. Deecke and other scholars, such as C. Pauli, G. Herbig and A. Torp, gave up altogether the external comparisons with other languages and devoted themselves exclusively to the internal study of Etruscan texts and their reciprocal relations. The inductive, internal or 'combinatory' method was thus born. New discoveries, such as the Capua tile and the manuscript wrappings of the mummy in the Zagreb museum, together with more up-to-date means of research such as the *Corpus Inscriptionum Etruscarum* (*C.I.E.*), begun in 1893 by Pauli and still in course of publication,[5] and the lexical indices drawn up by Lattes,[6] gave a vigorous momentum to research in this new direction. Much progress, mainly due to the work of A. Torp (*Etruskische Beiträge*, 1903–6), was made both in our knowledge of Etruscan grammar and in the interpretation of the texts, especially the shorter ones. More recently, the activity of other Etruscologists has done much to extend still further our knowledge of the subject. It is true that the etymological method, though superseded, has occasionally been used by scholars belonging to the 'combinatory' school (Deecke, Pauli, even Torp and, more recently, E. Vetter) and it was obstinately followed for some time by E. Lattes and E. Goldmann; nevertheless it is by now mainly relegated to those amateurish improvisations that continue to flourish with tenacious persistence on the borders of Etruscan studies and which have vainly sought to explain Etruscan by means of Greek, Hittite, Armenian, the Semitic languages, Egyptian, and so on.

Meanwhile research on the linguistic relationships of Etruscan was progressing independently of the actual work of interpretation. Such research was much assisted by the more reliable and broader criteria furnished by modern historical linguistics. The obvious though not very close similarities between Etruscan and certain Indo-European, Caucasian and Anatolian languages were explained in a number of ways: by postulating the existence, superimposition and survival of pre-Indo-European linguistic groups as understood by A. Trombetti; by recognizing in these similarities traces of a supposed proto-Indo-European stratum (P. Kretschmer)[7]; or, finally, as suggested by G. Devoto, as forming part of a peri-Indo-European structure, the result of the dissolution and transformation of an archaic Mediterranean linguistic substratum under the action of subsequent and repeated Indo-European infiltrations.[8] In each case it was a question of recognizing in Etruscan direct or indirect echoes of those pre-Indo-European Mediterranean languages that had already been largely extinguished in the course of the last stages of prehistory, and had remained unsubmerged only sporadically, as in the case of some of the Caucasian languages.[9] Toponymy – the study of place names – was mainly responsible for providing a concrete basis for these theories: there survive in many place names fossil elements of very ancient languages that have gradually revealed a measure of primitive Mediterranean linguistic unity and point to affinities uniting Etruscan with the eastern group of prehellenic languages and those of Asia Minor as well as with the pre-Indo-European linguistic layer of the Italian peninsula and islands. Only the language spoken in the Aegean island of Lemnos before the Athenian conquest was recognized (not without a certain amount of discussion) as being linked more closely to Etruscan (see pp. 72 ff.).[10]

The possibility of classifying Etruscan with some degree of precision among the linguistic groups surrounding the Mediterranean was destined to reopen, but upon new and well-defined bases, the problem of etymological comparisons as a tool in the interpretation of Etruscan texts. Alfredo Trombetti, who had already contributed so much to the genealogical classification of Etruscan, and who, by the great breadth of his linguistic erudition, was singularly well placed to attempt the arduous task of comparing little-known languages or linguistic remains, did, in fact, reintroduce the 'etymological' in conjunction with the 'combinatory' method in his *La Lingua etrusca* (1928). He succeeded in achieving some results before his premature death, especially in the morphological analysis of the language and in the interpretation of texts as pursued earlier by Torp; these results, however, did not fulfil the hopes that had been nourished. After his death, the methodological principles which he had expounded were misinterpreted, for they were too intimately linked with his personal capacities and scientific preparation; they prompted a fresh outbreak of amateurish attempts at finding

194

a solution. At the same time, official science appeared to adopt a policy of 'wait and see' for a few years.

Later developments in research are based on the deeper analysis of epigraphic data (B. Nogara, G. Buonamici, E. Vetter, H. Rix, R. Lambrechts, A. J. Pfiffig, M. Cristofani, etc.) and an intensification of the analytical study of morphology and phonetics (M. Pallottino, F. Slotty, H. Rix, C. De Simone, etc.). There have also been a number of attempts at interpretation along the traditional lines of the combinatory method: the most praiseworthy may be found in the work of S. P. Cortsen and E. Vetter. But the most exciting advances have been due to a radical and decisive change in critical outlook. With very few exceptions, all previous research had been conceived and conducted on the purely technical plane of linguistics: it hardly took into account the fact that a language is the living expression of the history and civilization of its speakers. F. Ribezzo was the first to point out the importance of historical sources of ancient literature as a tool in understanding the spiritual and institutional world of the Etruscans and, therefore, their texts. The notion of basing linguistic research on our knowledge of the historical background has led to the development of a concrete method that seeks to explain the structure and meaning of Etruscan texts by comparing them with Greek, Latin and Italic formulas and texts: both the known and the unknown are taken to reflect a common inheritance of traditions and ideas and to be roughly analogous in content and mode of expression. This 'bilingual method' has been applied by K. Olzscha and the author of the present work for the interpretation of the *liber linteus* (linen book) of the Zagreb mummy, of the Capua tile and of various votive and funerary inscriptions. Results already obtained undoubtedly show the opening of a new door to the interpretation of the language. The work of interpretation still continues on the basis of the combinatory method, although the external evidence, both direct and indirect, is steadily becoming more useful and may even take on an immediate and decisive value when, as in the case of the Pyrgi inscriptions, we have the fortune of having at our disposal an actual bilingual document.

In conclusion we may state that we now possess a common fund of lexical and grammatical notions on which we may rely to a greater or lesser extent, and that it is continually growing; that research is following a direction which is substantially agreed upon by the more experienced and serious specialists, independently of school or method. This is not the rigid, closed 'system' attacked in a few recent over-schematic – not to say ingenuous – attempts at a synthesis, e.g. the one put forward by H. Stoltenberg. It is a dynamic approach, still fluid in many details and open to every future possibility of progress. The validity of this direction for research can be measured in the light of the new discoveries, for they do not invalidate it but confirm it. The study of the Pyrgi bilingual inscriptions has definitely confirmed, through their Punic version, a number of hypotheses (e.g. the equivalence $ci =$ 'three') which had been accepted as highly probable by the majority of Etruscologists but were not yet supported by unambiguous external data. This new fact, which at first sight appears insignificant, since it does not affect widely-held beliefs, is indeed of prime methodological importance for the present and future history of Etruscan linguistic research. It allows us to follow calmly what appears to be – certainly and irreversibly – the right road in our arduous but fascinating task.[11]

CHAPTER 11 The Sources and the
Method

Present means and future prospects

The major obstacle to a full and accurate knowledge of Etruscan resides
in the scarcity, the brevity and the unilateral contents of the original
texts. Save for a few exceptional cases, the material at our disposal
consists exclusively of brief, monotonous funerary or votive inscriptions, containing little more than a few oft-repeated formulas and a
vocabulary restricted to certain limited aspects of Etruscan religious
life. With the loss of all traces of Etruscan literature, we are left
without any notion of the most lively part of the language, the
stock of expressions reflecting family, social and economic life,
abstract ideas and the structure of direct speech. We are thus obliged
to confess that even if we did have the 'technical' means of trans-
lating word for word all the texts in our possession, we should still
be very much in the dark concerning the fabric of the lexicon and
many aspects of the morphological and syntactical structure of the
language.

Every year, as the result of chance discoveries or systematic excavations, funerary and votive inscriptions are regularly brought to light in
the various sites of ancient Etruria. They are generally short, and
exhibit few variants except in the case of personal names.[1] In spite of
the apparent thinness of this material, it is often of considerable value,
especially for the light it throws on current analyses and discussions of
the more important known texts: a single new word or grammatical
form has been sufficient in some special cases to resolve doubts and
problems of many years' standing.[2]

A larger measure of good fortune has accompanied the search for
inscriptions during the last few years, although it should be said that
the greater scope and accuracy of recent archaeological research have
also played their part. Epigraphic finds have been particularly rewarding both with regard to their number (the result of new explorations at
Cerveteri, Tarquinia, Vulci, Bolsena, Orvieto, etc.) and to the exceptional nature, content and length of some of the documents that
have been discovered: e.g. the Archaic vase inscription of the so-called
'Poupé aryballos'; the gold and bronze tablets of the Pyrgi sanctuary;
the fragments of a lead tablet unearthed near Santa Marinella; the

197

dedicatory inscription in the tomb of the Claudii at Caere. These are discussed in detail below.[3]

These discoveries have revived the hope that the future, perhaps even the immediate future, may hold further unforeseeable surprises. It is likely that Etruria still hides a rich hoard of written documents. As we are beginning to recognize the existence of actual temple archives at Pyrgi and at Santa Marinella, we may well hope that a careful search on the sites of the major urban centres could lead to the discovery of epigraphic texts of a public, historico-commemorative or juridical character, some of which might perhaps be written in both Etruscan and Latin – which is quite likely for the later historical periods, when Etruria was dominated by or associated with Rome. At the same time we must not expect that new inscriptions, however substantial their length, or even bilingual inscriptions will necessarily provide us with an automatic solution to all the unresolved problems: the most recent discoveries have shown that, in some respects, the greater the amount of data, the larger the number of problems.[4] What is certain is that such discoveries will increase the scope and tempo of research on interpretation. But the absence of literary texts leaves a gap that will probably never be filled, and thus removes, for the present at least, any chance of our knowing Etruscan in the way we know the other languages of the classical world. Etruscan literary documents could in theory be discovered among the papyri of Egypt or Herculaneum, especially if we remember the truly miraculous find of an Etruscan text written on the linen wrappings of an Egyptian mummy. But the likelihood of another such find is tenuous and remote enough to be wholly discounted.

Direct and indirect sources

The sources of our knowledge of Etruscan can be clearly divided into those of direct and those of indirect origin.[5] The first – the texts of direct origin – do not derive from an uninterrupted manuscript tradition. They are wholly archaeological in character and are all inscribed upon monuments or objects, with the sole exception of the fragments of the book of the Zagreb mummy (Plate 96), also archaeological in provenance.

The exceptional importance of this document for the history of Etruscan civilization, and, more generally, for that of classical antiquity, cannot be overstressed. It is the only surviving sacral book on cloth (*liber linteus*) from the Greek and Italo-Roman world. Originally in the form of a roll (*volumen*), it was later cut into strips and used to wrap the mummy of an Egyptian woman in Ptolemaic or Roman times. It was probably discovered in Middle Egypt, though we have no record of the exact place. There is little doubt that this particular use of the 'book' was not the one originally intended, for important fragments of the original roll were lost in the process. We know nothing of the circumstances that led to the presence of an Etruscan religious book in Egypt. The mummy was brought to Europe by a Croatian traveller and later donated to the Zagreb National Museum, where J. Krall identified the writing on the wrappings as Etruscan. By fitting the separate strips together, it was possible to reconstruct a text consisting of at least twelve vertical columns: about 1,200 words more or less clearly and completely legible, to which may be added about 100 more that can be reconstructed with the help of the context. When account is taken of repetitions, the number of distinct words is reduced to little more than 500. Nevertheless, the Zagreb book is by far the longest and most important of the Etruscan texts in our possession.

The inscriptions have been discovered mainly in Tyrrhenian Etruria, though a few have also turned up in Campania, Latium, North Italy, Corsica and North Africa. They are carved or painted on architectural monuments, tomb walls, cippi, sarcophagi, urns, roof-tiles, statues, household objects, metal tablets, vases, and so on. All together there are about 10,000; but only very few are of any substantial length. Among the latter, some are in fact independent documents unconnected with the nature of the movable object on which they appear: the surfaces on which they are written function as occasional writing surfaces just like those made of perishable materials such as cloth or leather rolls, wooden tablets and diptychs which are frequently reproduced on Etruscan figured monuments but have not themselves survived, because of the action of our climate; in contrast, the Zagreb *liber linteus* was preserved by the dry climate of Egypt.

The longest inscription is on a roof-tile found at Capua and now in the Berlin Museum (Plate 97): it comprises 62 extant lines, divided into ten sections and containing almost 300 legible words. The second part of the text is much damaged; the writing is boustrophedic, running alternately from right to left and left to right. Another text, written on both faces of a long, ribbon-like lead tablet, unfortunately found broken, has come to light in a small sanctuary close to Santa Marinella (Plate 101): there are traces of at least 80 words, of which only half are wholly legible; the lettering of this inscription is very small indeed. A round thin plaque, also in lead, found at Magliano and now in the Museo Archeologico at Florence (*C.I.E.* 5237) contains a spiral inscription etched on both faces and reading towards the centre; at least 70 words can be counted (but it is sometimes difficult to decide whether a group of letters represents one or two words). Then there are the three gold tablets discovered in the Pyrgi sanctuary (Plates 12–14), outstanding both for their content and for their linguistic and historical importance. Two are in Etruscan, the third in Punic. The longer Etruscan inscription contains fifteen lines composed of 36 or 37 words; it corresponds to the Punic inscription, forming, as we know, a kind of bilingual text. The shorter is nine lines long and composed of fifteen words. In addition, there are sizeable documents on metal tablets, e.g. the *tabellae defixionis* – execratory tablets commending the recipient of a curse to the infernal deities (notable examples are those of Monte Pitti, *C.I.E.* 5211, and Volterra, *C.I.E.* 52) – and a few more of uncertain content.

Among truly epigraphic inscriptions, the most remarkable is the stone cippus (Plate 98), probably a boundary mark, now in the Perugia Museum (*C.I.E.* 4538). On two of its faces it features a fine long carved inscription comprising 46 lines and 130 words. A number of extended funerary inscriptions have also been found, e.g. the one on the sarcophagus of Laris Pulenas now in the Tarquinia Museum (*C.I.E.* 5430), inscribed on an open scroll held by the sculptured figure of the dead man and containing nine lines and 59 words. Others of equal length and importance have come to light painted on tomb walls at Tarquinia, but these are not so well preserved. Several inscriptions on tombs, sarcophagi and cippi contain a few lines of text and exhibit a certain variety in the words used; but the great majority consist merely of a few words composed in standard formulas. Votive inscriptions on movable objects may be sub-divided into an Archaic group, with special formulas of their own containing the name of the dedicator, and a later group where it is the name of the divinity that is prominent. But if we except the sizeable inscriptions on a few Archaic vases, votive inscriptions are generally short and stereotyped. Finally, we should mention the innumerable captions found alongside figures on tombs, painted vases and mirrors; inscriptions on coins, lead projectiles and other small objects; and various trade marks, which often include proper names.

Some mention of bilingual inscriptions has already been made.[6] The few extant funerary inscriptions in Etruscan and Latin show the correspondence of personal names but only very exceptionally contain elements that help to increase our knowledge of Etruscan vocabulary or morphology: e.g. the title *netśvis trutnvt*, or *netśvis trutnvt frontac*, translated as *haruspex fulguriator* in the Pesaro bilingual inscription (*C.I.I.* 69; see Plate 100)[7]; or the form *Cahatial*, the genitive of a *gens* name *Cahati*, translated as *Cafatia natus* in inscription *C.I.E.* 3763. Much richer and more complex is the information which the parallel Etruscan and Punic texts of Pyrgi have so far contributed and may still provide. Established correspondences have already thrown much light on, e.g., the object of the dedication (*ita tmia* = '*šr qdš* '*z*, 'this sacred place'), the names of the deity (*unial astres* = *lrbt l'štrt*, 'to (Uni-) Astarte') and of the dedicator (*θefariei velianas* = *tbrj wlnš*), the verb 'to give' (*turuce* = *jtn*, 'has given'), the introduction to the phrase explaining the dedication (*nac* = *k*, 'because . . .'), the length of time Thefarie Velianas held power (*ci avil* = *šnt šlš*, 'three years' or 'year three'), etc.

The indirect sources for the study of Etruscan are the following:

1. glosses and other information provided by classical and post-classical writers;
2. Etruscan elements that have passed into Latin, and common Etrusco-Italic elements;
3. Etruscan elements surviving in place names;
4. fragments of presumed Latin versions of original Etruscan texts.

The glosses are Etruscan words with a Latin or Greek translation: they may be found quoted haphazardly in texts by classical authors or gathered together to form actual glossaries. We possess about sixty such glosses, but their value in the interpretation of Etruscan texts is somewhat limited, just as in the case of Etrusco-Latin bilingual texts. Glosses of a varied nature appear in Varro (*De lingua latina*), in Verrius Flaccus (*De verborum significatione*, in the compendia of Festus and Paul the Deacon), in Isidore of Seville (*Etymologicum*), and especially in Hesychius's *Lexicon*; e.g. *arse verse* = *arce ignem* (Verrius Flaccus); ἄνδας, ἄνδαρ = north wind, eagle (Hesychius); δρούνα = command, power (Hesychius). Occasionally Etruscan words are quoted in the works of other authors, such as Livy, Strabo, Plutarch, Dio Cassius, Macrobius, Servius or John Lydus: e.g. ἄριμος = monkey (Strabo, XIII, 626), *capys* = falcon (Servius, *ad Aen.*, X, 145). The original form may be preserved intact or may be modified by a Greek or Latin ending: e.g. αἴσαρ = god (Dio Cassius), αἰσοί = gods (Hesychius). The reliability of such glosses may be checked by reference to the Etruscan texts themselves (*aiser*, 'gods'; *versum*, cf. *verse*, 'fire'?) or by a study of their form (e.g. *fala(n)do* = sky, according to Verrius Flaccus in Paul the Deacon: cf., for the root, such Etruscan words as *falaš, falzaθi*, and, for the ending, Etr. *aranθ*). In a few cases the authenticity of the Etruscan gloss appears to be belied by the Latin character of the word: e.g. δέα, κάπρα (Hesychius). Specialized vocabularies are represented by glosses of medicinal plant names (Dioscorides, though here too some of the names are Latin), and of the names of the months (Papias, in the *Liber Glossarum* of Leyden) which also seem to appear in Etruscan texts: e.g. *Aclus* = June (cf. *acale* in the Zagreb text). Phonetic and grammatical remarks, of very little value, may be

201

The Etruscans

found in Varro, in Agrecius's *Ars de orthographia*, and in Martianus Capella.[8]

A special study has been made by A. Ernout of those Etruscan elements that passed into Latin.[9] They are thought to be characterized by endings in *-na* (*atena, persona*: cf. Etr. *φersu*), in *-rna* (*santerna*), in *-mna* (*antemna*), in *-sa* (*favisa*: cf. Etr. *faviti*), in *-nt, -nd* (*flexuntes, mundus*: cf. Etr. *munθ*), in *-on* (*subulo*: Etr. *suplu*?; *fullo*: cf. Etr. *fulum-*), in *-it* (*veles, poples*), etc. The Etruscan derivation of certain words is explicitly stated by classical authors (*mantisa, histrio, lucumo, atrium*, etc.); in other cases it is hypothetical and may possibly be due to analogical formations, i.e. Latin words with endings imitating Etruscan derivatives; or again they may be remnants of the general pre-Indo-European substratum of Italy rather than actual borrowings from the Etruscan of historical times. On the other hand, an Etruscan origin may be more correctly suspected for Latin words with obscure etymologies and an Etruscan-looking ending, if related to the technical languages of religion, civil or military institutions and technology: such loan-words would be explained by the very strong cultural influence exerted by Etruria upon primitive Rome. There are also many examples where Etruscan probably acted as an intermediary between Greek and Latin: e.g. *groma* (an instrument used in direction finding and field measurement), from γνώμων. It is also possible that Etruscan may have had some limited influence on the phonetics and morphology of Latin. The whole question deserves renewed and more careful examination, if only for the help it may bring to the understanding of the language. Equally if not more obscure is the question of the possibility of Etruscan words surviving in the vocabulary of central Italian dialects; the hypothesis attributing an Etruscan origin to the aspiration of certain consonants in Tuscan dialects (the well-known *gorgia toscana*) has received the support of a number of linguists.[10]

Despite the fundamental difference between Etruscan and the Indo-European languages of Italy, there are a number of words and roots common to both: e.g. Etr. *sac-, sacri*: Lat. *sacer*; Etr. *eiser*, 'gods, deities': Umbrian *esono-*, Volscian *esari-*, 'sacred ceremonies, sacrifices'; Etr. *nefts*, 'nephew, grandson': Lat. *nepos*; Etr. *prumts*, 'great-nephew, great-grandson': Lat. *pronepos*; Etr. *vinum*: Lat. *vinum*; Etr. *cletram*: Umbrian *kletra*, 'trolley for sacred offerings'. These correspondences may be due to contacts established during the prehistoric period (as the reflexes of a common pre-Indo-European linguistic substratum, or as the result of very ancient Indo-European 'infiltrations' as understood by Devoto) or perhaps to reciprocal borrowings during the historical period. At any rate they throw much light upon the history and meaning of the Etruscan forms. The same phenomenon can

202

be recognized in connection with names of persons and gods. In the first group (masterfully treated by W. Schulze in *Zur Geschichte der lateinischen Eigennamen*, 1904, and more recently by H. Rix in *Das etruskische Cognomen*, 1963), the resemblance first appears in the fact that the formula is composed of two or three members (the *praenomen*, the name of the *gens* and, sometimes, the *cognomen*: Etr. *Aule Seiante Śinu*, Lat. *Marcus Tullius Cicero*). Moreover, the very forms (roots and internal suffixes) of a number of *praenomina* and a large number of *gens* names are identical in Etruscan and Latin, apart from phonetic and grammatical differences: e.g. Etr. *Aule*: Lat. *Aulus*; Etr. *Marce*: Lat. *Marcus*, among the *praenomina*; Etr. *Fapi*: Lat. *Fabius*; Etr. *Petruni*: Lat. *Petronius*; Etr. *Vete*: Lat. *Vettius*, among the *gens* names.

In the case of names of gods and goddesses a number of common elements are also observed: Etr. *Menerva*: Lat. *Minerva*; Etr. *Selvans*: Lat. *Silvanus*. These correspondences should be compared with such clearly marked divergences as Etr. *Tin, Tinia*: Lat. *Iuppiter*; Etr. *Fufluns*: Lat. *Liber*. Very ancient linguistic contacts are also revealed by correspondences of the type Lat. *Lar* (the name of a male genius) and Etr. *Laran, Larun* (male deity) and *Lasa* (female deity: in this case a possible oscillation between intervocalic *s* and *r* may be connected with the phenomenon of rhotacism). It is worth noting here that a single root may give rise to a great number of forms in Etruscan proper names. Several names of gods, both Etruscan and Latin, derive from the Greek; such names, together with a number of mythological names and cultural terms (e.g. names of vases), also derived from Greek, represent an invaluable source to our knowledge of Etruscan phonetics, since the various changes which they have undergone provide us with a clue to the phonetic tendencies and morphological exigencies of the language[11]; e.g.: Greek Ἀλέξανδρος: Etr. *Alcsentre, Elaχśantre, Elaχśntre, Elχsntre, Aleχsantre, Elcste*, etc.; Gk Κλυταιμνήστρα: Etr. *Cluθumusθa, Clutmsta*; Gk Ἑλένη: Etr. *Elina, Elinai, Elinei*.

Despite the rich collections made by S. Pieri and the monographs of P. Aebischer, V. Bertoldi, G. Bottiglioni and C. Battisti,[12] the study of the Etruscan toponymy of central and northern Italy is still a long way from providing us with systematic data and reliable conclusions. The fundamental difficulty lies in distinguishing the various layers and the various areas of diffusion of pre-Indo-European place names; for example, distinguishing place names of the 'Mediterranean' or 'palaeo-Etruscan' type (found also in central Italy, as in the case of derivatives of the roots *carra-, pala-, gav-*, etc.) from place names belonging to the Etruscan of historical times. Where the latter can be identified with absolute certainty, it may even be possible to use them to help assess the semantic value of certain Etruscan words, as attempted by Bertoldi with place names of the *falar-* type. Account should also be taken of the close relationship between place names and personal names, as indicated by Schulze. Names of Etruscan cities are particularly important in this respect, for their ancient forms are known to us through the writings of classical authors and from inscriptions: they often seem closely related to the name of a god or hero, e.g. **Tarχuna*, Tarquinia, with the hero *Tarχun-*, Tarchon; *Pupluna*, Populonia, with the god *Fuflun*, Bacchus; *Manθva-*, Mantua, with the god *Mantus*; etc.[13]

Finally, we should consider the hypothetical examples of Latin versions of original Etruscan texts. We already know that the main body of Etruscan sacred books was translated or abridged into Latin. In the congeries of indirect references and shortened or rewritten versions of Etruscan texts (some echoes of which have come down to us), we find passages which are of especial interest in the study of Etruscan literature and civilization, and which also throw some light on certain structures of the language: e.g. the fragment from the Vegonic books quoted by the *Gromatici* (Lachmann ed., I, pp. 350 ff.) giving the teachings of the Lasa Vegonia on the division of fields.[14]

Methods of research

After this review of the sources of our knowledge of Etruscan let us pass to the question of method. From the character of the documents in our possession and the retrospective examination of research conducted during the past decades, we may, as we have seen,[15] exclude the possibility of a complete understanding of Etruscan by means of an external agency, one or more known languages with which it could be compared (the etymological method). The fundamental basis of research remains, therefore, the direct examination of the texts in our possession, taking into account their purpose, the objects to which they refer, the figures that may accompany them and the onomastic formulas which they contain. Hence it is most important that an accurate archaeological estimate be made of the character, meaning and chronology of the objects or monuments connected with the inscriptions. The lexical and grammatical values thus inductively obtained should then be checked by combining texts and passages with one another, i.e. by checking the reliability of a first hypothesis by means of new tests. This is the classical procedure of the 'combinatory' method. If we discount its more rigid applications, which have frequently led to vague and sterile conjectures, the 'combinatory' method may still be used as a basic means of control and further research, even when examining information obtained from external sources.

Naturally, the information obtained by the internal inductive method is, by its very nature, a good deal less precise than what could be obtained from reliable etymological comparisons or glossaries and bilingual texts. In many cases, the function of a case ending is known only approximately or in part: in the word *Menervas*, found written on a vase, final *-s*, added to the name of the goddess Menerva, may just as easily be a genitive of possession or a dative of advantage or dedication. The same may be said of lexical values, since their differentiation is often generic, according to category, within the limits of *genus proximum* rather than those of *differentia specifica*. This is particularly the case with terms referring to concepts and actions relating to sacred ceremonies and public institutions. We know quite well, for example, that the word *sacni* stands for a sacred place or institution, but we cannot tell which term in Latin or in any other language is its exact equivalent.

In much the same way, we know of several verbs within the general concepts of 'to give', 'to offer', 'to sacrifice' (*tur-*, *men-*, *scuv-*, *mul-*, *al-*, *nunθ-*, etc.); but we cannot establish precise correspondences between these verbs and their probable Latin equivalents: *do*, *dono*, *reddo*, *lito*, *fero*, *supplico*, etc. Naturally, in the interpretation of words, the determination of meaning falls by degrees from a maximum of accuracy and probability to vague and generic working hypotheses on which it would be rash to build further hypotheses. The uncertainty characterizing certain complex hermeneutic constructions built up entirely by means of combinatory processes is in fact due to this piling of hypothesis upon hypothesis till the whole structure appears to lack any solid foundation.

The weightier role played by the inductive or 'combinatory' method does not exclude the use of deductions based upon external data. Glosses and bilingual texts have provided us with a few reliable lexical determinations: e.g. *ais* = god, *arim* = monkey, *netśvis* = *haruspex*, *ci* = three, etc. More data could be obtained from an intelligent sifting of the Latin lexical material of supposed Etruscan derivation, so long as it were carefully checked by means of the combinatory method. It would seem, for instance, that a connection might exist between Etruscan *munθ* and Latin *mundus*, which has no supporting Indo-European root.[16] However, the consequent translation of *munθ* as 'ornament' proposed for inscription *C.I.E.* 5470 (*calti suθiti munθ zivas murśl XX*, '... in this tomb, ornament of the dead, twenty sarcophagi'!) does not fit the precise, concrete language of Etruscan funerary inscriptions. On the other hand, several other inscriptions include words derived from the same root *mun-*: it seems from the context as if the meaning was rather that of 'place' (in the specific sense of Latin *locus*) or 'repository for the dead', which sense also fits the previous inscription. The connection with *mundus* might then be established (if at all) as indicated by F. Leifer,[17] by way of the special funerary and religious meaning of the Latin word which, besides signifying 'world' and 'ornament', also stood for 'pit communicating with the underworld'. This example will suffice to show the importance, first stressed by Ribezzo, of broadening our knowledge of the religious and institutional foundations of classical antiquity for a better understanding of Etruscan.

From examples of etymological analyses of single Etruscan words, prudently carried out by M. Hammarström (for *natis*, *netśvis*),[18] Devoto (for *aís*, *culsu*, etc.)[19] and others, we are inclined to believe that the old etymological method, as long as it is not considered as the only instrument capable of interpreting the whole of Etruscan by means of a known language (which, as we have already stated, has shown itself to be critically impossible), but is cautiously applied to single words or forms, is destined to furnish useful confirmations or even new contributions to the interpretation of Etruscan texts. In this connection we should not forget the possibility of a tentative, but as yet untried application of the methods of linguistic geography as practised in Italy by M. Bartoli: it may help to determine more accurately the position of Etruscan among the Mediterranean languages, and even perhaps to confirm, if only indirectly, some of its lexical and morphological values.

Side by side with the two traditional methods of Etruscan hermeneutics (etymological and combinatory), a new deductive principle has become established during the last thirty years as a major tool of research: the bilingual method. It operates in a completely different field from that of linguistic affinities and comparisons, tending instead to explain the meaning of words and phrases by using the same principle as the 'translators', i.e. bilingual texts or glossaries. Assuming that the Etruscan civilization was closely linked with the Greek and the Italic (as the comparative study of religion, art, customs, etc. clearly shows), and that such cultural affinities are also reflected by analogies in their modes of expression, in sacrificial, votive and funerary formulas, we are justified in concluding that in many cases an Etruscan text may be compared with a Greek, Latin or Italic text with presumably similar contents, and may be interpreted on the basis of such a comparison almost as if we were dealing with a bilingual inscription. Such a process was first applied by the present writer, establishing the meaning of the Etruscan pronoun *mi* (= I, me) by comparing the formulas inscribed on two vases found on Faliscan territory: one in Etruscan: *mi qutun lemausnas* ..., the other in Faliscan (i.e., for practical purposes, in archaic Latin): *eco quto ... euotenosio* ..., 'I [am] the pitcher of ...

Euotenus (name of the possessor) . . .' – identical expressions couched in two different languages. At about the same time, Olzscha recognized the great importance of Roman and Umbrian sacrificial formulas in the interpretation of Etruscan ritual texts, especially in the case of the longest and most important, that of the Zagreb mummy, to the interpretation of which he devoted studies of fundamental importance. Naturally, the bilingual method rests substantially upon the reciprocal translatability of words and expressions in Etruscan and Latin or Italic, i.e. upon the existence of those 'translated loan-words' which inevitably follow the close co-habitation of peoples of different tongues within a common cultural orbit (as in the case of Romance and Germanic speakers in the modern world). Such a correspondence existed between the Etruscan title *zilaθ meχl rasnal* and the Latin *praetor Etruriae*.[20] This new procedure, used in the spirit of the new 'historicist' directions taken by Etruscan hermeneutics, and applied cautiously and intelligently and without neglecting the assistance of the older, well-tried methods, opens up unhoped-for vistas of new conquests in this field.[21]

Naturally, its application will be most successful in those cases where the circumstances accompanying the find of the documents to be compared are such as to make them more like actual bilingual inscriptions. Similarity of textual content may range from that of Etruscan and Latin epitaphs belonging to the same family and found in the same tomb to that of documents where the contents are undoubtedly the same, as in the case of the Pyrgi tablets. At this point the use of an actual bilingual inscription as an 'external' source of light takes over from the bilingual method.[22]

Variations in time and space

It is chiefly owing to the work of E. Fiesel that the attention of scholars has been drawn to the problem of the internal evolution of the language during the seven centuries for which we have material.[23] The evolution of epigraphic Latin from Archaic to Imperial times is so evident and rapid a phenomenon that we may *a priori* suppose some similar developments in Etruscan. Hence the need always to keep in mind the date, be it only approximate, of each inscription: it may be determined from the characteristics of the monument concerned and of its accompanying objects, from the shape of the letters, etc. This attitude contrasts with the earlier habit of studying and combining texts without taking their relative ages into account. From both the palaeographic and the phonetic points of view notable differences can be found between Archaic (seventh to fifth centuries B.C.) and later inscriptions mostly contemporary with the Roman conquest and domination of Etruria (it is to this later period that the more important extant texts belong). As an example, we may quote the fall of unstressed vowels and the reduction of diphthongs in later texts: e.g. *turce* (archaic Etr. *turuce*), *zusleve* (archaic Etr. *zuslevai*).[24] In morphology too a number of noticeable differences are beginning to be observed: the genitive ending *-al* corresponds, in Archaic inscriptions, to *-a*.

It is likely that further studies will enable us to determine and recognize similar differences in the lexical and semantic fields, and provide us with an outline of the characteristics of Archaic Etruscan ('Ar. Etr.') and later or Neo-Etruscan ('N-Etr.')

Much the same remarks could be made with respect to problems concerning topographical variations in the language. The study of these phenomena is still less advanced than that of chronological variations. Only the completion of that great collection of Etruscan inscriptions, the *Corpus Inscriptionum Etruscarum*, which is to include the Etruscan regions of Campania and the Po valley, can provide sufficiently broad and reliable foundations for an attempt to disentangle regional – perhaps even dialectal – peculiarities in vocabulary, phonetics and grammar. Up to the present such research has proved extremely arduous owing to the rarity of preserved texts, especially in certain regions (e.g. northern Italy). Nor is it always possible to establish how far the peculiarities of certain inscriptions are the result of local differentiations or reflect a given stage in the development of the language: this is the case with the archaisms found in the Capua tile or those (palaeographic and orthographic in particular) of the Po valley inscriptions. It is probable, moreover, that the outlying districts of Etruria, conquered and flourishing in Archaic times, would tend to feature Archaic traits when compared with the central regions. Here the language developed rapidly towards a Neo-Etruscan which, without doubt, formed the basis of the literary κοινή of the Etrusco-Roman era. Even Neo-Etruscan, however, features a number of variants (e.g. in the treatment of sibilants) according to whether it was spoken in southern or in central and northern Etruria. It is such variants that have allowed us, for example, to establish that the text of the Zagreb mummy was written in the idiom of one of the central or northern cities (e.g. Chiusi or Perugia).[25]

CHAPTER **12** **The Results**

The alphabet

The identification and the reading of the symbols of the Etruscan alphabet are no longer a problem to the scholar: their phonetic values were gradually established between the seventeenth and the early nineteenth centuries by comparison with the Greek alphabets and with that of Latin. Since 1833, when R. Lepsius determined that the value of the Etruscan letter ✷ was *z*, the cycle of research has been considered closed as far as the alphabet is concerned: the correct and complete reading of inscriptions could be guaranteed in every case. A relatively recent discovery in this field should be recorded, however, for it has solved a marginal problem affecting one of the signs of the early Etruscan alphabet. This is the symbol ×, previously confused with *t*, but demonstrated with complete certainty by E. Fiesel to be a sibilant, which she transcribed as *ś*.[1] The reading of a number of Archaic inscriptions has been modified as a result: the symbol, in any case, is not very frequent.

The origin of the Etruscan alphabet has given rise to discussions that have not been completely settled. On the basis of the equivalence ↓ = χ, it has been classified among the western or 'red' Greek alphabets (A. Kirchhoff). Some scholars have postulated an ancient proto-Greek alphabet or have put forward even more improbable hypotheses.[2] The recent discovery of an inscription in Chalcidian characters on a Geometric eighth-century vase found at Pithekoussai (Ischia), however, has confirmed the traditional theory that the alphabet was first introduced into Central Italy by way of Cumae with the first Greek colonization of the area.[3]

It is certain that during the seventh century the Etruscans adopted a foreign alphabet of twenty-six letters, which is reproduced in its entirety on the margin of an ivory writing tablet found at Marsiliana d'Albegna (Plate 93), and also on a number of vases (see Plate 94), which are evidently didactic models. The practical use of this alphabet must have been the result of an elaborate process of adaptation to the needs of the recipient language. The letters *β*, *δ*, Phoenician *samek*, and *o* were discarded and do not appear in inscriptions, since they did not correspond to any of the sounds in the Etruscan phonetic system: the latter, in fact, lacked the series of voiced plosives, and the vowel o was not distinguished, at least originally, from u.[4] The letter γ was used to represent not the voiced velar plosive, absent from the Etruscan system, but the voiceless plosive (as also later with Latin c), together with κ and q, the use of which becomes rarer in later inscriptions.[5] The complementary symbol $\times$, which in the East Greek alphabets carried the value of χ, and in the western alphabets (and in Latin) that of the consonant cluster ks, occurs only in a few Archaic Etruscan inscriptions, with the value of a simple sibilant, $\acute{s}$. In the case of the labio-dental fricative f (different from the aspirated bi-labial consonant ϕ), the original alphabet lacked the appropriate symbol; at first, in the oldest texts, it was represented by the group vh[6]; later, as early as the sixth century but especially in later inscriptions, a new sign, 8, of uncertain origin, was introduced for it; it was placed last in the series of letters of the alphabet. The co-existence of the two sibilants **M** and **S** (corresponding respectively to the Phoenician letters *sade* and *šin*) is also worthy of note: it was justified by the existence in Etruscan of two allied sounds which, though occasionally confused or interchanged, were fundamentally distinct, and are now generally transcribed $\acute{s}$ and s.[7] As well as the adoption and the rejection of certain signs, the evolution of the Etruscan alphabet features a number of variations in the shapes of the letters, which permit the dating, at least approximately, of inscriptions. Figure 6 gives an outline of these changes.

In modern transcriptions of Etruscan the corresponding Latin letters are used, modified at times by diacritical signs, with the addition of the aspirates (*ph*, *th*, and *ch*), for which the Greek letters ϕ, θ, and χ are used.

Writing proceeds from right to left in the great majority of inscriptions, contrary to the usual direction of Greek and Latin writing. In a few rare cases, writing runs from left to right or changes direction with each new line. In the older inscriptions words are run together, whereas in later texts one or two dots are often interposed. An important discovery in the study of Etruscan arose from Vetter's researches on Venetic punctuation: working back from the latter to Archaic Etruscan inscriptions, he found the widespread application of a system where simple open syllables (e.g. *ma*, *lu*, *ke*, etc.) are considered 'normal' and are therefore left unpunctuated; whereas isolated letters, whether vowels or consonants, are distinguished by one or more dots. This system is common in some of the earlier vase inscriptions from southern Etruria, and is found even in such a relatively late document as the Capua tile. Is it perhaps a relic of a syllabic system of writing?[8] It is worth noting in this respect that an Archaic vase found at Cerveteri gives, in addition to the alphabet, a complete syllabary.

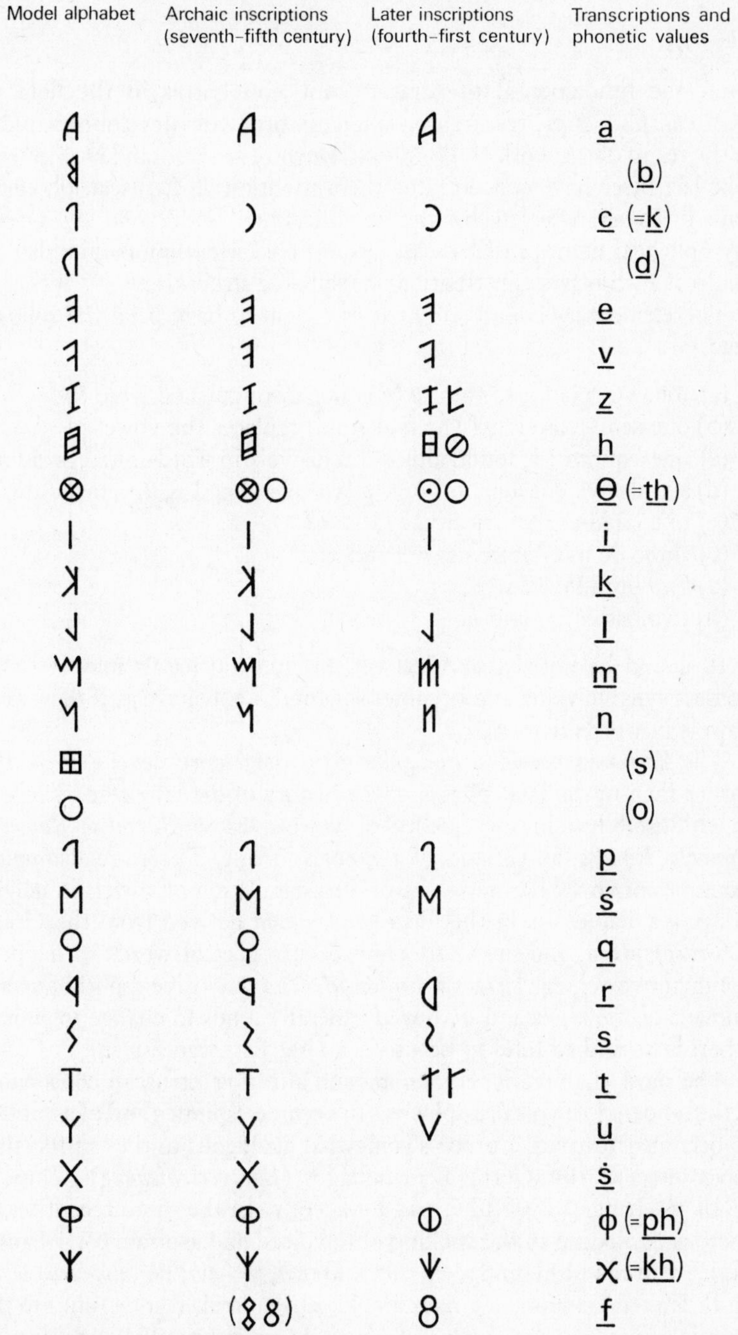

Model alphabet	Archaic inscriptions (seventh–fifth century)	Later inscriptions (fourth–first century)	Transcriptions and phonetic values
A	A	A	a
𐌁			(b)
ꓶ	)	C	c (=k)
ꓷ			(d)
ꓱ	ꓱ	ꓱ	e
ꓶ	ꓶ	ꓶ	v
I	I	ⵣ	z
𐌇	𐌇	𐌇⊘	h
⊗	⊗○	⊙○	θ (=th)
l	l	l	i
ꓘ	ꓘ		k
ꓩ	ꓩ	ꓩ	l
ꟽ	ꟽ	ꟿ	m
ꓩ	ꓩ	ꓵ	n
⊞			(s)
○			(o)
ꓶ	ꓶ	ꓶ	p
M	M	M	ś
ϙ	ϙ		q
ꓒ	ꓒ	ꓒ	r
ꕚ	ꕚ	ꕚ	s
T	T	ꓔꓩ	t
Y	Y	V	u
X	X		ś
Φ	Φ	Φ	φ (=ph)
Ψ	Ψ	Ψ	χ (=kh)
	(𐌚8)	8	f

Figure 6. Etruscan alphabets.

211

Phonetics

After the fundamental preparatory work by Lattes in the field of Etruscan phonetics, research on phonetic problems developed rapidly as the result of the work of Trombetti, Devoto, E. Fiesel and De Simone. The last three have concentrated their attention on Etruscan phonetic tendencies as revealed by the modifications undergone by Greek mythological names in Etruscan inscriptions. Mention should also be made of F. Slotty's contributions on syllable structure.[9]

The elementary sounds of Etruscan seem to have been the following:

(a) four vowels: *a*, *e*, *i* and *u* (*o* is not distinguished from *u*);
(b) one semi-vowel: *v* (which at times replaces the vowel *u*);
(c) one aspirate: *h*, found almost exclusively in word-initial position;
(d) six plosive consonants: *k*, *t*, *p* (voiceless) and *χ*, *θ*, *φ* (aspirates);
(e) one labio-dental fricative: *f*;
(f) three dental fricatives: *s*, *ś* and *z*;
(g) two liquids: *l* and *r*;
(h) two nasals: *m* and *n*.

It should be noted that fricatives, liquids and nasals may at times possess syllabic value and become 'sonants', i.e. behave as if they were vowels in words like *cnl*, *clθi*.

The Etruscan vowel system is a good deal more developed in the earlier than in the later phases of the history of the language. There is much instability in the quality of vowels, as in *Ràmaθa*, *Ràmeθa*, *Ràmuθa*, *Ràmθa*, all variants of a woman's name. There are also many examples of vowel harmony, i.e. of the assimilation of vowels in neighbouring syllables, as in the form *Cluθumusθa* derived from the Greek *Κλυταιμνήστρα*, and in the frequent occurrences of words with a predominant vowel, e.g. *siricima*, *Fuflunsul*, *acnanasa*. Five diphthongs are known: *ai*, *au*, *ei*, *eu* and *ui*, but *ai* generally tends to change to *ei* or *e*, whereas *au* and *eu* tend to become, in later Etruscan, *av* and *ev*.

The most characteristic phenomenon affecting Etruscan consonants is the tendency of voiceless plosives to become aspirates and of aspirates to become fricatives, a process somewhat analogous to the 'shifts' that have affected the Germanic languages (*Lautverschiebung*). Thus, *k* tends to change to *χ*, *t* to *θ*, and *p* to *φ* or *f*. In the more recent texts, there is oscillation in the spelling of unvoiced and aspirate consonants: both are used indifferently, e.g. *śuti* and *śuθi*, *zic-* and *ziχ*, *uple* and *uφle*. In the initial position, aspirates and fricatives weaken sometimes to the simple aspirate *h*: e.g. *Fasti* and *Hasti*. The absence of voiced plosives (*b*, *d* and *g*) in Etruscan may perhaps have been originally due to the

212

same phenomenon, i.e. they may have changed to the corresponding unvoiced consonants in prehistoric times.

In the matter of word-stress, the most noticeable and striking characteristic of Etruscan is the strong initial stress and consequent fall of unstressed vowels (syncope). It is most marked in Neo-Etruscan and results in the formation of complex consonant clusters and the development of sonants: e.g. Ar. Etr. *lautun*: N-Etr. *lautn*; Greek 'Αλέξανδρος: Etr. *Alexsantre*, *Elxsntre*.

Grammar

Considerable progress has also been made in the study of Etruscan morphology, although there are still vast areas of uncertainty or obscurity. We are indebted to Trombetti for stressing the importance of morphological phenomena in the interpretation of Etruscan, on the ground that the understanding of a text cannot be achieved merely by knowing the lexical values (i.e. the meaning of the word-roots), but requires also an accurate appreciation of syntactical relations and grammatical functions. Trombetti was the first to attempt, on a sound critical basis, the splitting of Etruscan words into their formative elements; and it is to him, as also to Rosenberg (within the framework of the combinatory method), that we owe the notion that the grammatical structure of Etruscan is distinct from that of the Indo-European languages. It is this difference which may explain some uncertainties and oscillations in word-formation and in word-endings, a certain lack of distinction between nominal and verbal forms, and even the anomalies that have been noticed in the construction of certain phrases (e.g. the apparent lack of a subject in the nominative case) that bedevil grammatical analyses based upon the model of more familiar languages. It is to solve this kind of problem that some scholars have formulated hypotheses on the 'passivity' of the Etruscan verb, of which more will be said later. But this whole question, large and complex as it is and still very obscure, merges into the problem of the very history of the language: the origin and correct classification of the structure of the oldest nucleus of the language and the likelihood of its gradual assimilation by the structure of neighbouring Indo-European languages.

With regard to word-formation, the cumulation of suffixes is a particularly interesting phenomenon. We define as 'morphological redetermination' (a term suggested by Trombetti) that group of facts pointing to a typical tendency of Etruscan grammar to reinforce or redetermine the syntactical function of a form by the cumulation of suffixes. For example, *Larθ*, a masculine personal name, becomes *Larθ-al* in the genitive, which, in its turn, may acquire another genitive

213

ending -*ś* to form *Larθ-al-ś*, used indifferently instead of *Larθ-al*. We may truly speak of an actual inflexion of forms that have already been grammatically inflected, with consequent change of meaning. This is the case of the so-called *genetivus genetivi* or double genitive, obtained by adding the suffix -*la* to a form in -*s*: e.g. *Vel Avleś*, 'Vel [son] of Avle' – genitive *Vel-uś Avles-la*, 'of Vel [son] of Avle'. These forms must be distinguished from a type of 'redetermined' genitive that does not involve change of meaning. A double genitive may in its turn be added to a redetermined genitive, producing complex forms where no less than three genitival suffixes are found superimposed upon each other: e.g. *Larθ-al-iś-la*, 'of [the son] of Larth'. Superimposed suffixes may be distinct in nature and function, as in the case of a locative added to a genitive: e.g. *Velsna-l-θi*, 'at Volsinii'; *uni-al-θi*, 'in Juno's [sanctuary]', from *Uni-al*, the genitive of *Uni*, 'Juno'. The concept of morphological redetermination, however repugnant it may appear to the structure of classical languages, has today been recognized by scholars as one of the most characteristic facets of Etruscan morphology.

The Etruscan noun does not possess a characteristic ending for the nominative, with the exception of a few masculine names of persons and gods that may take on an -*s* ending (genitive in origin?). Adjectives are formed by means of special suffixes, of which the most characteristic is -*na* (-*ina*, -*ena*). This is considered as the typical 'Etruscan' formative element, for it is also found in proper names, in place names, etc.: e.g. *śuθi*, 'tomb': *śuθi-na*, 'funerary'. Other derivational suffixes are -*u*, -*ie*, -*l*, -*c*, -*χva*. We may note the suffix -*θur*, which indicates appurtenance to a family unit or college: *velθinaθuraś*, 'of those belonging to the Velthina family'; *paχaθuras*, 'of the members of the confraternity of Bacchus', etc. Feminines show differentiation only in personal nouns (both proper and common), by means of special thematic suffixes and endings in -*i*, -*ia*, -*a*, and -*θa*: e.g. *pui, puia*, 'wife'; *Seθra*, the feminine form of *Seθre*, a *praenomen*; *Mutunai*, the feminine form of the gentilitial name *Mutuna*; *lautniθa*, 'freewoman', from *lautni*, 'freeman'. In the case of plural formations too, it is difficult to establish a rule: we know plural and collective nouns characterized by the suffixes -*r*, -*l*, and -*a*: e.g. *clan*, 'son': *clen-ar*, 'sons'; *murś*, 'sarcophagus': *murs-l*, 'sarcophagi'.

As for the declension of the noun, we are able to distinguish first of all an opposition between a thematic case, or nominative, and an 'oblique' case, characterized by the endings -*s* (-*ś*), -*si* (-*śi*), -*sa* (-*śa*) or -*l*, -*al*, -*la* (Ar. Etr. -*a*); this last suffix is generally used, as far as we can tell, with the value of a genitive of possession or attribution, and thus corresponds also to the Latin dative. The value of other nominal

214

suffixes is a good deal more obscure: *-i*, *-e;* *-t(i)* or *-θ(i)*; *-eri*. These seem at times to function as instrumental or locative suffixes, at times as datives of advantage, although forms with *-t(i)* and *-θ(i)* certainly possess a specifically locative value. The drawing up of actual regular paradigms of inflexions is not an easy task. Nevertheless it is possible to recognize series such as the following:

spur-	probably 'city'
spur-al	probably 'of the city'
spur-eθi	probably 'in the city'
śpur-eri	probably 'to [or for] the city'

We are able to distinguish two separate nominal groups or 'declensions', characterized by their genitive endings: one in *-s*, the other in *-l* (Ar. Etr. *-a*). To the first group belong all nouns ending in a vowel, with the exception of feminines in *-i*, and the majority of nouns ending in a consonant; to the second, feminines in *-i* and certain nouns, mostly personal, in *-s*, *-θ* or *-n*. E.g. for the first group, *hamφe*: gen. *hamφe-ś*; *Ramθa*: gen. *Ramθa-ś*; *fler*: gen. *fler-ś*; for the second group, *Uni*: gen. *Uni-al*; *Larθ*: gen. *Larθ-al*. We have already given some account of the phenomenon of morphological redetermination, which complicates and enriches the flexional system of the noun, although it should be remembered that such redeterminations are known to us almost exclusively from the personal name system.

The identification of the particles *mi*, *mini* with the personal pronoun of the first person (they were at first believed to be demonstratives), first made by Sittig and confirmed by the present author by the application of the method of 'bilingual' comparison, is now generally accepted.[10] From their use in inscriptions, particularly in votive inscriptions, it appears that *mi* is the nominative form (= *ego*) and *mini* the accusative (= *me*). We would thus seem to have proof of the existence in Etruscan of an accusative case, even though it may have been limited (or at some time restricted) to the pronominal system alone. The following probable demonstrative adjectives and pronouns are also known: *ca*, *eca* (Ar. Etr. *ica*), *ta* (Ar. Etr. *ita*), together with some of their declensional forms (e.g. *ca*, *cś*, *cla*, *cn*, *cei*, *clθi*, etc.; here too forms in *-n* appear to be accusatives). It is probable that demonstratives used as noun determinants came to be reduced to enclitic articles and incorporated in the noun: e.g. *esvi-tn*, *huslneś-tś*, *śacni-cla*, *śacni-cleri*, *śacni-cs-treś*, etc.

This peculiar phenomenon, first noticed by Torp, tends to increase the number and variety of declensional noun forms, already quite complex as the result of morphological redetermination: enclitic elements may take on the function of grammatical endings or create derivatives of the type *lautneś-cle*, 'gentilitial', literally 'in that of the family', from *lautn*, 'family'. Other particles such as *θi*, *χi*, *in*, *an*, *ipa*, etc. may have been demonstrative, relative or indefinite pronouns, but their use and interpretation are still far from clear. Compound particles such as *ancn*, *cnticnθ*, *ipeipa*, etc. should also be taken into account.

The problem of the Etruscan numerals is among the hardest and most debated in this field. Its starting-point resides in the identification of the first six digits with the six words written on the facets of the well-known Tuscania dice (Plate 95), now in the Bibliothèque Nationale in Paris. Although the correct equation of the two sets has for long been uncertain, the equivalences proposed by Torp can now be considered definite. They are: $θu = 1$, $zal = 2$, $ci = 3$, $śa = 4$, $maχ = 5$, $huθ = 6$. The only doubt that may persist concerns the identification of *huθ* as 6 or 4, owing to an ancient classical interpretation of the prehellenic place name Ὑττηνία as Τετράπολις.[11] Other numerals are represented by *semφ-*, *cezp-*, and *nurφ*. The word *zaθrum* is probably equivalent to 20. Multiples of 10 are formed by the addition of the suffix *-alc* or *alχ*: e.g. *cialχ*, *śealχ*, *cezpalχ-*, *muvalχ-*, etc. Counting appears to have proceeded additively as far as 6 (e.g. *huθiś zaθrumiś*, 'on the twenty-sixth [day]?') and subtractively from 7 to 9 (e.g. *esl-em-zaθrumiś*, 'on the eighteenth [day]'; cf. Greek δυῶν δέοντα εἴκοσι, Latin *duo-de-viginti*). Mention should also be made of numeral adverbs formed by the addition of the suffix *-z* or *-zi*: e.g. *ci-z*, 'thrice'. Forms like *zelur*, *zaθrumsne*, etc. are probably adjectives derived from numerals.

Many important questions arise from the study of the Etruscan verb. A nominal character was ascribed to it by Pauli; more recently it has been described as possessing a passive structure by Olzscha.[12] Many forms derived from verbal roots do in fact have the appearance and the endings of nouns, and also occasionally a passive value: e.g. *C.I.I.*, *Append.* 773: *mi mulu kaviiesi*, 'I have been dedicated by Kavie' or 'I [am the object] dedicated by Kavie' or even 'I [am] the votive offering of Kavie'. The most frequent among these forms end in a vowel (*tura*, *ture*, *turi*, *turu*, from a root *tur-*, 'to give'), or with a vocalized *-n* suffix (*śatena*, *nunθene*, *mulveni*, *zilaχnu*). Others, on the other hand, have suffixes that determine the verbal character of the form and specify its function, as in the case of the 'perfects' in *-ce*: *tur-ce*, 'has given', *lupu-ce*, 'has died' (cf. its equivalent *lupu*) or *muluvani-ce*, 'has dedicated'. The imperative is made up of the simple root, or of the root plus the ending *-θ*: *tur*, 'give!', *heχśθ*, 'place!', *nunθen* and *nunθen-θ* = Lat. *fac*, *facito*. Forms ending in *-sa* or *-śa* appear to have the value of a finite past or aorist: *teśamsa*, 'curavit'(?); whereas forms ending in *-as*

216

(-*aś*) or -*θas* (-*θaś*) may be interpreted as particles, or 'relatives' of the past: *sval-θas*, 'having lived, who has lived'. Finally, there is a suffix -*ri*, -*eri*, which expressed the concept of obligation or necessity, as in the Latin gerundive: *nunθ-eri* = Lat. *faciundum* [*est*]; a possible connection may exist with its homologue in the flexional system of the noun (*spur-eri*).

Very little is known for certain on adverbial expressions and copulative particles. It is generally difficult to distinguish between pronouns and pre- or postpositions. The old, fundamental discovery of the enclitic conjunction -*c*, corresponding to Latin -*que*, has been joined by that of enclitic -(*u*)*m*, analogous in meaning but generally used to co-ordinate sentences. The particle *etnam*, also found, it seems, in an enclitic form -*tnam*, has the value of an emphatic conjunction: it corresponded to Umbrian *inumek* and to Latin *item*, *etiam*. A few more adverbial or conjunctive particles are known, such as *θui*, 'here'; *matam*, 'above'(?); *iχ*, *iχnac*, 'as'; *nac*, 'how, why'; etc.

Little attention has so far been given to questions of syntax, word-order or style. Yet the texts seem to lend themselves to interesting observations under these headings, despite their thinness and the uncertainty of many of the data. Problems of this nature, moreover, are connected with the question of the originality of Etruscan linguistic structures. Generally speaking, the construction of the simpler, more easily analysable sentences shows remarkable analogies with Latin: e.g. a genitive precedes the noun it qualifies, the verb comes last in the sentence, etc. The best-known longer texts, those with a ritual content (Zagreb mummy, Capua tile), feature markedly analytical divisions and consist of short co-ordinated phrases.[13]

Interpretation of the texts

It would be true to say that the vast majority of Etruscan inscriptions in our possession can be read and understood without any difficulty. This is the case with the captions accompanying the figures on paintings and mirrors, the legends on coins, the names of owners written on single objects, and, especially, with funerary inscriptions. From these, the establishment of the syntactic value of certain inflexions (such as the genitive of the patronymic and matronymic) and the comparison of epitaphs of related persons buried in the same tomb have enabled us to establish from the very beginning the meaning of certain very common words such as *clan* = son, *seχ* = daughter, etc. At the same time, the meaning of the words for 'to live', 'to die', 'years', and 'age' were also fixed. Here is an example of the complete formula of a funerary inscription, with a literal translation:

Partunus	Vel	Velθurus	
Partunu	Vel	of Velthur	
Satlnal-c		Ramθas	clan
and of Satlnei		Ramtha	son
avils	lupu	XXIIX	
of years	dead	28	

(*C.I.E.* 5424)

i.e. 'Vel Partunu, son of Velthur and of Ramtha Satlnei, died when 28 years of age'.

Difficulties begin to arise when we pass to funerary inscriptions containing information on the life and career of the dead person, or inscriptions recording the dedication, foundation and furnishing of a tomb. Words of obscure and uncertain meaning begin to make their appearance, and their meanings become all the more arduous to determine as the etymological problems which they present are often rendered more complex by archaeological and historical difficulties. The combinatory method, even when assisted by the new bilingual processes, has not yet allowed us to pin down the value of, say, political, administrative or priestly titles that accompany the names of the dead, or the exact significance of sacral and funerary terms such as *sacni* (whence the verb *sacniśa*), *acazr*, etc. The value carried by the words for 'tomb', 'sarcophagus', 'to do', 'to give', etc., is, on the other hand, much clearer. Biographical funerary inscriptions are quite frequent, and may assume the character of Latin *elogia*, like the well-known inscriptions in the tombs of the Scipios. Here is a brief and simple example:

Aleθnas	Arnθ	Larisal	zilaθ
Alethna	Arnth	of Laris	*zilath*
Tarχnalθi	amce		
in Tarquinia	was		

(*C.I.I.*, *Suppl.*, III, 322)

i.e. 'Arnth Alethna, [son] of Laris: he was *zilath* (probably = *praetor*) in Tarquinia'. Here is a longer and more complex inscription:

Arnθ	Xurcles	Larθal	clan
Arnth	Churcle	of Larth	son [and]
Ramθas	Nevtnial	zilc	parχis
of Ramtha	of Nevtni	zilc	*parchis*
amce	marunuχ	spurana	
was	*maru*	civic	

cepen	tenu		avils
priest	held office(?)		of years
maxs semφalxls	*lupu*		
seventy-five(?)	dead		

(Fabretti, *C.I.I.* 2070)

i.e. 'Arnth Churcle, son of Larth and of Ramtha of Nevtni: he was *zilc parchis* (specification of one of the supreme magistratures), having [also] held the function of civic priest [of the college] of the *maroni*, died when seventy-five(?) years of age'. In these inscriptions, we meet titles of offices the precise meaning of which it is naturally impossible to determine (see, however, pp. 133 ff.). One of the longest biographical funerary inscriptions in our possession is, as we have already mentioned, the one carved on the sarcophagus of Laris Pulena (*C.I.E.* 5430). Beginning with a very full genealogical account of the dead man (going back to his great-grandfather), it lists the offices and religious honours of this important personage; but the text is unfortunately still very obscure, except for the introductory formula and a number of isolated words and expressions. It appears that Pulena was the author of books on divination (*zix neθśrac acasce*), had filled an important civic office in his native city of Tarquinia (*creals Tarxnalθ spureni lucairce*) and had been active in connection with the worship of the gods Catha, Pacha (Bacchus) and Culsu.

Some inscriptions refer more generally to the tomb, its owners, its foundation and furnishings, etc. Their commemorative nature is shown by the presence of dates, expressed by the name of the eponymous magistrate or magistrates of the city; e.g. at Tarquinia: *z[i]lci Vel[u]s Hulxniesi . . .*, 'when Vel Hulchnie was *zilc*' (*C.I.E.* 5388). Among the most complete and interesting inscriptions of this type there is one carved over one of two side niches of the San Manno hypogeum, near Perugia (*C.I.E.* 4116). We give here the first part, although there are some uncertainties about its interpretation:

cehen	*suθi hinθiu*	
this	underworld seat (= tomb)	
θueś	*sianś*	
of (or to) each	dead person(?)	
etve	*θaure*	
in the (?)	sepulchre	
lautneścle		
that of the family (= gentilitial)		
caresri	*auleś*	*larθial*
were built(?)	for Aule	[and] Larth

219

Precuθuraśi	*Larθialisvle*
belonging to the Precu	of Larth
Cestnal	*clenaraśi*
[and] of Cestnei	sons

i.e. 'The individual tombs built within this family vault (i.e. the side niches or *loculi*) are destined for Aule and Larth Precu, the children of Larth and Cestnei'. There follows a reference to the placing (*heczri*) of small urns (*murzua*) and other items.

The inscription of the great cippus of Perugia (*C.I.E.* 4538) is particularly noteworthy. From the time it was discovered in the nineteenth century, it has stimulated much interest among Etruscologists, with especially keen attempts to interpret it on the part of Torp, Trombetti, Ribezzo, Goldmann, Devoto, Kluge and others.[14] Two distinct families are recorded in the inscription, the Velthina and the Afuna, and explicit reference is made to the tomb of the Velthina (*Velθinaθuraś θaura*); the text also deals with public transactions or affairs (*raśneś, raśne*), land borders (*tularu*), measurements (*naper*), property (*acnina*), cessions (*turune, ścune* = 'he gave', or some similar phrase) and the writing of documents (*ziχuχe* = 'it was written'?). It is now almost impossible to doubt the juridical character of the text: it probably records a purchase-and-sale transaction or a donation of funerary properties, analogous perhaps to the *iura sepulcrorum* of certain Latin inscriptions. It is possible to explain not only single words, but whole phrases, though many obscurities, uncertainties and unsolved problems are scattered widely in the text, for there are still insufficient data to fix the accurate and precise translation of many words (e.g. *vaχr, tezan, fuśle, falaś, śpelθi*, etc.).

Votive inscriptions are the most common texts pertaining to the religious sphere. They are numerous on archaic vases and follow the classic formula:

mini	*mulvanice*	*Mamarce*
me	has dedicated	Mamarce
Velχanas		
Velchana		

(Cerveteri: *Notizie degli Scavi*, 1937, 388)

i.e. 'Mamarce Velchana dedicated me'.

These dedications include many forms and variants of the 'perfect' of the verb *mul-* (= Greek ἀνατίθημι); and other verbs with analogous meaning (e.g. *tur-, al-*, 'to give, to offer') also appear. The longer Archaic votive inscriptions on vases are usually extremely obscure, partly owing to the difficulty of separating the words from each other; they need not all be votive in character: some may be amatory or of some other nature, as in Greek, Latin and Faliscan Archaic graffiti. Particularly interesting is the spiral inscription traced on a small bucchero vase known as the 'Poupé aryballos', where the name of Turan (Aphrodite) or one of its derivatives is repeated three times.[15]

Neo-Etruscan dedications found on statuettes and other objects are generally easier to understand; next to the name of the dedicator, they often bear the name of the divinity to whom the offering is made. Here is an example:

ecn	*turce*	*Larθi*	*Leθanei*
this	has given	Larthi	Lethanei
alpnu	*Selvansl*		
as a gift	to Sylvan		

(*C.I.E.* 2403, on a bronze statuette)

Two Archaic dedicatory inscriptions stand out from the others for their content and importance. They are of uneven length and inscribed on two gold tablets found in the Pyrgi sanctuary together with an analogous inscription in Punic (Plate 13), corresponding to the longer of the two Etruscan texts (Plate 12). This proclaims the donation (*turuce*) of a sacred place or edifice (*tmia*), possibly also of a statue (*heramasve, heramve*?), to the goddess Uni, identified with the Phoenician goddess Astarte (*Unial Astres*), the donor being one Thefarie Velianas, designated by the Punic text as 'King over Cisra (i.e. Cerveteri)'. The circumstances and causes of the donation can be surmised from the Punic version, which alludes to a favour granted by Astarte to the dedicator; they seem to have some connection with three years (*ci avil*) of his supreme power (*zilacal*?). The shorter inscription (Plate 14) refers to the disposition and performance of certain rites in a given month (*tiurunias*) at the same holy place – an apparently yearly event (*vacl tmial avilχval*). Even if we discount the precious data they give on Etruscan religious life, the value of these documents is exceptional, for they are the first official contemporary historical sources to have come down to us by way of Etruscan epigraphy.[16]

The ribbon-like lead tablet found near Santa Marinella (Plate 101) is so damaged as to exclude the likelihood of a reconstruction and interpretation of the original. It is almost certainly a religious document, describing ceremonies and offerings (including votive offerings) and containing several words similar to those found in the important ritual texts of Capua and of the Zagreb mummy. By contrast, the text of the Magliano lens-shaped plaque, also in lead, is complete (*C.I.E.* 5237); it contains the names of gods (*cauθas, aiseras, marisl, calus, tins*) inserted within ritual prescriptions of an apparently funerary nature. In spite of numerous attempts, it is still impossible to offer even a partial translation of this text. Other inscribed lead tablets in our possession almost certainly consist of *tabellae defixionum*, i.e. the consecration to the infernal deities of persons whose death was desired. The most interesting, found at Monte Pitti, near Populonia (*C.I.E.* 5211), contains the curse of a freewoman upon a number of people partly related to one another. This type of document is well-known in the Greek and Roman worlds; but the bronze model of a liver found at Piacenza (already mentioned in the chapter on religion) is unique. It is inscribed with the names of gods, mostly abbreviated, in the appropriate spaces, presumably for the use of divinatory priests.

Finally we come to the two longest Etruscan texts in our possession: the Capua tile and the wrappings of the Zagreb mummy. Both these texts consist of rituals couched in the prescriptive formulas proper to a liturgical manual for the guidance of priests, a characteristic shared by the Umbrian texts of the Iguvine Tablets and by the Roman rituals handed down by literary sources (e.g. those contained in Cato's *de re rustica*). The difference lies in the nature of the ceremonies described. The Capua tile is closely connected with funerary rites performed in honour of infernal deities (*Suri, Leθam, Aφe-, Calu, Larun-, Fulinuśna, Natinusna(i), Seθum-*, etc.; but there is also mention of Tinia, Uni and, perhaps, Bacchus). Within the text, it is possible to distinguish brief sentences, rather uniform in structure, with the verb in the imperative, the indication of the blood or bloodless offering, preceded at times by a numeral and the name of the divinity in the genitive-dative case. But it is more difficult to determine the exact technical meaning (i.e. the correct translation) both of verbs expressing sacred acts (*acas-, picas-, sac-, tul, ilucu, apir-, utu, scuv-, fani-, nunθ*, etc.) and of the nouns describing the offering or the things offered (*vacil, tartiria, cleva, riθna, zusleva, turza*, etc.). Here, for example, is how the meaning of one of the prescriptive phrases may be dimly perceived:

Leθamsul	*ci*	*tartiria*
To [the god] Letham	three	*tartiria*
ci-m	*cleva*	
and also three	*cleva*	
acasri		
ought to be offered (or some similar phrase)		

The text probably also mentions the officiating priests (*cipen, celu*, etc.) and perhaps also the family (*lavtun*) of the dead man. It is possible, though not certain, that the rites mentioned are distributed along a calendar. We have already noted the likelihood that the Capua ritual may have some connection with the 'salvation' sacrifices contained in the *Libri Acherontici* and recorded by some late classical authors.[17]

Naturally the greatest effort in the deciphering of Etruscan has concentrated on the longest available text, the *liber linteus* of the Zagreb mummy, which, thanks to good editing, the evenness of the script and the regular word-division, the recentness of the language and frequent recurrence of words and formulas, offers the most favourable conditions for decipherment. The text was first studied with partial success by Lattes, Torp, Rosenberg and Trombetti; more recently, it has become the object of repeated and ever deeper probings on the part of Runes, Cortsen, Olzscha, Vetter, Pfiffig and the present author.[18]

The hypothesis that the text contains a funerary ritual in some way connected with ancient Egypt and with the mummy on which the wrappings were found has now been definitely discarded in favour of the view that it consists of a series of prescriptions connected with partly public ceremonies regulated by a religious calendar. The most notable section of the text consists of a liturgical sequence, repeated with small variants at least four times, in honour of the 'gods' (*eiser śi-c śeu-c*), of a god *in crapśti*, and of Neptune (*Neθunś*). As in the case of the Iguvine Tablets, the sacrifices were made on behalf of institutions of a religious nature (a sanctuary) or political (a city and people?), indicated by the words *śacnicleri cilθl śpureri meθlumeri-c enaś*. Less important paragraphs prescribe, more or less summarily, ceremonies in honour of other divinities (Veltha, Tin, Culsu and Uni). Each paragraph appears to be preceded by a date (day and month): e.g. *eslem zaθrumiś acale*, 'on the eighteenth of the month of *Acale* (June)'. Of the words found repeated in the text, some are understood with sufficient certainty and precision (e.g. *vinum* = 'wine'; *ais*, *eis* = 'god'; *fler* = 'sacrifice, offering'; *tur* = 'give'; etc.). Others are understood only in a general sense and no precise translation can be given with any certainty (e.g. *zeri*, *vacl*, *faśe*, *eśvi*, *zuśleva* = sacred ceremonies, offerings; *farθan*, *nunθen*, *θezin*, *tul* = technical verbs connected with religious worship etc.). Finally, there are many words about whose meaning there is much doubt and disagreement among scholars.

Here as elsewhere, the step most likely to lead to a complete understanding of the text consists in isolating the syntactic units corresponding to complete phrases, and identifying, as far as possible, the essential elements of these phrases: subject, verb or nominal predicate, and complements. To achieve this, much help is obtained from the isolation of conjunctive elements (e.g. the enclitic particles *-c* and *-um*, and conjunctions such as *etnam*, *iχ*, *nac*), and especially from the distinction of nominal and verbal forms and the definition of the syntactic functions of certain suffixes. In many cases, no satisfactory result has been attained or seems attainable, but in the most favourable instances the structure of the Etruscan text is revealed by the network of syntactic relations, and only the precise semantic content of lexical elements is missing. Thus in the phrase *cis-um pute tul θansur haθrθi repinθi-c* it is possible to recognize *tul* as a verb in the imperative, *θansur* as the object in the form of a plural noun and *haθrθi repinθi-c* as a locative or instrumental complement formed by two nouns, both probably in the plural possessing the same inflexion *-θi* and connected by an enclitic copula *-c*. Occasionally, however, even the semantic values of the component words may be arrived at with a greater or lesser degree of probability, so that the general meaning of the phrase can be made out, as if through a gradually lifting fog. Here are some examples:

(1) Column VIII, lines 3 ff.:
Celi
[the month of] *Celi* (September)
huθiś zaθrumiś
the twenty-sixth [day] (?)
flerχva
all the offerings

Neθunsl	*sucri*
to the god Neptune	should be declared (or similar verb)

θezeri-c . . .
and should be made . . .

(2) Column IX, lines 6 ff.:

raχθ	*tur*	*heχśθ*
to the left(?)	give	place

vinum	*trin*
the wine,	invoke (or propitiate)

flere Neθunśl	*un*	*mlaχ*
the god Neptune,	accomplish(?)	the vow,

nunθen	*zuśleve . . .*
sacrifice	with the offer of a *zuśleva* . . . (an animal?)

(3) Column XI, lines 14 ff.:

cntnam	*θesan*	*fler*
and on the same	morning	the offering

Veiveś	*θezeri*	*etnam*
to Vejove	should be made	and moreover

ais[na]	. . .	*iχ*
the divine service . . .		as on the [day]

huθiś zaθrumiś . . .
twenty-six(?) . . .

These examples, with their partial, tentative translations, give a fair idea of the procedures adopted in interpretative work and of its achievements and limitations. These criteria are being followed by the majority of authoritative specialists and result in slow but gradual progress.

The vocabulary

For reasons that we have already examined, our knowledge of Etruscan vocabulary is limited mainly to those words that concern the religious and funerary world, to terms relating to kinship or political and social organization, to a few notions on the division of time and to a very small number of other more general items.[19] To complete the data already given, there now follows an alphabetical list of Etruscan words with their certain or most likely meaning.

The list comprises both words documented directly from the texts and words reconstructed from the 'glosses' (these are marked by an asterisk). Since the scope of this selection is mainly linguistic, we have excluded proper names, whether personal, religious or mythological, and place names; but we have included names that probably have some generic meaning as well, and also words derived from proper names that have entered the common vocabulary. Words connected etymologically are grouped together. The flexional endings of nouns and verbs are shown in brackets after the root form. As a rule, wherever possible, the older forms are listed first.

acale (*Aclus*) name of month: 'June'

*acaleθur(?) (ἀγαλήτορα) 'boy', with perhaps some special meaning

acas (-a, -ce, -ri) 'to do, to offer'(?); *acazr* 'objects offered in the tomb'

avil (-s, -ś) 'year(s)'; *avilχva-* (-l) 'yearly, anniversary'(?)

aθre 'edifice' (related to Lat. *atrium*?); derived form(?): *atranes*

ais, aiś (plur.: *ais-er; -er-as, -er-aś*), *eis* (-er; -er-as, -er-aś) 'god' (αἰσοί, *aesar*); *aisna, eisna* 'divine, divine service', perhaps in the sense of a particular ceremony; *eisnev*(c)- priestly title; see also under *esvi-*

al (-a, -e, -(i)ce, -(i)qu, -χu, etc.) 'to give, donate'; *alpan, alpnu* 'gift'; *alφaze* 'offering'

am (-a, -e, -(u)ce) 'to be'

an, anc, ananc, ancn (relative?) pronouns

*anθa (ἄνδας, ἄνταρ) 'eagle', 'north wind'

apa 'father', *aφe-* (*aφe-s, -rs, afrs*) 'ancestors, *parentes*'; derived forms: *aper* (*apir-e, -es, -ase; -θe, -θe-s; aper-ucen*) sacred act, perhaps 'funerary sacrifice' (= Lat. *parentare*?); *aprinθu* (*aprinθvale*) sacral title(?)

225

ar (*-a*, *-aś(a)*, *-ce*, *-θ*, etc.), *er-* (*-ce*, *-s-ce*) verb of movement(?); also in ritual practices (with *arse verse* 'move away the fire'?)

*arac (ἄρακος) 'falcon'

*arim (ἄριμος) 'monkey'

asil part of sacred building, perhaps 'small pilaster, base' or the like (related to Lat. *assis*, *asser*?); probable derivative: *aślaχ*

aska (from Gk ἀσκός) name of vase

ati, *ati(v)u* (*atis*?) 'mother'; *ati nacn(v)a* 'grandmother'?

-c enclitic copula (= Lat. *-que*)

ca (*cen*, *cn*; *ces*, *cś*; *cal*, *cla*; *cei*, *ceia*; *calti*, *clθ(i)*, etc.); emphatic forms: *ica* (*ikan*, *ikam*), *eca* (*ecn*, *ecs*, *eclθi*) demonstrative adjective or pronoun: 'this'; used also enclitically as determinate article (*-ca*, *-can*, *-cn*, *-cas*, *-cś*, *-cla*, *-cle*, *-cleri*); compound forms: *cehen*, *catica*, *ceiθi(m)*, *cnticnθ*(?), *icecin*(?)

calusin, *calusna* derivatives of the name of the infernal deity *Calu*?

camθi title of magistracy; *canθ-* (*-e*, *-ce*) verb denoting the exercise of the magistracy

cape, *capi* (*cape-r*, *-ri*) name of container (related to Lat. *capis*?) and perhaps also (γάπος) 'cart'; adjectival form: *caperχva*; derivative: *capra* container, funerary urn

*capr- (*Cabreas*) name of month: 'April'

*capu (κάπυς) 'falcon'

car- (*kar-a*, *car-u*, *-es-ri*), *cer-* (*-en*, *-ine*; *-iχu*; *-iχun-ce*) 'to make, build'; derivatives: *caraθsle*, *cerur*, etc.

cezp numeral ('eight'?); *cezpalχ* (*-als*) decimal ('eighty'?); *cezpz* 'eight(?) times'; may be connected with *Chosfer*, name of month: 'October'

cel, *celi*, *celu*, *celu-cn* point of the compass(?) and (*Celius*) name of month: 'September'; *celu* priestly title

cep-ta (*-ar*), *cepen*, *cipen* (*cepen-e*) priestly title

ces-, *ceś-* (*-u*, *-eθ-ce*) 'to place', 'to be placed, to lie'

ceχa (*ceχe*) referring to sacred things: 'rite' or 'right'(??). Derivatives: *ceχane* (*-ri*: *zilχ ceχaneri* title); *ceχase* title of magistracy or priestly office; *ceχasieθur* 'belonging to the college of the *ceχase*'

cver, *cvera*, *-cvil*, *cvl* 'gift', thing offered or dedicated; also enclitically in the compounds *tins-cvil*, *tinś-cvil* 'offered to the god Tin' or perhaps generically 'votive offering' (and in the formation of the theophoric female *praenomen* *θan-cvil* *θan-χvil* = consecrated to the goddess Thana)

ci (*-s*, *-ś*) numeral: 'three'; *cialχ-*, *cealχ*, *celχ-* (*-us*, *-uś*, *-ls*) 'thirty'; *ciz*, *citz*, *cizi* 'three times'; possible derivatives: *cialaθ*, *cianil*, *ceanuθ*, etc.

cilθcva (-*l*, *cilθcve-ti*) derived form of the name of a deity or of the site of a sanctuary *cilθ*

clan (*clen*, *clen-s*, *clen-ś*; *clin-si*, *clen-si*, *clen-śi*; plur.: *clen-ar*, *clinii-ar-as*, *clen-ar-aśi*) 'son'

cleva offering

cletram object for the carrying of offerings (= Umbrian *kletra*)

culiχna, *χuliχna* (from Gk κύλικνος) name of vase

cupe (-*s*) (from Gk κύπη, Lat. *cupa*) name of vase, 'cup'

eca see *ca*

eθr- see *etr-*

ei, *ein*, *eiθ*, *eθ*, *eθl* pronominal particles (?); see also *ta*

eis see *ais*

elu- see *ilu-*

-em enclitic subtracting element in numerals: 'from'

epl see *pi*

eprθ- see *purθ-*

er- see *ar-*

esl-, *esal-* see *zal*

esc-, *esχ-* see *sc-*

esvi- (-*tn*, -*ś*) ceremony, sacrifice (to be connected with *ais*, *eis*?)

eśta(*c*), *eśtla* pronominal particles (?); see *ta*

etera, *eteri*, *etri* (*etera-ś*, *eterai*(*a*)*s*) name of a social class: 'client, serf'(?); *eterau*, *eterav* connected with the *etera*: *zilaθ eterav*, *camθi eterau* (cf. *zil eterai*(*a*)*s*) titles of magistracies connected with the *etera*

etva see *ta*

etnam conjunctive copula: 'and, also'; enclitically: -*tnam*

etr-, *eθr-* (*eθr-i*; -*se*; *etra-sa*) verb denoting some religious act (related perhaps with *tur*?); probable derivatives: *eter-ti*(*c*), *etrin-θi*

vacal, *vacil*, *vacl* sacred act or offering ('libation'?); derivative, or plural: *vaχr*

*velcitna (*Velcitanus*) name of month: 'March'

velznaχ 'Volsinian' (from *Velzna-* 'Volsinii')

vers- (*verse*) 'fire'; derivatives: *versie* name of container(?), *versin*

vertun, *vrtun* name of vase

vinum, *vinm* 'wine' (= Lat. *vinum*)

zal, *zel-*, *zl*, *es*(*a*)*l-* (*esal-s*) numeral: 'two'; *zaθrum*, *zaθrm-* (-*s*, -*is*, -*iś*) 'twenty'; *eslz* 'twice'; derivatives: *zelvθ*, *zelur*, *zelarvenas*, *zaθrumsne*

zar see *sa*

zeri (-*ś*) sacred act or thing, 'rite', juridical act(??)

ziva- (*-s*, *-ś*) '(the) dead'

zic-, *ziχ* (*ziχ-u*, *-ina*, *-ne*, *-uχe*, *-un-ce*) 'to write'; *ziχ* 'book'(?)

zil, *zili*, *zilac-* (*-al*), *zilc*, *zilci*, *zilχ*, *zilaθ* 'magistrate' and specific title of magistracy (= Lat. *praetor*?); *zilcθi*, *zilcti*, *zilcte* forms or derivatives denoting the magistrate in office; *zilχ-*, *zilaχ-* (*zilχ-nu*, *-nce*, *zilaχ-nu*, *-nve*, *-n(u)-ce*, *-n-θaś*) verb denoting the exercise of the magistracy

zusle, *zuśle* (*zusle-i*), *zusleva*, *zuśleva* (*zusleva-i*, *zuśleve-ś*) offering, animal victim(?)

hec-, *heχ* (*hec-i*, *-ia*, *-e*, *-ce*, *-z-ri*, *heχ-z*, *-śθ*) 'to place, to add' or similar verb

heramaśva, *heramve*, *herma*, *hermu*, *hermeri* words probably connected with the name of the god Hermes and which may have a common meaning: 'statue'?; **hermi-* (*Hermius*) name of month: 'August'

hinθa, *hinθu*, *hinθia*, *hinθie*, *hinθθin* indications of place(?) with special reference to the underworld; *hinθial* 'spirit, shade'

hiuls 'screech-owl'

huθ (*-s*, *-iś*) numeral: 'six' (or 'four'???); connected or derived forms: *huθte*, *huθzars*, *huteri*

hupni (*-ś*), *hupnina* (*hupnineθi*), *hupniva* chamber or repository, particularly in tomb

hus-, *huś-* (plur.: *hus-ur*, *huś-ur*, *hus-iur*) 'son, boy'; the following may be connected: *husl*, *husili*, *huslne* (*-ś-tś*), *husina*, perhaps in relation with the concept 'young man'; derivative: *huzrnatre* referring to the college of the *iuventus*(?)

θam- (*-(u)ce*) 'to place', 'to found'(?)

θanasa see *tanasa-*

θap- (*-icun*, *-inta(i)ś*) verb denoting a dedication or *devotio*; *θapn*, *θapna* (*-i*, *θapne-ś-tś*) probably sacrificial vase

θaur-, *θaura* (*θaur-uś*, *θaure*) 'tomb, sepulchre'; *θaurχ* 'funerary': *cepen θaurχ* title of funerary priest

*θevru (in *θevru-mineś* 'Minotaur') 'bull'

θez-, *tez*? (*θez-i*, *-in*, *-ine*, *-in-ce*, *-eri*) 'to make' (an offering or sacrifice)

θesan (*θesn-s*, *θesan-e*) 'morning, day' (also name of goddess: Thesan, the dawn); derived adjective: *θesnin*

θi (*-i*, *-l*) pronominal particle(?)

θu, *θun*, *tun-* (*θue-ś*?, *θun-ś*, *-i*?, *-t*?, *tun-t*?) numeral: 'one' and also 'alone'?; *θunz* 'once'; probable derivatives *θunśna*, *θunχer-* (*-ś*), *θunχul-* (*-e*, *-θe*, *-l*), *tunur*, *θufi*, *θueś*, *θuvas*, etc.

θucte name of month

θui adverb: 'here'

ica see *ca*

ic, *iχ* conjunctive or adverbial particle: 'how, and' (perhaps related with enclitical -*c*); compound: *iχnac*

ilu- (*ilu-cu*, -*cve*; *ila-cve*), *elu-* (-*ce*, -*ri*) verb denoting prayer or offering; perhaps possesses also some temporal meaning (*ilucve*, *ilacve* 'kalendae'?)

in, *inc*, *ininc* pronominal (relative?) particles; compounds: *inpa*, *inpein*

ipa (-*s*, -*l*, *ipe*, -*i*, -*ri*?) relative pronoun(??)

ita see *ta*

**itu-* (*idus*) 'to divide'(?), 'Ides'(?); derivative: *ituna*(?)

-*k* see -*c*

kape, *kapi* see *cape*, *capi*

kara see *car-*

klan see *clan*

lautun-, *lautn*, *lavtun*, *lavutn*, *lavtn* (*lautn-es*, *lautn-eś-cle*) 'family, gens'; other form, or derivative: *lavtunui*; *lautni*, *lavtni*, *lautuni*, *lavtuni* (*lautuni-ś*) 'of the family, gentilitial' and, as substantive, specifically 'free-man'; *lautna*, *lautnita*, *lavtniθa*, *lavtnita* 'free-woman'; compound: *lautn-eteri* 'free-man, client'(?)

lauc-, *luc-*, *lauχme*, *luχum-* (*lucumo*) probably 'king'; *lauχumna-* (*lauχumne-ti*) 'king's court'(?); *lucair-* (-*ce*) verb denoting the exercise of a power

lein- (-e) 'to die'(?)

leu 'lion, lioness'

leχtumuza (from Gk λέκυθος) name of vase

lupu (-*ce*, *lupv-enas*?) 'to die'

-*m*, -*um* enclitic copula

mac, *maχ* (*maχ-s*) numeral: almost certainly 'five'; derivatives: *macra*, *macnur*(?)

macstrev(*c*) title of magistracy (= Lat. *magister*: cf. the name *Macstrna*)

malena, *malstria* 'mirror'(?)

man, *mani*, *manim* (*man-θ*, *manim-eri*) 'the dead, Manes' (= Lat. *Manes*); *manin-* (-*ce*) verb denoting offerings to the Manes(?)

maru title of magistracy (= Lat. *maro*, Umbrian *maron-*); connected and derived forms: *marnu*, *marniu*, *marunu*, *marunuχ*, *maruχva*, *marunuχva*: *zilaθ maruχva*, *zilc marunuχva*, *marunuχva cepen*, etc. titles; *maru-* (*marv-as*) verb denoting the exercise of the magistracy

masan, *masn* name of month

matam, *matan* adverb: 'above' or 'before'(?)

229

meθlum (*-es, -eś; -eri; -θ, -t*) referring to the territory (of the State?) or to some other institutional concept

men- (*-a, -e, -u; -ece, -aχe; -aś*) verb denoting the act of offering; derivatives: *menica, menitla*

meχ (*-l*) political or institutional concept, probably '*populus*' (cf. *meθlum?*); *zilaθ meχl rasnal* (or *meχl(um) rasneas*) title (= *praetor Etruriae, praetor Etruriae XV populorum*)

mi, me- (*mi-ni, -ne, -na, me-ne*) first-person pronoun: 'I, me'; compound or derivative forms: *mipi, minpi(?)*

mlak-, malak, mlac, mlaχ (*mlak-a, -as, mlac-aś, mlaχ-as*), *mlaci-θa, mlaχ-(u)ta* 'votive gift, anathema' (possibly from *mulaχ*: see *mul*)

muvalχ- (*-ls*): numeral, decimal

mul- (*-a, -i, -u; -une, -veni; -eni-ke, -vani-ce, -vene-ke, -vunu-ke, -uvani-ce,* etc.) 'to offer as a vow or because of a vow, ἀνατίθημι'; derivatives *mulaχ, mlaχ, mulsle,* etc.

mun-, muni- (other forms or derivatives: *muni-s, -s-ta-s; -cle-θ, -cle-t, -ule-θ, -vle-θ; mun-sle; munθ*) place, tomb niche, tomb(?) (= Lat. *mundus?*)

mur (*-ce*) 'to be, to live in a place' (connected with Lat. *mora?*); probable derivative: *murs* (*murś-ś, -l*) 'urn, sarcophagus'

mutana, mutna (*mutne, mutnia-θi*) 'sarcophagus'

*mutu- (μούτουκα) 'thyme'

nac adverb or conjunction: 'as, because'

nap- (*nap-ti, nap-er*) measure(?) (cf. Lat. *napurae?*)

naplan name of vase (connected with Gk ναβλας, Lat. *nabl(i)um?*)

nes-, neś- (*-l, neś-s*) 'dead person'; derivatives *nesna, nesiθvas*

netśvis, netsviś 'haruspex'; *neθśrac* 'haruspicine': *ziχ neθśrac* probably = *liber haruspicinus*

nefts, nefś, nefiś 'nephew, grandson' (= Lat. *nepos*)

nuna (*-r*) 'offering'(?); *nunθ* (*-en, -ena; -en-θ; -eri*) verb denoting the sacrificing or the giving of an offering

nurφ- numeral; *nurφzi* adverb: '? times'

papa 'father'(??) or 'grandfather'(?); *papacś?, papals, papalś* (*papals-er*) other terms denoting kinship (but rather in a sense opposed to 'nephew'?)

par, parniχ, parχis terms connected with social conditions or with offices (= Lat. *par?*): *zilc parχis, zilaθ parχis* title of magistracy

parla name of vase (connected with Lat. *patera, patella?*; cf. *patna*); derivative: *parliu*

patna (from Gk πατάνη, Lat. *patina*) name of vase

paχaθur- (*-as*) 'bacchant, belonging to the college of bacchants' (from the name of the god *Paχa* 'Bacchus')

penθna, penθuna 'cippus, stone'(?)

pi particle: pre- or postpositional (also, enclitically, *-pi*) with the value of 'to, in, for'(?); the words *pul, epl* may perhaps be related, and possess analogous values(?)

picas (*-ri*) verb denoting an offering (cf. *acas*)

prumts, prumaθś, prumste 'great-nephew, great-grandson' (= Lat. *pronepos*)

pruχ- (*-ś*), *pruχum* (from Gk πρόχους) name of vase; derivative or variant form: *prucuna*

puθ- see *put-*

pui, puia, pulia (*puiian; pui-l*) 'wife'

pul see *pi*

pulumχva 'stars'(?); perhaps also in the sense of augural signs in connection with the foundation of a temple (if corresponding to Phoenician *kkbm*)

purθ, pruθ (?), *puruθn*(?), *purat*(*um*); *purθne, eprθne* title of magistracy (connected with Gk πρύτανις?); connected or derived forms: *eprθieva, eprθnev*(*c*), *purtśvana*; *purθśvavcti* denoting the magistrate in office; *purθvnce, φurθce* verbal forms denoting the exercise of the magistracy

put-, puθ- (*-s, put-e*), *putina, putiza* name of vase (connected with Lat. *potus*?) or perhaps more generically, container: 'well'(?) (cf. Lat. *puteus, puteal*?); *putere* (*-s*) (from Gk ποτήρ) name of vase

qutun, qutum (from Gk κώθων) name of vase

rasna, raśna, rasnea- (*rasna-s, rasnea-s, raśne-ś; rasna-l, raśna-l; raśne*) connected with Gk Ρασέννα 'Etruscans': 'Etruscan', 'Etruria'(?)

ril 'at the age of . . . years'

rumaχ 'Roman' (from *Ruma-* 'Rome')

sa, śa (*śa-ś, śa-s*) numeral: 'four' (or 'six'???; see Plate 102); *sealx-* (*-ls*) decimal derivative: *sazil*(?); *sar-* (*-iś*), *zar* connected form or another unconnected numeral, with *śarve zarve, śarvenas, śarśnaus* as probable derivatives

sac-, śac- (*sac-a, -ri*) verb denoting a sacred act or state; *sacni, sacniu, śacni-cn, śacni-tn* (*-cla, -tle, -cl-eri, -cś-treś*) sacred or consecrated place or thing: 'sanctuary'(?); derivative: *sacnitalte*(?); *sacnisa, sacniśa* verbal form: 'to consecrate'(?)

san-, śan-, sian-, san-iśva 'the dead'; *sian-ś, sanś-aś, san-śl, sian-śl,*

231

san-ulis, san-e(?) 'dead person, dead ancestor'(?); *santi, śanti* (*śanti-ś-tś*) title of (funerary?) priest

sar-, śar- see *sa*

śat-, saθ, śaθ (*śaθ-e; śat-ena, -ene; śaθ-aś*) verb denoting the act of placing or establishing(?)

sc-, scu-, ścu-, esχ-, escu- (*sce*?; *ścu-n, -na, -ne, scu-na, -nu; -n-si, -v-se; scv-etu; esχ-aθ, esχ-aθ-ce, escu-na*) 'to give, to place, to offer'(?); derivative: *sχuinia*(?)

sec, śec, seχ, śeχ (*śeχ-is, -iś*) 'daughter'

semφ- (*-ś*) numeral ('seven'?); *semφalχ-* (*-ls*) decimal ('seventy'?)

sval, 'alive'; *sval-* (*-ce; -as, -asi; -θ-as*), variant: *saval-* (*-θas*) 'to live'; possible cognates: *svel-, śvel-* (*-eri, śvel-ś-treś*) in the sense of living beings(?)

sl- see *zal-*

snenaθ 'maidservant, female companion' or similar value

śran, sren 'figure'(?); *śrencve, śrenχve* 'figured, ornamented'(?)

spet- (*-ri*) verb denoting a sacred act: 'to libate'(?) (connected with Gk σπένδω?)

spur-, śpur- (*-al; spur-eθi; spur-eri; -es-treś*, etc.) 'city'; *spurana, spureni* 'civic, of the city'; *spuriaze(s)* 'public'(?)

suc-, śuc- (*śuc-i, -ivn, -ri*) ritual act (cf. *sac-, śac-* ?)

suplu (Lat. *subulo*) 'flautist'

sut-, suθ, śuθ-, śt-(?) (*śuθ-ce, sut-anaś*) verb probably denoting the act of placing or of standing (cf. *śat-, saθ, śaθ*?); *śuti, suθi, śuθi* (*suθi-ś, śuθi-θ, śuθi-ti* etc.) with variants or derivatives *śuθu* (plur. *suθv-r*?), *suθil:* 'place, tomb'; *śutina, śuθina, sutna, śutna* 'pertaining to the tomb, funerary'

ta (*ten, tn, θn; teis, teiś; tei*), emphatic form: *ita* (*itan, itun; itas*?; *ital*), cf. also *eθ, eiθ, eθl,* demonstrative pronoun or adjective: 'this', used also enclitically as a determinate article (*-ta; -tn; -tś; -tla, -tle; -tra, -tre, -treś,* etc.); possible cognates (whether as base or derived or compound forms?) *etva* (*etve*), *eśta(c)* (*eśt-la*), *itanim, etanal,* etc.

tamera, tameru (*tamere-s-ca*) title; *tamiaθur-* (*-as*) college; *tesinθ tamiaθuras* 'warden of the members of the college of the *tamia-*'

*tamna or *θamna (δάμνος) 'horse'

tanasa-, θanasa (*tanasa-r*) 'actor (*histro*)' or performer in a rite; may be connected with *θanś* (*-ur*)

tev-, tv- (*tva*) 'to show, to see'(?); *tevaraθ* 'referee, judge in a competition'(?)

ten- (*-u, -ve; -ine; -θ-as, -θ-aś*) 'to act' in the sense of 'to exercise a magistracy' *teś-, tez*(?) (*-amsa*) 'to look after'(?) (cf. *θez-*?); *tesinθ* 'curator'; may perhaps be connected with the words *tezan, tesn-* (*-e, -ś*), *tesim, teśami-tn,* etc., of uncertain meaning

tin- (*-ś, -śi*) 'day' (also the name of the god Tin, with which it may be confused in the texts); derivative: *tinśi*

tiu, tiv-, tivr (*tiiur-ś, tivr-s*) 'moon, month'; variant or derivative forms: *tiuri-, tiurunias*

tmia (*-l*) sacred place or building: 'temple'(?)

-tnam see *etnam*

trin (*-θ, -θ-aśa*) verb denoting a sacred act of offering or prayer: 'to supplicate, to invoke'(?)

*truna or *θruna (δροὐνα) 'power, sovereignty'

trut, truθ (*trut-ana-śa*?) verb denoting a sacred act; probable derivatives: *trutnuθ, trutnvt* title of divinatory priest, '*fulguriator*' (*trutnvt fontac*??); *trutvecie*

tun- see *θu*

tuθi, tuti probably 'community, state' (cognate with Umbrian *tuta*?); variant or derivative forms: *tutin, tutim, tuθin; tuθiu; tuθina-* (*tuθineś*) 'pertaining to the state, public'(?)

tular, tularu 'limits, borders'

tur- (*-a, -e, -i, -u; -une; -u-ce, -un-ke, -i-ce, -ce, tiurke*) 'to give'; *turza* (*-i, -is*) offering

tuś (*-θi;* plur.: *-ur-θi*) funerary niche or repository; other forms or derivatives: *tuśuvas, tuśθuveś*(?); *tusurθir* (properly 'who are in the double urn', 'man and wife'?)

-um see *-m*

usil (*-s*) 'sun' and god of the sun (cf. Sabine *ausel-*); derivatives: *usli, uslane·*

ut-, uθ- (*ut-a; -us, -uśe; -in-ce; uθ-ari*?) verb denoting the action of giving

φersu 'mask, masked person' (= Lat. *perso-na*)

φurθce see *purθ-*

χia(?), *χi-* (*χia-s*?, *χi-ś*), *χim, χiem, χimθ, χimθm* particle, probably pronominal; derivative *χiśvlicś*(?)

favi- (*-ti*), *favin* 'temple vault, grave'

*falatu (*fala*(*n*)*do*) 'sky, heaven'; may be connected with *falau, falaś* (*falś-ti, falza-θi*), *falica, faluθras*

fanu sacred place (?) (= Lat. *fanum*?); *fan-* (*-u-śe, -u-śei; -eri*?, *-iri*) cognate verb: 'to consecrate'(?)

faśe (*-i*, *-iś*, *-iś*) type of sacrifice; derivatives: *fasle*; *faśena* name of vase

fler (*-ś*) 'offering, sacrifice'; *flere* (*-s*, *-ś*, *-ri*) 'god'; *flerχva* (*flerχve*) sacrificial rite to a god or the total offerings; *flerθce* derived verbal form

frontac 'pertaining to lightning'(?) (from Gk βροντή, in the title *trutnvt frontac*??), or ethnic adjective (from the name of a city: Ferentum??)

Supplementary Note

to the 1973 reprint of the sixth Italian edition

Etruscan studies today are remarkable for the quite unprecedented amount of research, discovery and publication that is taking place. As a consequence, knowledge is accumulating – and perspectives are changing – so fast and to such an extent that we are having to think in terms of a radical reshaping of accepted ideas about the Etruscan world. This extremely fluid situation renders full-scale revision of this book not merely difficult but inappropriate: any revision carried out now would very soon become obsolete under the pressure of new evidence and above all of new historical evaluations. The fact remains that five years have passed since the sixth Italian edition was published in 1968: this Note, added to the 1973 reprint, aims to provide readers with no more than a brief indication of the areas in which the most significant progress has been made in the meantime. Some amendments – factual, bibliographical and critical – have been incorporated in the individual chapters, or appended to them as 'Additional notes': it remains to provide an outline of the course of current developments as a whole and of the trends that are currently coming to the fore.

A wealth of new, interesting and unexpected information is coming out of the extended range of archaeological exploration. Whereas the usual targets for excavation – the great cities, such as Veii, Cerveteri, Tarquinia, Vulci, Roselle, Orvieto, Fiesole etc. – continue to be productive, the same is now also true of other types of site: the coastal settlements with their sanctuaries (first Pyrgi; and now Gravisca, the port of Tarquinia); and minor centres, like Acquarossa near Ferentum (prov. Viterbo) and Poggio Civitate near Murlo (prov. Siena). These sites are providing welcome evidence for Archaic domestic life and architecture which has not been destroyed by later superimpositions. In addition, and again in the interior, new and important discoveries have been made at Tuscania, Ischia di Castro and elsewhere: more detailed references will be found in the notes to Chapter Five.

Excavation, however, is not the only means by which our knowledge is being expanded: the past few years have seen a growing commitment of resources to programmes of field-survey and to the study – and publication – of previously unpublished material. In other words, we can now proceed to the historical evaluation of a considerable amount of information that was either insufficiently (or incorrectly) appreciated or inaccessible – and therefore completely unknown. In the main, these programmes are the result of the increased resources and organization associated with the plethora of old and new institutions that are actively collaborating in our field. Pride of place must be accorded to the Istituto di Studi Etruschi ed Italici in Florence, the principal co-ordinating body at the national and international levels, followed by the Centro di studi per l'archeologia etrusco-italica of the CNR (the Italian National Research Council), the Comitato per le attività archeologiche nella Tuscia, the Centro di studi etruschi and the Fondazione Faina at Orvieto, the Istituto per la storia di Bologna, the Comitato per Marzabotto, the Fondazione Lerici and the relevant Institutes in the Universities of Rome, Florence, Perugia, Pisa, Bologna and Milan, the foreign Schools in Rome (British, French, Swedish, American etc.), and of course the appropriate regional Antiquities Departments: the Soprintendenze alle Antichità for Southern Etruria, Tuscany, Umbria, Emilia and Romagna, Latium and Campania (Naples and Salerno). A few especially significant examples of research and publication undertaken by these bodies may be cited here: the system-atic publication of Italian Iron Age cemeteries; the reorganization and publication of the topographical collections in the Florence Archaeo-logical Museum, as a result of the restoration programme occasioned by the 1966 flood; the systematic planning and publication of the rock-sepulchres of Middle Etruria; the publication of the material from pre-Roman Capua; the resumption of work on the *Corpus Inscriptionum Etruscarum*. And so on.

The same desire for a more secure understanding of the material evidence itself is seen at the purely technical level. In museums, old restoration work has been investigated and revised, with important results; a CNR programme for the application of science to archae-ology is promoting the physical analysis of metal, wooden, amber and other finds; a laboratory for the scientific treatment of metals has been established in the Florence Archaeological Museum.

In general terms, it is now true to say that in all sectors of Etruscology there is a welcome and profitable tendency to establish the precise identity of the primary evidence itself. This takes the successive forms of intelligent collection of information, careful study and critical exegesis: these are now seen to be the essential prerequisites to histori-cal interpretation and synthesis. On the linguistic side, too, there is a similarly greater emphasis on the systematic collection and study of the inscriptions themselves, seen as the essential preliminary step to their interpretation. We are, in fact, witnessing an intellectual volte-face: the time is now past when the main aim of the Etruscan scholar was simply to propound a hypothesis or to arrive at a vigorously argued conclusion without any great attention to the broadest possible spectrum of relevant evidence. In this respect, one thinks in particular of the traditional controversies regarding the origin of the Etruscans, the 'originality' of Etruscan art, the language and the meaning of the texts. It is now seen that any solution to these problems can only be derived from an individual and collective concentration on the acquisition of precise and secure facts. Most unfortunately, the acceptance of this doctrine at the academic level has so far failed to stem the flow of uninformed writings and popular misconceptions about the Etruscans in the form of second-rate and second-hand syntheses compiled for the general public: most of them are of little value, and they need not concern us here.

Meanwhile, research, discussion and publication have increased apace in other fields of Italian archaeology and ancient history adjacent (in space and time) to Etruscan studies: the later prehistory of the peninsula, with particular reference to the cultures of the Bronze Age and the Bronze Age–Iron Age transition; the effects on the West of Mycenaean and post-Mycenaean enterprise; Greek and Phoenician colonial activity in Italy and the islands; study of the various Italic languages and cultures (especially in Lucania, Apulia and the Middle Adriatic area generally; the Veneti and Alpine peoples); the origins and early history of Rome. The progressively greater degree of precision that is being achieved in this vast area of 'background' provides a welcome reinforcement to – and a much needed sense of perspective in – the evaluation of our knowledge about the Etruscans and their civilization. Perhaps the most important result of this recent and current work in allied fields is the recognition and confirmation of the indissoluble spiritual, cultural and historical interdependence of the Etruscans and the range of experience and events that comprises the history of pre-Roman Italy as a whole. It follows that the concept of an 'Etruscan world' isolated, intrusive and virtually antithetic to an 'Italic world' is rapidly becoming a myth. The idea of Etruscology as an autonomous – indeed 'closed' – historical discipline is giving way to the broader-based and much more promising concept of 'Italic history' or 'history of Italic civilization' as a whole.

At the same time, the impressive quantity and quality of the evidence of all kinds that has emerged from Etruria in the last few years force us to question certain basic assumptions that are still taken for granted in much modern writing about Etruscan civilization. Not least by the present writer, that civilization has hitherto been considered as a phenomenon of secondary importance – on many counts, indeed, a satellite or modest imitation – in comparison with the great civilizations

237

of the East Mediterranean and of Greece; it has been tacitly assumed that Etruscan studies are devoid of any great general importance for the history of the ancient world at large (save as a prelude to the story of Roman Italy and of '*Romanità*' as a whole). But the sheer population and commercial significance of centres like Cerveteri and Vulci in the Archaic period, the enormous number of inscriptions that can be assigned to the seventh century (not less than that found in the various cities of contemporary Greece), the discovery of buildings like those at Poggio Civitate and Pyrgi, the growing mass of evidence for an extraordinarily refined, lively and complex art (arising particularly out of the discovery of new painted tombs at Tarquinia) – all these elements may be taken to substantiate the echoes of ancient tradition about the might of the Tyrrhenians, leading to a more positive assessment of the role of the Etruscans in the history of the Mediterranean between the eighth and the fifth centuries B.C.

It remains implacably true, however, that the Etruscans are not heralded by such voices as those of Homer, Sappho and Herodotus, with all that they mean for our contemporary Western culture: the memory of any conceivable spiritual adventure that accompanied the early flowering of Etruscan civilization was erased by its equally early decline. That is why the Etruscans and their remains are still remote, alien to ourselves and largely silent.

M.P.

Notes on the Text

A SHORT HISTORY OF ETRUSCAN STUDIES

1. A. Michaelis, *Ein Jahrhundert Kunstarchäologischer Entdeckungen*, 1908[2]; P. Ducati, 'La ricerca archeologica nell'Etruria', in *Atene e Roma*, 1913, pp. 277 ff.; E. Fiesel, *Etruskisch*, 1931; B. Nogara, *Gli Etruschi e la loro civiltà*, 1934, pp. 1 ff.; P. Ducati, *Le problème étrusque*, 1938, pp. 3 ff., and *Voci di Etruria*, 1939, pp. 173 ff.; R. Bloch, *Le Mystère étrusque*, 1956, pp. 3 ff. (translated by J. Hogarth as *The Etruscans*, Geneva and London, 1969); A. Hus, *Les Étrusques, peuple secret*, 1957, pp. 9 ff. See also G. Devoto, M. Pallottino, G. Caputo, 'In memoria di Luigi Lanzi', in *Studi Etruschi*, XXIX, 1961, pp. xix ff.; F. Magi, 'Il Museo Gregoriano Etrusco nella storia degli scavi e degli studi etruschi', in *Études Étrusco-italiques*, 1963, pp. 119 ff. For an over-all view of the history of Etruscan studies and the directions taken by research, see M. Pallottino, 'Introduzione alla civiltà degli Etruschi', in *Historia*, VI, 1957, pp. 1 ff.
2. See M. Pallottino, 'Scienza e poesia alla scoperta dell'Etruria', in *Quaderni A.C.I.*, 24, 1957, pp. 5 ff.
3. On the subject of one of the noisier attempts by an amateur to interpret the language, and on the debates that grew around it, see C. Battisti, *Polemica etrusca* (Biblioteca de 'Il Saggiatore', Florence, 1934). For some more recent cases, see the reviews in *Studi Etruschi*, XXII, 1952–3; XXV, 1957; XXX, 1962; XXXII, 1964; and also F. De Ruyt, 'De la méthode en étruscologie', in *Études Étrusco-italiques*, 1963, pp. 1 ff.

Part I

CHAPTER ONE: *Italy at the Dawn of History*

1. *Römische Geschichte*, I, 1881[7], pp. 44 ff.
2. See W. Helbig, *Die Italiker in der Po-ebene*, 1879; L. Pigorini, 'Le più antiche civiltà dell'Italia', in *Bullettino di Paletnologia Italiana*, XXIX, 1903, pp. 189 ff.
3. To mention only later works, cf.: E. Täubler, *Terremare und Rom*, 1926; V. Basanoff, 'Pomerium Palatinum', in *Memorie dell'Accademia dei Lincei*, 1939. The theory is exhaustively criticized by P. Barocelli in *Bullettino della Commissione archeol. comunale*, LXX, 1942, pp. 131 ff.
4. G. Sergi, *Italia. Le origini. Antropologia, cultura e civiltà*, 1919; *Le prime e le più antiche civiltà*, 1926; G. Patroni, *La preistoria (Storia politica d'Italia)*, 1937[1], 1951[2].

5. U. Rellini, *Le origini della civiltà italica*, 1929; 'La civiltà enea in Italia', in *Bullettino di Paletnologia Italiana*, LII, 1933, pp. 3 ff.

6. cf. G. Devoto, *Storia della lingua di Roma*, 1940, pp. 37 ff., 386 ff.

7. G. Patroni, 'L'indoeuropeizzazione dell'Italia', in *Athenaeum*, XVII, 1939, pp. 213 ff.; 'Espansioni e migrazioni', in *Archivio Glottologico Italiano*, XXXII, 1940, pp. 21 ff. For the idea of a political influence, following C. Jullian's theory of an 'Indo-European empire', cf. L. Homo, *L'Italie primitive et les débuts de l'impérialisme romain*, 1953², pp. 58 ff.

8. For these hypotheses and, more generally, for the most recent opinions on the arrival of the Indo-Europeans in Italy, see especially: F. Matz in *Neue Jahrbücher für Antike und Deutsche Bildung*, I, 1938, pp. 367 ff., II, 1939, pp. 32 ff., and *Klio*, XXXV, 1942, pp. 299 ff.; H. Krahe, *Die Indogermanisierung Griechenlands und Italiens*, 1949; G. Devoto, *Gli antichi Italici*, 1967³; F. Altheim, *Römische Geschichte*, I, 1951, pp. 13 ff.; L. Pareti, *Storia di Roma*, I, 1952, pp. 63 ff.; P. Laviosa Zambotti, *Il Mediterraneo, l'Europa, l'Italia durante la preistoria*, 1954; 'Le origini della civiltà di Villanova', in *Civiltà del ferro*, 1960, pp. 73 ff.; P. Bosch Gimpera, *El problema indoeuropeo*, 1960 (containing a full bibliography on the subject).

9. On the subject of pre-Roman Italy and its peoples as a whole, see J. Whatmough, *The Foundations of Roman Italy*, 1937; A. Furumark, *Det äldsta Italien*, 1947; M. Pallottino, 'Popolazioni storiche dell'Italia antica', in *Guida allo studio della civiltà romana antica*, 1952, pp. 71–90; L. Pareti, *Storia di Roma*, I, 1952, pp. 63 ff.; M. Pallottino in *Encyclopedia of World Art*, V, 1961, *s.v.* 'Etrusco-Italic Art', esp. cols. 100–112, and now *Civiltà artistica etrusco-italica*, 1971.

10. For the pre- and proto-history of Italy in general, see *Piccola guida della preistoria italiana*, 1965²; L. Bernabò Brea, *Sicily before the Greeks*, 1966²; D. H. Trump, *Central and Southern Italy before Rome*, 1966; C. E. Östenberg, *Luni sul Mignone e problemi della preistoria italiana*, 1967; R. Peroni, *Archeologia della Puglia preistorica*, 1967; *Atti del Iº Simposio di Protostoria d'Italia*, 1969; L. Barfield, *Northern Italy before Rome*, 1971. For more details on the Arene Candide sequence, L. Bernabò Brea, *Gli scavi della caverna delle Arene Candide*, I, 1946, and II, 1956; for Sicily and the Aeolian Islands, L. Bernabò Brea, M. Cavalier, 'Civiltà preistoriche delle Isole Eolie e del territorio di Milazzo', in *Bullettino di Paletnologia Italiana*, LXV, 1956, pp. 7 ff.; *Meligunìs-Lipara*, I, 1960; for south Italy before the Bronze Age, R. D. Whitehouse, 'The Early Neolithic of Southern Italy', in *Antiquity*, XLII, 1968, pp. 188 ff.; 'Settlement and economy in Southern Italy in the Neothermal period', in *Proceedings of the Prehistoric Society*, XXXIV, 1968, pp. 332 ff.; 'The Neolithic pottery of Southern Italy', in *Proceedings of the Prehistoric Society*, XXXV, 1969, pp. 267 ff.; for Beakers in Italy, D. Ridgway in *Antiquity*, XLVI, 1972, p. 52; for the Bronze Age in general, R. Peroni, *L'età del bronzo nella penisola italiana, I: L'antica età del bronzo*, 1971 (further volumes forthcoming); S. M.

Cassano and A. Manfredini in *Parola del Passato*, XXVII, 1972, pp. 344 ff.; for the Apennine culture, D. H. Trump, 'The Apennine culture of Italy', in *Proceedings of the Prehistoric Society*, XXIV, 1958, pp. 165 ff.; S. Puglisi, *La civiltà appenninica*, 1959; for Mycenaean material in Italy, Lord Wm. Taylour, *Mycenaean pottery in Italy and adjacent areas*, 1958; E. Macnamara, 'A group of bronzes from Surbo, Italy: new evidence for Aegean contacts with Apulia during Mycenaean III B and C', in *Proceedings of the Prehistoric Society*, XXXVI, 1970, pp. 241 ff.; L. Vagnetti, 'I Micenei in Italia: la documentazione archeologica', in *Parola del Passato*, XXV, 1970, pp. 359 ff.; for the *terremare*, G. Säflund, *Le terremare delle provincie di Modena, Reggio Emilia, Parma, Piacenza*, 1939; for the transition from Bronze to Iron Age, H. Müller-Karpe, *Beiträge zur Chronologie der Urnenfelderzeit Nördlich und Südlich der Alpen*, 1959 (and subsequent discussions: see note 12, below); R. Peroni, 'Per una definizione dell'aspetto culturale "subappenninico" come fase cronologica a se stante', in *Memorie dell'Accademia dei Lincei*, VIII, 1959; 'Per uno studio dell'economia di scambio nel quadro dell'ambiente culturale dei secoli intorno al 1000 a.C.', in *Parola del Passato*, XXIV, 1969, pp. 134 ff.; for the sequence, M. Pallottino, 'Proposta di una classificazione e di una terminologia delle fasi culturali del bronzo e del ferro in Italia', in *Atti del VI° Congresso Intern. Scienze Preistoriche e Protostoriche*, II, 1965, pp. 396 ff. See also the Italian fascicules of the *Inventaria Archaeologica* and *Prähistorische Bronzefunde* series.

11. Radiocarbon dating laboratories are active in Italy at the Universities of Pisa and Rome, and since 1970 in Florence; results are published regularly in *Radiocarbon*: I, 1959, pp. 103 ff.; III, 1961, pp. 99 ff.; VI, 1964, pp. 77 ff.; VII, 1965, pp. 213 ff.; VIII, 1966, pp. 401 ff.; IX, 1967, pp. 346 ff.; X, 1968, pp. 350 ff.; XI, 1969, pp. 482 ff.; XII, 1970, pp. 599 ff.; XIII, 1971, pp. 395 ff.; XV, 1973, pp. 165 ff., 382 ff., 479 ff. See also H. L. Thomas, *Near Eastern, Mediterranean and European Chronology*, 1967, pp. 86 ff., Chart II: 8 a–b; C. E. Östenberg, *Luni sul Mignone e problemi della preistoria italiana*, 1967, pp. 54 ff., 128 ff., 283 ff.; R. Peroni, 'Per una revisione critica della stratigrafia di Luni sul Mignone e della sua interpretazione', in *Atti del I° Simposio di Protostoria d'Italia*, 1969, pp. 167 ff.

12. On these problems see H. Müller-Karpe, *Beiträge zur Chronologie der Urnenfelderzeit Nördlich und Südlich der Alpen*, 1959, discussed from south of the Alps by M. Pallottino, 'Sulla cronologia dell'età del bronzo finale e dell'età del ferro in Italia', in *Studi Etruschi*, XXVIII, 1960, pp. 11 ff., and from north of the Alps by J. D. Cowen, 'The Late Bronze Age chronology of Central Europe', in *Antiquity*, XXXV, 1961, pp. 40 ff.; see also N. K. Sandars, 'From Bronze Age to Iron Age: a sequel to a sequel', in J. Boardman, M. A. Brown, T. G. E. Powell (eds.), *The European Community in Later Prehistory: Studies in honour of C. F. C. Hawkes*, 1971, pp. 3 ff., and G. von Merhart, *Hallstatt und Italien*, 1969 (a posthumous collection of papers edited by G. Kossack).

13. For the terms 'proto-Latial' and 'proto-Golaseccan', see respectively

M. Pallottino, 'Le origini di Roma', in *Archeologia Classica*, XII, 1960, pp. 1 ff. and F. Rittatore, in *Rivista di Scienze Preistoriche*, XV, 1960, pp. 216 ff.

14. On Italian Iron Age cultures in general, see F. v. Duhn, F. Messerschmidt, *Italische Gräberkunde*, I, 1924, II, 1939; D. Randall-MacIver, *Villanovans and Early Etruscans*, 1924; *The Iron Age in Italy*, 1927; F. Messerschmidt, *Bronzezeit und frühe Eisenzeit in Italien*, 1935; U. Rellini and G. Säflund in *Studi Etruschi*, XII, 1938, pp. 9 ff.; G. Kaschnitz-Weinberg, in *Handbuch der Archäologie*, II, 2, 1950, pp. 364 ff.; *Civiltà del ferro. Studi pubblicati nella ricorrenza centenaria della scoperta di Villanova*, 1960; H. Hencken, *Tarquinia, Villanovans and Early Etruscans*, 1968; papers on Veii by J. Close-Brooks and D. Ridgway in *Notizie degli Scavi*, 1965, pp. 53 ff., and *Studi Etruschi*, XXXV, 1967, pp. 311 ff.; I. Pohl, *The Iron Age Necropolis of Sorbo at Cerveteri*, 1972; R. Peroni (ed.), *Studi sulla cronologia delle civiltà di Este e Golasecca*, forthcoming. For the latest studies and discoveries, see also the articles and notices in the following journals: *Bullettino di Paletnologia Italiana, Notizie degli Scavi, Rivista di Scienze Preistoriche, Studi Etruschi*. On the question of the appearance of the Villanovan culture at Fermo in the Marche and in southern Italy, see G. Annibaldi in *Bullettino di Paletnologia Italiana*, LXV, 1956, pp. 229 ff.; C. P. Sestieri in *Studi Etruschi*, XXVIII, 1960, pp. 73 ff.; *Mostra della Preistoria e della Protostoria nel Salernitano, Catalogo*, Salerno, 1962; *Archäologische Forschungen in Lukanien*, I: K. Kilian, *Untersuchungen zu früheisenzeitlichen Gräbern aus dem Vallo di Diano*, 1964; idem, *Früheisenzeitliche Funde aus der Südostnekropole von Sala Consilina*, 1970; J. de la Genière, *Recherches sur l'Âge du Fer en Italie Méridionale: Sala Consilina*, 1968; B. D'Agostino in *Studi Etruschi*, XXXIII, 1965, pp. 671 ff., and in *Mélanges École Française de Rome*, LXXXII, 1970, pp. 571 ff.

15. cf. M. Pallottino, 'Sulle facies culturali arcaiche dell'Etruria', in *Studi Etruschi*, XIII, 1939, pp. 85 ff.

16. A summary of research in this field will be found in B. Gerola, 'Substrato mediterraneo e latino', in *Studi Etruschi*, XVI, 1942, pp. 345 ff.; P. Kretschmer, in *Glotta*, XXVIII, 1940, pp. 231 ff.; XXX, 1943, pp. 84 ff.; F. Ribezzo, 'Sulla originaria unità linguistica e culturale dell'Europa mediterranea', in *Atti del I° Congresso Intern. di Preistoria e Protostoria Mediterranea* (1950), 1952, pp. 185 ff.; G. Devoto, 'Le fasi della linguistica mediterranea', in *Studi Etruschi*, XXIII, 1954, pp. 217 ff.; XXIX, 1961, pp. 175 ff.; C. Battisti, *Sostrati e parastrati nell'Italia preistorica*, 1959; J. Hubschmid, *Mediterrane Substrate*, 1960; G. Devoto, 'La linguistica mediterranea', in *Scritti Minori*, II, 1967, pp. 11 ff.

17. In *Studi Etruschi*, XVII, 1943, pp. 359 ff.; XVIII, 1944, pp. 187 ff.; XXXI, 1963, pp. 93 ff.

18. cf. M. Pallottino, *La Sardegna nuragica*, 1950, pp. 22 ff., p. 28; J. Hubschmid, *Sardische Studien*, 1953.

19. Among more recent studies, see H. Krahe, *Die Indogermanisierung Griechenlands und Italiens*, 1949; G. Devoto, *Gli antichi Italici*, 1967[3],

pp. 41 ff.; H. Krahe, *Sprache und Vorzeit*, 1954; H. Hencken, *Indo-European Languages and Archaeology = American Anthropological Association Memoir* No. 84, 1955; V. Pisani, 'Le lingue indoeuropee in Grecia e in Italia', in *Rendiconti dell'Istituto Lombardo di Scienze e Lettere*, LXXXIX, 1956, pp. 1 ff.; E. Pulgram, *The Tongues of Italy. Prehistory and History*, 1958, pp. 69 ff. cf. also G. Devoto, *Scritti minori*, I, 1958, II, 1967; V. Pisani, *Saggi di linguistica storica*, 1959; C. Battisti, *Sostrati e parastrati nell'Italia preistorica*, 1959.

20. cf. J. Whatmough, *The Foundations of Roman Italy*, 1937; E. Pulgram, *The Tongues of Italy. Prehistory and History*, 1958, pp. 182 ff.; V. Pisani, *Le lingue dell'Italia antica oltre il latino*, 1964[2]. In the notes that follow we shall only provide the most important bibliographical references not included or not given sufficient weight in these manuals.

21. U. Schmoll, *Die vorgriechischen Sprachen Siziliens*, 1958; G. Devoto, 'Siculo e protolatino', in *Studi Etruschi*, XXVII, 1959, pp. 141 ff.

22. This is F. Ribezzo's hypothesis (in *Rivista Indo-greco-italica*, XVI, 1932, pp. 29 ff.; XX, 1936, pp. 222 etc.); it has been accepted by Devoto and by other scholars.

23. L. R. Palmer, *The Latin Language*, 1955.

24. H. Krahe, *Die Sprache der Illyrier*, II (C. De Simone, J. Untermann), 1964; O. Parlangeli, *Studi messapici*, 1960.

25. E. Vetter, *Handbuch der italischen Dialekte*, I, 1953; G. Bottiglioni, *Manuale dei dialetti italici*, 1954; A. De Franciscis, O. Parlangeli, *Gli Italici del Bruzio nei documenti epigrafici*, 1960.

26. It is represented essentially by the Novilara stele, for which see G. Camporeale, G. Giacomelli in *I Piceni e la civiltà etrusco-italica*, pp. 93 ff.; M. Durante in *Ricerche linguistiche*, V, 1963, pp. 65 ff.

27. cf. P. Kretschmer, in *Glotta*, XXX, 1943, pp. 168 ff.

28. G. B. Pellegrini, A. L. Prosdocimi, *La lingua venetica*, 1967.

29. cf. G. Devoto, *Storia della lingua di Roma*, pp. 1 ff.; L. R. Palmer, *The Latin Language*, 1955, pp. 3 ff.

30. F. Altheim postulated the existence of a primitive Latin substratum spread over the region between the Euganean hills and the Val Camonica; this substratum was then overlaid, according to this theory, by Venetic, of supposed Illyrian origin (*Römische Geschichte*, I, 1951, pp. 14 ff., with references to the author's preceding works). This hypothesis, however, is based on epigraphic documents of no value for the purpose of demonstrating this.

31. G. Devoto, in *Studi Etruschi*, XXI, 1950–51, p. 175; XXVII, 1959, p. 149; *Gli antichi Italici*, pp. 51 ff., 65 ff.; 'Le origini tripartite di Roma', in *Athenaeum*, XXXI, 1953, pp. 335 ff.

32. On the concept of an Italic *ethnos* as the end-product of a long, slow process, see U. Rellini, in *Bullettino di Paletnologia Italiana*, 1939, p. 126. For the ideas expressed in the following pages, see M. Pallottino, 'Le origini storiche dei popoli italici', in *X° Congresso Internazionale di Scienze Storiche, Relazioni, II*, 1955, pp. 3 ff.

33. See especially P. Laviosa Zambotti, 'I Balcani e l'Italia nella preistoria',

in *Origines* (*Raccolta di scritti in onore di G. Baserga*), 1954, pp. 161 ff.; some of the statements in this article are to be read with caution, but it is useful for the collection of primary material contained in it.

34. L. Bernabò Brea, *Sicily before the Greeks*, 1966 [2].
35. For these aspects, see H. Müller-Karpe, *Vom Anfang Roms*, 1959, pp. 43 ff.
36. On these problems, see G. A. Mansuelli, 'Formazione delle civiltà storiche nella pianura padana orientale. Aspetti e problemi', in *Studi Etruschi*, XXXIII, 1965, pp. 3 ff.
37. On Italic cultures and peoples in general, see M. Pallottino, *Civiltà artistica etrusco-italica*, 1971. Lucania: *Popoli anellenici in Basilicata* (exhibition catalogue), 1971. The Middle Adriatic: *Antiche civiltà d'Abruzzo* (exhibition catalogue), 1969; V. Cianfarani, *Culture adriatiche d'Italia. Antichità tra Piceno e Sannio prima dei Romani*, 1970; M. Pallottino in *Adriatica praehistorica et antiqua. Miscellanea Novak*, 1970, pp. 285 ff. The Sabines: *Civiltà dei Sabini nella valle del Tevere* (exhibition catalogue), 1973. The Samnites: E. T. Salmon, *Samnium and the Samnites*, 1967.

Additional Note to Chapter One

The cultural and economic development of Etruria in the Final Bronze Age and the Bronze Age–Iron Age transition period (eleventh–ninth centuries B.C.) is demonstrated by the discoveries at Luni sul Mignone and by the tumuli with 'Protovillanovan' graves found – together with impressive walling – at Crostoletto di Lamone in the middle valley of the Fiora: *Nuovi Tesori dell'Antica Tuscia*, 1970, pp. 16–18.

CHAPTER TWO: *The Problem of Etruscan Origins*

1. A history of the problem will be found in P. Ducati, *Le problème étrusque*, 1938. The whole question of Etruscan origins is also treated in the following monographs (which include full bibliographical data): L. Pareti, *Le origini etrusche*, 1929; F. Schachermeyer, *Etruskische Frühgeschichte*, 1929; M. Pallottino, *L'origine degli Etruschi*, 1947; F. Altheim, *Der Ursprung der Etrusker*, 1950. See also M. Pallottino, 'Nuovi studi sul problema delle origini etrusche (bilancio critico)', in *Studi Etruschi*, XXIX, 1961, pp. 3 ff. Much primary material is also collected in H. Hencken, *Tarquinia, Villanovans and Early Etruscans*, 1968, pp. 603 ff., and summarized in the same author's *Tarquinia and Etruscan Origins*, 1968. Hencken admits that he has arrived at 'a somewhat different result from my Italian colleagues', and his version of the migration story has been criticized: see the review by M. Pallottino in *Studi Etruschi*, XXXVI, 1968, pp. 493 ff., and also R. Bloch in *Aufstieg und Niedergang der römischen Welt*, I, 1972, pp. 363 ff.
2. Even in one of his last studies: 'L'origine degli Etruschi', in *Antiquitas*, II, 1947, pp. 75 ff.
3. 'Les Étrusques, peuple d'orient', in *Cahiers d'histoire mondiale*, I, 1954, pp. 328 ff.

4. That Etruscan belonged to a 'Tyrrheno-Etruscan' linguistic complex of Aegean origin was reaffirmed by H. Krahe, *Sprache und Vorzeit*, 1954, pp. 153 ff.

5. For a supposedly early dating of eastern influences at Populonia, see K. R. Maxwell-Hyslop, in *Proceedings of the Prehistoric Society*, XXII, 1956, pp. 126 ff.

6. 'Über den Ursprung der Etrusker', in *Historia*, VI, 1957, pp. 10 ff.

7. *Revue des Études Anciennes*, LI, 1949, pp. 201 ff.; *La colonisation grecque de l'Italie méridionale et de la Sicile dans l'antiquité*, 1957², pp. 497 ff.

8. See also G. A. Wainwright, 'The Teresh, the Etruscans and Asia Minor', in *Anatolian Studies*, IX, 1959, pp. 197 ff.

9. 'Archaeological Evidence for the Origin of the Etruscans', in *A Ciba Foundation Symposium on Medical Biology and Etruscan Origins*, 1958, pp. 29 ff.; 'A view of Etruscan origins', in *Antiquity*, XL, 1966, pp. 205 ff.; *Tarquinia, Villanovans and Early Etruscans*, 1968, pp. 603 ff. In this last work, Hencken develops a theory suggesting two succeeding waves of eastern immigrants: the first represented by the Villanovans, i.e. the Tyrrhenians in the sense they are understood in Säflund's or Bérard's hypotheses; the second placed at the very beginning of the Orientalizing period.

10. 'The Problem of Etruscan Origins', in *Harvard Studies in Classical Philology*, LXIV, 1959, pp. 1 ff.

11. Also in his *Storia di Roma*, I, 1952, pp. 63 ff.

12. *Glotta*, XXX, 1943, pp. 213 ff.

13. M. Pallottino, 'Tradizione etnica e realtà culturale dell'Etruria, Umbria e Romagna prima della unificazione augustea', in *Relazioni della XXVIII Riunione della Società Italiana per il Progresso delle Scienze*, V, 1940, pp. 81 ff. On the Tyrrhenians and the Pelasgians, see also the following note, and note 1 on p. 247.

14. See M. Pallottino, 'Erodoto autoctonista?', in *Studi Etruschi*, XX, 1948–9, pp. 11 ff. Other scholars exclude the name of Cortona (Korton) from Herodotus's original text and prefer to read the name of Kreston, a city near the Chalcidice peninsula in northern Greece: cf. H. Hencken, *Tarquinia, Villanovans and Early Etruscans*, 1968, pp. 613 ff.

15. On the sources and the problem of the *Trš.w* see F. W. v. Bissing, 'Die Überlieferung über die Turuscha', in *Wiener Zeitschrift für die Kunde des Morgenlandes*, XXXV, 1928, pp. 177 ff.

16. For the Orientalizing civilization in general, see F. Poulsen, *Der Orient und die frühgriechische Kunst*, 1912; L. Pareti, *La tomba Regolini-Galassi e la civiltà dell'Italia centrale nel sec. VII av. Cr.*, 1947; M. Pallottino, 'Orientalizing Style', in *Encyclopedia of World Art*, X, cols. 782–96; G. Camporeale, *I commerci di Vetulonia in età orientalizzante*, 1969; I. Strøm, *Problems concerning the origin and development of the Etruscan Orientalizing style*, 1971. It should be remembered that the Greeks responsible for the spread of the Orientalizing civilization were unlikely to be Phocaeans, as thought by Pareti, but rather Rhodians and Chalci-

dians: cf. *Studi Etruschi*, XX, 1948–9, pp. 335 ff. Concerning Urartu and Anatolian influences, see M. Pallottino, 'Urartu, Greece and Etruria', in *East and West*, IX, 1958, pp. 29 ff.; E. Akurgal, 'Urartu medeniyeti (Urartäische Kunst)' in *Anatolia*, IV, 1959, pp. 67 ff.; B. B. Piotrovskiy, *Urartu: the Kingdom of Van and its art*, 1967.

17. C. Pauli, *Eine vorgriechische Inschrift von Lemnos* (*Altitalischen Forschungen*, 1886, 1894); E. Nachmanson, *Die vorgriechische Inschriften von Lemnos*, and G. Karo, 'Die "Tyrsenische" Stele von Lemnos', in *Athenische Mitteilungen*, XXXIII, 1908, pp. 47 ff.; L. Pareti, *Le origini etrusche*, pp. 89 ff.; S. P. Cortsen, 'Die lemnische Inschrift', in *Glotta*, XVIII, 1929–30, pp. 101 ff.; J. Friedrich, *Kleinasiatische Sprachdenkmäler*, 1932, pp. 43 ff.; B. Hrozny, 'Die Inschrift von Lemnos', in *Studi Etruschi*, IX, 1935, pp. 127 ff.; S. P. Cortsen, 'L'inscription de Lemnos', in *Latomus*, II, 1938, pp. 3 ff.; P. Kretschmer, 'Die tyrrhenischen Inschriften der Stele von Lemnos', in *Glotta*, XXIX, 1941, pp. 89 ff.; H. Rix, 'Eine morphosyntaktische Übereinstimmung zwischen Etruskisch und Lemnisch: die Datierungsformel', in *Studien zur Sprachwissenschaft und Kulturkunde . . . für W. Brandenstein*, 1968, pp. 213 ff.

18. The other known inscriptions are only very brief and scratched on sherds; they are practically useless from the linguistic point of view. See A. Della Seta, in *Scritti in onore di B. Nogara*, 1937, pp. 199 ff.

19. A. Trombetti, *La lingua etrusca*, 1928; E. Fiesel, *Etruskisch*, 1931, p. 63. P. Meriggi ('Osservazioni sull'etrusco', in *Studi Etruschi*, XI, 1937, pp. 129 ff.) re-examined the close relationship between Etruscan and Lydian but produced no valid results.

20. Equally without critical foundation is the most ambitious attempt so far to relate Etruscan to Hittite by placing it fully in the context of the languages of Asia Minor: this was undertaken in a painstaking study by W. Georgiev (*Hethitisch und Etruskisch. Die hethitische Herkunft der etruskischen Sprache*, 1962, and in more recent works): cf. *Studi Etruschi*, XXXII, 1964, pp. 223 ff.

21. Some scholars have tended to seek the original homeland of the Etruscans in southern Asia Minor, between Rhodes, Cyprus and Syria, in complete contrast with ancient tradition: see Å. Åkerström, *Der geometrische Stil in Italien*, 1943, pp. 156 ff.

22. On Lemnos, see D. Mustilli, 'La necropoli tirrenica di Efestia', in *Annuario Scuola Ital. d'Atene*, XV, XVI, 1938. For Asia Minor, cf. H. Th. Bossert, *Altanatolien*, 1942; K. Bittel, *Grundzüge der Vor- und Frühgeschichte Kleinasiens*, 1950²; E. Akurgal, *Die Kunst Anatoliens*, 1961. On Sardis, see G. M. Hanfmann, 'Sardis und Lydien', in *Abhandlungen der Akademie der Wissenschaft und Literatur in Mainz, Geistes- und Sozialwiss. Kl.*, 1960, pp. 449 ff.

23. U. Antonielli, in *Bullettino di Paletnologia Italiana*, L–LI, 1930–31, pp. 191 ff. P. G. Gierow, *The Iron Age Culture of Latium*, I, 1966, p. 326, Fig. 92 no. 22; II, 1, 1964, p. 209, Fig. 123 no. 19.

24. R. S. Young, in *American Journal of Archaeology*, LXII, 1958, pp. 139

ff.; M. Pallottino, in *East and West*, IX, 1958, pp. 29 ff.; E. Akurgal, in *Anatolia*, IV, 1959, pp. 67 ff.

25. cf. E. Fiesel, *Etruskisch*, 1931, pp. 65 ff., who also quotes U. Wilamowitz's authoritative opinion on the subject.

26. For some Aegean reflections in the proto-Latial, Protovillanovan and Villanovan cultures, see note 35 on p. 244, and H. Hencken, *Tarquinia, Villanovans and Early Etruscans*, 1968, II, pp. 462 ff., 532 ff., 568 ff. Actual traces of Mycenaean commerce have been found in Etruria: a few allegedly Mycenaean sherds have recently been found in a 'Sub-Apennine' level at Luni on the Mignone river, in the interior of south Etruria (C. E. Östenberg, *Luni sul Mignone*, 1967, pp. 128 ff.). So far, such evidence is extremely rare when compared with the wealth of such finds in southern Italy (see above, pp. 42 ff. and 59 ff.). Even so, Mycenaean navigation would not be sufficient to demonstrate the actual immigration into Etruria of peoples from the Aegean or Near East.

27. See, among others, V. Pisani, *Le lingue dell'Italia antica oltre il latino*, 1964[2], pp. 303 ff., 326.

28. See below, pp. 97 ff.

29. See above, pp. 58 ff.

30. See M. Pallottino, *L'origine degli Etruschi*, 1947, pp. 113 ff.

31. See especially C. F. C. Hawkes, 'The Problem of the Origins of the Archaic Cultures in Etruria and its Main Difficulties', in *Studi Etruschi*, XXVII, 1959, pp. 363 ff.

32. See below, pp. 84 ff.

33. See M. Pallottino, *L'origine degli Etruschi*, 1947, pp. 111 ff.; H. Hencken, *Tarquinia, Villanovans and Early Etruscans*, 1968, pp. 492 ff., 541 ff., 568 ff.

34. See also C. F. C. Hawkes, in the work cited in note 31 above; and note 13 to Chapter Four below.

Additional Note to Chapter Two

The whole problem of Etruscan origins is critically re-examined in depth by J. Heurgon, *Rome et la Méditerranée occidentale jusqu'aux guerres puniques*, 1969, pp. 363–71. He uses particularly convincing arguments to support his view that the Etruscans were in Etruria already by Villanovan times: and he connects the origin of the Etruscans with traditions about the Pelasgians, involving possible migrations by sea at the end of the Bronze Age (this was the thesis of J. Bérard: see above, pp. 67, 75). The recent discovery of evidence for a Mycenaean presence in Etruria would appear to be relevant.

CHAPTER THREE: *The Etruscans and the Sea*

1. The traditions concerning the adventures of the Tyrrheno-Pelasgians and the historical foundation of these traditions are discussed by J. Bérard in *Revue des Études Anciennes*, LI, 1949, pp. 224 ff., and in *Studies Presented to D. M. Robinson*, I, 1951, pp. 135 ff. See also F.

Lochner-Hüttenbach, *Die Pelasger*, 1960 (useful for sources and bibliography, but unreliable in its conclusions); H. Hencken, *Tarquinia, Villanovans and Early Etruscans*, 1968, pp. 607 ff., 649. See also notes 13 and 14 on p. 245.

2. The demonstration of a proto-Etruscan colonization of Spain, attempted by A. Schulten ('Los tirsenos en España', in *Ampurias*, II, 1940; *Tartessos*, 1945) on the basis of toponymy, has no reliable foundation. These hypothetical linguistic relationships and the analogies between place names found in Lusitanian inscriptions and in the Tyrrheno-Pelasgic world (cf. *Glotta*, XVIII, 1930, p. 106; *Klio*, XXXIII, 1940, pp. 83 ff.; *Glotta*, XXIX, 1941, pp. 90 ff.) can, if at all, be explained by referring back to older, prehistoric contacts (cf. my review of O. F. A. Menghin, 'Migrationes Mediterraneae', in *Doxa*, III, 1950, pp. 266 ff.).

3. For Gaul and Spain, see M. Almagro, 'Los hallazgos de bucchero etrusco hacia occidente y su significación', in *Boletín Arqueol. de la Sociedad Arqueol. Tarraconense*, XLIX, 1949, pp. 1 ff., with a bibliography of previous studies; M. Pallottino, in *Archeologia Classica*, I, 1949, pp. 80 ff.; F. Benoit, *Recherches sur l'hellénisation du Midi de la Gaule*, 1965, pp. 51 ff. (this includes all the most recent finds and conclusions). For Greece and the Mediterranean east, see G. Karo, 'Etruskisches in Griechenland', in *Archaiologike Ephemeris*, 1937, pp. 316 ff.; E. Kunze, 'Etruskische Bronzen in Griechenland', in *Studies Presented to D. M. Robinson*, I, 1951, pp. 736 ff.; E. Gjerstad, *The Swedish Cyprus Expedition*, IV, 2, 1948, p. 404; B. B. Shefton, in *Perachora*, II, 1962, pp. 385 ff.

4. E. Benveniste, 'Notes étrusques', in *Studi Etruschi*, VII, 1933, pp. 245 ff.

5. cf. A. Taramelli, 'Sardi ed Etruschi', in *Studi Etruschi*, III, 1929, pp. 43 ff.; G. Lilliu, in *Studi Sardi*, VIII, 1948, pp. 19 ff.; M. Pallottino, *La Sardegna nuragica*, 1950, pp. 37 ff.; G. Lilliu, *La civiltà dei Sardi*, 1963, pp. 173, 229 ff., 282.

6. R. Bartoccini, in *Atti del VII Congresso Internazionale di Archeologia Classica*, 1961, II, pp. 257 ff. (Plate XVII).

7. See note 3 above.

8. S. Bastianelli, in *Studi Etruschi*, XVI, 1942, pp. 248 ff.

9. See note 40 on p. 258.

10. S. Paglieri, 'Origine e diffusione delle navi etrusco-italiche', in *Studi Etruschi*, XXVIII, 1960, pp. 209 ff.

11. Discovered at Tarquinia, near the temple known as the 'Ara della Regina', with other historically interesting fragments; see M. Pallottino, 'Uno spiraglio di luce sulla storia etrusca: gli "Elogia Tarquiniensia"', in *Studi Etruschi*, XXI, 1950–51, pp. 147 ff.; M. Torelli, 'Un nuovo attacco fra gli Elogia Tarquiniensia', in *Studi Etruschi*, XXXVI, 1968, pp. 467 ff.

12. On the possibility of interpreting Aristotle's comment as referring to the actual archaic institution of an exchange of civic rights among allied cities, see M. Sordi, *I rapporti romano-ceriti e l'origine della civitas sine suffragio*, 1960, pp. 115 ff.

13. See J. Jehasse, *Aléria grecque et romaine*, 1963; F. Benoit, *Recherches sur l'hellénisation du Midi de la Gaule*, pp. 44 ff.; J. and L. Jehasse, *La nécropole préromaine d'Aléria*, Paris, 1973. For a discussion of the problem of an actual historical presence of the Etruscans in Corsica, see also the works cited in note 16 below.

14. G. Colonna, G. Garbini, M. Pallottino, L. Vlad Borelli, 'Scavi nel santuario etrusco di Pyrgi. Relazione preliminare della settima campagna, 1964, e scoperta di tre lamine d'oro inscritte in etrusco e in punico', in *Archeologia Classica*, XVI, 1964, pp. 49 ff.; G. Colonna, 'Il santuario di Pyrgi alla luce delle recenti scoperte', in *Studi Etruschi*, XXXIII, 1965, pp. 191 ff.; G. Pugliese Carratelli, 'Intorno alle lamine di Pyrgi', ibid., pp. 221 ff.; M. Pallottino, 'Rapporti fra Greci, Fenici, Etruschi ed altre popolazioni italiche alla luce delle recenti scoperte', in *Accademia Nazion. dei Lincei, Quaderno no. 87*, 1966, pp. 13 ff.; J. Heurgon, 'The Inscriptions of Pyrgi', in *Journal of Roman Studies*, LVI, 1966, pp. 1 ff. For further discussion and bibliography, see *Le lamine di Pyrgi = Accademia Nazion. dei Lincei, Quaderno no. 147*, 1970, and M. Pallottino, 'Nota sui documenti epigrafici rinvenuti nel santuario', in *Pyrgi. Scavi nel santuario etrusco (1959–1967)*, *Notizie degli Scavi*, 1970, *II Supplemento* (1973), pp. 730 ff.

15. Apart from historical sources for this battle, we have contemporary epigraphic documents in the Etruscan helmets dedicated by the Syracusans at Olympia as tithe of the plunder: *Inscr. Grecae*, 510; *Bulletin de Correspondence Hellénique*, LXXXIV, 1960, p. 721, fig. 12.

16. On the historical problems relating to the sea expansion of Etruria and its relationship with Greek colonies and Carthage, see M. Pallottino, *Gli Etruschi*, 1940[2], pp. 73 ff.; E. Colozier, 'Les Étrusques et Carthage', in *Mélanges de l'École Française de Rome*, 1953, pp. 63 ff.; J. Bérard, *La colonisation grecque de l'Italie méridionale et de la Sicile dans l'antiquité*, 1957[2], pp. 258, 266 ff., 297; N. N. Zalesski, 'Etruski i Karfagen', in *Drevnii Mir*, Moscow, 1962, pp. 520 ff.; J. Jehasse, 'La "victoire à la Cadméenne" d'Hérodote (I, 166) et la Corse dans les courants d'expansion grecque', in *Revue d'Études Anciennes*, LXIV, 1962, pp. 269 ff.; M. Pallottino, 'Les relations entre les Étrusques et Carthage du VIIe au IIIe siècle av. J.-Chr.', in *Cahiers de Tunisie*, XLIV, 1963, pp. 23 ff.; F. Benoit, *Recherches sur l'hellénisation du Midi de la Gaule*, pp. 35 ff.; G. Vallet, F. Villard, 'Les Phocéens et la fondation de Hyélè', in *Parola del Passato*, XXI, 1966 (*Velia e i Focei in Occidente*), pp. 166 ff.; J.-P. Morel, 'Les Phocéens en Occident: certitudes et hypothèses', ibid., pp. 378 ff.; J. Heurgon, *Rome et la Méditerranée occidentale jusqu'aux guerres puniques*, 1969; *Nuovi studi su Velia = Parola del Passato*, XXV, 1970; recent numbers of *Kokalos*. Concerning the discoveries at Pyrgi, see the works cited in note 14 above, and further bibliography in *Archeologia Classica*, XVIII, 1966, pp. 279 ff., and *Göttingische Gelehrte Anzeigen*, CCXX, 1968, pp. 64 ff.; concerning the Etruscan colonization in Italy and especially in Campania, see N. N. Zalesski, *K istorii etrusskoi kolonizacii Italii v. VII–VI vv do n.e.* ['On the history of the Etruscan

colonization of Italy in the 7th–6th centuries B.C.'], 1965; concerning the Etruscan, Phoenician and Greek trade-routes between the eighth and sixth centuries B.C., see L. Breglia, 'Le antiche rotte del Mediterraneo documentate da monete e pesi', in *Rendiconti dell' Accademia di Napoli*, XXX, 1955, pp. 211 ff.; on sea trade in the Tyrrhenian and through the straits of Sicily, see G. Vallet, *Rhégion et Zancle*, 1958. For the contributions made by the Etruscan cities to Rome during the second Punic war, see below, pp. 181 ff.

CHAPTER FOUR: *The Etruscans and Italy*

1. On the spread of Etruscan and Italic objects, and on Etrusco-Italic confluences north of the Alps, see E. Genthe, *Über den etruskischen Tauschhandel nach dem Norden*, 1874; Å. Åkerström, 'Der Schatz von Hassle', in *Opuscula Archaeologica*, II, 1941, pp. 174 ff.; D. B. Harden, 'Italic and Etruscan Finds in Britain', in *Atti del I° Congresso Intern. di Preistoria e Protostoria Mediterranea*, 1952, pp. 315 ff.; J. Gy. Szilágyi, 'Zur Frage des Etruskischen Handels nach dem Norden', in *Acta Antiqua Hungariae*, I, 1953, 3–4, pp. 419 ff.; O. Klindt Jensen, *Bronzekedelen fra Brå*, 1953; P. J. Riis, 'The Danish Bronze Vessels of Greek, Early Campanian and Etruscan Manufactures', in *Acta Archaeologica*, XXX, 1959, pp. 1 ff.; O. H. Frey, in *Mostra dell' Etruria Padana e della città di Spina*, 1960, II, pp. 147 ff.; B. Stjernquist, 'Ett svenst praktfynd med sydeuropeiska bronser', in *Proxima Thule*, 1962, pp. 71 ff.
2. *Der Ursprung der Etrusker*, 1950.
3. 'Cere all'epoca della sua annessione a Roma', etc., in *Atti del II° Congresso di Studi Romani*, 1931, pp. 411 ff. This thesis was taken up again by L. Pareti in *La tomba Regolini-Galassi*, 1947, pp. 8 ff., and by other scholars.
4. *Notizie degli Scavi*, 1930, pp. 335 ff.
5. See M. Pallottino, 'Appunti di protostoria etrusca e latina', in *Studi Etruschi*, XIX, 1940, pp. 27 ff.
6. On the problem of the relations between Etruscans and other peoples of ancient Italy, see G. Devoto, in *Historia*, VI, 1957, pp. 23 ff.; on the interior of southern Etruria, see G. Colonna, 'L'Etruria meridionale interna dal villanoviano alle tombe rupestri', *Studi Etruschi*, XXXV, 1967, pp. 3 ff.
7. For these problems, see M. Pallottino, in *Archeologia Classica*, XVI, 1964, pp. 104 ff.
8. See M. Pallottino, *Tarquinia* = *Monumenti Antichi dell' Accademia dei Lincei*, XXXVI, 1937, cols. 245 ff., 367 ff.
9. See G. Colonna, in *Studi Etruschi*, XXIX, 1961, pp. 76 ff.
10. The presence of Etruscan inscriptions in Piedmont (cf. M. Buffa, 'Iscrizioni etrusche nel territorio del popolo ligure', in *Memorie dell'- Accademia Lunigianese*, XV, 1934) has raised the question of an Etruscan colonization of the valleys of the Tanaro and of the Stura as far as the outskirts of Cuneo. On the frontier between Etruscans and Ligurians, cf. also N. Lamboglia, in *Studi Etruschi*, X, 1936, pp. 137 ff.

11. See above, pp. 80 and 84.
12. *Campanien*, 1879.
13. Ancient sources record an unsuccessful attack against Cumae by Etruscan forces reinforced with Umbrian and Daunian contingents in the year 524 B.C. (Dionysius of Halicarnassus, VII, 3 ff.), and the naval battle of 474 B.C., for which see above, p. 90. On the activities of the eighth-century Euboeans on Ischia and in Campania and Etruria, see the 'Atti dell'Incontro di studi sugli inizi della colonizzazione greca in Occidente, Napoli-Ischia 1968' in *Dialoghi di Archeologia*, III, 1969, pp. 3 ff. (discussions opened by J. Boardman, G. Buchner, W. Johannowsky, E. Lepore, D. Ridgway, G. Vallet); see also D. Ridgway, 'The first Western Greeks: Campanian coasts and Southern Etruria', in *Greeks, Celts and Romans* (ed. C. and S. Hawkes), 1973, pp. 5 ff.
14. On the subject of the Etruscan domination of Campania, see J. Heurgon, *Recherches sur l'histoire, la religion et la civilisation de Capoue préromaine*, 1942; A. Maiuri, *Saggi di varia antichità*, 1954, pp. 11 ff., 111 ff., 241 ff.; M. Pallottino, in *Parola del Passato*, XI, 1956, pp. 81 ff.; N. N. Zalesski, *K istorii etrusskoi kolonizacii Italii v. VII–VI vv do n.e.* (see note 16 on p. 249 above). See also M. W. Frederiksen, 'Campanian cavalry: a question of origins', in *Dialoghi di Archeologia*, II, 1968, pp. 3 ff.
15. On these recent discoveries, see *Mostra della preistoria e della protostoria nel Salernitano. Catalogo*, 1962; M. Napoli, B. D'Agostino, W. Johannowsky, in *Studi Etruschi*, XXXIII, 1965, pp. 661 ff.; B. D'Agostino, in *Notizie degli Scavi*, 1968, pp. 75 ff. On the Orientalizing dish of Pontecagnano, similar to the ones found at Cerveteri and Palestrina, see A. Vaccaro, 'La patera orientalizzante da Pontecagnano presso Salerno', in *Studi Etruschi*, XXXI, 1963, pp. 241 ff.; on Etruscan inscriptions at Vico Equense and at Pontecagnano, see *Studi Etruschi*, XXXVI, 1968, pp. 226 ff.; on Marcina, see B. D'Agostino, in *Dialoghi di Archeologia*, II, 1968, pp. 139 ff.
16. On the question of the Etruscans at Pompeii, see A. Sogliano, *Pompei nel suo sviluppo storico*, I, 1927; A. Boëthius, 'Gli Etruschi in Pompei', in *Symbola Philologica O. A. Danielsson dicata*, Uppsala, 1932; G. Patroni, in *Studi Etruschi*, XV, 1941, pp. 109 ff.
17. A. Maiuri, *Saggi di varia antichità*, pp. 244 ff.
18. See M. Pallottino, 'Le origini di Roma', in *Archeologia Classica*, XII, 1960, pp. 1 ff., 'Fatti e leggende (moderne) sulla più antica storia di Roma', in *Studi Etruschi*, XXXI, 1963, pp. 3 ff., and 'Le origini di Roma; considerazioni critiche sulle scoperte e sulle discussioni più recenti', in *Aufstieg und Niedergang der römischen Welt*, I, 1972, pp. 22 ff.; A. Momigliano, 'An Interim Report on the Origins of Rome', in *Journal of Roman Studies*, LIII, 1963, pp. 95 ff.; A. Alföldi, *Early Rome and the Latins*, 1965. These articles confute E. Gjerstad's attempt to move the Tarquin dynasty and the period of Etruscan influence on Rome forward in time to the end of the sixth and the first half of the fifth century.

19. M. Pallottino, 'La iscrizione arcaica su vaso di bucchero rinvenuta ai piedi del Campidoglio', in *Bullettino Archeol. Comunale*, LXIX, 1941; 'Rivista di epigrafia etrusca', in *Studi Etruschi*, XXII, 1952–3, pp. 309 ff.; XXXIII, 1965, pp. 505 ff.; C. De Simone, 'Zur altetruskischen Inschrift aus Rom', in *Glotta*, XLVI, 1968, pp. 207 ff. An Etruscan inscription had already been found at Satricum in Latium (*Studi Etruschi*, XIII, 1939, pp. 427 ff.). See also M. Torelli, 'L'iscrizione "latina" sulla coppa argentea della tomba Bernardini', in *Dialoghi di Archeologia*, I, 1967, pp. 38 ff.; cf. M. Pallottino in *Studi Etruschi*, XXXV, 1967, pp. 569 ff.

20. The most recent discussions on the subject may be found in L. Pareti, in *Studi Etruschi*, V, 1931, pp. 147 ff.; A. Momigliano, *L'opera dell'Imperatore Claudio*, 1932, pp. 30 ff.; M. Pallottino, in *Studi Etruschi*, XIII, 1939, pp. 456 ff. and in *Gli Etruschi*, 1947², pp. 108 ff., 270; S. Mazzarino, *Dalla monarchia allo stato repubblicano: Ricerche di storia romana arcaica*, 1945, pp. 184 ff.; L. Pareti, *Storia di Roma*, I, 1952, pp. 310 ff.; P. De Francisci, *Primordia Civitatis*, 1959, pp. 638 ff.; A. Alföldi, *Early Rome and the Latins*, pp. 212 ff.

21. On the Veii inscription, see *Studi Etruschi*, XIII, 1939, pp. 455 ff. The name Avle Vipina appears quoted, perhaps already as a heroic personage, on a fifth-century painted cup from Vulci: see J. Heurgon, in *Mélanges Carcopino*, 1966, pp. 515 ff.

22. On the relations between Rome, Etruscans and Latins in the sixth and fifth centuries, see A. Alföldi, *Early Rome and the Latins*, 1965. On the Samnites, see E. T. Salmon, *Samnium and the Samnites*, 1967.

23. N. N. Zalesski, *Etruski v severnoi Italii* ['The Etruscans in north Italy'], 1959; 'Spina e l'Etruria Padana' (*Atti del I° Convegno di Studi Etruschi*), 1959; *Mostra dell'Etruria Padana e della città di Spina*, Bologna, I, 1961²; II, 1960, with preceding bibliography; G. A. Mansuelli, R. Scarani, *L'Emilia prima dei Romani*, 1961; M. Pallottino, 'Gli Etruschi nell'Italia del Nord: nuovi dati e nuove idee', in *Hommages à Albert Grenier* (*Collection Latomus*, LVIII), 1962, pp. 77 ff.; G. A. Mansuelli, 'Formazione delle civiltà storiche nella pianura padana orientale. Aspetti e problemi', in *Studi Etruschi*, XXXIII, 1965, pp. 3 ff.

24. On the Celts in Italy and the chronology of their invasion, see A. Grenier, *Les Gaulois*, 1951, pp. 114 ff.; J. Bayet, *Tite-Live. Histoire Romaine*, V, 1954, pp. 159 ff.; J. Moreau, *Die Welt der Kelten*, 1958, pp. 26 ff. A period of peaceful co-existence, *regnante Tarquinio*, between Celtic intruders and natives in valley outposts leading to central Italy has recently been proposed by G. Bermond Montanari: see her excavation reports on S. Martino in Gattara, in *Notizie degli Scavi*, 1969, pp. 5 ff. and *Studi Etruschi*, XXXVII, 1969, pp. 213 ff. On the date of the Gallic burning of Rome, see M. Sordi, *I rapporti romano-ceriti e l'origine della civitas sine suffragio*, 1960, pp. 25 ff.

25. See above, p. 75.

26. See L. Banti, in *Studi Etruschi*, V, 1931, pp. 163 ff., and *Luni*, 1937. See also note 10 on p. 250.

27. See K. Olzscha, *Interpretation der Agramer Mumienbinde*, 1939, pp. 3 ff.; M. Pallottino, 'Sulla lettura e sul contenuto della grande iscrizione di Capua', in *Studi Etruschi*, XX, 1948–9, pp. 159 ff.
28. See below, pp. 134 ff.
29. See below, p. 134.
30. On the importance and spread of the Etruscan alphabet in north Italy, see G. B. Pellegrini, in *Tyrrhenica. Saggi di studi etruschi*, 1957, pp. 145 ff.; *Spina e l'Etruria Padana (Atti del I° Convegno di Studi Etruschi)*, 1959, pp. 181 ff.
31. See F. Altheim, E. Trautmann, *Vom Ursprung der Runen*, 1939 (to be read with caution); J. G. Février, *Histoire de l'écriture*, 1948, pp. 513 ff.
32. On the Roman conquest of Etruria, see M. Pallottino, *Gli Etruschi*, 1940², pp. 182 ff.; A. Passerini, *Roma alla conquista dell'Italia*, 1942; L. Pareti, *Storia di Roma*, I, pp. 451 ff., 563 ff.; A. J. Pfiffig, *Die Ausbreitung des römischen Städtewesens in Etrurien und die Frage der Unterwerfung der Etrusker*, 1966; W. V. Harris, *Rome in Etruria and Umbria*, 1971.

Part 2

CHAPTER FIVE: *Cities and Cemeteries of Etruria*

1. J. Bradford, 'Etruria from the Air', in *Antiquity*, XXI, 1947, pp. 74 ff., and *Ancient Landscapes. Studies in Field Archaeology*, 1957; C. M. Lerici, *Alla scoperta delle civiltà sepolte. I nuovi metodi di prospezione archeologica*, 1960; *A Great Adventure of Italian Archaeology 1955–1965*, 1965.
2. Topographical surveys have recently been particularly well developed for southern Etruria through the work of the British School at Rome (cf. J. B. Ward-Perkins, in *Papers of the British School at Rome*, XXVI, 1955, pp. 44 ff.; *Journal of Roman Studies*, XLVII, 1957, pp. 139 ff.; and regular progress reports in *Antiquity* since 1963) and of the Library of Aerial Photography of the Italian Ministry of Education. Other bodies involved in topographical work (surveys and publications) are the Comitato per le attività archeologiche nella Tuscia and the Centro di studi per l'archeologia etrusco-italica. New discoveries are reported regularly in *Studi Etruschi* and *Notizie degli Scavi*, and the following pair of recent exhibition catalogues are valuable: *Arte e Civiltà degli Etruschi*, Turin, 1967; *Nuovi Tesori dell'antica Tuscia*, Viterbo, 1970. See also *Corpus Inscriptionum Etruscarum (C.I.E.)*, II, sect. I, 4 (ed. M. Cristofani, 1970).
3. On this problem, see C. M. Lerici, *Italia sepolta*, 1962.
4. G. Dennis's *Cities and Cemeteries of Etruria*, 1883³, descriptive, erudite and well written, is still the fundamental work of reference on the topography, history and archaeology of Etruscan sites. See also H. Nissen,

Italische Landeskunde, 1883–1902; A. Solari, *Topografia storica dell'-Etruria*, I–IV, 1915–20; the brief introductory chapters to the collected inscriptions of the various cities and territories found in the *Corpus Inscriptionum Etruscarum*; the reports on excavations and discoveries published in *Studi Etruschi*; and, more recently, M. Santangelo, *Musei e monumenti etruschi*, 1960; H. H. Scullard, *The Etruscan Cities and Rome*, 1967; L. Banti, *Il mondo degli Etruschi*, 1969². For recent discoveries in southern Etruria, see C. M. Lerici, *Nuove testimonianze dell'arte e della civiltà etrusca*, 1960; *Repertorio degli scavi e delle scoperte archeologiche nell'Etruria meridionale (1939–1965)*, I, 1969 (ed. A. Sommella Mura); II (*1966–70*), 1972 (ed. G. Brunetti Nardi). Reference to these general works should be understood in the following notes when there is no reference to more specialized monographs.

5. On Etruscan Rome, with special reference to the archaeological evidence, see I. Scott Ryberg, *An Archaeological Record of Rome from the Seventh to the Second Century B.C.*, 1940; E. Gjerstad, *Early Rome*, I–IV, 1953–66; M. Pallottino, in *Archeologia Classica*, XII, 1960, pp. 1 ff., and *Studi Etruschi*, XXXI, 1963, pp. 3 ff. (with bibliography to date); G. Colonna, 'Aspetti culturali della Roma primitiva: il periodo orientalizzante recente', *Archeologia Classica*, XVI, 1964, pp. 1 ff.; H. H. Scullard, *The Etruscan Cities and Rome*, 1967. See also above, pp. 96 ff.

6. See the reports by various authors in *Notizie degli Scavi*, 1919, pp. 8 ff.; 1929, pp. 325 ff.; 1953, pp. 29 ff.; in *Le Arti*, I, 1938–9, pp. 402 ff.; II, 1939–40, pp. 17 ff.; in *Monumenti Antichi dell'Accademia d'Italia*, XL, 1944, cols. 177 ff.; in *Latomus*, VIII, 1949, pp. 37 ff.; in *Bollettino d'Arte*, 1952, pp. 147 ff.; in *Opuscula Archaeologica*, VII, 1952, pp. 50 ff.; in *Papers of the British School at Rome*, XXVII, 1959, pp. 38 ff.; and A. De Agostino, *Veio (Itinerari dei Musei e Monumenti d'Italia)*, 1965. For the Villanovan cemetery of Quattro Fontanili, excavated by an Italo-British team, see the excavation reports in *Notizie degli Scavi*, 1963, pp. 77 ff.; 1965, pp. 49 ff.; 1967, pp. 87 ff.; 1970, pp. 178 ff., and papers by J. Close-Brooks and D. Ridgway, ibid., 1965, pp. 53 ff., and *Studi Etruschi*, XXXV, 1967, pp. 311 ff. For the topography of Veii, see J. Ward-Perkins, *Veii. The Historical Topography of the Ancient City* = *Papers of the British School at Rome*, XXIX, 1961; A. Kahane, L. M. Threipland, J. Ward-Perkins, *The Ager Veientanus, North and East of Veii* = ibid., XXXVI, 1968. See also M. Pallottino, *La scuola di Vulca*, 1945; A. De Agostino on the Tomba delle Anatre, *Archeologia Classica*, XV, 1963, pp. 219 ff.; M. Cristofani and F. Zevi on the Tomba Campana, ibid., XVII, 1965, pp. 1 ff.; M. Cristofani, *Veio. Le tombe da Monte Michele nel Museo Archeologico di Firenze*, 1969; L. Vagnetti, *Il deposito votivo di Campetti a Veio*, 1971.

7. The translation is from G. Dennis, *Cities and Cemeteries of Etruria*, 1883, I, p. 16.

8. On Cerveteri, see R. Mengarelli, in *Studi Etruschi*, I, 1927, pp. 145 ff.; IX, 1935, pp. 83 ff.; X, 1936, pp. 77 ff.; XI, 1937, pp. 77 ff.; L. Pareti, *La tomba Regolini-Galassi e la civiltà dell'Italia centrale nel sec. VII av.*

Cr., 1947; M. Pallottino, *La necropoli di Cerveteri* (*Itinerari dei Musei e Monumenti d'Italia*), 1968[7]; B. Pace, R. Vighi, G. Ricci, M. Moretti, 'Caere, scavi di Raniero Mengarelli', in *Monumenti Antichi dell'Accademia dei Lincei*, XLII, 1955; M. Cristofani, *La Tomba delle Iscrizioni di Cerveteri*, 1965; F. Roncalli, *Le lastre dipinte di Cerveteri*, 1966; M. Moretti, *Tomba Martini Marescotti*, 1966; *Materiali di Antichità Varia, V: Concessioni alla Fondazione Lerici*, 1966; I. Pohl, *The Iron Age necropolis of Sorbo at Cerveteri*, 1972.

9. Preliminary reports in *Archeologia Classica* from IX, 1957, onwards, *passim*; *Notizie degli Scavi*, 1959, pp. 143 ff.; *Studi Etruschi*, XXXIII, 1965, pp. 191 ff.; XXXIV, 1966, pp. 175 ff.; for further bibliography, see *Archeologia Classica*, XVIII, 1966, pp. 279 ff., *Göttingische Gelehrte Anzeigen*, CCXX, 1968, pp. 64 ff., and *Le lamine di Pyrgi*, in *Accademia Nazion. dei Lincei, Quaderno no. 147*, 1970; and now *Pyrgi. Scavi nel santuario etrusco (1959–1967)*, *Notizie degli Scavi*, 1970, II Supplemento (1973).

10. S. Bastianelli, 'Il territorio tolfetano nell'antichità', in *Studi Etruschi*, XVI, 1942, pp. 229 ff.; *Civitavecchia, Pagine di storia e di archeologia*, 1961. On centres within the eastern and northern edges of the Tolfa hills, see below, pp. 115 ff.; on the Coste de Marano and other hoards, R. Peroni, *Inventaria Archaeologica: Italia, 1, Ripostigli del Massiccio della Tolfa*, 1961.

11. M. Pallottino, *Tarquinia* = *Monumenti Antichi dell'Accademia dei Lincei*, XXXVI, 1937; P. Romanelli, *Tarquinia. La necropoli e il museo* (*Itinerari dei Musei e Monumenti d'Italia*), 1940. For later discoveries, see P. Romanelli, in *Bollettino d'Arte*, 1948, pp. 54 ff.; *Notizie degli Scavi*, 1948, pp. 133 ff.; C. M. Lerici, *Prospezioni archeologiche a Tarquinia. La necropoli delle tombe dipinte* [1959]; M. Moretti, *Nuovi monumenti della pittura etrusca a Tarquinia*, 1966; on the new painted tombs, see G. A. Mansuelli, in *Revue Archéologique*, I, 1967, pp. 41 ff., and M. Cristofani in *Dialoghi di Archeologia*, I, 1967, pp. 288 ff.

12. M. Torelli, in *Notizie degli Scavi*, 1971, pp. 195 ff., and 'Il santuario di Hera a Graviscaʼ, in *Parola del Passato*, XXVI, 1971, pp. 44 ff.; A. W. Johnston, 'The rehabilitation of Sostratos', ibid., XXVII, 1972, pp. 416 ff.

13. See *Bollettino dell'Istituto Centrale del Restauro*, 2, 1950; 3–4, 1951; 17–18, 1954; 34–5, 1958.

14. S. Gsell, *Fouilles dans la nécropole de Vulci*, 1891; F. Messerschmidt, *Die Nekropolen von Vulci*, 1930; R. Bartoccini, 'Tre anni di scavi a Vulci [1956–8]', in *Atti del VII° Congresso Internazionale di Archeologia Classica*, II, 1961, pp. 257 ff.; 'Il grande tempio di Vulci', in *Études Étrusco-Italiques*, 1963, pp. 9 ff.; S. Paglieri, 'Una stipe votiva vulcente', in *Rivista dell'Istit. Nazion. di Archeologia e Storia dell'Arte*, 1960, pp. 74 ff.; G. Colonna, 'Il ciclo etrusco-corinzi dei rosoni: contributo alla conoscenza della ceramica e del commercio vulcente', *Studi Etruschi*, XXIX, 1961, pp. 47 ff.; *Materiali di Antichità Varia*, II: *Materiale concesso alla Soc. Hercle*, 1964; ibid., III: *Materiale concesso a Francesco*

Paolo Bongiovi, 1964; G. Riccioni and M. T. Falconi Amorelli, *La Tomba della Panatenaica di Vulci*, 1968; A. Hus, *Vulci étrusque et étrusco-romaine*, 1971.

15. See above, p. 96.

16. On Capena and its region, see E. Stefani, in *Monumenti Antichi dell'-Accademia dei Lincei*, XLIV, 1958; G. D. B. Jones, 'Capena and the Ager Capenas', in *Papers of the British School at Rome*, XXX, 1962, pp. 116 ff.; ibid., XXXI, 1963, pp. 100 ff. On the Faliscans, W. Deecke, *Die Falisker*, 1888; G. Giacomelli, *La lingua falisca*, 1963; R. Hirata, *L'onomastica falisca e i suoi rapporti con la latina e l'etrusca*, 1967. For the archaeological remains of these areas (mostly kept at the Villa Giulia Museum in Rome), see especially A. Della Seta, *Museo di Villa Giulia*, 1918, pp. 37 ff.

17. G. Duncan, 'Sutri (Sutrium)', in *Papers of the British School at Rome*, XXVI, 1958, pp. 63 ff.; ibid., XXXII, 1964, pp. 38 ff.

18. G. Foti, *Museo Civico di Viterbo. Guida delle raccolte archeologiche, etrusche e romane*, 1957; L. Rossi Danielli, *Gli Etruschi nel Viterbese*, I *Ferento*, 1960 (to be consulted only for details and illustrations of the material). See also C. F. Giuliani, in *Quaderni dell'Istituto di Topografia Antica*, II, 1966, pp. 5 ff. (Norchia), pp. 61 ff. (Bolsena and Ferento).

19. G. Rosi, 'Sepulchral Architecture as Illustrated by the Rock Façades of Central Etruria', in *Journal of Roman Studies*, XV, 1925, pp. 1 ff.; XVII, 1927, pp. 59 ff.; H. Kock, E. v. Mercklin, C. Weickert, 'Bieda', in *Römische Mitteilungen*, XXX, 1915, pp. 161 ff.; A. Gargana, *La necropoli repustre di S. Giuliano* (*Monumenti Antichi dell'Accademia dei Lincei*), 1929; R. Bianchi Bandinelli, *Sovana*, 1929; E. Colonna di Paolo and G. Colonna, *Castel d'Asso*, 1970, and *Norchia*, forthcoming. On the hinterland of Etruria in general, see G. Colonna, 'L'Etruria meridionale interna dal villanoviano alle tombe rupestri', *Studi Etruschi*, XXXV, 1967, pp. 3 ff. Tuscania: S. Quilici Gigli, *Forma Italiae: Tuscana*, 1970.

20. *San Giovenale. Etruskerna landet och folket. Svensk forskning i Etrurien*, 1960 (reissued in English as *Etruscan Culture. Land and People*, 1962), and *Notizie degli Scavi*, 1960, pp. 1 ff.; 1961, pp. 103 ff.

21. L. Gasperini, 'Monterano. Un centro minore dell'Etruria meridionale', in *Études Étrusco-Italiques*, 1963, pp. 19 ff.

22. G. Matteucig, *Poggio Buco. The Necropolis of Statonia*, 1951; G. Barto-loni, *Le tombe da Poggio Buco nel Museo Archeologico di Firenze*, 1971.

23. R. Bloch, *Recherches archéologiques en territoire volsinien de la proto-histoire à la civilisation étrusque*, 1972. For epigraphic discoveries, see *Studi Etruschi*, XXXIV, 1966, pp. 165 ff., 310 ff., 337 ff.; see also W. V. Harris, 'The Via Cassia and the Via Traiana Nova between Bolsena and Chiusi', *Papers of the British School at Rome*, XXXIII, 1965, pp. 113 ff., and S. T. Buchicchio, 'Note di topografia antica sulla Volsinii romana', *Römische Mitteilungen*, LXXVII, 1970, pp. 19 ff.

24. P. Perali, *Orvieto etrusca*, 1928; S. Puglisi, *Studi e ricerche su Orvieto*

etrusca, 1934; M. Bizzarri, *Orvieto etrusca, arte e storia*, 1967, and in *Studi Etruschi*, XXX, 1962, pp. 1 ff.; XXXIV, 1966, pp. 3 ff.; see also ibid., XXXVIII, 1970, pp. 3 ff.; G. Camporeale, *La collezione alla Querce. Materiali archeologici orvietani*, 1970.

25. On the archaeological discoveries in this district, see especially A. Mazzolai, *Mostra Archeologica del Museo Civico di Grosseto*, 1958; *L'età del ferro nella Etruria Marittima*, 1965.

26. F. E. Brown, 'Cosa. I, History and Topography', and F. E. Brown, E. Hill Richardson, L. Richardson Jr, 'Cosa. II, The Temples of the Arx', in *Memoirs of the American Academy in Rome*, XX, 1951; XXVI, 1960; useful summary in E. T. Salmon, *Roman Colonization under the Republic*, 1969, pp. 29 ff.

27. O. W. v. Vacano, in *Römische Mitteilungen*, LXVIII, 1961, pp. 38 ff.; *Notizie degli Scavi*, 1961, pp. 251 ff.; 1962, pp. 285 ff.; 1965, pp. 30 ff. See also P. Sommella, in *Quaderni dell'Istituto di Topografia Antica*, III, 1967, pp. 11 ff.

28. A. Minto, *Marsiliana d'Albegna*, 1921.

29. A. Minto, 'Per la topografia di Heba etrusca e romana', in *Studi Etruschi*, IX, 1935, pp. 11 ff.; 'Saturnia etrusca e romana', in *Monumenti Antichi dell'Accademia dei Lincei*, XXX, 1925.

30. R. Bianchi Bandinelli, 'Roselle', in *Atene e Roma*, VI, 1925, pp. 35 ff.; R. Naumann, F. Hiller, 'Rusellae', in *Römische Mitteilungen*, LXVI, 1959, pp. 1 ff.; C. Laviosa, in *Studi Etruschi*, XXVII, 1959, pp. 33 ff.; XXVIII, 1960, pp. 289 ff.; XXIX, 1961, pp. 31 ff.; XXXI, 1963, pp. 39 ff.; XXXIII, 1965, pp. 49 ff.; XXXIX, 1971, pp. 521 ff.; P. Bocci, ibid., XXXI, 1963, pp. 453 ff.; XXXIII, 1965, pp. 109 ff.; A. Mazzolai, *Roselle e il suo territorio*, 1960.

31. I. Falchi, *Vetulonia*, 1891; *Studi Etruschi*, V, 1931, pp. 13 ff.; XXI, 1950–51, pp. 291 ff.; XXXI, 1963, pp. 435 ff.; XXXIV, 1966, pp. 239 ff.; *Notizie degli Scavi*, 1966, pp. 18 ff.; G. Camporeale, *La Tomba del Duce*, 1967; *I commerci di Vetulonia in età orientalizzante*, 1969.

32. D. Levi, in *Monumenti Antichi dell'Accademia dei Lincei*, XXXV, 1933.

33. A. Minto, *Populonia. La necropoli arcaica*, 1922; *Populonia*, 1943; 'L'antica industria mineraria in Etruria ed il porto di Populonia', in *Studi Etruschi*, XXIII, 1954, pp. 291 ff.; A. De Agostino, 'Nuovi contributi all'archeologia di Populonia', in *Studi Etruschi*, XXIV, 1955–6, pp. 255 ff.

34. R. Bianchi Bandinelli, 'Clusium', in *Monumenti Antichi dell'Accademia dei Lincei*, XXX, 1925; D. Levi, *Il Museo Civico di Chiusi*, 1935.

35. C. Shaw, *Etruscan Perugia*, 1939; A. M. Pierotti, M. Calzoni, 'Ricerche su Perugia etrusca, la città e la necropoli urbana', in *Studi Etruschi*, XXI, 1950–51, pp. 275 ff.; F. Santi, *Perugia*, 1950. For the region, see L. Banti, in *Studi Etruschi*, X, 1936, pp. 97 ff.

36. A. Neppi Módona, *Cortona etrusca e romana*, 1925.

37. On this problem, see T. Dohrn, in *Atti del I° Convegno di Studi Umbri*, Gubbio, 1964, pp. 197 ff., and in *Bollettino d'Arte*, XLIX, 1964, pp. 27 ff.; G. C. Susini, in *Archeologia Classica*, XVII, 1965, pp. 141 ff.

The Etruscans

38. *Studi Etruschi*, I, 1927, pp. 99 ff.; VI, 1932, pp. 533 ff.; G. Devoto, 'Arezzo', in *Atti Accademia Petrarca di Arezzo*, XXXIV, 1947-8, pp. 60 ff.

39. F. Magi, 'Contributi alla conoscenza di Fiesole etrusca', in *Atene e Roma*, X, 1930, pp. 83 ff.; G. Maetzke, 'Il nuovo tempio tuscanico di Fiesole', in *Studi Etruschi*, XXIV, 1955-6, pp. 277 ff.; G. Caputo, G. Maetzke, 'Presentazione del rilievo di Fiesole antica', in *Studi Etruschi*, XXVII, 1959, pp. 41 ff. For Florence, see C. Hardie, *Journal of Roman Studies*, LV, 1965, pp. 122 ff.

40. G. Caputo, 'Gli "athyrmata" orientali della Montagnola e la via dell'Arno e transappenninica', in *Arte antica e moderna*, 1962, pp. 58 ff.; and 'La Montagnola di Quinto Fiorentino. L'"orientalizzante" e le tholoi dell'Arno', in *Bollettino d'Arte*, 1962, pp. 115 ff.; *Studi Etruschi*, XXXVIII, 1970, pp. 367 ff.; F. Nicosia, *Il Tumulo di Montefortini e la Tomba dei Boschetti a Comeana*, 1966.

41. L. Consortini, *Volterra nell'antichità*, 1950 (to be consulted with caution).

42. A. De Agostino, in *Studi Etruschi*, XXVII, 1959, pp. 27 ff.; K. M. Phillips and A. Talocchini, *Poggio Civitate: the Archaic Etruscan sanctuary*, 1970.

43. For Etruscan Campania, see notes 12-17 on p. 251 above. For Capua, M. Bonghi Jovino, *Capua preromana: Terrecotte votive*, I, 1965; II, 1972; F. Parise Badoni, *Capua preromana: ceramica campana a figure nere*, 1968. M. Bonghi Jovino, R. Donceel, *La necropoli di Nola preromana*, 1970.

44. A. Grenier, *Bologne villanovienne et étrusque*, 1912; P. Ducati, *Storia di Bologna. I tempi antichi*, 1928; G. A. Mansuelli, 'La terza Bologna', in *Studi Etruschi*, XXV, 1957, pp. 31 ff.

45. E. Brizio, *Guida alle antichità della villa e del Museo di Marzabotto*, 1886, republished 1928; P. E. Arias, 'Considerazioni sulla città etrusca a Pian di Misano (Marzabotto)', in *Atti e Memorie della Deput. di Storia Patria per le Provincie di Romagna*, III, 1953; J. B. Ward-Perkins, *Town Planning Review*, 1955-6, pp. 133 ff.; recent excavations, *Studi Etruschi*, XXXVI, 1968, pp. 115 ff.; XXXVIII, 1970, pp. 215 ff.; XXXIX, 1971, pp. 217 ff.

46. S. Aurigemma, *Il R. Museo di Spina*, 1935; P. E. Arias, N. Alfieri, *Spina*, 1958; P. E. Arias, N. Alfieri, *Spina. Il Museo Archeologico di Ferrara*, 1960. Recent bibliography in D. Ridgway, *Archaeological Reports for 1967-68*, pp. 46 f.

47. For the Etruscan Po valley in general, see above, p. 97, and note 23 on p. 252.

CHAPTER SIX: *The Political and Social Organization of Etruria*

1. On problems concerning the political and social organization of Etruria, see especially: K. O. Müller, W. Deecke, *Die Etrusker*, I, pp. 319 ff.; also A. Solari, *La vita pubblica e privata degli Etruschi*, 1928; J. Heurgon, *La vie quotidienne chez les Étrusques*, 1961 [*Daily Life of the Etruscans*, 1964].

2. They have been utilized to this end especially in the works of A. Rosenberg, *Der Staat der alten Italiker*, 1913; S. P. Cortsen, *Die etruskischen Standes- und Beamtentitel, durch die Inschriften beleuchtet*, 1925; F. Leifer, *Studien zum antiken Ämterwesen, I, Zur Vorgeschichte des römischen Führeramts*, 1931; S. Mazzarino, *Dalla monarchia allo stato repubblicano : ricerche di storia romana arcaica*, 1945; P. De Francisci, 'Intorno all'origine etrusca del concetto di imperium', in *Studi Etruschi*, XXIV, 1955–6, pp. 19 ff.; M. Pallottino, 'Nuovi spunti di ricerca sul tema delle magistrature etrusche', in *Studi Etruschi*, XXIV, 1955–6, pp. 45 ff.; J. Heurgon, 'L'État étrusque', in *Historia*, VI, 1957, pp. 63 ff.; P. De Francisci, *Primordia Civitatis*, 1959; R. Lambrechts, *Essai sur les magistratures des républiques étrusques*, 1959; B. Liou, *Praetores Etruriae XV populorum (Étude d'épigraphie)*, 1969. On the relevance to this question of the Pyrgi discoveries, see M. Pallottino, in *Archeologia Classica*, XVI, 1964, pp. 104 ff.
3. F. Altheim, *Der Ursprung der Etrusker*, pp. 61 ff.
4. See L. Pareti, 'La disunione politica degli Etruschi e i suoi riflessi storici e archeologici', in *Rendiconti Pont. Accademia di Archeologia*, VII, 1929–31, pp. 89 ff. This thesis was put forward again, by G. A. Camporeale in *Parola del Passato*, XIII, 1958, pp. 5 ff.
5. See G. Devoto, in *Studi Etruschi*, VI, 1932, pp. 243 ff.
6. On the question of the existence of tribes in Etruria (though they cannot notionally be identified with the tribes of historical times), see H. Rix, in *Beiträge zur Namenforschung*, VII, 1956, p. 153, and G. Forni, in *Studi in onore di E. Betti*, 1961, III, p. 203.
7. S. P. Cortsen, *Die etruskischen Standes- und Beamtentitel*, 1925, p. 126. For the origin and meaning of the title *purθ-*, see below, p. 134.
8. L. Bonfante Warren, 'Roman triumphs and Etruscan kings: the changing face of the triumph', *Journal of Roman Studies*, LX, 1970, pp. 49 ff.; and also 'Etruscan dress as historical source: problems and examples', in *American Journal of Archaeology*, LXXV, 1971, pp. 277 ff.
9. See A. M. Colini, *Il fascio littorio*, 1932, pp. 5 ff.
10. See especially P. De Francisci, in *Studi Etruschi*, XXIV, 1955–6, p. 34.
11. See H. G. Bucholz, *Zum Herkunft der Kretischen Doppelaxt, Geschichte und auswärtige Beziehungen eines minoischen Kultsymbols*, 1959.
12. For a distinction between the primitive religious concept of sovereignty (*auctoritas*) and an essentially military power of more recent origin (*imperium*), see S. Mazzarino, *Dalla monarchia allo stato repubblicano*, 1945, pp. 208 ff., pp. 216 ff. On the whole question, see also P. De Francisci's article cited in note 10 above.
13. See G. De Sanctis, *Storia dei Romani*, I, 1907, pp. 224 ff.; E. Pais, *Storia di Roma dalle origini all'inizio delle guerre puniche*, II, 1926, pp. 296 ff. A bibliography on these questions will be found in P. De Francisci, 'La comunità sociale e politica romana primitiva', in *X° Congresso Internazionale di Scienze Storiche, Relazioni*, II, 1955, pp. 61 ff., in his article cited in note 10 above, and in *Primordia Civitatis*, 1959.
14. See S. Mazzarino, *Dalla monarchia allo stato repubblicano*; L. Pareti,

Storia di Roma, I, 1952; P. De Francisci, *Primordia Civitatis*; R. Werner, *Der Beginn der römischen Republik*, 1963.

15. See M. Pallottino, in *Archeologia Classica*, XVI, 1964, pp. 106 ff.
16. See M. Pallottino, *Gli Etruschi*, 1940[2], pp. 208 ff.
17. See F. Sartori, *Problemi di storia costituzionale italiota*, 1953, pp. 105 ff., 116 ff.
18. Arguments in favour of this correspondence are given by M. Pallottino, in *Studi Etruschi*, XXIV, 1955–6, pp. 64 ff.
19. On these problems, see especially S. Mazzarino, in *Historia*, VI, 1957, pp. 110 ff.; T. Frankfort and J. Heurgon, in *Latomus*, XVIII, 1959, pp. 3 ff., 713 ff.; H. Rix, *Das etruskische Cognomen*, 1963, pp. 325 ff.
20. For the sources, see K. O. Müller, W. Deecke, *Die Etrusker*, I, pp. 120, 351 ff.
21. See F. Slotty, 'Zur Frage des Mutterrechtes bei den Etruskern', in *Archiv Orientální*, XVIII, 1950 (*Symbolae F. Hrozny*, V), pp. 262 ff.
22. L. Bonfante Warren, 'The Women of Etruria', in *Arethusa*, VI, 1973, pp. 91 ff., and more briefly in *Archaeology*, XXVI, 1973, pp. 242 ff.

CHAPTER SEVEN: *The Etruscan Religion*

1. The following are among those who have devoted themselves to the subject: C. Thulin, G. Herbig, R. Pettazzoni, C. Clemen, G. Furlani, C. C. van Essen, H. M. R. Leopold, B. Nogara, G. Q. Giglioli, A. Grenier, R. Herbig, S. Weinstock and J. Heurgon.
2. G. Q. Giglioli, 'La religione degli Etruschi', in *Storia delle Religioni*, II, 1962[5], pp. 281 ff.; A. Grenier, *Les religions étrusque et romaine* ('*Mana*', *Les religions de l'Europe ancienne*), 1948. Both works are easy to consult and contain all the preceding bibliography. Briefer treatments may be found in: M. Pallottino, 'La religione degli Etruschi', in *Le religioni del mondo*, edited by N. Turchi, 1950[2], pp. 313 ff.; R. Herbig, *Götter und Dämonen der Etrusker*, 1965[2], and 'Zur Religion und Religiosität der Etrusker', in *Historia*, VI, 1957, pp. 123 ff.
3. H. J. Rose, 'On the Relations between Etruscan and Roman Religion', in *Studi e materiali di Storia delle Religioni*, IV, 1928, pp. 161 ff.
4. The attempt to connect certain aspects of Etruscan religion (divination, ecstasy, belief in the journey to the underworld, asexuality or bisexuality, bells, etc.) with shamanistic ideas and practices (W. Muster, 'Der Schamanismus bei den Etruskern', in *Frühgeschichte und Sprachwissenschaft*, edited by W. Brandenstein, 1948, pp. 60 ff.) rests upon very slender arguments; for such motifs are very widely spread throughout the world, and it is extremely doubtful whether at least some of them were native to Etruria.
5. The concept of *lasa*, a name common to a number of female demi-goddesses, which have in some cases been identified by the Greeks and Romans with the nymphs, has been improperly extended by modern archaeologists to include female daemons from the other world. There has also been a mistaken attempt to deny the existence of minor deities

by that name and to substitute in their stead a single great goddess *Lasa* (R. Enking, 'Lasa', in *Römische Mitteilungen*, LVII, 1942, pp. 1 ff.).

6. On this divinity, see R. Pettazzoni, 'La divinità suprema della religione etrusca', in *Studi e materiali di Storia delle Religioni*, IV, 1928, pp. 207 ff., where the hypothesis is advanced that the god was a local *gens* form of the sky god *Tin* (Jupiter). On the origin of the names *Vertumnus-Voltumnus*, see G. Devoto, in *Studi Etruschi*, XIV, 1940, pp. 275 ff.

7. Now in the Museo Nazionale di Villa Giulia at Rome: see G. Q. Giglioli, in *Archeologia Classica*, IV, 1952, pp. 189 ff.

8. On Hercle, see J. Bayet's classic study, *Herclé. Étude critique sur les principaux monuments relatifs à l'Hercule étrusque*, 1926.

9. On the names of Etruscan divinities, see also H. L. Stoltenberg, *Etruskische Götternamen*, 1957 (to be consulted with much caution).

10. See *Studi Etruschi*, XX, 1948–9, pp. 253 ff. An old hypothesis that *aisera* (genitive *aiseras*) was a feminine singular noun equivalent to 'goddess', or the actual name of a goddess, rather than the plural of *ais*, 'god', has been revived by A. J. Pfiffig and G. Devoto (cf. *Studi Etruschi*, XXXII, 1964, pp. 131 ff.). Their arguments, however, do not seem very convincing, at least as far as the Zagreb mummy text is concerned.

11. See L. Banti, 'Il culto del cosiddetto tempio "dell'Apollo" a Veio e il problema delle triadi etrusco-italiche', in *Studi Etruschi*, XVII, 1943, pp. 187 ff.

12. C. O. Thulin, 'Die etruskische Disciplin', in *Göteborgs Högskolas Årsskrift*, 1905, 1906, 1909. See also note 2 on p. 262.

13. See R. Pettazzoni, in *Studi Etruschi*, I, 1927, pp. 195 ff.; G. Furlani, in *Studi e materiali di Storia delle Religioni*, IV, 1928, pp. 243 ff.; VI, 1930, pp. 9 ff.; *Studi Etruschi*, V, 1931, pp. 203 ff.; *Tyrrhenica*, 1957, pp. 61 ff.; J. Nougayrol, in *Comptes-rendus de l'Académie des Inscriptions et Belles Lettres*, 1955, pp. 509 ff.

14. See M. Pallottino, ' "Partecipazione" e senso drammatico nel mondo figurato degli Etruschi', in *Arti Figurative*, 1946, pp. 149 ff.; and R. Enking, *Etruskische Geistigkeit*, 1947 (to be consulted with caution).

15. See C. O. Thulin, 'Die Götter des Martianus Capella und der Bronzeleber von Piacenza', in *Religionsgeschichtl. Versuche und Vorarbeiten*, III, 1, 1906, pp. 60 ff.; S. Weinstock, 'Martianus Capella and the Cosmic System of the Etruscans', in *Journal of Roman Studies*, XXXVI, 1946, pp. 101 ff.; A. Grenier, *Les religions étrusque et romaine*, pp. 18 ff., 34 ff.; M. Pallottino, 'Deorum sedes', in *Studi in onore di A. Calderini e R. Paribeni*, III, 1956, pp. 223 ff.

16. See S. Weinstock, 'Templum', in *Römische Mitteilungen*, XLVII, 1932, pp. 95 ff.

17. *C.I.I.* 6: see M. Pallottino, *Testimonia Linguae Etruscae* (*T.L.E.*), n. 697. This unusual epigraphic document has been thoroughly re-examined. S. Ferri (in *Rendiconti dell'Accademia dei Lincei*, XIII, 1958, pp. 323 ff.) rejects the correspondence between *frontac*, which had been connected with the Greek βροντή, 'thunder', and the title *fulguriator*. Ferri considers *frontac* to be an ethnic name referring to the priest's native

city: Ferento, in southern Etruria, where the same *gens* name is attested. M. Lejeune (in *Revue d'Études Latines*, XL, 1962, pp. 160 ff.) reads *frθntac*, and sees a relation with the title *purθne* (for which see p. 134 above). V. Pisani (in *Le lingue dell'Italia antica oltre il latino*, 1964², p. 225) goes so far as to believe that the non-Latin text of the bilingual inscription is not in Etruscan but in north Picene, because of its similarities with the Novilara stele; these undoubted similarities, however, may be explained as the result of prolonged contacts between Etruscan and local dialects in this frontier area.

18. This invalidates the parallel with Christianity drawn by T. Zielinski in *Studi e materiali di Storia delle Religioni*, IV, 1928, pp. 179 ff.
19. See F. Cumont, *Lux perpetua*, 1949.
20. A. Brelich, in *Dissertationes Pannonicae*, I, 7, 1937, pp. 80 ff.
21. On these problems, see also J. Bayet, 'Idéologie et plastique, II. La sculpture funéraire de Chiusi', in *Mélanges d'Archéologie et d'Histoire*, 1960, pp. 35 ff.
22. F. De Ruyt, *Charun, démon étrusque de la mort*, 1934.
23. J. M. Blázquez Martínez, 'Caballos en el infierno etrusco', in *Ampurias*, XIX–XX, 1957–8, pp. 31 ff.
24. See below, pp. 199 and 222.
25. See A. Bruhl, *Liber Pater*, 1953, to which should be added the epigraphic documentation: see M. Pallottino, in *Studi Etruschi*, XXV, 1957, pp. 604 ff.
26. See p. 138.
27. For the shape of the temple, see pp. 160 ff.
28. See pp. 198 ff. and 222 ff.
29. See pp. 201 and 225 ff.
30. A model of a *lituus* in sheet bronze has recently been found in a tomb at Cerveteri: see *Kunst und Leben der Etrusker*, Vienna, 1966, pp. 25 ff. and fig. 2.
31. Individual problems concerning Etruscan religion and religious iconography are discussed in relation with material recovered from votive deposits by Q. F. Maule and H. R. W. Smith in *Votive Religion at Caere: Prolegomena*, Univ. of California Press, 1959.

CHAPTER EIGHT: *Literature and the Arts*

1. B. Nogara, *Gli Etruschi e la loro civiltà*, 1934, pp. 405 ff.; J. Heurgon, *La vie quotidienne chez les Étrusques*, 1961, pp. 270 ff. [*Daily Life of the Etruscans*, 1964, pp. 237 ff.].
2. For a complete account and an interpretation of classical sources on the sacred literature of the Etruscans, see especially C. O. Thulin, 'Die etruskische Disciplin', in *Göteborgs Högskolas Årsskrift*, 1905, 1906, 1909. On individual problems and their religious content, see among others the following: S. Weinstock, 'C. Fonteius Capito and the Libri Tagetici', in *Papers of the British School at Rome*, XVIII, 1950, pp. 44 ff., and 'Libri Fulgurales', ibid., XIX, 1951, pp. 122 ff.; A. Piganiol,

'Sur le calendrier brontoscopique de Nigidius Figulus', in *Studies in Roman Economic and Social History in Honour of Allan Chester Johnson*, 1951, pp. 79 ff.; J. Heurgon, 'The Date of Vegoia's Prophecy', in *Journal of Roman Studies*, XLIX, 1959, pp. 41 ff.; A. J. Pfiffig, 'Eine etruskische Prophezeiung', in *Gymnasium*, LXVIII, 1961, pp. 55 ff.

3. See E. Bormann, in *Jahreshefte der Österr. Archäol. Inst.*, II, 1899, pp. 219 ff.; M. Pallottino, *Tarquinia = Monumenti Antichi dell'Accademia dei Lincei*, XXXVI, 1937, col. 561, and in *Studi Etruschi*, XXI, 1950–51, pp. 167 ff.; J. Heurgon, in *Latomus*, XII, 1953, pp. 402 ff.

4. See S. Mazzarino, 'Le droit des Étrusques', in *Iura*, XII, 1961, pp. 24 ff.

5. See B. Nogara, *Gli Etruschi e la loro civiltà*, 1934, pp. 425 ff.

6. K. O. Müller, W. Deecke, *Die Etrusker*, 1887, II, pp. 200 ff.; P. Ducati, *Etruria antica*, 1927, pp. 167 ff.; F. Behn, *Musikleben in Altertum und frühen Mittelalter*, 1954, especially pp. 127 ff.; G. Fleischauer, *Musik des Altertums*, II, 5: *Etrurien und Rom*, 1961, pp. 160 ff.

7. For a connection between pipe playing and the 'primitive' spirituality of the Etruscans, see R. Enking, *Etruskische Geistigkeit*, 1947.

8. A useful collection of documents on Etruscan dancing can be found in M. A. Johnstone, *The Dance in Etruria*, 1956.

9. On Etruscan art, the following general works and the bibliographies they contain are of fundamental importance: P. Ducati, *Storia dell'arte etrusca*, 1927; G. Q. Giglioli, *L'arte etrusca*, 1935; P. J. Riis, *An Introduction to Etruscan Art*, 1953; the critical essay by T. Dohrn, *Grundzüge etruskischer Kunst*, 1958; and the two encyclopaedia articles by R. Bianchi Bandinelli, 'Etrusca, arte', in *Enciclopedia dell'Arte Antica*, III (1960), and by M. Pallottino, 'Etrusco-Italic art', in *Encyclopedia of World Art*, V (1961). The following are also useful for the rich (often recently discovered) material they contain and for their critical framework: *Mostra dell'Arte e della Civiltà Etrusca*, Milan, 1955²; *Kunst und Leben der Etrusker*, Cologne, 1956²; *Arte e Civiltà degli Etruschi*, Turin, 1967 (also in Swedish and Austrian editions, 1966). See also the following summaries: M. Pallottino and H. Jucker, *Etruscan Art*, 1955 (also in French and German editions); A. Frova, *L'arte etrusca*, 1957; R. Bloch, *L'art étrusque*, 1959; see also note 32 below, and most recently M. Pallottino, *Civiltà artistica etrusco-italica*, Florence, 1971; R. Bianchi Bandinelli and A. Giuliano, *Les Étrusques et l'Italie avant Rome*, Paris, 1973.

10. On the subject of Etruscan architecture, besides the works quoted above, see especially A. Andrén, *Architectural Terracottas from Etrusco-Italic Temples*, 1939–40, and *Osservazioni sulle terrecotte architettoniche etrusco-italiche (Lectiones Boëthianae, I)*, 1971; G. Patroni, *Architettura preistorica generale ed italica. Architettura etrusca*, 1946; L. Polacco, *Tuscanicae dispositiones*, 1952 (to be consulted with care: see *Studi Etruschi*, XXII, 1952–3, pp. 558 ff.); A. Andrén, 'Origine e formazione dell'architettura templare etrusco-italica', in *Rendiconti della Pontificia Accademia di Archeologia*, XXXII, 1959–60, pp. 21 ff.; A. Boëthius and

J. B. Ward-Perkins, *Etruscan and Roman Architecture*, 1970. For architectural models, see R. Staccioli, *Modelli di edifici etrusco-italici, I, Modelli votivi*, 1969. See also *La città etrusca e italica pre-romana (Atti del Convegno di Bologna, 1966)*, 1970.

11. See F. E. Brown, in *Memoirs of the American Academy in Rome*, XX, 1951, pp. 102 ff.

12. R. Naumann, F. Hiller, in *Römische Mitteilungen*, LXVI, 1959, pp. 3 ff.

13. A. Minto, 'Pseudocupole e pseudovolte nell'architettura etrusca delle origini', in *Palladio*, III, 1939, pp. 1 ff.

14. F. Messerschmidt, 'Das Grabmal des Porsenna', in *Das neue Bild der Antike*, 1942, II, pp. 53 ff.

15. Metal coverings (Vitruvius, II, 3, 5) must be considered exceptional and limited to small and unusually rich buildings.

16. The chronological classification of Etrusco-Italic temple decorations into 'phases' is due to A. Della Seta, *Museo di Villa Giulia*, 1918, pp. 120 ff. Further refinements will be found in A. Andrén, *Architectural Terracotta from Etrusco-Italic Temples* (see note 10 above), pp. cxxx ff., and M. Pallottino, in *Bullettino Archeologico Comunale*, LXVIII, 1940, p. 253. On the temple decoration system, see also A. Minto, in *Studi Etruschi*, XXII, 1952-3, pp. 9 ff. For Pyrgi, see *Notizie degli Scavi*, 1959, pp. 143 ff. and especially pp. 246 ff.; *Studi Etruschi*, XXXIII, 1965, pp. 191 ff.; *Archeologia Classica*, XVIII, 1966, pp. 97 ff.

17. Stone rather than wooden columns seem to be attested already at the two Pyrgi temples (fifth century B.C.): see *Archeologia Classica*, XVIII, 1966, pp. 268 ff.

18. A. Ciasca, *Il capitello detto eolico in Etruria*, 1962.

19. It is difficult to decide whether this feature is an Etruscan innovation (in the direction of 'realism') or a survival of proto-Hellenic models. For the second hypothesis, see P. Zancani Montuoro, in *Palladio*, IV, 1940, pp. 49 ff.

20. Apart from the general works on Etruscan art already cited, see also: P. Ducati, *La scultura etrusca*, 1935; G. M. A. Hanfmann, *Altetruskische Plastik*, 1936; L. Goldscheider, *Etruscan sculpture*, 1941 (Phaidon); P. J. Riis, *Tyrrhenika. An Archaeological Study of Etruscan Sculpture in the Archaic and Classical Periods*, 1941; G. M. A. Hanfmann, *Etruskische Plastik*, 1956. For marble sculpture in Etruria, see A. Andrén, 'Marmora Etruriae', in *Antike Plastik*, VII, pp. 7 ff.

21. K. Olzscha, *Interpretation der Agramer Mumienbinde*, 1939, pp. 20 ff.; *Bollettino d'Arte*, 1964, pp. 115 ff.

22. See A. Andrén, *Architectural Terracottas . . .* (see note 10 above).

23. R. Herbig, *Die jüngeretruskischen Steinsarkophage*, 1952.

24. H. Brunn, G. Körte, *I rilievi delle urne etrusche*, 2 vols., 1870–1916; J. Thimme, 'Chiusinische Aschenkisten und Sarkophage der Hellenistichen Zeit', in *Studi Etruschi*, XXIII, 1954, pp. 25 ff.; XXV, 1957, pp. 87 ff.

25. L. Banti, 'Bronzi arcaici etruschi', in *Tyrrhenica*, 1957, pp. 77 ff.

26. M. Pallottino *et al.*, *L'arte delle situle dal Po al Danubio*, 1961.

27. Y. Huls, *Ivoires d'Étrurie*, 1957.
28. On Etruscan painting, see: F. Weege, *Etruskische Malerei*, 1921; F. Poulsen, *Etruscan Tomb Paintings*, 1922; F. Messerschmidt, *Beiträge zur Chronologie der etruskischen Wandmalerei*, I, 1928; M. Pallottino, *Etruscan Painting*, 1952; H. Leisinger, *Malerei der Etrusker*, 1953 (to be consulted only for the illustrations); A. Rumpf, *Malerei und Zeichnung* (*Handbuch der Archäologie*, 6), 1953.
29. C. M. Lerici, *Prospezioni archeologiche a Tarquinia. La necropoli delle tombe dipinte*, 1959, and *Nuove testimonianze dell'arte e della civiltà etrusca*, 1960; M. Moretti, *Nuovi monumenti della pittura etrusca a Tarquinia*, 1966.
30. See p. 112 above.
31. J. D. Beazley, *Etruscan Vase-Painting*, 1947.
32. For a comprehensive view of the problem, see J. Martha, *L'art étrusque*, 1889, p. 614; A. Della Seta, 'Antica arte etrusca', in *Dedalo*, I, 1920–21, pp. 559 ff.; C. Anti, 'Il problema dell'arte italica', in *Studi Etruschi*, IV, 1930, pp. 151 ff.; G. Kaschnitz-Weinberg, 'Bemerkungen zur Struktur der altitalischen Plastik', in *Studi Etruschi*, VII, 1939, pp. 135 ff.; R. Bianchi Bandinelli, *Storicità dell'arte classica*, 1950², pp. 77 ff., pp. 93 ff., pp. 115 ff. (see also the 1st ed., pp. 257 ff.); M. Pallottino, 'Sul problema delle correlazioni artistiche fra Grecia ed Etruria', in *Parola del Passato*, V, 1950, pp. 5 ff.; and 'Per una nuova prospettiva della storia dell'arte antica', etc., in *Archivio de Prehistoria Levantina*, IV, 1953, p. 259 (and the works cited in note 9 above); R. Bloch, 'L'art étrusque et son arrière plan historique', in *Historia*, VI, 1957, pp. 53 ff.; T. Dohrn, *Grundzüge etruskischer Kunst*, 1958; C. C. van Essen, *Précis d'histoire de l'art antique en Italie*, 1960; G. Kaschnitz Weinberg, *Das Schöpferische in der römischen Kunst*, 1961.
33. See M. Pallottino, ' "Partecipazione" e senso drammatico nel mondo figurato degli Etruschi', in *Arti Figurative*, II, 1946, pp. 149 ff.
34. *The Swedish Cyprus Expedition*, IV, 2: E. Gjerstad, *The Cypro-Geometric, Cypro-Archaic and Cypro-Classical Periods*, 1949, pp. 93 ff., 117 ff., 364 ff.
35. See G. Rodenwaldt, 'Über den Stilwandel in den Antoninischen Kunst', in *Abhandl. der Preuss. Akademie der Wissensch., Phil.-Hist. Klasse*, 1935, and 'Römische Reliefs Vorstufen zur Spätantik', in *Jahrbuch des Deutsch. Archäol. Instituts*, LV, 1940, pp. 12 ff.; M. Pallottino, *Civiltà romana, arte figurativa e ornamentale*, 1940, pp. 81 ff.; R. Bianchi Bandinelli, 'Tradizione ellenistica e gusto romano nella pittura pompeiana', in *La critica d'arte*, IV, 1941, pp. 3 ff.

CHAPTER NINE: *Life and Customs*

1. A general treatment of the subject-matter of this chapter will be found in A. Solari, *La vita pubblica e privata degli Etruschi*, 1928; J. Heurgon, *Daily Life of the Etruscans*, 1964; A. Pfiffig, 'Zur Sittengeschichte der Etrusker', in *Gymnasium*, LXXI, 1964, pp. 17 ff.

The Etruscans

2. We are dealing here with largely unpublished material now in the Museum of Villa Giulia in Rome. Objects found at Vulci are mentioned in *Studi Etruschi*, III, 1929, pp. 109 ff. For other wooden objects, see *Studi Etruschi, Indici dei Volumi* I–XXX, 1968, s.v. 'legno' in the Indice per materia, p. 338.

3. See C. O. Thulin, *Die etruskische Disciplin. III, Die Ritualbücher*, 1909, pp. 3 ff.

4. See F. Castagnoli, *Ippodamo di Mileto e l'urbanistica a pianta ortogonale*, 1956 [English ed.: *Orthogonal Town Planning in Antiquity*, Cambridge, Mass., 1971].

5. See M. Pallottino, 'Le origini di Roma', in *Archeologia Classica*, XII, 1960, pp. 1 ff.

6. See above, pp. 97 and 122 ff. and the accompanying notes.

7. See above, pp. 158 ff.

8. On Etruscan town-planning in general, see P. Lavedan, J. Hugueney, *Histoire de l'urbanisme. Antiquité*, 1966[2], pp. 296 ff., discussed by R. A. Staccioli, 'Urbanistica etrusca', in *Archeologia Classica*, XX, 1968, pp. 141 ff.

9. G. Patroni, 'L'origine della domus', in *Rendic. Accad. Lincei*, V, XI, 1902, pp. 467 ff.; A. Gargana, 'La casa etrusca', in *Historia*, 1934, pp. 204 ff.; G. Patroni, *Architettura preistorica generale ed italica. Architettura etrusca*, 1941, pp. 294 ff.

10. G. M. A. Richter, *The Furniture of the Greeks, Etruscans and Romans*, 1966.

11. P. Ducati, in *Monumenti antichi dei Lincei*, XXIV, 1916, col. 401 ff.

12. See A. Stenico, 'Studi interpretativi sulla "Tomba dei rilievi" di Cerveteri', in *Studi Etruschi*, XXIII, 1954, pp. 195 ff.

13. The subject of sport in ancient Etruria is studied in R. Passamonti, 'Giochi e gare', in *Vita Italiana*, VIII, 1957, n. 24, pp. 75 ff.; *Lo sport nella storia e nell'arte*, 1960.

14. G. Q. Giglioli, 'L'oinochoe di Tragliatella', in *Studi Etruschi*, III, 1929, pp. 111 ff.

15. Similar combats may be seen at the Tombs of Pulcinella and of the Olympic Games. See G. Becatti, F. Magi, *Le pitture delle tombe degli Auguri e del Pulcinella (Monumenti della pittura antica scoperti in Italia)*, 1955; R. Bartoccini, C. M. Lerici, M. Moretti, *La tomba delle Olimpiadi*, 1959.

16. On Etruscan mining and metallurgy, see G. D'Acchiardi, in *Studi Etruschi*, I, 1927, pp. 411 ff.; III, 1929, p. 397; see also *Studi Etruschi*, XI, 1937, pp. 305 ff.; XV, 1940, pp. 315 ff.; XX, 1950, pp. 303 ff.; XXII, 1952–3, pp. 291 ff.; XXIII, 1954, pp. 291 ff.; XXV, 1957, pp. 305 ff.; XXVII, 1959, pp. 191 ff.; L. Cambi, 'La metallurgia etrusca', in *Tyrrhenica*, 1957, pp. 97 ff.

17. See note 3 on p. 248.

18. See P. Fraccaro, 'La malaria e la storia degli antichi popoli classici', in *Atene e Roma*, XXII, 1919, pp. 57 ff.; N. Toscanelli, *La malaria nell'-antichità e la fine degli Etruschi*, 1927; on surface drainage by *cuniculi*,

266

see S. Judson and A. Kahane, *Papers of the British School at Rome*, XXXI, 1963, pp. 74 ff.

19. On Etruscan weights and coins, see A. Sambon, *Les monnaies antiques de l'Italie*, 1903–6, pp. 12 ff.; S. L. Cesano, 'Note di numismatica etrusca', in *Atti e Memorie dell'Istituto Italiano di Numismatica*, VIII, 1934, pp. 71 ff.; L. Breglia, in *Rendiconti dell'Accademia di Napoli*, XXX, 1955, pp. 211 ff.

20. See M. Pallottino *et al.*, *L'Arte delle situle dal Po al Danubio*, 1961, pp. 84 ff.

21. See note 15 on p. 249.

22. See M. Pallottino, 'Uno specchio di Tuscania e la leggenda etrusca di Tarchon', in *Rendiconti dell'Accademia dei Lincei*, 1930, pp. 47 ff., and *Studi Etruschi*, X, 1936, p. 463, plate 50.

23. On Etruscan jewellery, its techniques and forms, see G. Becatti, *Oreficerie antiche*, 1955; E. Coche De La Ferté, *Les bijoux antiques*, 1955; *Studi Etruschi*, XXII, 1952–3, pp. 199 ff., 203 ff.; XXIV, 1955–6, pp. 353 ff.; *Kunst und Leben der Etrusker*, Cologne, 1956, pp. 46 ff.; G. Piccardi, S. Bordi, 'Sull'oreficeria granulata etrusca', in *Studi Etruschi*, XXIV, 1955–6, pp. 353 ff.; *Ori e argenti dell'Emilia antica. Catalogo*, Bologna, 1958; *Ori e argenti dell'Italia antica*, Turin, 1961.

Part 3

CHAPTER TEN: *The Problem of Etruscan*

1. The content of the following chapters is for the most part a development of materials already treated in more succinct form in my article 'Gli studi sulla lingua etrusca nelle loro condizioni attuali' (*Archivio Glottologico Italiano*, XXXII, 1940), and later in *Was wissen wir heute von der etruskischen Sprache?*, Zurich, 1955 (reprinted in *Kunst und Leben der Etrusker*, Cologne, 1956, pp. 28 ff.) and in another article, 'Il problema della lingua etrusca' (in *Le Meraviglie del Passato*, 1958[5], II, pp. 283 ff.). The following pages also contain a number of data and observations that are new, the result of the very important epigraphical discoveries made in recent years (see pp. 197 ff.). We should add, however, that since these data are still being actively studied, the conclusions can only be provisional.

2. For these problems see J. Friedrich, *Entzifferung verschollener Schriften und Sprachen*, 1954, which gives a brief and accurate synthesis of the question of the interpretation of Etruscan; see also P. E. Cleator, *Lost Languages*, 1959.

3. See above, pp. 90, 111, 201–2, 221.

4. For these new prospects in the study of Etruscan, see M. Pallottino, 'L'ermeneutica etrusca tra due documenti-chiave', in *Studi Etruschi*, XXXVII, 1969, pp. 79 ff.

5. The first volume (1893–1902) contains inscriptions found at Fiesole, Volterra, Siena, Arezzo, Cortona, Chiusi and Perugia. Of the second

volume, four fascicules have been published: Section I, fasc. I, 1907 (Orvieto and Bolsena); fasc. 2, 1923 (Coastal Etruria from Populonia to Vulci); fasc. 3, 1936 (Tarquinia); Section II, fasc. I, 1912 (Faliscan territory). A supplement (1919–21) was also published containing the text of the Zagreb mummy. C. Pauli's collaborators in this work were O. A. Danielsson, B. Nogara, G. Herbig and E. Sittig. In preparation are a fascicule on the inscriptions of southern Etruria (excluding Tarquinia) and some of the fascicules on the *instrumentum*; fascicules dedicated to Campania, the Po valley, the rest of the *instrumentum* and the supplements and indices are still in project.

6. E. Lattes, 'Saggio di un indice lessicale etrusco', in *Memorie dell'Accademia d'Archeologia e Lettere di Napoli*, I, 1908; II, 1911; III, 1918; *Rendiconti del R. Istituto Lombardo*, XLV, 1912, pp. 303 ff., 351 ff., 412 ff.; *Memorie del R. Istituto Lombardo*, XXIII, 1914. This invaluable work is unfortunately incomplete and difficult to consult, buried as it is in various local journals. The work is now being completely revised and brought up-to-date in a large-scale scientific lexicon of the Etruscan language by the Istituto di Etruscologia e di Antichità Italiche of the University of Rome, with the collaboration of the Istituto di Studi Etruschi ed Italici in Florence. Meanwhile the word-index to M. Pallottino's *Testimonia Linguae Etruscae*, 1968[2], may be consulted for all but proper names.

7. See *Glotta*, XVIII, 1940, pp. 260 ff.; XXX, 1943, pp. 213 ff.

8. G. Devoto, 'Pelasgo e peri-indoeuropeo', in *Studi Etruschi*, XVII, 1943, pp. 359 ff.; 'Etrusco e peri-indoeuropeo', in *Studi Etruschi*, XVIII, 1944, pp. 187 ff.; XXXI, 1963, pp. 93 ff.

9. A new attempt at a general classification of Etruscan was recently undertaken by M. Durante in *Studi Micenei ed Egeo-anatolici*, VII, 1968, pp. 7 ff.

10. The chief workers in this field have been F. Ribezzo, A. Trombetti, B. Terracini, G. Devoto, V. Bertoldi and G. Alessio.

11. On the history and methods of research on Etruscan, see E. Fiesel, *Etruskisch*, 1931, and surveys by S. P. Cortsen and E. Vetter, in *Glotta*, XXIII, pp. 144 ff.; XXVIII, pp. 117 ff.; XXXV, pp. 270 ff.; M. Pallottino, in *Doxa*, III, 1950, pp. 29 ff.; F. Ribezzo, in *Studi Etruschi*, XXII, 1952–3, pp. 105 ff.; K. Olzscha, in *Historia*, VI, 1957, pp. 34 ff.; H. Rix, in *Göttingische Gelehrte Anzeigen*, 217, 1965, pp. 68 ff.; M. Pallottino, in *Studi Etruschi*, XXXVII, 1969, pp. 79 ff.

CHAPTER ELEVEN: *The Sources and the Method*

1. They are regularly published, with comments, in the 'Rivista di epigrafia' in the yearly issues of *Studi Etruschi*.

2. Particularly instructive in this context is the example of the small but important contributions made by the study of a number of funerary inscriptions recently discovered at Tarquinia: see *Studi Etruschi*, XXXI, 1964, pp. 107 ff.

3. For these more recent discoveries, see *Studi Etruschi*, XXVIII, 1960, pp. 479 ff.; XXX, 1962, pp. 136 ff. and 283 ff.; XXXI, 1963, pp. 175 ff.; XXXII, 1964, pp. 107 ff. and 161 ff.; XXXIII, 1965, pp. 469 ff.; XXXIV, 1966, pp. 175 ff., 307 ff. and 395 ff.; XXXV, 1967, pp. 516 ff.; *Archeologia Classica*, XVI, 1964, pp. 49 ff.; XVIII, 1966, pp. 291 ff. Among these finds there is an inscription at Tarquinia which mentions a personage connected in some way with Hannibal's campaigns: see A. J. Pfiffig, in *Studi Etruschi*, XXXV, 1967, pp. 613 ff.

4. See above, p. 190.

5. For published collections of the material, see note 5 on p. 267, and note 3 above; and M. Pallottino, *Testimonia Linguae Etruscae*, 1968², which also includes the glosses.

6. See above, pp. 190 ff.

7. On the question of *frontac*, see above, p. 146, and note 17 on p. 261.

8. cf. G. Buonamici, *Fonti di storia etrusca tratte dagli autori classici*, 1939, pp. 354 ff.

9. 'Les éléments étrusques du vocabulaire latin', in *Bulletin de la Société linguistique*, XXX, 1930, pp. 82 ff.

10. For the hypothesis, see C. Merlo, in *Studi Etruschi*, I, 1927, pp. 303 ff.; P. Mingazzini, in *Studi Etruschi*, XXIV, 1955–6, pp. 343 ff.; against it, see G. Rohlfs, in *Indogermanische Forschungen*, LXVIII, 1963, pp. 295 ff.

11. cf. G. Devoto, in *Studi Etruschi*, I, 1927, pp. 255 ff.; E. Fiesel, *Namen des griechischen Mythos im Etruskischen*, 1928; C. De Simone, *Die griechischen Entlehnungen im Etruskischen*, 1968–70.

12. *Studi Etruschi*, vols. I ff.

13. M. Pallottino, in *Scritti in onore di B. Nogara*, 1937, pp. 341 ff.

14. cf. B. Nogara, *Gli Etruschi e la loro civiltà*, 1933, p. 420; on the date of the fragment, see J. Heurgon, in *Journal of Roman Studies*, XLIX, 1959, pp. 41 ff. See also note 2 on p. 262.

15. See above, pp. 192 ff.

16. See A. Walde, J. B. Hofmann, *Lateinisches etymologisches Wörterbuch*, II, 1954, *s.v. mundus*.

17. *Studien zum antiken Ämterwesen*, I, 1931.

18. *Glotta*, XI, 1921, pp. 213 ff.

19. *Studi Etruschi*, V, 1931; VII, 1933, etc.

20. See above, pp. 126 ff.

21. On the bilingual method and its applications, see M. Pallottino, in *Studi Etruschi*, VII, 1933, p. 241; K. Olzscha, 'Die Sprache der Etrusker. Probleme und neue Wege der Deutung', in *Neue Jahrbücher für Wissenschaft und Jugendbildung*, XII, 1936, pp. 97 ff.; *Interpretation der Agramer Mumienbinde*, 1939, pp. 3 ff.; M. Pallottino, in *Studi Etruschi*, XIII, 1939, pp. 331 ff.; XX, 1948–9, pp. 159 ff.; 'Nuovi orientamenti nello studio dell'etrusco', in *Archiv Orientální*, XVIII, 4, 1950 (*Symbolae Hrozný*, V), pp. 159 ff.; and also in *Studi Etruschi*, XXII, 1952–3, pp. 128 ff.; XXIV, 1955–6, pp. 45 ff.; XXVI, 1958, pp. 49 ff.; *Studi in onore di G. Funaioli*, 1955, pp. 299 ff. See also note 11 on p. 268.

22. Recent examples of linguistic research undertaken with the help of

electronic computers have prompted some scholars (notably A. J. Pfiffig) to apply the new techniques to the study of Etruscan. An attempt to extend the techniques to the whole of the lexical corpus of Etruscan, based unfortunately on materials that had not been critically edited, has given definitely negative results in the work by M. Fowler and R. G. Wolf, *Materials for the Study of the Etruscan Language*, 1965; see M. Cristofani, in *Studi Etruschi*, XXXIV, 1966, pp. 436–40.

23. *Atti del Iº Congresso Internazionale Etrusco*, pp. 187 ff.
24. The lettering pertaining to the phonetic system of Archaic Etruscan has been systematically illustrated by F. Slotty, *Beiträge zur Etruskologie, I: Silbenpunktierung und Silbenbildung im Altetruskischen*, 1952.
25. cf. *Studi Etruschi*, XI, 1937, pp. 206 ff.

CHAPTER TWELVE: *The Results*

1. In *American Journal of Philology*, 1936, pp. 261 ff.
2. On the whole question of the origin of the Etruscan alphabet, see G. Buonamici, *Epigrafia etrusca*, pp. 133 ff., with bibliography; see also M. Guarducci, in *Studi Etruschi*, XIV, 1940, pp. 281 ff.; R. Carpenter, in *American Journal of Archaeology*, XLIX, 1945, pp. 452 ff.; K. Olzscha, in *Historia*, VI, 1957, pp. 34 ff.; G. Vallet, *Rhégion et Zancle*, 1958, p. 182; M. Cristofani, in *Annali Scuola Normale di Pisa*, s. II, XXXVIII, 1969, pp. 99–112.
3. See G. Buchner and C. F. Russo, in *Rendiconti dell'Accademia dei Lincei*, 1955, pp. 215 ff.
4. Some of these letters are very occasionally encountered in Etruscan inscriptions, especially in the most recent ones; their use is certainly due to the influence of the Latin alphabet: see G. Buonamici, *Epigrafia etrusca*, pp. 166 ff., 189 ff.
5. The Latin use of the letter *c*, derived from Greek γ, is certainly due to Etruscan influence. In Archaic times there probably also existed small differences in the pronunciation of the letters *c*, *q*, and *k*, as attested by their use with the different vowels: *c* was normally followed by the front vowels *i* and *e*, *k* by the middle vowel *a*, and *q* by the back vowel *u*.
6. This digraph is also encountered in primitive Latin inscriptions: e.g. on the Palestrina fibula (*C.I.L.*, I², 3), where the word *vhevhaked* should be read *fefaked*.
7. See M. Pallottino, in *Studi Etruschi*, XXXV, 1967, pp. 161 ff.
8. E. Vetter, in *Glotta*, XXIV, pp. 114 ff.; XXVII, pp. 157 ff.; G. Buonamici, 'L'interpunzione sillabica . . .', in *Studi Etruschi*, XVI, 1942, pp. 263 ff.; F. Slotty, *Beiträge zur Etruskologie, I: Silbenpunktierung und Silbenbildung im Altetruskischen*, 1952; A. J. Pfiffig, in *Kadmos*, II, 1963, pp. 142 ff. Slotty tends to ascribe the phenomenon to purely phonetic causes: objections to this view will be found in K. Olzscha, in *Gnomon*, 1953, pp. 271 ff.; M. Pallottino, in *Studi Etruschi*, XXII, 1952–3, pp. 478 ff.; see also K. Olzscha, in *Historia*, VI, 1957, pp. 34 ff.
9. op. cit. (see note 8 above).

10. See above, pp. 206 ff., and S. P. Cortsen, in *Glotta*, XXVI, 1937, pp. 10 ff.

11. See K. Olzscha, in *Neue Jahrbücher für Wissenschaft und Jugendbildung*, 1963, p. 105; M. Pallottino, in *Studi Etruschi*, XXX, 1962, p. 304; XXXII, 1964, pp. 121 ff.

12. K. Olzscha, *Interpretation der Agramer Mumienbinde*, 1939, pp. 103 ff., and *Tyrrhenica*, 1957, pp. 135 ff.; see also V. Pisani, *Archivio Glottologico*, XXXIV, 1942, pp. 116 ff., where the Etruscan verb is described as possessing an 'intransitive' character.

13. On Etruscan phonetics, morphology and syntax, see M. Pallottino, *Elementi di lingua etrusca*, 1936, with the modifications required by recent progress in the subject (see in particular the volumes of *Studi Etruschi*). More recent syntheses on the grammatical structure of Etruscan (with excessively rigid and axiomatic attempts at an interpretation of its phenomena, often on unverified assumptions) have been published by H. L. Stoltenberg, *Etruskische Sprachlehre mit vollständigem Wörterbuch*, 1950 (see *Studi Etruschi*, XXII, 1952–3, pp. 474 ff.) and *Die Sprache der Etrusker. Laut, Wort und Satz*, 1958.

14. See especially the contributions published in *Studi Etruschi*, VIII, 1934, pp. 217 ff.; X, 1936, pp. 191 ff., 289 ff.; XI, 1937, pp. 495 ff. (the proceedings of a conference at Florence in 1936 on the text of the cippus); XXIX, 1961, pp. 111 ff.; XXX, 1962, pp. 355 ff.

15. *Studi Etruschi*, XXVIII, 1960, pp. 479 ff.; *Études étrusco-italiques*, 1963, pp. 247 ff.

16. See *Archeologia Classica*, XVI, 1964, pp. 49 ff. (especially pp. 76 ff.); see also above, *passim*, and, for the literature, *Archeologia Classica*, XVIII, 1966, pp. 279–82.

17. See F. Ribezzo, in *Parola del Passato*, I, 1946, pp. 286 ff.; M. Pallottino, 'Sulla lettura e sul contenuto della grande iscrizione di Capua', in *Studi Etruschi*, XX, 1948–9, pp. 159 ff.; K. Olzscha, 'Götterformeln und Monatsdaten in der grossen etruskischen Inschrift von Capua', in *Glotta*, XXXIV, 1954, pp. 71 ff. (but see also *Studi Etruschi*, XXVI, 1958, pp. 74 ff.).

18. See *Studi Etruschi*, Vols. VI ff.; E. Vetter, *Etruskische Wortdeutungen*, I, 1937; K. Olzscha, *Interpretation der Agramer Mumienbinde*, 1939, and in *Glotta*, XXX, 1948, pp. 105 ff.; XXXII, 1953, pp. 283 ff.; in *Tyrrhenica*, 1957, pp. 122 ff.; in *Aegyptus*, 1959, pp. 340 ff.; E. Vetter, 'Zur Lesung der Agramer Mumienbinde', in *Anzeiger der Österreichische Akad. der Wissenschaften, Phil.-Hist. Klasse*, 1955, pp. 252 ff. (with new further readings discovered by infra-red photography); A. J. Pfiffig, *Studien zu den Agramer Mumienbinde* (Österreichische Akad. der Wissenschaften), 1963.

19. See Müller-Deecke, *Die Etrusker*, 1871, II, pp. 508 ff.; S. P. Cortsen, *Vocabulorum etruscorum interpretatio*, in *Nord. Tidsskrift f. filol. Fjerderæke*, VI, 1917, pp. 165 ff.; A. Trombetti, *La lingua etrusca*, 1928, pp. 211 ff.; M. Pallottino, *Elementi di lingua etrusca*, 1936, pp. 87 ff.; E. Vetter, *Etruskische Wortdeutungen*, I, 1937; K. Olzscha, *Interpretation*

der Agramer Mumienbinde, 1939, pp. 210 ff.; H. L. Stoltenberg, *Etruskische Sprachlehre mit vollständigem Wörterbuch*, 1950 (with reservations as to many of the proposed translations); M. Pallottino, *Testimonia Linguae Etruscae*, 1968[2] (for the glosses and a lexical index); and in *Kunst und Leben der Etrusker*, Cologne, 1956, pp. 34 ff., and 'Saggio di un vocabolario etrusco', in *Le Meraviglie del Passato*, 1958[5], pp. 297 ff.; H. L. Stoltenberg, *Etruskische Namen für Seinformer und Sachen*, 1959 (for which, see above). In the word-list given on pp. 225 ff., we have included the substantial contribution made by the epigraphic discoveries of the last few years (see above, p. 269, note 3).

Additional Note to Part Three

In 1969, the Istituto di Studi Etruschi ed Italici held an international colloquium to examine the progress and organization of research into the Etruscan language (*Atti del colloquio sul tema : le ricerche epigrafiche e linguistiche sull'etrusco*, Florence, 1973). A. J. Pfiffig, *Die Etruskische Sprache*, 1969, is a general monograph and includes all the essential bibliographical and critical information available up to the date of its publication: it should, however, be used with some caution. A number of the statements contained in it are subjective, and Pfiffig is a traditionalist in his application of the combinatory method and of grammatical schemes (on the inadvisability, at least for the time being, of allegedly or apparently definitive syntheses, see above, p. 191). The truth of the matter is that our ideas about the Etruscan language and its interpretation are currently in a phase of profound and even radical transformation: this is a direct result of the recent prodigious increase in the quality of epigraphic material available, and of the Pyrgi discoveries. For examples of new trends in Etruscan language studies see M. Pallottino, 'L'ermeneutica tra due documenti-chiave', in *Studi Etruschi*, XXXVII, 1969, pp. 79–81; H. Rix, 'Die moderne Linguistik und die Beschriebung des Etruskischen', in *Kadmos*, X, 1971, pp. 150–70.

The collection and publication of the raw material for study is symbolized by the reappearance of *Corpus Inscriptionum Etruscarum*, after an interval of several decades, under the joint auspices of the Istituto di Studi Etruschi ed Italici and the Academy of Sciences in Berlin (fasc. II, section II, 4, was published recently; for future plans see *Studi Etruschi*, XXXIX, 1971, pp. 472 ff.). See also: C. De Simone, *Die griechischen Entlehnungen im Etruskischen*, 2 vols., 1968–70; S. Pieri, *Toponomastica della Toscana Meridionale e dell'arcipelago toscano*, 1969; M. Pallottino, *Testimonia Linguae Etruscae*, second edition, 1968. At the moment, scholars are working mainly on problems of epigraphy and of proper names in the Archaic period (see G. Colonna in *Mélanges de l'École Française de Rome*, 1970, pp. 637 ff.; J. Heurgon, ibid., 1971, pp. 9 ff.), and of phonetics (C. De Simone, op. cit.). A particularly interesting funerary inscription from Cerveteri could now be added to my list of sample texts given above, pp. 218 ff.: *Studi Etruschi*, XXXVII, 1969, pp. 79 ff.

Notes on the Plates

by David Ridgway

The following abbreviations have been used in these Notes:

ACE   *Arte e Civiltà degli Etruschi* (exhibition catalogue), Turin, 1967
Arch. Class.   *Archeologia Classica*
Dial. di Arch.   *Dialoghi di Archeologia*
Giglioli   G. Q. Giglioli, *L'Arte etrusca*, Milan, 1935
JRS   *Journal of Roman Studies*
MAAR   *Memoirs of the American Academy in Rome*
Mélanges   *Mélanges d'Archéologie et d'Histoire de l'École Française de Rome*
Mon. Ant.   *Monumenti Antichi*
Not. Scavi   *Notizie degli Scavi*
Nuovi Tesori   *Nuovi Tesori dell'antica Tuscia* (exhibition catalogue), Viterbo, 1970
Par. Pass.   *La Parola del Passato*
PBSR   *Papers of the British School at Rome*
Rend. Linc.   *Rendiconti . . . dell'Accademia dei Lincei*
Röm. Mitt.   *Mitteilungen des Deutschen Archäologischen Instituts, Römische Abteilung*
St. Etr.   *Studi Etruschi*

1. A tomb at Tarquinia in the eighteenth century: Plate VII in Part One of James Byres, *Hypogaei, or sepulchral caverns of Tarquinia, the capital of antient Etruria*, London, 1842. James Byres (1734–1817) of Tonley, Aberdeenshire, was an antiquary and dealer in Rome for nearly forty years, until *c.* 1790; his pupils included Edward Gibbon, and his *coups* the Portland Vase for Sir William Hamilton. The plates only of his projected volume on Tarquinia were edited and published after his death by Frank Howard. See further H. Möbius, 'Zeichnungen etruskischer Kammergräber und Einzelfunde von James Byres', *Röm. Mitt.*, LXXIII–LXXIV, 1966–7, pp. 53–71 and Plates 19–31. The chamber figured here is the outer room of the Tomba della Mercareccia (or 'dei Rilievi': the friezes were sculptured in low-relief, and are no longer extant), of the Hellenistic period, *c.* third–second century B.C. The ceiling recalls Vitruvius's *cavum aedium displuviatum*, in which the roof had a central aperture and sloped outwards in four directions.

2. Villanovan trench-graves (*tombe a fossa*) in the Quattro Fontanili cemetery at Veii: D. Ridgway, *Archaeological Reports for 1967–68*, p. 35,

273

Figure 6. The cemetery was rediscovered in the course of the British School at Rome's long-term programme of field-survey in southern Etruria; note the evidence for modern deep ploughing. Excavation at Quattro Fontanili, by the British School and the Rome University Institute of Etruscology, began in 1961. These graves are for inhumations. The plan of the cemetery as a whole shows that it developed outwards from the earlier *tombe a pozzo* (for cremations) in the centre, and this succession is naturally valid for the relative chronology of the objects found in the graves: J. Close-Brooks, *Not. Scavi*, 1965, p. 54, Figure 3 (ossuaries: cf. Plate 3 below) and p. 61, Figure 7 (fibulas).
Photo: British School at Rome.

3. Villanovan biconical ossuary from the Grotta Gramiccia West cemetery at Veii: J. B. Ward-Perkins (ed.), *Veii = PBSR*, XXIX, 1961, Plate 25. Ht 36 cm. Handmade biconical ossuaries, or cinerary urns, of coarse pottery (impasto) with incised linear decoration are characteristically used for cremation burials of both the 'northern' and 'southern' Villanovan cultures. The urns usually have lids in the form either of a one-handled impasto bowl (*ciotola*) or of a helmet in bronze or impasto, and were interred in small well-like shafts covered by stone slabs (*tombe a pozzo*).
Photo: British School at Rome.

4. Villanovan bronzes from Vulci: R. Bartoccini, *Atti VII Cong. Int. Arch. Class. 1958*, 1961, Plate 2, Figure 3; M. T. Falconi Amorelli, *La collezione Massimo*, 1968, Nos. 22, 21, 24; *ACE* Nos. 6, 4, 5. Sword: length 44 cm.; urn: ht with lid 53 cm.; flask: ht 32·5 cm. These three pieces were allegedly found in the same late-eighth-century tomb in the Cavalupo cemetery, and form part of the collection presented to the Villa Giulia by a local landowner, Prince Vittorio Massimo, in 1955. The T-hilted short sword, complete with scabbard, is a particularly fine and well-preserved example: the type has a long history in Sicily, which is probably more immediately significant for Etruria than the undoubted Near Eastern similarities. The flask is a bronze version of a pottery type that goes back to the Late Bronze Age in Syria and Palestine. The relation of the Villanovan examples to this tradition is not easy to establish in any but the most general terms: the ridge and boss decoration is no less typical of Villanovan sheet-metalwork than the large and small bosses seen on the urn – the shape of which is clearly derived from earlier impasto models, such as Plate 3 above. The use of sheet bronze in Etruria follows the onset of Greek colonization in central and southern Italy in the early eighth century: the reappearance of bronze plate body-armour in Greece towards the end of the same century has been seen as the result of renewed contact with central Europe and the transmission, via Italy, of the appropriate metallurgical skills to the Aegean.
Rome: Museo Nazionale di Villa Giulia; photo: Soprintendenza alle Antichità dell'Etruria Meridionale.

5. Villanovan horned animal-bird askos from the Benacci cemetery, Bologna, datable to the late eighth–early seventh century. Pottery askoi like this are representative of the early stage of 'plastic art', and there are parallels in bronze for the little warrior. The odd combination of the horns and plump bird-like body of the larger beast contrasts strangely with the more reasonable (and purely animal) shape of the horse on its back. Somewhat similar examples are known from southern Etruria (Bisenzio and Veii): for full discussion of the type, and of related zoomorphic forms, see H. Hencken, *Tarquinia, Villanovans and Early Etruscans*, II, 1968, pp. 519 ff.

   Bologna: Museo Civico; photo: Soprintendenza alle Antichità dell'Emilia e Romagna.

6. Cypro-Phoenician gilded silver bowl from the Orientalizing-period Bernardini Tomb at Palestrina: *ACE* No. 21. Ht 18·8 cm. The six long-necked silver serpents were perhaps attached to the rim by the owner rather than the maker. The decoration consists of four horizontal bands and a central medallion. The figures are incised with some details embossed in low-relief before the gilding: the scenes – soldiers on the march, country life, hunting – make up 'a strange medley, suggesting Africa, Egypt, and the Aegean combined in a fantastic dream' (Randall-MacIver). See further: C. D. Curtis, *The Bernardini Tomb = MAAR*, III, 1919, pp. 34 ff. and Plates 12–18.

   Rome: Museo Nazionale di Villa Giulia; photo: Soprintendenza alle Antichità dell'Etruria Meridionale.

7. Gold pectoral from the Orientalizing-period Regolini-Galassi tomb at Cerveteri: L. Pareti, *La Tomba Regolini-Galassi*, 1947, Plate 9 and pp. 190 ff. This large gold plaque covered the breast of the corpse from the neck downwards. The dense *repoussée* decoration in concentric zones includes numerous human and animal figures, palmettes etc. – all typical of the Orientalizing repertoire.

   Vatican: Museo Etrusco Gregoriano; museum photo.

8. Cinerary urn of silver-plated sheet bronze from the Orientalizing-period Tomba del Duce at Vetulonia: G. Camporeale, *La Tomba del Duce*, 1967, No. 127, Plates 35–8, pp. 141 ff.; idem, *I commerci di Vetulonia in età orientalizzante*, 1969, p. 86, Plate 28. Ht 42 cm.; length 63 cm.; breadth 37 cm. The shape – a rectangular box, or hut, with gabled 'roof' – the decorative technique and the motifs themselves suggest that the piece was made in southern Etruria, most probably at Cerveteri, at the end of the seventh century.

   Florence: Museo Archeologico; photo: Soprintendenza alle Antichità dell'Etruria.

9. Funerary stele from Kaminia, Lemnos. The inscription is written in the dialect spoken on the island before it was conquered by the Athenians under Miltiades in the late sixth century: it is the only piece of writing found outside Italy that has a certain affinity with Etruscan.

For discussion and bibliography, see pp. 72 ff., and note 17 on Chapter Two.

Athens: National Museum; photo: Rome University, Istituto di Etruscologia e Antichità Italiche.

10. Naval battle painted on an Etruscan vase of the first half of the sixth century from Cerveteri: E. Pottier, *Vases antiques du Louvre*, 1897, D.150, p. 40, Plate 34. The scene is probably inspired by contemporary episodes in the struggle for maritime supremacy in the West.

Paris: Musée du Louvre; museum photo.

11. Stone cippus with Greek inscription of the late sixth century from Gravisca, the port of Tarquinia: M. Torelli, *Par. Pass.*, XXVI, 1971, pp. 55 ff.; idem, *Not. Scavi*, 1971, p. 241, Figure 57. The cippus had been reused to cover a fourth-century drainage channel, and was found in 1970 in the excavation of the sanctuary of Hera at Gravisca. This excavation has furnished the first tangible confirmation of resident Greeks in Etruria from *c.* 580 onwards – though it is clear that the phenomenon began much earlier: A. A. Blakeway, 'Demaratus', *JRS*, XXV, 1935, pp. 129–49. Among the early votive offerings in the Gravisca sanctuary is a bronze lamp in the form of a miniature boat, made in Sardinia: G. Lilliu, *Not. Scavi*, 1971, pp. 289 ff. The 'Sostratos' of the inscription has been tentatively equated by the excavator with a successful Greek merchant, mentioned by Herodotus, who traded with Tartessos in southern Spain.

Photo: Soprintendenza alle Antichità dell'Etruria Meridionale.

12–14. The three inscribed gold tablets found in 1964 at the Etruscan sanctuary of Pyrgi: *Not. Scavi, II Suppl. 1970*, 1973, Plate IV (colour). 12: 18·5 cm. × 8·1 cm.; 13: 19·3 cm. × 9·2 cm.; 14: 19·2 cm. × 9·5 cm. The tablets had been deliberately folded and hidden in a niche between the two temples; note the holes for nails (some were found, of gold) with which they had presumably been affixed to the walls or doors, most probably of Temple B. The two longer texts – 12, with sixteen lines in Etruscan, and 13, with eleven lines in Punic – are parallel (though not identical) in content: they refer to Thefarie Velianas, the ruler of Cerveteri, and the dedication by him of a holy place sacred to the Phoenician goddess Astarte (equivalent to the Etruscan Uni) in the third year of his reign, apparently in return for a favour granted to him. The precise months (and in the case of the favour, the day) are given in the Punic tablet, 13; the longer Etruscan tablet, 12, specifies commemorative ritual procedures, which are further defined in the shorter Etruscan text, 14. These inscriptions are of the first importance for the study not only of the Etruscan language but also of Etruscan history: they provide documentary evidence for the acceptance by an Etruscan ruler of the religion of a Phoenician goddess in his territory *c.* 500–480, and thus have an obvious bearing on the treaties of Carthage with the Etruscans (Aristotle, *Politics*, III, 5.10) and with Rome (Polybius, III, 22). The context of the tablets was described by G.

Colonna, *Arch. Class.*, XVI, 1964, p. 53 f., and the first major discussion appeared ibid., pp. 58–117 (M. Pallottino, G. Garbini). See further (in English): J. Heurgon, 'The inscriptions of Pyrgi', *JRS*, LVI, 1966, pp. 1–15.

Rome: Museo Nazionale di Villa Giulia; photos: Soprintendenza alle Antichità dell'Etruria Meridionale.

15. Fragmentary Latin inscription found at Tarquinia in 1948; one of a collection of early Imperial 'eulogies' inscribed on the base of statues or honorific monuments. Remarkably, these *Elogia Tarquiniensia* commemorate the heroes of a much earlier, Etruscan, tradition. This one recalls the career of a member of the *gens* Spurinna (this identification arises out of a join noticed recently by M. Torelli): 'as praetor he led an army against C(aere). He took another to Sicily, as the first Etruscan to lead an army across the sea, and was decorated with an eagle and gold crown for his victory'. The Sicilian episode has been connected with the Etruscan 'original invasion' (*sic*: incredible); a date in the sixth or early fifth century is much more probable, 'but even more important than the precise date is the fact that here we have a piece of Tarquinian history, otherwise unknown, preserved until the days of the Roman Empire' (H. H. Scullard). See further: P. Romanelli, *Not. Scavi*, 1948, pp. 260 ff.; M. Pallottino, *St. Etr.*, XXI, 1950–51, pp. 147 ff.; M. Torelli, *St. Etr.*, XXXVI, 1968, pp. 467 ff.

Tarquinia: Museo Nazionale; photo: Soprintendenza alle Antichità dell'Etruria Meridionale.

16. Etruscan bronze helmet found in the sanctuary at Olympia in 1817 and presented to the British Museum by King George IV in 1823. The Greek inscription reads: '(Dedicated by) Hieron the son of Deinomenes and the Syracusans to Zeus, (plunder) from the Tyrrhenians at Cumae'. Hieron defeated the fleet of the Etruscans and their Carthaginian allies off Cumae in 474 B.C.: Pindar, *Pythian Odes*, I, 72. The helmet was not originally intended to be a votive offering: it was most probably worn by an Etruscan during the battle.

London: British Museum; museum photo.

17–19. *Inscriptions on pottery from Rome*

17. Small bucchero plate, with Etruscan inscription, from the foot of the Capitol: M. Pallottino, *Bulletino Archeologico Comunale*, LXIX, 1941, pp. 101 ff. This, and other inscribed pieces from the Palatine and the Forum Boarium (cf. Plates 18, 19), bear witness to the importance of the Etruscan element in the population of Rome at the time of the Tarquins.

18. Impasto sherd with Etruscan inscription, found in 1963 in the sacred area of Sant'Omobono in the Forum Boarium: M. Pallottino, *St. Etr.*, XXXIII, 1965, pp. 505 ff. The script, especially the *q* and the four-stroke sigma (left), is typical of southern Etruria, particularly Cerveteri, and the Faliscan territory. The piece is dated by its context to the end

of the seventh–beginning of the sixth century (equivalent in traditional terms to the reign of Tarquinius Priscus), and is thus the earliest Etruscan inscription found in Rome: and, indeed, the earliest piece of writing of any kind found there.

19. Bucchero sherd with a very early Latin inscription, also found in 1963 at Sant'Omobono: M. Torelli, *Quaderni dell'Istituto di Topografia Antica*, V, 1968, pp. 75 ff. The piece is dated by its context to the middle of the sixth century. For a brief account of the excavation which produced both this and the preceding sherd, see G. Ioppolo in E. Gjerstad, *Early Rome*, IV: 2, 1966, pp. 399 f.; and, for the historical background, M. Pallottino, 'Fatti e leggende (moderne) sulla più antica storia di Roma', *St. Etr.*, XXXI, 1963, pp. 3 ff.

    Rome: Musei Capitolini; museum photos.

20. Battle scene in the painted François Tomb, Vulci: Giglioli, CCLXVI, 2. It shows the Etruscan hero Mastarna (far left) and the Vibenna brothers: among their adversaries is a Tarquin of Rome. The scene recalls events of the sixth century in Etruscan and Roman history. For the chronology of the painting, which has been much discussed, M. Cristofani has recently argued well for a date in the second half of the fourth century: *Dial. di Arch.*, I, 1967, pp. 186 ff.

    Rome: Torlonia collection; photo: Rome University, Istituto di Etruscologia e Antichità Italiche.

21. Funerary stele from Bologna, showing the journey to the nether regions (centre) and combat between an Etruscan horseman and a Celtic warrior: P. Ducati, *Mon. Ant.*, XX, 1911, col. 615 and Plate 4; idem, *Storia dell'arte etrusca*, 1927, p. 358 ff. and Figure 404. The piece is dated to the end of the fifth century, and thus affords a glimpse of the Celtic expansion into the Po valley.

    Bologna: Museo Civico; photo: Soprintendenza alle Antichità dell'Emilia e Romagna.

22. The 'Hypogeum of the Volumni' at Perugia: this tomb reproduces the interior of a house, and contains the cinerary urns of a family of the second and first centuries B.C. It is characteristic of the last phase of Etruscan civilization, on the eve of its definitive assimilation into the Roman world. See further: A. von Gerkan and F. Messerschmidt, 'Das Grab der Volumnier bei Perugia', *Röm. Mitt.*, LVII, 1941, pp. 122 ff. and Plate 9.

    Photo: Anderson-Mansell Collection.

23. Pottery from Tomb 10 at San Martino in Gattara (prov. Ravenna): G. Bermond Montanari, *St. Etr.*, XXXVII, 1969, pp. 219 ff. and Plate 44a; *Not. Scavi*, 1969, pp. 20 ff. and p. 21, Figure 27. The tomb-group, of the fifth century, contained many bronzes – including a single Etruscan greave and a 'Negau' helmet, typical of Celtic cemeteries in Northern Italy. The vases illustrated here include a pottery 'Schnabel-

kanne', a small two-handled jug (with parallels in southern Etruria) and two Attic red-figured kylikes mended in antiquity. The combination of finds in this cemetery points to an early period of peaceful co-existence between trans-Alpine immigrants – Celts – and the local population, characterized on the part of the former by the acquisition of Etruscan bronzes and Attic pottery. The Celts might indeed have been attracted south by the prospect of commerce with the Etruscans: the Romagna valleys afford an easy route to Central Italy. See further: *St. Etr.*, cit., pp. 213–28.

Bologna: Museo Civico; photo: Soprintendenza alle Antichità dell'Emilia e Romagna.

24–7. *'Aerial photographs' of relief-models of Etruscan cities*

24. *Veii*. The modern roads show up very well, as do the thinner and more sinuous lines of the streams. The broken white lines along the upper edge of the plateau (the site of the city) correspond to the visible sections of the town wall. The small plateau to the south is the site of the modern hamlet of Isola Farnese; below this is the Portonaccio area, site of the sanctuary 'of the Apollo' outside the city. The rectangular area to the south-east is Piazza d'Armi. The city is surrounded by its cemeteries: Quattro Fontanili lies to the north (top centre of this photograph). On the topography of Veii, see further: J. B. Ward-Perkins (ed.), *Veii = PBSR*, XXIX, 1961; A. Kahane *et al.*, *The Ager Veientanus, North and East of Veii = PBSR*, XXXVI, 1968.

25. *Cerveteri*. The Etruscan city, Caere, was sited on the long central plateau, the edge of which is delineated by the continuous white line; only a fraction of the same area is occupied by the modern village. The Fosso Manganello, to the north-west, divides the plateau from the Banditaccia area and its cemetery – note the characteristic tumuli; the Fosso della Mola, to the south-east, separates it from the vast cemetery of Monte Abatone. The Sorbo area, with its earlier burials, is in the valley to the south. See further: J. Bradford, *Ancient Landscapes*, 1957, pp. 116–31.

26. *Tarquinia*. The modern town (called Corneto until 1872) is situated on the western extremity of the Monterozzi plateau, which is covered with tombs (more than 6,000 have been found by geophysical methods in recent years, of which more than sixty are painted). Of the tumuli shown here, only the two largest (the Doganaccia tumuli), to the south, are still extant. On the far side of the Fosso San Savino, the ancient city stood on a plateau, Pian di Civita: this is surrounded by steep slopes. The temple known as the 'Ara della Regina', seen here as a white rectangle, was built in the late fourth–early third century on the outskirts of the ancient city. Beyond the city to the east, Villanovan cemeteries occupy a series of knolls (*poggi*). See further: M. Pallottino, *Tarquinia = Mon. Ant.*, XXXVI, 1937, cols. 39–122; Bradford, op. cit., pp. 131–9; H. Hencken, *Tarquinia, Villanovans and Early Etruscans*,

The Etruscans

I, 1968, pp. 5–18; C. M. Lerici, *Una grande avventura dell'archeologia moderna*, 1965.

27. *Vulci*. The plateau on which the ancient city was situated, west of the winding course of the Fiora, is bounded by a white line. Princely plundering of the cemeteries began in 1828, and has now been succeeded by clandestine and unscientific excavation: the areas affected – George Dennis estimated that by 1856 more than 15,000 tombs had been opened – lie to the north of the city, and to the east of the Fiora, where the Cuccumella tumulus is visible. Note (top) the medieval castle and the Ponte dell'Abbadia – a bridge resting on what may be Etruscan foundations. See further: R. Bartoccini, *Atti VII Cong. Int. Arch. Class. 1958*, 1961, pp. 257 ff.

    Rome University: Museo di Etruscologia; photos: Rome University, Istituto di Etruscologia e Antichità Italiche.

28. Veii: the Vignacce valley, on the south side of the plateau (facing Isola Farnese: cf. Plate 24), running from the Cremera valley to a postern in the middle of the south side of the city: J. B. Ward-Perkins (ed.), *Veii = PBSR*, XXIX, 1961, Plate 17a. There are the remains of a small cemetery in the east side (right) of the valley; the ruin in the background is modern. See further: Perkins, op. cit., pp. 13, 73–5.
    Photo: British School at Rome.

29. Norchia: section of the cemetery along the Fosso Pile, showing the arrangement in stories of the architectural façades typical of the 'rock sepulchres' in the hinterland of Middle Etruria. See further: G. Rosi, *JRS*, XV, 1925, pp. 1–59, and XVII, 1927, pp. 59–96 *passim*; E. Colonna di Paolo and G. Colonna, *Norchia (Le necropoli rupestri dell'Etruria meridionale*, II), forthcoming (the same authors' *Castel d'Asso* was published in 1970).
    Photo: Soprintendenza alle Antichità dell'Etruria Meridionale.

30. Funerary stele of Avle Feluske (the name is written on the right side of the 'frame'), from Vetulonia: Giglioli, LIX, 1. The stele bears an incised representation of a warrior, with round shield and long-crested helmet, brandishing a double axe. In Etruria, the latter feature – as earlier in both the East and the Mediterranean – was not only an instrument or weapon but also a symbol of political and religious power. The Warrior's Tomb, to which the stele belongs, is a circle-grave (a form typical of Vetulonia) dated to the late seventh–early sixth century. cf. Plate 31.
    Florence: Museo Archeologico.

31. Model of *fasces*, from the Tomb of the Lictor (another circle-grave) at Vetulonia, consisting of a bundle of iron rods surmounted by an axe of the same type as that seen on the Avle Feluske stele (Plate 30). Tradition associated the origin of this symbol of sovereignty with the Etruscans; it was used by the Romans as the outward sign of the power defined

by them as *imperium*. Silius Italicus, writing in the first century A.D. (*Punica*, VIII, 483 ff.), attributes the invention of the *fasces* to Vetulonia: the fact that the only surviving Etruscan specimen has been found there 'certainly does nothing to weaken the tradition' (H. H. Scullard). See further: P. de Francisci, *St. Etr.*, XXIV, 1955–6, pp. 34 ff.

Florence: Museo Archeologico; photo: Soprintendenza alle Antichità dell'Etruria.

32. Roman marble relief of Imperial date from Cerveteri, with 'personifications' of three Etruscan cities or 'peoples' (Vetulonia, Vulci, Tarquinia). The relief is far from complete; it probably figured the twelve (or fifteen, by Roman times) principal city-states assigned by tradition to the Etruscan League. In historical times, the character of the League was mainly religious; in the earlier period it probably had a more specifically political significance. Bibliography in *Rend. Linc.*, 1930, p. 66.

Rome: Museo Lateranense; photo: Musei e Gallerie Pontificie.

33. Bronze statuette – 'Lady with a pomegranate' – said to have been found at Piombino: R. S. Teitz, *Masterpieces of Etruscan Art*, 1967, No. 59. Ht 20·3 cm. The diadem and pomegranate (in the left hand) have been compared to Etruscan representations of goddesses: in particular of Turan (the Etruscan Aphrodite), and also of Persephone and Hera. The stance owes much to classical Greek models: the curling toes of the boots are typically Etruscan (and find parallels in contemporary tomb-painting), as is the rather solid general appearance. The context of the piece is not known: it should be dated to the middle of the fifth century B.C.

Harvard University: Fogg Art Museum; museum photo.

34. Bronze mirror from Vulci, with incised decoration on the back, dating probably from the third century B.C.: Giglioli, CCXCVI, 4. In the upper register, divinities with their Etruscan names: Tinia (= Zeus) on his throne, Hercle (with club) presenting the spirit Epiur to him, flanked by Turan (left) and Thelna (right). In the lower register, Greek mythological characters: Agamemnon, Menelaus, Helen (centre: on throne), Paris-Alexander, Ajax, and winged female spirits: another spirit is seen below, in the exergue.

Paris: Bibliothèque Nationale; photo: Rome University, Istituto di Etruscologia e Antichità Italiche.

35. Bronze statuette of a war-god, probably Maris (Mars, corresponding to the Greek Ares): Giglioli, CCXXI, 2. He wears a scaled Etruscan cuirass with broad lapels over a brief tunic, greaves and a helmet with a large crest and raised cheek-pieces; the usual round shield is on his left arm, and his right hand probably held a sword or dagger rather than a lance.

Florence: Museo Archeologico; photo: Soprintendenza alle Antichità dell'Etruria.

36. Incised bronze mirror of the third century from Volterra, showing the Etruscan myth of Hercle being suckled by Uni (Juno) in the presence of other mythical and divine beings: G. Monaco, *Rendiconti della Pontificia Accademia di Archeologia*, VIII, 1932, pp. 163 ff. The same myth is represented in various ways on other mirrors of the fourth and third centuries – usually with a younger and beardless Hercle: G. A. Mansuelli, *St. Etr.*, XIX, 1946–7, pp. 57 f., 122, and ibid., XX, 1948–9, pp. 76 ff.
   Florence: Museo Archeologico.

37. Incised bronze mirror of the third century from Tuscania, showing Pava Tarchies (Tages?) instructing the hero Tarchunus (Tarchon) in the art of divination. M. Pallottino, *Rend. Linc.*, 1930, pp. 49 ff.
   Florence: Museo Archeologico.

38. Bronze model of a sheep's liver, from Gossolengo near Piacenza. The upper face is incised with divine names in compartments, corresponding to the division of the heavens according to the *Etrusca disciplina*: it was probably used for divination. See further: G. Körte, *Röm. Mitt.*, XX, 1905, pp. 348 ff.; G. Buonamici, *Epigrafia etrusca*, 1932, pp. 359 ff. and Plate 41. See above, p. 145, Figure 5.
   Piacenza: Museo Civico; photo: Soprintendenza alle Antichità dell'Emilia e Romagna.

39. Bronze statuette of an augur (*haruspex*) wearing his typical costume: long tunic, cloak with embroidered edge (fastened with a fibula on the chest) and a high conical hat – cf. the hat worn by Pava Tarchies on the incised mirror (Plate 37). M. Pallottino, *Rend. Linc.*, 1930, pp. 55 ff. and Plate 2.
   Vatican: Museo Etrusco Gregoriano; photo: Musei e Gallerie Pontificie.

40. Pottery cinerary urn from Chiusi: Giglioli, LXI, 1. The lid is in the form of a human head. Ossuaries like this are typical of cemeteries in the Chiusi area in the seventh and sixth centuries, and are usually called 'canopic urns' because of their superficial resemblance to jars from Canopus in Egypt; they occur in bronze as well as pottery, and are sometimes placed on circular chairs. See further: J. Bayet, *Mélanges*, LXXII, 1960, pp. 35 ff.
   Arezzo: Museo Archeologico; photo: Alinari.

41. Top of a bronze candelabrum of the fifth century from Spina: Hermes conducting the soul of a woman to the nether regions. *Mostra Arte Civiltà Etrusca*, Milan, 1955, No. 557.
   Ferrara: Museo Archeologico; photo: Soprintendenza alle Antichità dell'Emilia e Romagna.

42. Archaic gravestone from Chiusi, with laying-out scene in low-relief: Giglioli, CXLVI.
   Munich: Museum antiker Kleinkunst; photo: Rome University, Istituto di Etruscologia e Antichità Italiche.

43. Lid of a terracotta urn of the Hellenistic period: Giglioli, CCCXIV. The dead person is represented as a banqueter, accompanied by a female figure – perhaps a daemon. The scene appears to reflect the pessimistic concept of death, widespread in the last centuries of Etruscan civilization, as the sojourn of the soul in an underworld populated by shades and daemons. *Mostra Arte Civiltà Etrusca*, Milan, 1955, No. 409.

    Volterra: Museo Guarnacci; photo: Soprintendenza alle Antichità dell'Etruria.

44. Detail from the Tomba dell'Orco at Tarquinia: Giglioli, CCXLVIII, 1. The monstrous daemon Tuchulcha appears in Avernus, among the shades of the heroes of old. M. Pallottino, *Etruscan Painting*, 1952, pp. 111 ff.

    Photo: Soprintendenza alle Antichità dell'Etruria Meridionale.

45. Terracotta daemon's mask from Orvieto: Giglioli, CCLVIII, 1; *ACE* No. 325. The mask is hollow at the back, and could thus be hung on the wall of a tomb, or on the side of a sarcophagus. The face is identified with that of the daemon Charun, the Etruscan version of the Charon of Greek mythology. This representation (cf. Virgil's description, *Aeneid*, VI, 298–301) should be dated to the fourth century.

    Orvieto: Museo Faina; photo: Rome University, Istituto di Etruscologia e Antichità Italiche.

46. Tarquinia, Tomba Cardarelli: painted frieze on the right wall showing a dancer, a lyre-player, a young cup-bearer and a man playing the wine-throwing (Gr. *kóttabos*) game with a companion on the opposite wall. M. Moretti, *Nuovi monumenti della pittura etrusca*, 1966, pp. 96 ff.

    Photo: Soprintendenza alle Antichità dell'Etruria Meridionale.

47. A stretch of the extant city walls at Volterra: Giglioli, LVI, 2. They were built in the Archaic period, extended in the fifth–fourth centuries, and subsequently repaired and remade at various times. The area enclosed is much larger than that occupied by the actual town – modern or Etruscan.

    Photo: Rome University, Istituto di Etruscologia e Antichità Italiche.

48. Cerveteri, the Banditaccia cemetery: tumuli along the main cemetery road. These conical mounds of earth, resting on drum-shaped moulded bases carved out of the natural rock, each cover one or more underground chambers – not necessarily contemporary. Tumuli like this, which are today particularly characteristic of Cerveteri, were once a feature of the landscape at Tarquinia – and, to a lesser extent, at Vulci and Veii too. See further: Various authors, *Caere: scavi di Raniero Mengarelli* = *Mon. Ant.*, XLII, 1955, *passim*, and J. Bradford, op. cit. under Plate 25 (*q.v.*), above.

    Photo: David Ridgway.

49. Funerary *aedicula* at Populonia. Each of the great cities of Etruria had

its own particular type of tomb: characteristic of Populonia are large
tumuli with bases built in stone (not cut out of the tufo, as at Cerveteri)
and tombs – like the one illustrated here – in the form of a small shrine
or *aedicula*, made of squared blocks of local sandstone.
Photo: Soprintendenza alle Antichità dell'Etruria.

50. Quinto Fiorentino: the Montagnola tholos tomb of the seventh century
B.C. The dry stone walling is covered with a mound of earth; a *dromos*
leads to the inside, where there is a vestibule with two small lateral
rooms and a large circular grave chamber covered by a corbelled dome.
G. Caputo, *Bollettino d'Arte*, XLVII, 1962, pp. 115 ff.
Photo: Soprintendenza alle Antichità dell'Etruria.

51. Pyrgi: ground-plan of the sanctuary at two crucial stages of its development. Top: the situation *c.* 500 B.C., showing Temple B and the
adjacent complex ('Sacred Area C'). Bottom: the situation fifty years
later, *c.* 450 B.C., when Temple A had been added, together with a
monumental entrance to the precinct for the road from Cerveteri. The
gold tablets (Plates 12–14 above) were found at point 'L'; the three
black dots indicate pits containing archaeological material and animal
bones. For bibliography, see note 14 on Chapter Three.
Drawing: Soprintendenza alle Antichità dell'Etruria Meridionale.

52. Etrusco-Italic temples. *1:* the 'Tuscan' temple with three *cellae* (left,
ground-plan; right, front and side elevations), as described by Vitruvius,
De Architectura, III, 3:5, and IV, 7:1–5, and attested in the Archaic
period at Veii, Pyrgi, Orvieto, Fiesole, Marzabotto, Rome etc. Ground-
plans: *2:* temple of Dea Marica at Minturno. *3:* Pyrgi, Temple B – a
single *cella* preceded by a broad portico and surrounded by a *peristasis*.
4: Orvieto, the Belvedere temple. *5:* Tarquinia, the 'Ara della Regina'
temple.

53. Decorative details of Etruscan architecture. *1:* scheme of terracotta
ornamentation of Archaic wooden temple roofs – A: *acroterion*; B:
antefixes; C: slabs on the visible ends of the longitudinal beams; D:
continuous frieze of facing slabs (*antepagmentum*). Columns: *2:* 'Tuscan'. *3:* 'Aeolic'. *4:* 'Composite'. See further: A. Andrèn, *Architectural
Terracottas from Etrusco-Italic Temples*, Lund, 1940.

Note: Plates 52 and 53 are taken from M. Pallottino, *Civiltà artistica etrusco-
italica*, 1971, pp. 75 and 77 respectively. An earlier version of this
book appeared in English *s.v.* 'Etrusco-Italic Art' in the McGraw-
Hill *Encyclopedia of World Art*, V, 1961, cols. 100 ff.; on temple
architecture, see especially cols. 126 ff.

54. Small terracotta model of a temple of the Etrusco-Roman period (first
half of the first century B.C.), from a votive deposit at Vulci: R. A.
Staccioli, *Modelli di edifici etrusco-italici*, I, 1968, Plate 12. From the
Archaic period onwards, temples, or parts of them – particularly the
roof and its decoration – were often reproduced as cinerary urns or

votive stone and terracotta models; this is of considerable help in filling out the regrettably scanty literary and archaeological evidence for the appearance of the originals.

Rome: Museo Nazionale di Villa Giulia; photo: Soprintendenza alle Antichità dell'Etruria Meridionale.

55. Castel d'Asso – view of tombs 25–8: E. Colonna di Paolo and G. Colonna, *Castel d'Asso* (*Le necropoli rupestri dell'Etruria meridionale*, I), 1970, Plate 176. Typical view of a 'rock sepulchre', showing façades carved in the natural rock face; the actual burial-chambers, of various dimensions but usually quite small, are hollowed out below the level of the road. Cemeteries of this type give us an idea of the external appearance of Etruscan houses and towns: the tombs at Cerveteri tell us more about the interiors. cf. Plate 29 above.

Photo: Soprintendenza alle Antichità dell'Etruria Meridionale.

56. Terracotta cinerary urn from Chiusi: R. S. Teitz, *Masterpieces of Etruscan Art*, 1967, No. 5. The container for the ashes is surmounted by two tiers of hollow figures, mounted individually over pegs, with a griffin-protome on each of the four handles. The main figure on the lid presumably represents the deceased. The context of the piece is not known: it should probably be assigned to the second half of the seventh century. Other similar large cinerary urns with standing human figures are also known from Chiusi: Giglioli, LXIV, LXV (the Paolozzi and Gualandi urns).

Philadelphia: University Museum; museum photo.

57. A lion in *nenfro* (local grey tufo), found in 1963 at Ischia di Castro, not far from Vulci, and datable to the middle of the sixth century: *ACE* No. 308. This is a good example of an Archaic type common in the Vulci area. The inspiration is probably of ultimately East Greek origin; in this particular piece, there are also elements that recall Orientalizing taste. For Etruscan lions in general see further: W. Llewellyn Brown, *The Etruscan Lion*, 1960; for Archaic sculpture in general see further: A. Hus, *La statuaire en pierre étrusque archaïque*, 1961.

Ischia di Castro: Antiquarium Comunale; photo: Soprintendenza alle Antichità dell'Etruria Meridionale.

58. *Nenfro* slab, with figured relief decoration, typical of the late Orientalizing period at Tarquinia. Slabs like this are mostly found broken or reused in tombs, and their original function is much discussed; it seems likely that they were doors. See further: M. Pallottino, *Tarquinia = Mon. Ant.*, XXXVI, 1937, cols. 197 ff.

Tarquinia: Museo Nazionale; photo: Soprintendenza alle Antichità dell'Etruria Meridionale.

59. A Campana slab: Giglioli, CVIII, 2. One of a series of painted terracotta slabs with probably mythical scenes. They were originally

intended – presumably – as interior decorations for sacred or civil buildings, and were subsequently reused (and cut down to size) for a tomb at Cerveteri. Date: *c.* 525. Pieces of a slightly older series, also from Cerveteri, are in the British Museum (the Boccanera slabs) and the Villa Giulia. See further: F. Roncalli, *Le lastre dipinte da Cerveteri*, 1965.

Paris: Musée du Louvre; museum photo.

60. Tarquinia, Tomba del Barone: Giglioli, CXV. Frieze on the back wall: it is one of the finest examples of painting in the typical Ionic-Etruscan style, *c.* 500 B.C. M. Pallottino, *Etruscan Painting*, 1952, pp. 55 ff.

Photo: Alinari-Mansell Collection.

61. The Apollo of Veii: one of the most famous, and typical, examples of Ionic-Etruscan art, *c.* 500 B.C. The statue, modelled by hand and painted, was one of a group on the roof of a temple in the Portonaccio area of Veii (see Plate 24 above). The group was probably the work of the only Etruscan artist known to us by name – Vulca, who was invited to Rome to make the statue of Jove for the temple on the Capitol. See further: M. Pallottino, *La scuola di Vulca*, 1945.

Rome: Museo Nazionale di Villa Giulia; photo: Soprintendenza alle Antichità dell'Etruria Meridionale.

62. Head of a warrior: *ACE* No. 318. Ht 23 cm. Fragment of a terracotta decorative figure from an Archaic temple at Veii – perhaps part of a monumental *acroterion* like the Apollo (Plate 61). Like the Apollo, it displays the stylistic characteristics of the 'School of Vulca'. Beginning of the fifth century.

Rome: Museo Nazionale di Villa Giulia; photo: Soprintendenza alle Antichità dell'Etruria Meridionale.

63. High-relief from the back pediment of Temple A at Pyrgi, showing two episodes from the 'Seven against Thebes' story: Tydeus gnaws the head of the dying Melanippus, as Athena (left) recoils in disgust; Zeus (centre) strikes down the arrogant Capaneus. Date: *c.* 470. M. Pallottino, *Arch. Class.*, X, 1958, pp. 319 ff., and XI, 1959, Plate 90; G. Foti, *Not. Scavi*, 1959, pp. 170 ff.; G. Colonna in *Not. Scavi, II Suppl. 1970*, 1973.

Rome: Museo Nazionale di Villa Giulia; photo: Soprintendenza alle Antichità dell'Etruria Meridionale.

64. Large antefix (cf. Plate 53, 1B) from Pyrgi in the form of a Silenus-head framed by a shell decorated with lotus-flowers – a refined example of the 'Severe' style: *ACE* No. 315. Ht 50·5 cm. A line of these, alternating with maenad-heads, decorated the long sides of Temple A. Date: 470–460.

Rome: Museo Nazionale di Villa Giulia; photo: Soprintendenza alle Antichità dell'Etruria Meridionale.

65. Lid of a limestone sarcophagus from Chianciano (near Chiusi), showing the deceased – a young man – as a banqueter, under the watchful eye of the goddess of destiny and of death; Giglioli, CCXXXV. Sculpture of the Classical period: second half of the fifth century.
Florence: Museo Archeologico; photo: Alinari.

66. The 'Chimaera of Arezzo': Giglioli, CCXXVIII. A large bronze statue of the first half of the fourth century, discovered and restored in Renaissance times. This is the monster slain by the hero Bellerophon, on his winged horse Pegasus – the myth was popular in Etruscan art from Archaic times onwards. This piece was probably part of a group that included Bellerophon. See further: W. Llewellyn Brown, *The Etruscan Lion*, 1960, pp. 155 ff.
Florence: Museo Archeologico; photo: Alinari-Mansell Collection.

67. Terracotta male head from Veii: L. Vagnetti, *Il deposito votivo di Campetti a Veio*, 1971, Plate 23, type D-III. Ht 24·8 cm. This head was found in the partially excavated Campetti votive deposit, along with more than three thousand other offerings, principally terracotta figurines and heads mass-produced in the local clay: the heads were made in two-piece (back and front) moulds. The cult of the Campetti sanctuary has not been identified with certainty, although the Etruscan equivalent (name not known) of Ceres has been suggested. The sanctuary was in use between the end of the sixth and the middle of the first centuries: the piece illustrated is one of the few terracottas in the deposit that have been attributed to the century following the Roman conquest of Veii in 396.
Rome: Museo Nazionale di Villa Giulia; photo: Soprintendenza alle Antichità dell'Etruria Meridionale.

68–71. *Figured terracotta decoration from temples of the Classical and Hellenistic periods*

68. Pair of winged horses from the 'Ara della Regina' temple at Tarquinia: P. Romanelli, *Le Arti*, I, 1938–9, p. 436 and Plates 131 ff.; idem, *Not. Scavi*, 1948, pp. 254 ff.; *Mostra Arte Civiltà Etrusca*, Milan, 1955, No. 1. Date: fourth–third centuries.
Tarquinia: Museo Nazionale; photo: Anderson-Mansell Collection.

69. Female head from a high-relief group on Temple A at Pyrgi – the source of the Archaic group in Plate 63 above: *Nuovi Tesori*, p. 61, No. 41 (and colour plate C). This piece, datable to the second half of the fourth century, shows signs (or rather echoes) of the teachings of Skopas and Praxiteles.
Rome: Museo Nazionale di Villa Giulia; photo: Soprintendenza alle Antichità dell'Etruria Meridionale.

70. Head of a youth from the temple at Lo Scasato, Falerii: *ACE* No. 327. Another example of the eclectic nature of early Hellenistic sculpture

(late fourth–beginning of third centuries), showing the influence of Praxiteles, Lysippus and especially Skopas.

Rome: Museo Nazionale di Villa Giulia; photo: Soprintendenza alle Antichità dell'Etruria Meridionale.

71. Head of a bald and bearded man from the Belvedere temple at Orvieto: Giglioli, CCCXXVI; G. M. A. Hanfmann, *Etruskische Plastik*, 1956, p. 15. Fourth–third centuries.

Orvieto: Museo dell'Opera del Duomo; photo: Rome University, Istituto di Etruscologia e Antichità Italiche.

72. Bronze statuette of a youthful Hercules from Poggio Castiglione: *ACE* No. 329. Ht 27·5 cm. Sculpture of the late Classical–Hellenistic period: the influence of Lysippus is noticeable in the smooth and elongated body; the face is more typically Etruscan. The god, wearing his traditional lion-skin, holds a drinking-horn in one hand, and probably a *patera* (now lost) in the other.

Florence: Museo Archeologico; photo: Soprintendenza alle Antichità dell'Etruria.

73. Terracotta urn found at Vignagrande near Chiusi in 1858: R. S. Teitz, *Masterpieces of Etruscan Art*, 1967, No. 94. In the reclining portrait of the deceased on the cover, the artist has succeeded in capturing a mood of 'grim, disillusioned meditation on the vanity of life' (Hanfmann). Of the three relief scenes on the urn itself, the most ambitious is that on the front, shown here: a mythological battle between Greeks and barbarians, against a background of Ionic columns surmounted by a Doric frieze. The architectural elements, and in particular parallels with the Great Frieze of the Altar at Pergamon, suggest a date in the middle of the second century.

Worcester, Mass.: Art Museum; museum photo.

74. Detail of the relief-decoration of a large krater (wine bowl) of the late fourth–early third century, found recently in the rich Tomba dei Curunas at Tuscania (Madonna dell'Olivo cemetery): *Nuovi Tesori*, pp. 64 ff., No. 43. This chamber-tomb was rich in bronze and pottery, and also yielded a number of important carved *nenfro* sarcophagi. The motifs shown on the piece illustrated are marine: dolphins, and a rare appearance in Etruscan art of the octopus.

Rome: Museo Nazionale di Villa Giulia; photo: Soprintendenza alle Antichità dell'Etruria Meridionale.

75. The 'Capitoline Brutus': Giglioli, CCLIV, CCLV. A bronze bust, probably of an Etruscan personage of the early third century, but traditionally held to be Lucius Iunius Brutus (the founder of the Roman Republic in 510). See further: P. J. Riis, *An Introduction to Etruscan Art*, 1953, pp. 126 ff. (with bibliography).

Rome: Musei Capitolini; museum photo.

76. Portrait of Avle Meteli: Giglioli, CCCLXIX. A bronze statue of

the second–first century, traditionally held to be an honorific civil monument to a so-called 'Orator' (in Italian '*L'Arringatore*'). The accompanying inscription suggests, however, a more religious significance. The provenance is usually given as Sanguineto on Lake Trasimene: but there is good reason to suppose that the piece was found near Perugia. See further: T. Dohrn, *Bollettino d'Arte*, XLIX, 1964, pp. 27 ff.; G. C. Susini, *Arch. Class.*, XVII, 1965, pp. 141 ff.

Florence: Museo Archeologico; photo: Alinari.

77. Male portrait-head of terracotta, modelled by hand and painted, from the votive deposit at Pian di Civita, Tarquinia: *A C E* No. 365. Sculpture of the Hellenistic period: late second century. The happy combination of Greek teaching and local tradition bears witness to the ability of the Tarquinian artists even at this late stage.

Tarquinia: Museo Nazionale; photo: Soprintendenza alle Antichità dell'Etruria Meridionale.

78. Form of a primitive Etruscan house, reproduced in an exceptional late Villanovan sheet-bronze hut-urn from Vulci: *Nuovi Tesori*, pp. 18 ff., No. 9. The piece is richer in detail than the numerous pottery examples.

Rome: Museo Nazionale di Villa Giulia; photo: Soprintendenza alle Antichità dell'Etruria Meridionale.

79. Limestone urn from the territory of Chiusi, of the Hellenistic period (second–first centuries B.C.). Like many other stone urns of the period, this one is a more or less faithful representation of the external form of an Etruscan house. A view of one of the short sides shows two stories (the upper one is an open loggia), a gabled roof and a decorated pediment. The representation is probably not as exact as many have thought: it is more likely to be a mixture of genuine architectural features and purely decorative motifs. See further: R. A. Staccioli, 'L'urna etrusca "a palazzetto" del Museo Archeologico di Firenze', *Arch. Class.*, XIX, 1967, pp. 293 ff.

Florence: Museo Archeologico; photo: Soprintendenza alle Antichità dell'Etruria.

80. Interior of an Etruscan house of the Archaic period, reproduced in the Tomba dell'Alcova in the Banditaccia cemetery at Cerveteri: Giglioli, CCXL.

Photo: Rome University, Istituto di Etruscologia e Antichità Italiche.

81. Interior and furniture of an Etruscan house, reproduced in the Tomba degli Scudi e delle Sedie (Tomb of the Shields and Chairs) in the Banditaccia cemetery at Cerveteri. *Mon. Ant.*, XLII, 1955, cols. 1065 ff., Figure 6.

Photo: Soprintendenza alle Antichità dell'Etruria Meridionale.

82. Detail of the Hellenistic-period Tomba dei Rilievi in the Banditaccia cemetery at Cerveteri, showing various items of domestic equipment

in painted relief on the walls and columns. See further: *Mon. Ant.*, XLII, 1955, cols. 893 ff.

Photo: Soprintendenza alle Antichità dell'Etruria Meridionale.

83. Detail of the Hellenistic-period (late-third-century) Tomba dei Caronti at Tarquinia: a painted door, flanked by two demoniac figures named as 'Charun Chunchulis' and 'Charun Huths'. This tomb is one of many recently discovered at Tarquinia: M. Moretti, *Nuovi monumenti della pittura etrusca*, 1966, pp. 300 ff. It affords an interesting insight into the Etruscan view of Greek religion and mythology ('Charun' is the Etruscan form of the Greek 'Charon' – Italian 'Caronte'). See further: *St. Etr.*, XXX, 1962, pp. 290–93 (L. Cavagnaro Vanoni) and pp. 303 f. (M. Pallottino).

Photo: Soprintendenza alle Antichità dell'Etruria Meridionale.

84. Underside of a large bronze lamp of the fifth century, with relief decoration, found near Cortona in the eighteenth century: it was clearly meant to be hung from a ceiling. Giglioli, CCXXX.

Cortona: Museo dell'Accademia Etrusca; photo: Alinari.

85. The 'Situla della Pania' – an ivory vessel of the late seventh century, from a tomb in the area of Chiusi: the carved decoration of human figures and animals is Orientalizing in inspiration. See further: W. Llewellyn Brown, *The Etruscan Lion*, 1960, pp. 49 ff., and in general Y. Huls, *Ivoires d'Étrurie*, 1957.

Florence: Museo Archeologico; photo: Soprintendenza alle Antichità dell'Etruria.

86. Etrusco-Corinthian wine amphora of the late Orientalizing period, found in 1968 in a rich tomb at Vulci (Osteria cemetery), and datable to the period 630–580: *Nuovi Tesori*, pp. 34 ff., No. 20. Ht 82 cm. The painting is in three colours (black, red and purple), and has been assigned to the 'Bearded Sphinx Painter' – the first recognizable personality in the great tradition of vase-painting at Vulci that lasted from the late seventh century to the last decades of the sixth. On the painter, see further: F. Zevi, *St. Etr.*, XXXVII, 1969, pp. 39 ff.

Rome: Museo Nazionale di Villa Giulia; photo: Soprintendenza alle Antichità dell'Etruria Meridionale.

87. Group of bucchero vases from a rich sixth-century tomb found intact at Trevignano Romano on the shores of Lake Bracciano in 1965: *ACE*, pp. 45 ff. (various Nos.). Bucchero is a particularly characteristic type of Etruscan pottery: the black (or grey) appearance of the surface and inside was obtained by a special method of firing. The shapes often imitate metal forms. See further: N. Hirschland Ramage, 'Studies in early Etruscan bucchero', *PBSR*, XXXVIII, 1970, pp. 1 ff.

Rome: Museo Nazionale di Villa Giulia; photo: Soprintendenza alle Antichità dell'Etruria Meridionale.

88. Bronze vase-stand, with vases: G. Camporeale, *Not. Scavi*, 1966, p. 37,

Figure 20. This was found in a fossa-grave in the Vetulonia area, in association with a variety of imported and locally-made Orientalizing material typical of the area and datable to the late seventh–early sixth centuries. The vases were found in position: the stand is of a type frequently identified as a candelabrum.

Florence: Museo Archeologico; photo: Soprintendenza alle Antichità dell'Etruria.

89. Archaic limestone urn from Chiusi, with a relief frieze apparently depicting a wedding: Giglioli, CXLII. The heads of the bride and groom are covered by a ritual canopy, and musical accompaniment is provided by the double-flute-player on the left.

Chiusi: Museo Civico; photo: Soprintendenza alle Antichità dell'-Etruria.

90. Detail of the Tomba degli Auguri (Tomb of the Augurs) at Tarquinia, of the Archaic period, showing aspects of the funeral games. M. Pallottino, *Etruscan Painting*, 1952, pp. 37 ff.

Photo: Soprintendenza alle Antichità dell'Etruria Meridionale.

91. Etruscan silver coins from Populonia: (1) tetradrachm, with chimaera, of the fifth–fourth century; (2) didrachm, with gorgon head, of the fourth century. *Mostra Arte Civiltà Etrusca*, Milan, 1955, Nos. 154, 156.

Florence: Museo Archeologico; photo: Soprintendenza alle Antichità dell'Etruria.

92. Bronze situla (wine-bucket) used as an ossuary in the cemetery at the Certosa convent, Bologna: M. Pallottino *et al.*, *Mostra dell'arte delle situle dal Po al Danubio*, 1961, No. 17; J. V. S. Megaw, *Art of the European Iron Age*, 1970, No. 24. Ht 32·7 cm. The context of the piece is early-fifth-century: its associations included an Attic black-figure lekythos, *c.* 490–480, and a pair of typical 'Certosa' fibulas. Four bands of relief decoration illustrate cavalry and infantry soldiers carrying a variety of equipment (their presence suggests a certain degree of military preparedness in the Po valley at this time), a religious procession, scenes from country life, and, at the bottom, a series of lions and other animals that recall the Orientalizing stage of Greek art – in fact the whole 'Peace and War' antithesis in the zonal arrangement is reminiscent of the Oriental background. This fascinating document of everyday life is an important component in the remarkable 'Situla Art' that grew up on buckets and metalwork generally around the head of the Adriatic from the early sixth century onwards.

Bologna: Museo Civico; museum photo.

93. Ivory writing tablet found at Marsiliana d'Albegna in a mid-seventh-century context: G. Buonamici, *Epigrafia etrusca*, 1934, pp. 101 ff. A model Etruscan alphabet (twenty-six letters) is engraved down one side. Traces of applied gold leaf, previously unnoticed, were found on

the back of the tablet during recent restoration in the laboratory set up in the Florence Museo Archeologico to repair the enormous amount of material (including 14,000 metal objects and 12,000 vases) damaged there in the flood of 1966.

Florence: Museo Archeologico; photo: Soprintendenza alle Antichità dell'Etruria.

94. The 'Formello Alphabet' – one of the earliest Etruscan alphabets: a complete set of letters is incised round the neck of this typically Archaic small bucchero amphora from Formello (i.e. Veii).

Rome: Museo Nazionale di Villa Giulia; photo: Soprintendenza alle Antichità dell'Etruria Meridionale.

95. Pair of ivory dice, 23 mm. cube, most probably from a tomb in the Tuscania area. Their six sides are inscribed with two or three Etruscan letters each: $hu\theta - \theta u$, $ma\chi - zal$, $ci - \acute{s}a$ on opposing surfaces. These dice letters are confirmed as spelt numerals by the funerary and kindred formulas of inscriptions containing numbers expressed in figures and in spelt forms. See further: J. Wilkins, 'Etruscan numerals', *Trans. Philological Society*, 1962, pp. 51 ff.; M. Pallottino, *St. Etr.*, XXXII, 1964, pp. 107 ff.

Paris: Cabinet des Médailles, Bibliothèque Nationale; museum photo, by courtesy of BBC *Chronicle*.

96. The Zagreb mummy – an Egyptian mummy, the cloth bindings of which were taken from a book (*liber linteus*) written in Etruscan. The subject-matter consists of ritual prescriptions and a liturgical calendar: this is the longest Etruscan text extant. How it came to be used as the bindings of a mummy is not known. For full discussion and bibliography see pp. 198 ff. and 223 ff. above.

Zagreb: National Museum; photo: from *Corpus Inscriptionum Etruscarum*, *Suppl*. I, Plate V.

97. The Capua tile, with a long Etruscan inscription concerning a funerary ritual in honour of the gods of the underworld. G. Buonamici, *Epigrafia etrusca*, 1934, p. 84.

Photo: Rome University, Istituto di Etruscologia e Antichità Italiche.

98. The Perugia cippus, with a long Etruscan inscription, probably concerning a purchase-and-sale transaction or a donation of funerary properties. G. Buonamici, *Epigrafia etrusca*, 1934, pp. 378 ff.

Perugia: Museo Archeologico; photo: Alinari-Mansell Collection.

99. Attic red-figure kylix from a tomb at Tarquinia: under the foot an incised votive inscription in Etruscan to the Dioscuri. M. Pallottino and M. Hammarström, *St. Etr.*, V, 1931, pp. 244 ff., 363 ff.

Tarquinia: Museo Nazionale; photo: Soprintendenza alle Antichità dell'Etruria Meridionale.

100. Cinerary urn of the Etrusco-Roman period, from Pesaro, with the style

and titles of the deceased inscribed in both Latin and Etruscan: a rare example of a bilingual inscription, on which see p. 146 above.

Pesaro: Museo Olivieriano; photo: from R. A. Staccioli, *La lingua degli etruschi*, 1967, Plate 11.

101. An unusually long Etruscan inscription written on a lead sheet (about ninety words, of which about a third are complete). It was found in a pit near the temple in recent (1964–6) excavations at the sanctuary of Santa Marinella, not far from Pyrgi. The subject-matter of the inscription, dated by the excavator to the early fifth century, is comparable to that of the Capua tile. See further: M. Torelli, *Arch. Class.*, XVIII, 1966, pp. 283–91 (with linguistic comments by M. Pallottino, pp. 291–9), and *St. Etr.*, XXXV, 1967, pp. 331–52.

Rome: Museo Nazionale di Villa Giulia; photo: Soprintendenza alle Antichità dell'Etruria Meridionale.

102. Funerary inscriptions painted on the walls of the third–second-century Tomba degli Anina at Tarquinia; each refers to a member of the Anina family. No. 2 is particularly important, because it uses formulas and words that are unusual in the normal run of funerary inscriptions: in addition, it seems to suggest that the word *sa* (line 4, right) means 'six'. See further: M. Pallottino, *St. Etr.*, XXXII, 1964, pp. 107 ff.

Photo: Soprintendenza alle Antichità dell'Etruria Meridionale.

Notes on Further Reading

by David Ridgway

The original Italian edition of this book contains a short bibliography of basic works and collections of papers. For the English edition, it seems appropriate to add a few relevant items written in English, and to include brief notes, mainly for the benefit of students, on the consultation of the more advanced literature, particularly in Italian. Monographs on individual sites and aspects of Etruscan civilization will be found in the notes to the previous chapters; only a very few of them are repeated here.

I. *General works on the Etruscans*

L. Banti   *Il mondo degli Etruschi*
Rome: Editrice Primato, 1960
Rome: Biblioteca di Storia Patria, 1969[2]
(Slight changes only in the second edition; illustrations better in the first)

J. Heurgon   *Daily Life of the Etruscans*
London: Weidenfeld & Nicolson, 1964

K. O. Müller and   *Die Etrusker*, 2 vols.
  W. Deecke   Stuttgart: Heitz, 1877
Graz: Akademische Druck-u. Verlagsanstalt, 1965 (ed. A. J. Pfiffig)

B. Nogara   *Gli Etruschi e la loro civiltà*
Milan: Hoepli, 1933

M. Pallottino   *Gli Etruschi*
Rome: Colombo, 1940[2]

——   *Civiltà artistica etrusco-italica*
Florence: Sansoni, 1971
(A paperback revision of the author's article 'Etrusco-italici centri' in *Enciclopedia Universale dell'Arte*, V, cols. 135 ff. = 'Etrusco-Italic Art' in the McGraw-Hill *Encyclopedia of World Art*, V, 1961, cols. 100 ff.)

M. Renard   *Initiation à l'étruscologie*
Brussels: Lebègue, 1941

E. Richardson   *The Etruscans: their art and civilization*
Chicago and London: The University of Chicago Press, 1964

H. H. Scullard   *The Etruscan Cities and Rome*
('Aspects of Greek and Roman Life' series)
London: Thames & Hudson, 1967

D. Strong   *The Early Etruscans*

294

Notes on Further Reading

('Life in Ancient Lands' series)
London: Evans Brothers, 1968

O.-W. von Vacano *The Etruscans in the Ancient World*
London: Edward Arnold, 1960
Bloomington: Indiana University Press, 1965 (paperback)

See also:

M. Lopes Pegna *Saggio di bibliografia etrusca*
Florence: Olschki, 1953

(To be used with discretion)

Collections of papers, and encyclopedia articles:
Atti del I° Congresso Internazionale Etrusco
Florence: Rinascimento del Libro, 1928
Etruscan Culture : land and people
New York and Malmö: Columbia University Press and Allhem, 1962
Études Étrusco-Italiques. Mélanges pour le 25e anniversaire de la chaire d'Étruscologie à l'Université de Louvain
Louvain, 1963
Historia : Zeitschrift für alte Geschichte, VI, 1957, pp. 1 ff.
Tyrrhenica : Saggi di studi etruschi
Milan: Istituto Lombardo, Accademia di Scienze e Lettere, 1957
Aufstieg und Niedergang der römischen Welt (ed. H. Temporini), I: 1, 2, 1972 (to be continued)
Berlin and New York: Walter de Gruyter

Individual centres and aspects of Etruscan civilization are treated in the seven volumes of the *Enciclopedia dell'Arte Antica* (Rome: Istituto della Enciclopedia Italiana, 1958–66) and the *Supplemento 1970*, 1973; the articles on Etruscan and Italic art have been reprinted as a separate fascicule: R. Bianchi Bandinelli, R. Peroni and G. Colonna, *Arte Etrusca e Arte Italica*, 1963.

Articles on broader themes appear in the *Enciclopedia Universale dell'Arte* (Venice–Rome: Istituto per la Collaborazione Culturale = *Encyclopedia of World Art* (New York, Toronto, London: McGraw-Hill, 15 vols., 1958–68): s.v. 'Archaic art', 'Etrusco-Italic art' (see M. Pallottino, above), 'Greek art, western', 'Mediterranean protohistory', 'Orientalizing style', etc.

II. *Etruria*

G. Dennis *The Cities and Cemeteries of Etruria*, 2 vols.
London: John Murray, 1883 ³

('In several instances, Dennis's descriptions of sites, compiled from his own field-work, still remain the best available . . . For him, field-work was the natural continuance by other means of work in the study' – J. Bradford, in *Antiquity*, XXII, 1948, pp. 160 ff.)

P. Ducati *Etruria antica*, 2 vols.
Milan: Paravia, 1927

A. Solari *Topografia storica dell'Etruria*, 4 vols.
Pisa: Spoerri, 1915–20

295

III. *Specialized works in English on single topics*

J. D. Beazley	*Etruscan Vase-Painting* (Oxford Monographs on Classical Archaeology) Oxford: Clarendon Press, 1947
——	'The world of the Etruscan mirror' *Journal of Hellenic Studies*, LXIX, 1949, pp. 1 ff.

A. Boëthius and
  J. B. Ward-
  Perkins
	Etruscan and Roman Architecture
	('Pelican History of Art' series)
	Harmondsworth: Penguin Books, 1970

W. L. Brown	*The Etruscan Lion* (Oxford Monographs on Classical Archaeology) Oxford: Clarendon Press, 1960

(Discussed at length in English by M. Pallottino in *Antiquity*, XXXVI, 1962, pp. 201 ff.)

W. V. Harris	*Rome in Etruria and Umbria* (Oxford Classical and Philosophical Monographs) Oxford: Clarendon Press, 1971
H. Hencken	*Tarquinia, Villanovans and Early Etruscans*, 2 vols. (American School of Prehistoric Research, Bulletin 23) Cambridge, Mass.: Peabody Museum, 1968

(Important reviews: M. Pallottino in *Studi Etruschi*, XXXVI, 1968, pp. 493 ff.; J. Close-Brooks in *Journal of Roman Studies*, LX, 1960, pp. 238 ff.; and see G. Bartoloni and F. Delpino, 'Per una revisione critica della prima fase villanoviana di Tarquinia', in *Rendiconti Lincei*, ser. viii, XXV, 5-6, 1970, pp. 217 ff.)

Q .F. Maule and H. R. W. Smith	*Votive religion at Caere: Prolegomena* (University of California Publications in Classical Archaeology) Berkeley: University of California Press, 1959
M. Pallottino	*Etruscan Painting* ('The Great Centuries of Painting' series) Geneva: Skira, 1952
G. M. A. Richter	*The Furniture of the Greeks, Etruscans and Romans* London: Phaidon, 1966
P. J. Riis	*Tyrrhenika: an archaeological study of the Etruscan sculptors of the Archaic and Classical periods* Copenhagen: Munksgaard, 1941
——	*An Introduction to Etruscan Art* Copenhagen: Munksgaard, 1953
E. T. Salmon	*Samnium and the Samnites* Cambridge University Press, 1967

(Discussed by M. W. Frederiksen in *Journal of Roman Studies*, LVIII, 1968, pp. 224 ff.)

I. Strøm	*Problems concerning the origin and early development of the Etruscan Orientalizing style*, 2 vols.

(Odense University Classical Studies)
Odense University Press, 1971
For Greek colonization in Italy see:
T. J. Dunbabin   *The Western Greeks*
                    Oxford: Clarendon Press, 1948
J. Boardman   *The Greeks Overseas*
                    Harmondsworth: Penguin Books, 1974[2]
For Attic vases in Etruria and elsewhere in Italy, see the individual sites in the indexes in:
J. D. Beazley   *Attic Black-figure Vase-painters*, 1956
——   *Attic Red-figure Vase-painters*, 1963[3]
——   *Paralipomena*, 1971
                    Oxford: Clarendon Press

The 'Ancient Peoples and Places' series published by Thames & Hudson, London, includes nine volumes – of unequal value – on the pre-Roman archaeology of Italy and the adjacent islands: L. Barfield, *Northern Italy*, 1971; L. Bernabò Brea, *Sicily before the Greeks*, 1966[2]; R. Bloch, *The Etruscans*, 1958 (but see J. Boardman in *Antiquity*, XXXIII, 1959, pp. 142 f.), and *The origins of Rome*, 1960; J. D. Evans, *Malta*, 1959; M. Guido, *Sardinia*, 1963; H. Hencken, *Tarquinia and Etruscan Origins*, 1968; D. Trump, *Central and Southern Italy*, 1966; A. G. Woodhead, *The Greeks in the West*, 1962.

IV. *Exhibitions and Museums*

Good catalogues of important post-war exhibitions include:
      Mostra dell'Arte e della Civiltà Etrusca, Milano 1955
      Milan, 1955[2]
  = *Kunst und Leben der Etrusker, Köln 1956*
      Cologne, 1956
      Mostra dell'Etruria Padana e della città di Spina, 2 vols.
      Bologna, 1960
      Kunst und Kultur der Etrusker
      Vienna, 1966
  = *Etruskernas konst och Kultur*
      Stockholm, 1967
  = *Arte e Civiltà degli Etruschi*
      Turin, 1967
      M. A. Del Chiaro, *Etruscan Art from West Coast Collections*
      The Art Gallery, University of California, Santa Barbara, 1967
      R. S. Teitz, *Masterpieces of Etruscan Art*
      Worcester Art Museum, Worcester, Mass., 1967
      D. G. Mitten and S. F. Doeringer, *Master Bronzes from the Classical World*
      Fogg Art Museum, St Louis and Los Angeles, 1967–8
Among the best publications of permanent museum collections are:
J. D. Beazley and   *La Raccolta Benedetto Guglielmi nel Museo Gregoriano*
  F. Magi   *Etrusco*, 2 vols.

297

The Etruscans

W. Helbig
    (Monumenti Vaticani di Archeologia e d'Arte)
Vatican City, 1939–41
Führer durch die öffentlichen Sammlungen klassischer Altertümer in Rom (revised edition), I, 1963 (Musei Vaticani); II, 1966 (Musei Capitolini etc.); III, 1969 (Museo Nazionale di Villa Giulia, pp. 466–862); IV, 1972 (Museo Ostiense etc.)
Tübingen: Verlag Ernst Wasmuth/Deutsches Archäologisches Institut

H. B. Walters
    Catalogue of the bronzes in the British Museum, Greek, Roman and Etruscan, 1899, and *Catalogue of the Greek and Etruscan vases*, I, 2, 1912
London: Trustees of the British Museum

(There are similar British Museum catalogues of engraved gems, finger rings, etc.; see also the two small books by Sybille Haynes, *Etruscan Bronze Utensils*, 1965, and *Etruscan Sculpture*, 1971.)

V. *Learned Journals*

The principal journal concerned with all aspects of Etruscan studies is *Studi Etruschi*, directed by L. Banti and A. Neppi Módona, and published by the Istituto di Studi Etruschi e Italici in Florence. Original contributions are divided between the sections labelled I, History – Archaeology – Religion; II, Language and Epigraphy; III, 'Naturalistica' (which includes technology); IV, Excavation papers. Other regular features include brief preliminary notes on new discoveries and excavations in progress, the publication of collections of Etruscan and Italic material in Italian and foreign museums, and a systematic review of new epigraphic material. A detailed analytical index to the first thirty volumes (1927–62), by G. Giacomelli, was published in 1968. In addition, the Florence publishing house of Olschki produces two monograph series on behalf of the Istituto di Studi Etruschi:

Biblioteca di Studi Etruschi

1. G. Giacomelli	*La lingua falisca*, 1963
2. A. J. Pfiffig	*Die Ausbreitung des römischen Stadtwesen in Etrurien*, 1966
3. R. Hirata	*L'onomastica falisca e i suoi rapporti con la latina e l'etrusca*, 1967
4. R. Lambrechts	*Les inscriptions avec le mot 'tular' et les bornages étrusques*, 1970
5. G. Camporeale	*La collezione alla Querce: materiali archeologici orvietani*, 1970

Monumenti Etruschi

1. G. Camporeale	*La Tomba del Duce* (Vetulonia), 1967
2. M. Cristofani	*Le tombe da Monte Michele nel Museo Archeologico di Firenze* (Veii), 1969

3. G. Bartoloni   *Le tombe da Poggio Buco nel Museo Archeologico di Firenze*, 1971
4. F. Delpino   *Le tombe da Bisenzio nel Museo Archeologico di Firenze*, forthcoming

Archeologia Classica, directed by M. Pallottino, is published for the Scuola Nazionale di Archeologia of Rome University, and contains much of Etruscan archaeological interest. An associated monograph series is published by Sansoni in Florence:

Studi e Materiali di Etruscologia e Antichità Italiche

A. Ciasca   *Il capitello detto eolico in Etruria*, 1962
M. Cristofani   *La Tomba delle Iscrizioni a Cerveteri*, 1965
M. Bonghi Jovino   *Capua preromana. Terrecotte votive* I, 1965; II, 1972
F. Roncalli   *Le lastre dipinte da Cerveteri*, 1966
F. Parise Badoni   *Capua preromana. Ceramica campana a figure nere*, 1968
R. A. Staccioli   *Modelli di edifici etrusco-italici. I modelli votivi*, 1968
G. Camporeale   *I commerci di Vetulonia in età orientalizzante*, 1969
G. Colonna   *Bronzi votivi umbro-sabellici a figura umana. I, periodo arcaico*, 1970
L. Vagnetti   *Il deposito votivo di Campetti a Veio*, 1971
P. G. Guzzo   *Le fibule in Etruria dal VI al I secolo a.C.*, 1973
A. Rallo   *Lasa. Iconografia ed esegesi*, forthcoming

The Istituto di Topografia Antica of Rome University publishes papers on the multi-period fieldwork carried out by its members in Etruria and elsewhere in the *Quaderni dell'Istituto di Topografia Antica*; and the same Institute has recently assumed responsibility for *Forma Italiae*, instituted in 1926. Ten volumes of the new series, published in Rome by De Luca for the Unione Accademica Nazionale, have appeared between 1966 and 1973; some of them (e.g. S. Quilici Gigli, *Tuscana*, 1970) are directly relevant to Etruscan studies.

The results of important excavations in Etruria (and the rest of Italy), usually with a minimum of exegesis, have been published annually since 1876 in *Notizie degli Scavi di Antichità*, produced in Rome by the Accademia Nazionale dei Lincei. Ampler accounts of individual centres (e.g. Narce, 1894; Tarquinia, 1937; Cerveteri, 1955) and their material will be found in *Monumenti Antichi*, also published by the Lincei and shortly to become a monograph series. Papers on a variety of Etruscan subjects appear in other Lincei series (the *Memorie*, *Rendiconti* and *Quaderni*), in a number of other national journals and in the *Rendiconti della Pontificia Accademia di Archeologia*.

In the English-speaking world, papers of Etruscan interest appear from time to time in the *American Journal of Archaeology* and the *Journal of Roman Studies*: both also carry specialist reviews and notices of books, and the former has a regular 'Archaeological News' section, which includes a 'News Letter from Rome'. *Archaeological Reports*, published in London by the Hellenic Society and the British School at Athens, contains occasional surveys of work in Central Italy and Etruria (No. 14, 1967–8: by D. Ridgway) and in South Italy and Sicily (No. 19, 1972–3, and previous issues: by A. D. Trendall). Illustrated accounts of work in progress in the regional 'Soprintendenze alle Antichità' are also published at intervals in *Bollettino d'Arte*, the organ of the Direzione Generale delle Antichità e Belle Arti of the Italian Ministry of Education.

Classified bibliographical information is published regularly in *L'Année Philologique*, *Archäologische Bibliographie* (suppl. *Jahrbuch des Deutschen Archäologischen Instituts*) and in the *Fasti Archeologici*.

Foreign Academies, Institutes and Schools in Rome are actively engaged in various fields of Etruscan research; the principal journals published by them are:

Mélanges d'Archéologie et d'Histoire de l'École Française de Rome, published since 1971 in two sections: 'A' (*Antiquité*) and 'M' (*Moyen Age, Temps Modernes*)

Memoirs of the American Academy in Rome

Mitteilungen des Deutschen Archäologischen Instituts, Römische Abteilung ('*Röm. Mitt.*')

Papers of the British School at Rome

Skrifter utgivna av Svenska Institut i Rom (contents usually in English, German or Italian), subdivided into a variety of journals (*Opuscula Archaeologica*, *Opuscula Romana*) and multi-volume monographs (including A. Andrén, *Architectural Terracottas from Etrusco-Italic Temples*, 1939–40; E. Gjerstad, *Early Rome*, 1953 onwards; P. G. Gierow, *The Iron Age culture of Latium*, 1964 onwards, etc.)

Index

References to the section of Notes on the Text (pp. 239–72) are given in the form 'Ch. 1 n. 34', 'Short History n. 1', etc. References to the plates and the Notes on the Plates (pp. 273–93) are given as 'Pl. 20 n.' etc.

1. Historical and geographical subjects

Aborigines, 37, 60
l'Accesa, lake, 117
Acerra, 95, 122
Achaea, 69, 70
Acqua Rossa, 235
Adige, river and region, 53, 54, 75
Adria, 83, 97, 123
Adriatic:
  area and culture, 45, 47, 59–63, 67, 80, 97, 99
  languages, 52, 54, 55, 237
Aegean:
  area and culture, 42, 43, 50–51, 70, 73, 75
  languages, 67, 68, 69, 77, 78
Aegeo-Asianic linguistic layer, 50, 51
Aegeo-Tyrrhenian linguistic layer, 75
Aeneas, 60, 64
Aeolian Is., 42, 60, 84, 89
Aeolis, 69, 73, 169
Aeolus, 60
Aequi, 63
Aesaronenses, 86
Africa, North, 83, 131, 199
Agamemnon, Pl. 34 n.
Aita (Hades), 143
Ajax, Pl. 34 n.
Alalia, 89
Alban Hills, 45, 47, 52, 61
Albano Laziale, Tomba dei Horatii e dei Curiatii, 160
Albegna river, 116, 117
Alexander VI, Pope, 106
Alfedena, 47
Allumiere, 45, 112

Alps, the, 51, 61, 65, 91
  area and culture, 47, 62, 101, 164, 237
Alsium, 111
Anatolia, 42, 61, 73, 74
Ansedonia: see Cosa
Apennine:
  culture, 40, 42, 57, 58, 76, 80
  'folk', 37, 62
Apennines, the, 52, 76, 97–8, 107, 121
Apollo, Apulu, Aplu, 142
Apollo of Veii, 110, 163, 167, 169, Pl. 61 n., Pl. 62 n.
Apuli, 41, 62
Apulia, 62, 80, 101
  cultures of, 42, 44, 45, 47, 61
  language of, 52, 237
Arcadia, 69
Arene Candide, 42
Arezzo, 94, 105, 108, 120, 127
  architecture and industry of, 158, 159, 177, 181
  political development of, 133, 136
Argolid, the, 69
Ariminum: see Rimini
Arimna, Arimnestus, 93
Aristodemus of Cumae, 132
Armenia, 71
Arno river, 91, 120–21
Arnoaldi period, 49
Artemis, Aritimi, Artumes, 142
Arval brothers, poem of, 191
Asciano, 121
Ascoli, 47
Asia Minor, 21, 70, 74, 83
  languages of, 50, 51, 65, 67–9, 73
Astarte: see Uni

Index

Atestine culture, 47, 76
Athens, 82, 169, 182
Attica, 69, 72
  pottery, 86, 90, 177
Atys, 64, 74
Aucnus, Ocnus, 97
Augustus, 41, 82, 109
Aulestes, 97
Aulus Vibenna: *see* Vibenna
Ausonian period, 42–4
Ausonii, 47, 52, 60, 61
Ausonius, 60
Avernus, Pl. 44 n.
Avle Feluske, 130, Pl. 30 n.
Avle Metelle, 120, Pl. 76 n.

Bacchus, Pacha, 134, 149, 152
Balearic Is., 83
Balkans, the, 41, 42, 51, 59–61, 68
Basque language and peoples, 50, 51, 68
Bell Beaker culture, 42
Bellerophon, Pl. 66 n.
Belmonte Piceno, 47
Benacci I and II periods, 49
Bettona (Vettona), 101
Bisenzio (Visentium), 27, 115, 127, 172, 181, 184, Pl. 5 n.
Bismantova, 45
Blera, 28, 115, 127, 175
Boeotia, 69
Boii, 98. *See also* Celts
Bologna, Pl. 5 n., Pl. 21 n., Pl. 92 n.
  cemeteries of, 27, 28, 48, 49, 76
  as a centre, 97, 122, 123, 164, 174
Bolsena lake, 114, 115, 197
Bomarzo (Polimartium), 114
Bonaparte, Lucien, 25, 105
Bovolone, 44
Bracciano lake, 110, 114
Brauron, 82
Bronze Age cultures, 38–44, 58, 59, 61, 67–8, 115, 237
Bruschi Tomb, 178
Bruttii, 63
Bruttium, 55
Brutus, 167, Pl. 75 n.

Caelius Vibenna: *see* Vibenna
Caere: *see* Cerveteri
Caesena: *see* Cesena
Cafate, L., 146

Cagli, 101
Calabria, 45, 52, 55
Caletra, 117
Camars: *see* Chiusi
Camerlingate, the, 106
Camertes, 92
Ca' Morta, 47
Campana, G. P., 25
Campania, 27, 87
  Etruscan influence on, 91, 94–101
    passim, 122, 161, 180
  Iron Age culture of, 43, 45, 48
  language in, 52–5, 63, 65, 151, 199, 208
  people, 60, 61
Campano-Lucania area, 85
Canale, 46
Canegrate, 44
Canino, 113
Cannatello, 46
Canopus, Pl. 40 n.
Capena, 114
Capestrano, 47
Capodifiume, 48
Capua, 27, 28, 95, 101, 122, 174
Capua tile, 28, 95, 139, 142, 149, 152, 154, 193, 195, 199, 208, 210, 217, 221, 222, Pl. 97 n.
Carbon-14 dating, 43
Carrara, 158
Carthage, 82, 83, 89, 90, 99, Pls. 12–14 n.
Casaglia, 121
Casal Marittimo, 121, 159
Casinalbo, 44
Cassibile-Dessueri phase, 44
Castel d'Asso, 115, 175, Pl. 55 n.
Castelletto Ticino, 47
Castellina, 121
Castelluccio, 42
Castel San Mariano, 119
Catha, 134
Caucasus, languages of, 65, 192, 194
Cecina river, 121
Ceicna (Cecina) *gens*, 136
Celto-Ligurian people, 63
Celts, the, 53, 59, 62, 79, 98, 101, Pl. 23 n.
Cenomani, 98. *See also* Celts
Ceres, Pl. 67 n.
Certosa:
  culture, 97, 122
  situla, 122, 130, 164, 182–5, Pl. 92 n.

Cerveteri, 27, 28, 48, 70, 80, 85–7, 127, 272 (Additional Note), Pl. 8 n., Pl. 10 n., Pl. 15 n., Pl. 18 n., Pl. 51 n., Pl. 55 n., Pl. 125 n., Pl. 132 n.
art, 165, 172, 175, 176, 184
Banditaccia cemetery, 110–11, Pl. 25 n., Pl. 48 n.
Boccanera slabs, Pl. 59 n.
epigraphic evidence, 197, 210
Etruscan centre, 92–6 *passim*, 107, 110–12, 181, 238
Fosso Manganello, Pl. 25 n.
Fosso della Mola, Pl. 25 n.
Tomba dell'Alcova, Pl. 80 n.
Tomba dei Claudii, 198
Tomba Regolini-Galassi, 185, Pl. 7 n.
Tomba dei Rilievi, 178, Pl. 82 n.
Tomba degli Scudi e delle Sedie, Pl. 81 n.
Cesena (Caesena), 123
Charun, Charon, 149, Pl. 45 n., Pl. 83 n.
Chianciano, 118, Pl. 65 n.
Chianti, 121
Chiavari, 48
Chimaera of Arezzo, 106, 120, 182, Pl. 66 n.
Chiusi, 27, 28, 92, 105, Pl. 40 n., Pl. 42 n., Pl. 56 n., Pl. 85 n., Pl. 89 n.
art and architecture of, 129, 159, 165, 176, 177, 184
Etruscan centre, 94, 108, 118–19, 127, 181
Granduca tomb, 159
Tomba della Scimmia (Tomb of the Monkey), 180, 185
urns, 148, 163, 164, 168, 175, 176, 179, 184
Cilnii *gens*, 136
Città della Pieve, 118
Civita Castellana: *see* Falerii
Civita Musarna, 115
Clusium: *see* Chiusi
Colline Metallifere, 118
Comacchio, 123
Comeana tumulus, 121
Conelle di Arcevia, 42
Copenhagen, Helbig Museum, 27
Copper Age, 38, 39, 42
Corchiano, 114
Corinthian pottery, 49, 177
Corneto: *see* Tarquinia

Corpus Inscriptionum Etruscarum, 29, 193, 208, 236, 272 (Additional Note)
Corpus Inscriptionum Italicarum, 26, 29, 192
Corsica, 83, 85, 86, 89, 199
Corsini chair, 176
Cortona, 24, 25, 28, 69, 105, 106
art and architecture of, 159, 177, 181, Pl. 84 n.
Etruscan Academy at, 106, 120
Etruscan centre, 108, 127
mausoleum, La Tanella di Pitagora, 120
Corythus, 105, 106
Cosa, 116, 158
Coste del Marano hoard, 112
Cremera river, 109
Crespellano, 44
Crete, 69, 130
Crostoletto di Lamone, 244 (Additional Note)
Croton, 69
Cumae:
culture of, 46, 61, Pl. 16 n.
Greek settlement of, 43, 95, 209
politics of, 90, 97, 132
Cuneo, Ch. 4 n. 10
Cutilia lake, 63
Cypro-Phoenician, 71
Cyprus, 71, 73, 83, 87, 170

Danai, 70
Danube area, 39–47, 51, 59–61, 68, 77, 80
Dardani, 70
Daunians, 47, 62
Diana style of pottery, 42
Diomedes, 60
Dionysius of Syracuse, 87, 111
Dioscurides, the (Castor and Pollux), 143, Pl. 99 n.
Direzione Generale delle Antichità e Belle Arti, 107
Dolciano, 118
Duenos vase, 96, 191

Echetia, 127
Egypt, 43, 67, 70, 71, 148
Eileithyia, Leucothea, 111, 142
Elba, 85, 86, 87, 181
Elea (Velia), 89

Index

Elymi, the, 52
Emilia, 27, 45, 47, 48, 63, 66, 80, 99
Epiur, Pl. 34 n.
Erinyes, 149
Este, 45, 47, 62, 80, 122
Etruscan League, 87, 125
Euboea, 95
Europe, 40, 50, 100, 101

Fabriano, 47
Falerii, 27, 101, 114, Pl. 70 n.
Falerii Novi (Santa Maria di Falleri), 114
Faliscan territory:
  art and architecture of, 100, 161, 164, 177
  culture and language of, 47, 52, 61, 92, Pl. 18 n.
Falisci, the, 114
Felsina: see Bologna
Ferento (Ferentum), 114–15, 234, Ch. 7 n. 17
Fermo, 48
Feronia, 114
Fescennium, 155
Ficoroni cista, 82
Fiesole, 27, 108, 120–21, 127, 130
  art and architecture of, 159, 160, 164
Finocchito, 46
Fiora river, 107, 113, 115, Pl. 27 n.
Florence, 121, 127
  la Montagnola tomb, 121
  Museo Archeologico, 25, 27, 29–30, 236
Fontanella Mantovana, 45
Fordongianus, 86
Forum cippus, the, 191
Fossakultur: see Trench-grave culture
France, 79, 83
Fratte di Salerno, 95

Gaudo, 42
Gaul, 79, 117
Geometric:
  period, 44
  pottery, 45, 47, 62, 73
Germanic invasions, 79
Gibbon, Edward, Pl. 1 n.
Gioia del Colle, 42
Gnaeus Tarquinius Romanus, 96
Golasecca, 45, 47, 62, 101
Gordion, 74

Gortyna, 69
Gortynia, 69
Gortys, 69
Gossolengo, Pl. 38 n.
Gravisca, 87, 112, 235, Pl. 11 n.
Greece, culture of, 40, 41, 83, 87, 150, 161, 162–71, 174. See also Greek
Greek:
  colonies, 48, 61, 71, 73, 74, 84, 85, 88, 89, 237
  cultural influences, 81, 82, 99, 141, 149, 155, 156, 162–71
  language, 50, 52–3, 68, 73, 77, 100, 134
  pottery, 25, 71, 72, 74, 86, 111, 113, 177, 182
  See also Greece
Grosseto, 27, 76, 117
Gyrton, 69

Hades, 149
Hamilton, Sir William, Pl. 1 n.
Heba: see Magliano
Hebrew, 192
Helen, Pl. 34 n.
Hera: see Uni
Herakles, Hercle, Hercules, 142, Pl. 34 n., Pl. 36 n., Pl. 72 n.
Herculaneum, 95, 122
Hermes, Mercury, Turms, Pl. 41 n.
Hiero, Hieron, 183, Pl. 16 n.
Himera, 90
Hispano-Caucasian languages, 50, 54

Iapodes, 62
Iapuzkus, 62
Iapyges, 47, 60, 61, 62
Iberian peninsula, 51, 68, 79
Iguvine Tablets, 62, 99, 146, 191, 222, 223
Illyria, 41, 61
Illyrian-Balkan languages, 52
Imbros, 64, 67
Indo-European languages, 38–40, 50–60, 65–8, 75–81 passim, 93, 192–4, 202, 213
Insubres, 98. See also Celts
Ionia, 72, 73, 125, 169, 177, 185
Irnthi, 95
Iron Age, 40, 41–9 passim, 57, 59, 62, 63, 65
Ischia, 43, 95, 209

Ischia di Castro, 115, 235, Pl. 57 n.
Isola Farnese, 109, Pl. 24 n., Pl. 28 n.
   See also Veii
Istituto di Corrispondenza Archeo-
   logica, 26, 106
Istituto di Studi Etruschi ed Italici,
   30, 31, 272 (Additional Note), 236
Istria, 62
Itali, 47, 52, 61
Italic:
   languages, 92, 93, 134
   eastern, 52–6, 62, 63
   western, 54–5, 60, 61
   peoples, 37–9, 40–42, 57, 58, 65–8,
     76–8, 101
Italus, 60

Jove, Jupiter, Zeus, 142, 143
Juno: *see* Uni

Kaminia, 72, Pl. 9 n.
Kyrton, 69

Lagozza style pottery, 42
Lapis Niger cippus, 96
Laris(s)a, 69
Larth Ninie stele, 130
La Tène culture, 98
Latial culture, 61, 76, 92
Latin language, 37, 40, 50, 52–6, 73,
   96, 100, 114, 134, 202
Latin-Ausonian, 54. *See also* Proto-
   Latin; Italic (western)
Latins, the, 47, 60–61, 63, 64, 76, 80,
   97, 99, 100
Latium, 27, 43–9 *passim*, 53, 55, 65, 72,
   80, 94–101 *passim*, 107, 127, 161,
   199
Lemnos, 64, 65, 67, 69, 72–5, 194, Pl.
   9 n.
Lepontic dialect, 53, 100
Lesbos, 69
Leucothea, Eileithyia, Uni, 111, 142
Liguria, 42, 45, 51–3, 77, 89
Ligurians, the, 62, 79, 98, 99
Lipari, 45, 60, 61
Liparus, 60
Lombard lakes, 53
Lombardy, 45
Lucani, 63
Lucania, 48, 52, 55, 237
Luni, 98, 127, 161

Luni sul Mignone, 115, 244 (Additional
   Note)
Lycians, the, 70, 73
Lydia, 64, 70, 73, 156
Lydians, the, 64, 69, 70, 73, 137
Lysippus, Pl. 70 n., Pl. 72 n.

Macedonia, 69
Macstrna: *see* Mastarna
Magliano, 117, 142, 143, 199, 221
Mania, 143
Mantua, Mantova, 97, 98, 123, 128
Mantus, 143
Marche, the, 62
Marcina, 95, 122
Maremma, 32, 107, 182
Maris, Mars, Ares, 100, 141, 142, Pl.
   35 n.
Marsi, the, 63
Marsiliana d'Albegna, 28, 105, 117, 127,
   209, Pl. 93 n.
Marzabotto, 27, 97, 122
   architecture and plan of, 146, 151,
     160, 174, 176
Massalia (Marseilles), 89
Massa Marittima, 105, 117
Mastarna, 96, 113, 132
Mediterranean languages, 50, 68, 131
Melpum, 97
Menelaus, Pl. 34 n.
Menerva, Minerva, Athene, 100, 142,
   143
Mercatello, 116
Merneptah, 67
Mesopotamia, 71, 143
Messapians, 47, 62
Messapic language, 52–5, 62
Messina, straits of, 91
Michelangelo, 106
Mignone river, 115
Milazzo, 43, 45, 61
Miltiades, 72, Pl. 9 n.
Minoan civilization, 39
Minturno, Pl. 52 n.
Modena, 97, 123
Montalto di Castro, 113
Monte Abatone, 110, Pl. 25 n.
Monte Argentario, 45, 107, 116
Monte Cetona, 44
Monte Pitti, 200, 222
Montepulciano, 118
Monterano, 115

Index

Monterozzi hill, 112, Pl. 26 n.
Monti Cimini, 114
Monti Sabatini, 114
Monza, 44
Morgeti, 47, 52
Mutina: *see* Modena
Mycenaean civilization, 40, 42–4, 59–61, 131, 175, 237, 247 (Additional Note)

Narce, 27, 114
Naxos, 74
Near East, 73, 74, 178
Neolithic Age, 38, 39, 42, 58, 59
Nepi (Nepet), 114, 127
Nethun, Neptune, 100
Nocera, 95, 122
Nola, 95, 122
Norchia, 115, 175, Pl. 29 n.
Nortia, 116
Novilara, 47, 62
Numana, 47
Nuraghi, 85

Oenotri, 47, 52
Oenotrius, 60
Olympia, 93, 183, Pl. 16 n.
Ombrone river, 117, 121
Opici, 47, 52, 61
'Orator' of Perugia, 106, 163, Pl. 76 n.
Orbetello lagoon, 116
Orientalizing phase, 27, 48–9, 65–6, 69–75, 86–7, 97, 122, 169, 177, 185
  art, 113, 164, 165, 168, Pl. 7 n., Pl. 8 n., Pl. 58 n., Pl. 85 n., Pl. 86 n.
  tombs, 85, 95, 110, 121, Pl. 50 n., Pl. 88 n.
Orte (Horta), 92, 114
Orvieto, 27, 44, 94, 105, 126, 197
  art and architecture of, 116, 160, 165, Pl. 45 n., Pl. 52 n., Pl. 71 n.
  Cannicella cemetery, 116
  Crocefisso del Tufo, 116
  Porano tomb, 116
  Sette Camini tombs, 116
Oscan language, 37, 63, 100
Osco-Umbrian, 52, 56. *See also* Umbro-Sabellic; Italic (eastern)

Paestum, 101, 122
Paglia river, 107
Palestine, Pl. 4 n.

Palestrina, 49, 74, 95, 176, Pl. 6 n.
Palombara Sabina, 45
Pania, 118
Pantalica North and South phases, 42, 44, 46
Paris-Alexander, Pl. 34 n.
Parma, 97, 123
Pava Tarchies, Pl. 37 n.
Peithesa, 127
Pelasgians, 37, 64, 67, 69, 70, 73, 82, 247 (Additional Note)
Pelasgic, Raeto-Tyrrhenian linguistic wave, 51
Peligni, 63
Peloponnese, 169
Pergamon, Pl. 73 n.
Peri-Indo-European, 50
Persephone (Phersipnai), 143, Pl. 33 n.
Perugia:
  art and architecture of, 158, 164, 169, 177
  an important centre, 94, 108, 119–20, 127, 181
  cippus, 200, Pl. 98 n.
  Hypogeum dei Volumnii, 119, Pl. 22 n., Pl. 76 n.
  Museo Etrusco-Romano, 25
  Palazzone cemetery, 119
  Porta di Augusto, 159
  Porta Marzia, 119, 159
  San Manno Hypogeum, 119, 159, 219
Pesaro, 53, 146, 200
Peschiera culture, 42
Peucetians, the, 47, 61
Philelphus, 106
Phocaeans, the, 74, 89
Phoenicians, the, 52, 73, 83, 87, 89, 90, 111, 131, 237
  alphabet, 209, 210. *See also* Punic
Phrygia, 74
Piacenza, 97, 123
  the bronze liver, 139, 142, 144, 145, 222, Pl. 38 n.
Pianello della Genga, 43, 45, 61
Picene:
  region, 45, 47, 48, 99
  dialect, north, 53, 62
  dialect, south, 52, 62
Picenum, 27, 52–3, 62, 63, 98, 101
Piedmont, 45, Ch. 4 n. 10
Pila, 120
Piombino, Pl. 33 n.

Pisa, 86, 127
Pithekoussai (Ischia), 209
Pitigliano, 115
Pitino, 47
Placentia: see Piacenza
Po valley, Pl. 92 n.
    cultures of, 38, 45, 47, 61, 62
    Etruscanization of, 65, 76, 91, 94, 97, 98, 121, 122, 182
    language, 100, 208
Poggio Buco (Statonia?), 115
Poggio Castiglione, 117, Pl. 72 n.
Poggio Civitate, 121, 235, 238
Poggio Colonna, 117
Poggio Gaiella, 118
Poggio Renzo, 118
Polada culture, 42
Pompeian house, 175, 176
Pompeii, 95, 122, 174
Pontecagnano, 48, 49, 95
Ponte San Pietro, 45
Populonia, 27, 28, 48, 159, 178, 182, Pl. 49 n., Pl. 91 n.
    centre, 80, 107, 117–18, 127
    mineral resources, 85–7, 181
Porsenna, Lars, 94, 97, 119, 129, 160
Portland vase, the, Pl. 1 n.
Porto Baratti, 118
'Poupé aryballos', 197, 221
Praxiteles, Pl. 69 n., Pl. 70 n.
Pre-Indo-European languages, 49–51, 56, 68, 75, 77, 98, 194
Protogeometric period, 44
Proto-Indo-European languages, 50
Proto-Italic languages, 56, 61, 77
Proto-Latin, 54, 56, 58, 68, 92. See also Italic (western)
Protovillanovan:
    cemeteries, 41, 43, 66, 244 (Additional Note)
    culture, 45, 57, 58, 62, 63, 76, 80, 92, 112, 115
    'people', 37, 68, 84
Pulenas, Laris, 200, 219
Punic language, 90, 190, 196, 200–201, Pls. 12–14 n.
Punicum, 111
Pyrenees, 51
Pyrgi, 27, 87, 111, 235
    architecture of, 116, 142, 158, 160, 161, 198, 238, Pl. 51 n., Pl. 52 n., Pl. 63 n., Pl. 64 n., Pl. 69 n.

tablets, 90, 93, 132, 190, 195–6, 197, 198, 200, 207, 221, 272 (Additional Note), Pls. 12–14 n.

Quinto Fiorentino, 87, 121, 159, Pl. 50 n.

Raetians, 51, 53, 62, 65, 75, 77, 100
Raeto-Tyrrhenian, Raeto-Pelasgic languages, 51, 68
Ramesses III, 67
Rasenna people, 64, 65, 75, 126
Ravenna, 97, 123
Reggio, 44
Remedello, 42
Remus, 39
Renaissance, the, 23, 106, 192
Reno river, 122
Rhodes, 71, 177
Rieti, 63
Rimini, 97, 98, 123
Rinaldone, 42, 59
Riserva del Truglio, 74
Romagna, the, 46, 48, 63, Pl. 23 n.
Romance languages, 68
Roma quadrata, 39
Rome, 37, 237
    art and architecture, 96, 101
    as a centre, 95–7, 108–9
    culture, 45, 47, 61–3, 66, 82, 91, 92
    politics, 120, 126, 131, 132, 135
    religion, 139, 143, 150, 151
    Capitoline, 82, 96, 109, 160, 163, 167, Pl. 17 n., Pl. 61 n.
    Esquiline, 109
    Forum Boarium, S. Omobono in, 96, 109, Pls. 17–19 n.
    Museo Etrusco Gregoriano, 25, 26
    Museo Villa Giulia, 27
    Palatine, 39, 96, Pl. 17 n.
    Torlonia collection, 113
    Velabrum Quarter, 109
Romulus, 39
Roselle, 27, 107, 117, 127, 158, 175, 181

Sabelli, 47
Sabines, the, 47, 55, 63, 109
Sala Consilina, 48
Salentine peninsula, 52
Salerno, 47, 63, 80, 95, 122
Samnites, the, 45, 47, 52, 55, 63, 97, 99
Samos, 82
Sangallo, Giuliano da, 119

Index

San Giovenale, 27, 115
San Giuliano, 115
Sanguineto, Pl. 76 n.
San Marino, 48
San Martino in Gattara, Pl. 23 n.
Santa Maria di Capua Vetere, 122. *See also* Capua
Santa Marinella, 197, 198, 199, 221, Pl. 101 n.
Sant'Andrea Priu, 86
San Valentino, 119
Sardinia, 42, 83, 85, 130, Pl. 11 n.
  languages of, 50–51, 54, 70
Sardinian Sea, battle of, 89
Sardis, 73
Sarno valley, 46, 61
Sarteano, 118
Sasso di Furbara, 45, 112
Satre, Saturn, 100
Satricum, 101
Saturnia, 27, 28, 117, 158
Sàvena-San Vitale period, 49
Scipio Africanus, 180
Scipio family, 133, 218
Scoglio del Tonno, 39
Sele river, 95
Selvan, Silvanus, 100
Senones, 98. *See also* Celts
Serraferlicchio, 42
Servius Tullius, 96, 132
Sesto Calende, 47
Sesto Fiorentino, 121
Sethlans, 142
Sican-Ligurian, 51
Sicans, the, 46, 52
Sicels, Siculi, 46, 47, 52–6, 60, 61, 70
Sicily, 39, 42–6, 51–2, 161, Pl. 4 n., Pl. 15 n.
Siculus, 60
Siena, 24, 27, 106, 121, 127
Skopas, Pl. 69 n., Pl. 70 n.
Sorbo river, 110, Pl. 25 n.
Sorrento, 95, 122
Sostratos, 112
Sovana, 28, 115, 127
Spain, 83
Sparta, 131
Sperandio, 119
Spina, 27, 70, 87, 97, 122–3, Pl. 41 n.
Spurinna, 89, Pl. 15 n.
Statonia, 28, 127
Sticciano, 45

Sub-Apennine culture, 44, 57
Suessula, 122
Sutri, Sutrium, Suthri, 114, 127
Switzerland, 39
Syracuse, 90, Pl. 16 n.
Syria, 71, 73, 131, Pl. 4 n.

Tages, 154
Tarchon, Tarchunus, 97, Pl. 37 n.
Tarquinia (Corneto), 27, 28, 48, 86, 105, 106, 127, Pl. 48 n.
  art and architecture of, 158, 161, 164, 165, 175, 238, Pl. 32 n., Pl. 58 n., Pl. 99 n.
  centre, 80, 85, 87, 94, 107, 112–13
  language, 93, 126, 154, 197, Pl. 15 n.
  Ara della Regina, 112, 160, Pl. 26 n., Pl. 52 n., Pl. 68 n.
  La Civita, 112, Pl. 26 n., Pl. 77 n.
  Doganaccia tumuli, Pl. 26 n.
  Fosso San Savino, Pl. 26 n.
  Tomba degli Anina, Pl. 102 n.
  Tomba degli Auguri, 179, 180, 185, Pl. 90 n.
  Tomba del Barone, 169, Pl. 60 n.
  Tomba Cardarelli, Pl. 46 n.
  Tomba dei Caronti, Pl. 83 n.
  Tomba dei Carri (Tomb of the Chariots), 112, 179
  Tomba di Francesca Giustiniani, 179
  Tomba dei Giocalieri (Tomb of the Jugglers), 180
  Tomba delle Iscrizioni, 157, 179
  Tomba dei Leopardi, 179, 185
  Tomba del Letto Funebre (Tomb of the Funeral Couch), 179
  Tomba della Mercareccia, 176, Pl. 1 n.
  Tomba della Nave (Tomb of the Ship), 112
  Tomba degli Olimpiadi, 112, 179
  Tomba dell'Orco, Pl. 44 n.
  Tomba della Scrofa Nera (Tomb of the Black Sow), 112
  Tomba degli Scudi (Tomb of the Shields), 178
  Tomba del Triclinio, 112, 179
Tarquinius Priscus, 128, Pl. 18 n.
Tarquins, the, 95, 96, 97, 109
Tarquitius Priscus (or Tuscus), 154
Tartessos, 112, Pl. 11 n.
Telamon, 117, 161
Terni, 45, 47

Terramara, 37–40, 42, 44, 58, 68
Thefarie Velianas, 90, 94, 132, 201, 221,
    Pls. 12–14 n.
Thelna, Pl. 34 n.
Thessaly, 69
Tiber river, 54, 61, 81, 91, 92, 114, 116,
    119
Timmari, 43, 45
Tin, Tinia, 142, Pl. 34 n.
Tivoli, 47, 63
Todi, 101
Tolfa hills, 43, 45, 61, 76, 87, 112, 115,
    181
Torre Castelluccia, 43, 44, 61
Torre Galli, 46
Trasimene lake, 119, 120
Trench-grave culture, 47
Trento, 75
Trevignano Romano, Pl. 87 n.
Troad, the, 69
Trojans, the, 64, 74
Trš.w, Tyrrhenians, 67, 70, 71
Tuchulcha, 149, Pl. 44 n.
Turan, Aphrodite, 131, 141, 142, 221,
    Pl. 33 n., Pl. 34 n.
Turms, Mercury, 142
Tuscania (Tuscana), 115, 127, 235, Pl.
    37 n., Pl. 74 n.
  dice, 216, Pl. 95 n.
Tyrrha, Torrhebus, 70
Tyrrhenians, Tyrsenoi, Tyrrhenoi, 64,
    69, 70, 74, 78, 81, 82–90, 238
Tyrrhenian Sea area, 52–6, 63, 66–8, 73,
    77, 79, 82–92 passim, 94, 101, 199
Tyrrhenus, 64, 70

Umbria, 27, 45–7
  languages of, 37, 52, 62, 134
  people of, 63, 66, 76, 78, 98–100, 143
Umbro-Sabellian, 55, 56, 58, 62, 63, 99,
    100
Umbro-Sabellic, 52–4, 68. See also
    Osco-Umbrian; Italic (eastern)
Uni, Astarte, Juno, Hera, 82, 90, 100,
    111, 112, 142, 143, 201, 221, Pls.
    12–14 n., Pl. 33 n., Pl. 36 n.
Urartu, 71, 74
Uri, Urina (Hyria?), 95
Urnfield cultures, 44, 59, 61, 80

Val d'Elsa, 121
Val di Magra, 98

Val d'Ossola, 53
Valle Pega: see Spina
Valle Trebba: see Spina
Vanth, Moira, 149
Vegoia, Begoe, 154, 204
Veii, 27, 48, 105, 127, 133, Pl. 24 n.
  art and architecture of, 160, 161, 165,
    175, Pl. 5 n., Pl. 62 n., Pl. 67 n.
  centre, 80, 107, 109–10
  language, 92, 96
  Campetti area, 110, Pl. 67 n.
  Cremera valley, Pl. 28 n.
  Formello, Pl. 94 n.
  Grotta Gramiccia cemetery, Pl. 3 n.
  Piazza d'Armi, Pl. 24 n.
  Portonaccio, 109–10, 165, Pl. 24 n.,
    Pl. 61 n.
  Quattro Fontanili cemetery, Pl. 2 n.,
    Pl. 24 n.
  Tomba delle Anatre, 110
  Tomba Campana, 110
  Vignacce valley, Pl. 28 n.
Velcha, 95
Velchan, Vulcan, 100
Veli, Pl. 48 n.
Velletri, 101
Velsu, 95
Veltha, Veltune, Vertumnus, Voltumna,
    141
Veneti, the, 41, 98, 99
  culture of, 47, 62, 76, 80, 101, 237
  language of, 53, 55–6
Veneto, the, 45, 99
Venus, Turan, Aphrodite, 131
Verucchio, 48
Vestini, 63
Vesuna, Vesona, 100
Vetralla, 115
Vetulonia, 27, 48, 96, 105
  art and architecture of, 117, 130, 158,
    175, Pl. 32 n., Pl. 88 n.
  centre, 80, 107, 117, 127
  mineral resources, 85–7, 181
  Tomba del Duce, Pl. 8 n.
  Tomba del Littore, Pl. 31 n.
  Pietrera tumulus, 117
Vibenna brothers, Aulus and Caelius,
    96, 113
Vico lake, 114
Vignagrande, Pl. 73 n.
Vignanello, 114
Villanova, 27

Index

Villanovan, 27, 37, 174
  cemeteries, 110, 112, 118, 120, 122
  culture, 43, 45-9, 63, 65-8, 71, 72, 76-7, 80, 81, 84-6, 97
  urns, 148, 175
Vipina brothers: see Vibenna
Viterbo (Surina?), 115
  Tomba della Cipollara, 106
Volnius, 155
Volsci, the, 55, 63, 97
Volsinii (Bolsena), 27, 107, 115-16, 126, 127, 133, 136, 158
Volterra, 24, 25, 105, 106
  art and architecture of, 158, 164, 177, Pl. 36 n., Pl. 47 n.
  centre, 94, 108, 121, 127, 181
  inscription, 200
  politics, 133, 136
  Guerruccia cemeteries, 121
  Porta dell'Arco, 121, 159
Voltumna, 115, 125, 126, 151
Vulca, 97, 163, Pl. 61 n.
Vulci, 27, 28, 96, 106
  art and architecture of, 85, 165, 169, 172, 177, Pl. 32 n., Pl. 48 n., Pl. 54 n., Pl. 78 n.
  centre, 48, 80, 85, 86, 93, 107, 113-14, 116, 127, 181, 238
  inscriptions, 197
  Cavalupo cemetery, Pl. 4 n.
  la Cuccumella tumulus, 113, Pl. 27 n.
  François tomb, 96, 113, Pl. 20 n.
  Osteria cemetery, Pl. 86 n.
  Ponte dell'Abbadia, Pl. 27 n.

Wedgwood, Josiah, 31

Zagreb mummy, 28, 129, 139, 142-3, 151, 152, 154, 193, 195, 198-9, 201, 207, 208, 217, 221, 222-3, Pl. 96 n.
Zeus, Pl. 16 n.

2. Ancient authors

Aeschylus, 156
Agrecius, 202
Anticleides, 64
Aristotle, 89, 178, Pls. 12-14 n.
Arnobius, 138, 142, 143, 149
Athenaeus, 82, 156, 179, 180
Ausonius, 83

Caecina, 142
Cato, 91, 99, 222
Censorinus, 155
Cicero, 82, 93
Claudius, 96

Dio Cassius, 201
Diodorus Siculus, 83, 87, 90, 97, 182
Dionysius of Halicarnassus, 64, 65, 66, 83, 96, 97, 109, 125, 126, 138, Ch. 4 n. 13
Dioscorides, 201

Ephorus, 74, 84
Euripides, 156
Eustathius, 82

Festus, 96, 109
Flaccus, Verrius, 201
Florus, 129

Hellanicus, 64, 69
Hesychius, 201
Herodotus, 64, 65, 66, 70, 73, 74, 89, 112, 137, Pl. 11 n.
Homer, 84
Homeric Hymns, 82, 84

Isidore, 138, 201

Livy, 91, 92, 97, 98, 109, 116, 125, 133, 138, 150, 157, 180

Macrobius, 129
Martianus Capella, 143, 144, 145, 149

Nigidius Figulus, 143

Palaephatus, 83
Papias, 201
Pausanias, 93
Philochorus, 83
Pindar, 90, Pl. 16 n.
Plautus, 179
Pliny, 83, 95, 96, 143, 144, 163, 182
Plutarch, 82, 96
Pollux, 182
Polybius, 89, Pls. 12-14 n.
Procopius, 116
Propertius, 109

Seneca, 142, 147
Servius, 85, 87, 91, 96, 97, 125, 128, 149, 201
Silius Italicus, 129, Pl. 31 n.
Sophocles, 156
Stephanus of Byzantium, 83
Strabo, 64, 74, 76, 83, 84, 85, 89, 95, 98, 201
Suidas, 140

Tacitus, 96

Varro, 96, 97, 109, 141, 142, 143, 155, 163, 201
Virgil, 64, Pl. 45 n.
Vitruvius, 160, Ch. 8 n. 15, Pl. 1 n., Pl. 52 n.

Zonaras, 116

3. Modern authors

Åberg, N., 28, 43
Aebischer, P., 203
Åkerström, Å., 43, 66, Ch. 2 n. 21, Ch. 4 n. 1
Akurgal, E., Ch. 2 n. 16, n. 22
Alessio, G., 49, Ch. 10 n. 10
Alfieri, N., Ch. 5 n. 46
Alföldi, A., 29, Ch. 4 n. 18, n. 20, n. 22
Almagro, M., Ch. 3 n. 3
Altheim, F., 29, 92, Ch. 1 n. 8, n. 30, Ch. 2 n. 1, Ch. 4 n. 31, Ch. 6 n. 3
Amorelli, M. T. Falconi, Ch. 5 n. 14, Pl. 4 n.
Andrén, A., 28, Ch. 8 n. 10, n. 16, n. 20, n. 22, Pl. 53 n., 300
Annibaldi, G., Ch. 1 n. 14
Annius of Viterbo, 24, 106, 192
Anti, C., 28, Ch. 8 n. 32
Antonielli, U., 68, 77, Ch. 2 n. 23
Arias, P. E., Ch. 5 n. 45, n. 46
Ascoli, G. I., 40
Aurigemma, S., Ch. 5 n. 46

Banti, L., 28, 29, Ch. 4 n. 26, Ch. 5 n. 35, Ch. 7 n. 11, Ch. 8 n. 25, 294, 298
Barfield, L., Ch. 1 n. 10, 297
Barocelli, P., Ch. 1 n. 3
Bartoccini, R., Ch. 3 n. 6, Ch. 5 n. 14, Ch. 9 n. 15, Pl. 4 n., Pl. 27 n.

Bartoli, M., 206
Bartoloni, G., 296, 299
Basanoff, V., Ch. 1 n. 3
Bastianelli, S., Ch. 3 n. 8, Ch. 5 n. 10
Battisti, C., 203, Short History n. 3, Ch. 1 n. 16, n. 19
Bayet, J., Ch. 4 n. 24, Ch. 7 n. 8, n. 21, Pl. 40 n.
Beazley, J. D., 28, Ch. 8 n. 31, 296, 297
Becatti, G., Ch. 9 n. 15, n. 23
Behn, F., Ch. 8 n. 6
Beloch, J., 29, 95
Benoit, F., Ch. 3 n. 3, n. 13, n. 16
Benveniste, E., Ch. 3 n. 4
Bérard, J., 67, 75, 247 (Additional Note), Ch. 3 n. 1, n. 16
Bermond Montanari, G., Ch. 4 n. 24, Pl. 23 n.
Bernabò Brea, L., 42, 60, Ch. 1 n. 10, n. 34, 297
Bertoldi, V., 49, 203, 204, Ch. 10 n. 10
Betham, Sir William, 20–21
Bianchi Bandinelli, R., 28, 167, Ch. 5 n. 19, n. 30, n. 34, Ch. 8 n. 9, n. 32, n. 35, 295
von Bissing, F. W., Ch. 2 n. 15
Bittel, K., Ch. 2 n. 22
Bizzari, M., Ch. 5 n. 24
Blakeway, A. A., Pl. 11 n.
Blázquez Martínez, J. M., Ch. 7 n. 23
Bloch, R., 28, 29, 66, Short History n. 1, Ch. 2 n. 1, Ch. 5 n. 23, Ch. 8 n. 9, n. 32
Boardman, J., Ch. 1 n. 12, Ch. 4 n. 13, 297
Bocci, P., Ch. 5 n. 30
Boëthius, A., Ch. 4 n. 16, Ch. 8 n. 10, 296
Bonghi Jovino, M., Ch. 5 n. 43, 299
Bopp, F., 25
Bordi, S., Ch. 9 n. 23
Borelli, L. Vlad, Ch. 3 n. 14
Bormann, E., Ch. 8 n. 3
Bosch Gimpera, P., Ch. 1 n. 8
Bossert, H. Th., Ch. 2 n. 22
Bottiglioni, G., 203, Ch. 1 n. 25
Bradford, J., Ch. 5 n. 1, Pl. 25 n., Pl. 26 n., Pl. 48 n.
Brandenstein, W., Ch. 7 n. 4
Brea: see Bernabò Brea, L.
Breglia, L., Ch. 3 n. 16, Ch. 9 n. 19
Brelich, A., Ch. 7 n. 20

Index

Brizio, E., 27, 66, 67, 76, Ch. 5 n. 45

Brown, F. E., Ch. 5 n. 26, Ch. 8 n. 11

Brown, M. A., Ch. 1 n. 10

Brown, W. Llewellyn, Pl. 57 n., Pl. 66 n., Pl. 85 n., 296

Bruhl, A., Ch. 7 n. 25

Brunetti Nardi, G., Ch. 5 n. 4

Brunn, H., 26, 28, Ch. 8 n. 24

Buchicchio, S. T., Ch. 5 n. 23

Buchner, G., Ch. 4 n. 13, Ch. 12 n. 3

Bucholz, H. G., Ch. 6 n. 11

Buffa, M., Ch. 4 n. 10

Bugge, S., 26, 192

Buonamici, G., 29, 195, Ch. 11 n. 8, Ch. 12 n. 2, n. 4, n. 8, Pl. 38 n., Pl. 93 n., Pl. 97 n., Pl. 98 n.

Buonarroti, F., 24, 106

Byres, J., Pl. 1 n.

Calzoni, M., Ch. 5 n. 35

Cambi, L., Ch. 9 n. 16

Camporeale, G., Ch. 1 n. 26, Ch. 2 n. 16, Ch. 5 n. 24, n. 31, Ch. 6 n. 4, Pl. 8 n., Pl. 88 n., 298, 299

Canina, L., 25, 26

Caputo, G., Short History n. 1, Ch. 5 n. 39, n. 40, Pl. 50 n.

Carducci, G., 105

Carpenter, R., Ch. 12 n. 2

Cassano, S. M., Ch. 1 n. 10

Castagnoli, F., Ch. 9 n. 4

Cavagnaro Vanoni, L., Pl. 83 n.

Cavalier, M., Ch. 1 n. 10

Caylus, A. C. Ph. de, 24

Cesano, S. L., Ch. 9 n. 19

del Chiaro, M. A., 297

Chierici, G., 39

Cianfarani, V., Ch. 1 n. 37

Ciasca, A., Ch. 8 n. 18, 299

Cleator, P. E., Ch. 10 n. 2

Clemen, C., 138, 140, Ch. 7 n. 1

Close-Brooks, J., Ch. 1 n. 14, Ch. 5 n. 6, Pl. 2 n., 296

Coche de la Ferté, E., Ch. 9 n. 23

Coli, U., 29

Colini, A. M., Ch. 6 n. 9

Colini, G. A., 39

Colonna, G., Ch. 3 n. 14, Ch. 4 n. 7, n. 9, Ch. 5 n. 5, n. 14, n. 19, 272 (Additional Note), Pls. 12–14 n., Pl. 63 n., 295, 299

Colonna di Paolo, E., Ch. 5 n. 19, Pl. 29 n., Pl. 55 n.

Colozier, E., Ch. 3 n. 16

Conestabile, G. C., 192

Consortini, L., Ch. 5 n. 41

Corssen, W., 26, 67, 192, 193

Cortsen, S. P., 29, 195, 223, Ch. 2 n. 17, Ch. 6 n. 2, n. 7, Ch. 10 n. 11, Ch. 12 n. 10, n. 19

Cowen, J. D., Ch. 1 n. 12

Cristofani, M., 195, Ch. 5 n. 2, n. 6, n. 8, n. 11, Ch. 11 n. 22, Ch. 12 n. 2, Pl. 20 n., 298, 299

Cumont, F., Ch. 7 n. 19

Curtis, C. D., Pl. 6 n.

D'Acchiardi, G., Ch. 9 n. 16

D'Agostino, B., Ch. 1 n. 14, Ch. 4 n. 15, Ch. 5 n. 6

Danielsson, O. A., Ch. 10 n. 5

De Agostino, A., Ch. 5 n. 6, n. 33, n. 42

Deecke, W., 17, 26, 27, 29, 31, 193, Ch. 5 n. 16, Ch. 6 n. 1, n. 20, Ch. 8 n. 6, Ch. 12 n. 19, 294

De Francisci, P., 29, Ch. 4 n. 20, Ch. 6 n. 2, n. 10, n. 13, n. 14, Pl. 31 n.

De Franciscis, A., Ch. 1 n. 25

Della Seta, A., 28, 66, Ch. 2 n. 18, Ch. 5 n. 16, Ch. 8 n. 16, n. 32

Delpino, F., 296, 299

Dempster, T., 24, 106

Dennis, G., 20, 21, 26, 32, Ch. 5 n. 4, n. 7, Pl. 27 n., 295

De Ruyt, F., Short History n. 3, Ch. 7 n. 22

De Sanctis, G., 29, 68, 76, Ch. 6 n. 13

De Simone, C., 195, 212, Ch. 1 n. 24, Ch. 4 n. 19, Ch. 11 n. 11, 272 (Additional Note)

Devoto, G., 41, 49, 50, 54, 56, 60, 68, 77, 194, 202, 206, 212, 220, Short History n. 1, Ch. 1 n. 6, n. 8, n. 16, n. 19, n. 21, n. 29, n. 31, Ch. 4 n. 6, Ch. 5 n. 38, Ch. 6 n. 5, Ch. 7 n. 6, n. 10, Ch. 10 n. 8, n. 10, Ch. 11 n. 11

Doeringer, S. F., 297

Dohrn, T., 28, Ch. 5 n. 37, Ch. 8 n. 9, n. 32, Pl. 76 n.

Donceel, R., Ch. 5 n. 43

Ducati, P., 28, 29, 31, 66, 76, Short History n. 1, Ch. 2 n. 1, Ch. 5 n. 44,

Ch. 8 n. 9, n. 20, Ch. 9 n. 11, Pl. 21 n., 295

von Duhn, F., 27, 28, 67, Ch. 1 n. 14

Dunbabin, T. J., 297

Duncan, G., Ch. 5 n. 17

Durante, M., Ch. 1 n. 26, Ch. 10 n. 9

Enking, R., Ch. 7 n. 5, n. 14, Ch. 8 n. 7

Ernout, A., 202

van Essen, C. C., 28, Ch. 7 n. 1, Ch. 8 n. 32

Evans, J. D., 297

Fabretti, A., 25, 26, 29, 192, 219

Falchi, I., 130, Ch. 5 n. 31

Fea, C., 25

Ferri, S., Ch. 7 n. 17

Février, J. G., Ch. 4 n. 31

Fiesel, E., 29, 73, 207, 209, 212, Short History n. 1, Ch. 2 n. 19, n. 25, Ch. 10 n. 11, Ch. 11 n. 11

Fleischauer, G., Ch. 8 n. 6

Forni, G., Ch. 6 n. 6

Foti, G., Ch. 5 n. 18, Pl. 63 n.

Fowler, M., Ch. 11 n. 22

Fraccaro, P., Ch. 9 n. 18

Frankfort, T., Ch. 6 n. 19

Frederiksen, M. W., Ch. 4 n. 14, 296

Fréret, N., 65

Frey, O. H., Ch. 4 n.1

Friedrich, J., Ch. 2 n. 17, Ch. 10 n. 2

Frova, A., Ch. 8 n. 9

Furlani, G., Ch. 7 n. 1, n. 13

Furumark, A., Ch. 1 n. 9

Gamurrini, F., 26, 192

Garbini, G., Ch. 3 n. 14, Pls. 12-14 n.

Gargana, A., Ch. 5 n. 19, Ch. 9 n. 9

Gasperini, L., Ch. 5 n. 21

Gell, W., 26

de la Genière, J., Ch. 1 n. 14

Genthe, E., Ch. 4 n. 1

Georgiev, W., Ch. 2 n. 20

Gerhard, E., 26

von Gerkan, A., Pl. 22 n.

Gerola, B., Ch. 1 n. 16

Ghirardini, G., 66

Giacomelli, G., Ch. 1 n. 26, Ch. 5 n. 16, 298

Giambullari, P. F., 192

Gierow, P. G., Ch. 2 n. 23, 300

Giglioli, G. Q., 29, 138, Ch. 7 n. 1, n. 2,

n. 7, Ch. 8 n. 9, Ch. 9 n. 14, Pl. 20 n., Pl. 29 n., Pl. 34 n., Pl. 35 n., Pl. 40 n., Pls. 42-5 n., Pl. 47 n., Pl. 56 n., Pl. 59 n., Pl. 65 n., Pl. 71 n., Pl. 75 n., Pl. 76 n., Pl. 81 n., Pl. 84 n., Pl. 89 n.

Giuliani, C. F., Ch. 5 n. 18

Giuliano, A., Ch. 8 n. 9

Gjerstad, E., Ch. 3 n. 3, Ch. 5 n. 5, Ch. 8 n. 34, Pl. 19 n., 300

Goldmann, E., 193, 220

Goldscheider, L., Ch. 8 n. 20

Gori, A. F., 24, 106

Grenier, A., 28, 138, Ch. 4 n. 24, Ch. 5 n. 44, Ch. 7 n. 1, n. 2, n. 15

Gsell, S., 28, Ch. 5 n. 14

Guarducci, M., Ch. 12 n. 2

Guarnacci, M., 24

Guido, M., 297

Guzzo, P. G., 299

Hammarström, M., 206, Pl. 99 n.

Hanfmann, G. M. A., 28, Ch. 2 n. 22, Ch. 8 n. 20, Pl. 71 n., Pl. 73 n.

Harden, D. B., Ch. 4 n. 1

Hardie, C., Ch. 5 n. 39

Harris, W. V., Ch. 4 n. 32, Ch. 5 n. 23, 296

Hawkes, C. F. C., Ch. 2 n. 31, n. 33

Haynes, S., 298

Helbig, W., 27, 39, 76, Ch. 1 n. 2, 298

Hencken, H., 28, 44, 67, Ch. 1 n. 14, n. 19, Ch. 2 n. 1, n. 9, n. 14, n. 26, Ch. 3 n. 1, Pl. 5 n., Pl. 26 n., 296, 297

Herbig, G., 26, 66, 193, Ch. 7 n. 1, Ch. 10 n. 5

Herbig, R., 28, 67, Ch. 7 n. 1, n. 2, Ch. 8 n. 23

Heurgon, J., 28, 29, 247 (Additional Note), Ch. 3 n. 14, n. 16, Ch. 4 n. 14, n. 21, Ch. 6 n. 1, n. 2, n. 19, Ch. 7 n. 1, Ch. 8 n. 1, n. 2, n. 3, Ch. 9 n. 1, Ch. 11 n. 14, 272 (Additional Note), 294

Hiller, F., Ch. 5 n. 30, Ch. 8 n. 12

Hirata, R., Ch. 5 n. 16, 298

Hirschland Ramage, N., Pl. 87 n.

Hofmann, J. B., Ch. 11 n. 16

Hogarth, J., Short History n. 1

Homo, L., 29, Ch. 1 n. 7

Howard, F., Pl. 1 n.

Hrozny, B., Ch. 2 n. 17

Hubschmid, J., Ch. 1 n. 16, n. 18

Hugueney, J., Ch. 9 n. 8

Index

Huls, Y., 29, Ch. 8 n. 27, Pl. 85 n.
Hus, A., 29, Short History n. 1, Ch. 5 n. 14, Pl. 57 n.
Huxley, A., 32

Inghirami, F., 25, 26
Ioppolo, G., Pl. 19 n.

Jehasse, J., Ch. 3 n. 13, n. 16
Johannowsky, W., Ch. 4 n. 13, n. 15
Johnston, A. W., Ch. 5 n. 12
Johnstone, M. A., Ch. 8 n. 8
Jones, G. D. B., Ch. 5 n. 16
Jucker, H., Ch. 8 n. 9
Judson, S., Ch. 9 n. 18
Jullian, C., Ch. 1 n. 7

Kahane, A., Ch. 5 n. 6, Ch. 9 n. 18, Pl. 24 n.
Karo, G., 43, Ch. 2 n. 17, Ch. 3 n. 3
Kaschnitz-Weinberg, G., 28, 167, Ch. 1 n. 14, Ch. 8 n. 32
Kilian, K., Ch. 1 n. 14
Kirchhoff, A., 209
Klindt Jensen, O., Ch. 4 n. 1
Kluge, T., 220
Koch, H., 28, Ch. 5 n. 19
Konow, S., 192
Körte, G., 26, 28, 66, 67, Ch. 8 n. 24, Pl. 38 n.
Kossack, G., 43
Kossinna, G., 38
Krahe, H., Ch. 1 n. 8, n. 19, n. 24, Ch. 2 n. 4
Krall, J., 199
Kretschmer, P., 50, 51, 68, 77, 194, Ch. 1 n. 16, n. 27, Ch. 2 n. 17
Kunze, E., Ch. 3 n. 3

Lamboglia, N., Ch. 4 n. 10
Lambrechts, R., 195, Ch. 6 n. 2, 298
Lanzi, L., 24–5, 192
Lattes, E., 26, 67, 72, 192, 193, 223, Ch. 10 n. 6
Lavedan, P., Ch. 9 n. 8
Laviosa, C., Ch. 5 n. 30
Laviosa Zambotti, P., Ch. 1 n. 8, n. 33
Lawrence, D. H., 32
Leifer, F., 206, Ch. 6 n. 2
Leisinger, H., Ch. 8 n. 28
Lejeune, M., Ch. 7 n. 17
Leopold, H. M. R., Ch. 7 n. 1

Lepore, E., Ch. 4 n. 13
Lepsius, R., 209
Lerici, C. M., Ch. 5 n. 1, n. 3, n. 4, n. 11, Ch. 8 n. 29, Ch. 9 n. 15, Pl. 26 n.
Levi, D., 28, Ch. 5 n. 32, n. 34
Lilliu, G., Ch. 3 n. 5, Pl. 11 n.
Liou, B., Ch. 6 n. 2
Lochner-Hüttenbach, L., Ch. 3 n. 1
Lopes Pegna, M., 295

Macnamara, E., Ch. 1 n. 10
Maetzke, G., Ch. 5 n. 39
Maffei, S., 24
Magi, F., Short History n. 1, Ch. 5 n. 39, Ch. 9 n. 15, 297
Maiuri, A., 95, Ch. 4 n. 17
Manfredini, A., Ch. 1 n. 10
Mansuelli, G. A., 29, Ch. 1 n. 36, Ch. 4 n. 23, Ch. 5 n. 11, n. 44, Pl. 36 n.
Mariani, L., 66
Martha, J., 26, 28, 192, Ch. 8 n. 32
Matteucig, G., 28, Ch. 5 n. 22
Matz, F., Ch. 1 n. 8
Maule, Q. F., Ch. 7 n. 31, 296
Maxwell-Hyslop, K. R., Ch. 2 n. 5
Mazzarino, S., 29, Ch. 4 n. 20, Ch. 6 n. 2, n. 12, n. 14, n. 19, Ch. 8 n. 4
Mazzolai, A., Ch. 5 n. 25, n. 30
Megaw, J. V. S., Pl. 92 n.
Mengarelli, R., 92, Ch. 5 n. 8
Menghin, O. F. A., Ch. 3 n. 2
von Mercklin, E., 28, Ch. 5 n. 19
von Merhart, G., 43, 44, Ch. 1 n. 12
Meriggi, P., Ch. 2 n. 19
Merlo, C., Ch. 11 n. 10
Messerschmidt, F., 28, Ch. 1 n. 14, Ch. 5 n. 14, Ch. 8 n. 14, n. 28, Pl. 22 n.
Meyer, E., 68
Micali, G., 25, 26
Michaelis, A., Short History n. 1
Migliarini, M. A., 25, 192
Milani, L. A., 30
Mingazzini, P., Ch. 11 n. 10
Minto, A., 28, 30, 31, Ch. 5 n. 28, n. 29, n. 33, Ch. 8 n. 13, n. 16
Mitten, D. G., 297
Möbius, H., Pl. 1 n.
Modestov, B., 66
Momigliano, A., Ch. 4 n. 18, n. 20
Mommsen, T., 37
Monaco, G., Pl. 36 n.
Montelius, O., 28, 43, 66

Moreau, J., Ch. 4 n. 24

Morel, J.-P., Ch. 3 n. 16

Moretti, M., 28, Ch. 5 n. 8, n. 11, Ch. 8 n. 29, Ch. 9 n. 15, Pl. 46 n., Pl. 83 n.

Müller, K. O., 17, 25, 27, 29, 31, 65, 66, 67, Ch. 6 n. 1, n. 20, Ch. 8 n. 6, Ch. 12 n. 19, 294

Müller-Karpe, H., 44, Ch. 1 n. 10, n. 12, n. 35

Muster, W., Ch. 7 n. 4

Mustilli, D., Ch. 2 n. 22

Nachmanson, E., Ch. 2 n. 17

Napoli, M., Ch. 4 n. 15

Naumann, R., Ch. 5 n. 30, Ch. 8 n. 12

Neppi Módona, A., 28, Ch. 5 n. 36, 298

Nicosia, F., Ch. 5 n. 40

Niebuhr, B. G., 25, 65, 66, 67

Nissen, H., 28, Ch. 5 n. 4

Noël des Vergers, A., 26, 32

Nogara, B., 29, 31, 195, Short History n. 1, Ch. 7 n. 1, Ch. 8 n. 1, n. 5, Ch. 10 n. 5, Ch. 11 n. 14, 294

Nougayrol, J., Ch. 7 n. 13

Olzscha, K., 29, 195, 216, 223, Ch. 4 n. 27, Ch. 8 n. 21, Ch. 10 n. 11, Ch. 11 n. 21, Ch. 12 n. 2, n. 8, n. 11, n. 12, n. 17, n. 18, n. 19

Orioli, F., 25

Orsi, P., 39

Östenberg, C. E., Ch. 1 n. 10, n. 11, Ch. 2 n. 26

Pace, B., Ch. 5 n. 8

Paglieri, S., Ch. 3 n. 10, Ch. 5 n. 14

Pais, E., Ch. 6 n. 13

Pallottino, M., 28, 29, 195, 215, 223, Short History n. 1, n. 2, Ch. 1 n. 9, n. 10, n. 12, n. 13, n. 15, n. 18, n. 32, n. 37, Ch. 2 n. 1, n. 13, n. 14, n. 16, n. 24, n. 30, n. 33, Ch. 3 n. 3, n. 5, n. 11, n. 14, n. 16, Ch. 4 n. 5, n. 7, n. 8, n. 14, n. 18, n. 19, n. 20, n. 23, n. 27, n. 32, Ch. 5 n. 5, n. 6, n. 8, n. 10, Ch. 6 n. 2, n. 15, n. 16, n. 18, Ch. 7 n. 2, n. 14, n. 15, n. 17, n. 25, Ch. 8 n. 3, n. 9, n. 16, n. 26, n. 32, n. 33, n. 35, Ch. 9 n. 5, n. 20, n. 22, Ch. 10 n. 1, n. 4, n. 6, n. 11, Ch. 11 n. 5, n. 13, n. 21, Ch. 12 n. 7, n. 8, n. 11, n. 13,

n. 17, n. 19, 272 (Additional Note), Pls. 12–14 n., Pl. 15 n., Pls. 17–19 n., Pl. 26 n., Pl. 37 n., Pl. 39 n., Pl. 44 n., Pl. 53 n., Pl. 58 n., Pl. 60 n., Pl. 61 n., Pl. 63 n., Pl. 83 n., Pl. 90 n., Pl. 92 n., Pl. 95 n., Pl. 99 n., Pl. 101 n., Pl. 102 n., 294, 295, 296, 299

Palmer, L. R., Ch. 1 n. 23, n. 29

Pareti, L., 29, 31, 41, 68, 72, 76, Ch. 1 n. 8, n. 9, Ch. 2 n. 1, n. 16, n. 17, Ch. 4 n. 3, n. 20, Ch. 5 n. 8, Ch. 6 n. 4, n. 14, Pl. 7 n.

Parise Badoni, F., Ch. 5 n. 43, 299

Parlangeli, O., Ch. 1 n. 24, n. 25

Passamonti, R., Ch. 9 n. 13

Passeri, G. B., 24, 106

Passerini, A., Ch. 4 n. 32

Patroni, G., 39–41, 66, Ch. 1 n. 4, n. 7, Ch. 4 n. 16, Ch. 8 n. 10, Ch. 9 n. 9

Pauli, C., 26, 193, 216, Ch. 2 n. 17, Ch. 10 n. 5

Pellegrini, G. B., Ch. 1 n. 28, Ch. 4 n. 30

Perali, P., Ch. 5 n. 24

Peroni, R., Ch. 1 n. 10, n. 11, n. 14, Ch. 5 n. 10, 295

Pettazzoni, R., Ch. 7 n. 1, n. 6, n. 13

Pfiffig, A. J., 195, 223, Ch. 4 n. 32, Ch. 7 n. 10, Ch. 8 n. 2, Ch. 9 n. 1, Ch. 11 n. 3, n. 22, Ch. 12 n. 8, n. 18, 272 (Additional Note), 298

Phillips, K. M., Ch. 5 n. 42

Piccardi, G., Ch. 9 n. 23

Pieri, S., 203, 272 (Additional Note)

Pierotti, A. M., Ch. 5 n. 35

Piganiol, A., 66, Ch. 8 n. 2

Piggott, S., 20

Pigorini, L., 27, 39–40, 76, 77, Ch. 1 n. 2

Piotrovskiy, B. B., Ch. 2 n. 16

Pisani, V., Ch. 1 n. 19, n. 20, Ch. 2 n. 27, Ch. 7 n. 17, Ch. 12 n. 12

Pittioni, R., 41

Pohl, I., Ch. 1 n. 14, Ch. 5 n. 8

Pokorny, H., 41

Polacco, L., Ch. 8 n. 10

Pottier, E., 67, Pl. 10 n.

Poulsen, F., Ch. 2 n. 16, Ch. 8 n. 28

Powell, T. G. E., Ch. 1 n. 10

Prosdocimi, A. L., Ch. 1 n. 28

Pugliese Carratelli, G., Ch. 3 n. 14

Puglisi, S., Ch. 1 n. 10, Ch. 5 n. 24

Pulgram, E., Ch. 1 n. 19, n. 20

315

Index

Quilici Gigli, S., Ch. 5 n. 19, 299

Rallo, A., 299
Randall MacIver, D., 28, Ch. 1 n. 14, Pl. 6 n.
Rellini, U., 39, 40, Ch. 1 n. 5, n. 14, n. 32
Renard, M., 29, 294
Ribezzo, F., 31, 49, 51, 54, 68, 77, 195, 206, 220, Ch. 1 n. 16, n. 22, Ch. 10 n. 10, n. 11, Ch. 12 n. 17
Ricci, G., 28, Ch. 5 n. 8
Richardson, E. H., Ch. 5 n. 26, 294
Richardson, L., Jr, Ch. 5 n. 26
Richter, G. M. A., Ch. 9 n. 10, 296
Ridgway, D., Ch. 1 n. 10, n. 14, Ch. 4 n. 13, Ch. 5 n. 6, n. 46, Pl. 2 n., 300
Riegl, A., 167
Riis, P. J., 28, Ch. 4 n. 1, Ch. 8 n. 9, n. 20, Pl. 75 n., 296
Rittatore, F., Ch. 1 n. 13
Rix, H., 29, 136, 195, 203, Ch. 2 n. 17, Ch. 6 n. 6, n. 19, Ch. 10 n. 11, 272 (Additional Note)
Rodenwaldt, G., Ch. 8 n. 35
Rohlfs, G., Ch. 11 n. 10
Romanelli, P., Ch. 5 n. 11, Pl. 15 n., Pl. 68 n.
Roncalli, F., Ch. 5 n. 8, Pl. 59 n., 299
Rose, H. J., Ch. 7 n. 3
Rosenberg, A., 213, 223, Ch. 6 n. 2
Rosi, G., Ch. 5 n. 19, Pl. 29 n.
Rossi Danielli, L., Ch. 5 n. 18
Rumpf, A., Ch. 8 n. 28
Runes, M., 223
Russo, C. F., Ch. 12 n. 3
Ryberg, I. Scott, Ch. 5 n. 5

Säflund, G., 28, 43, 67, Ch. 1 n. 10, n. 14
Salmon, E. T., Ch. 1 n. 37, Ch. 4 n. 22, Ch. 5 n. 26, 296
Sambon, A., Ch. 9 n. 19
Sandars, N. K., Ch. 1 n. 12
Santangelo, M., 28, Ch. 4 n. 4
Santi, F., Ch. 5 n. 35
Sartori, F., Ch. 6 n. 17
Scarani, R., Ch. 4 n. 23
Schachermeyer, F., 29, 67, Ch. 2 n. 1
Schlegel, F., 25
Schmoll, U., Ch. 1 n. 21
Schuchhardt, C., 68

Schulten, A., Ch. 3 n. 2
Schulze, W., 203, 204
Scullard, H. H., Ch. 5 n. 4, n. 5, Pl. 15 n., Pl. 31 n., 294
Sergi, G., 39, Ch. 1 n. 4
Sestieri, C. P., Ch. 1 n. 14
Shaw, C., Ch. 5 n. 35
Shefton, B. B., Ch. 3 n. 3
Sittig, E., 215, Ch. 10 n. 5
Slotty, F., 29, 195, 212, Ch. 6 n. 21, Ch. 11 n. 24, Ch. 12 n. 8
Smith, H. R. W., Ch. 7 n. 31, 296
Sogliano, A., Ch. 4 n. 16
Solari, A., 28, 29, Ch. 5 n. 4, Ch. 6 n. 1 Ch. 9 n. 1, 295
Sommella, P., Ch. 5 n. 27
Sommella Mura, A., Ch. 5 n. 4
Sordi, M., Ch. 3 n. 12, Ch. 4 n. 24
Staccioli, R. A., Ch. 8 n. 10, Ch. 9 n. 8 Pl. 54 n., 299
Stefani, E., Ch. 5 n. 16
Stenico, A., Ch. 9 n. 12
Stjernquist, B., Ch. 4 n. 1
Stoltenberg, H. L., 195, Ch. 7 n. 9, Ch. 12 n. 13, n. 19
Strøm, I., Ch. 2 n. 16, 296
Strong, D., 294
Sundwall, J., 28, 43
Susini, G. C., Ch. 5 n. 37, Pl. 76 n.
Szilágyi, J. Gy., Ch. 4 n. 1

Talocchini, A., Ch. 5 n. 42
Taramelli, A., Ch. 3 n. 5
Täubler, E., Ch. 1 n. 3
Taylour, Lord William, Ch. 1 n. 10
Teitz, R. S., Pl. 33 n., Pl. 56 n., Pl. 73 n., 297
Terracini, B., Ch. 10 n. 10
Thimme, J., Ch. 8 n. 24
Thomas, H. L., Ch. 1 n. 11
Thomsen, V., 192
Threipland, L. M., Ch. 5 n. 6
Thulin, C. O., Ch. 7 n. 1, n. 12, n. 15, Ch. 8 n. 1, Ch. 9 n. 3
Torelli, M., Ch. 3 n. 11, Ch. 4 n. 19, Ch. 5 n. 12, Pl. 11 n., Pl. 15 n., Pl. 19 n., Pl. 101 n.
Torp, A., 29, 193, 194, 215, 220, 223
Toscanelli, N., Ch. 9 n. 18
Trautmann, E., Ch. 4 n. 31
Trendall, A. D., 300
Trombetti, A., 29, 49, 50, 68, 77, 194,

212, 213, 220, 223, Ch. 2 n. 19, Ch. 10 n. 10, Ch. 12 n. 19
Trump, D. H., Ch. 1 n. 10, 297

Undset, I., 27
Untermann, J., Ch. 1 n. 24

von Vacano, O. W., 29, Ch. 5 n. 27, 295
Vaccaro, A., Ch. 4 n. 15
Vagnetti, L., Ch. 1 n. 10, Ch. 5 n. 6, Pl. 67 n., 299
Vallet, G., Ch. 3 n. 16, Ch. 4 n. 13, Ch. 11 n. 2
Vermiglioli, G. B., 25, 192
Vetter, E., 29, 193, 195, 210, 223, Ch. 1 n. 25, Ch. 10 n. 11, Ch. 12 n. 8, n. 18, n. 19
Vighi, R., 28, Ch. 5 n. 8
Villard, F., Ch. 3 n. 16
Visconti, E., 25
Vitellius, L., 106

Wainwright, G. A., Ch. 2 n. 8
Walde, A., Ch. 11 n. 16
Walters, H. B., 298

Ward-Perkins, J. B., 67, Ch. 5 n. 2, n. 6, n. 45, Ch. 8 n. 10, Pl. 3 n., Pl. 24 n., Pl. 28 n., 296
Warren, L. Bonfante, Ch. 6 n. 8, n. 22
Weege, F., 28, Ch. 8 n. 28
Weickert, C., 28, Ch. 5 n. 19
Weinstock, S., Ch. 7 n. 1, n. 15, n. 16, Ch. 8 n. 2
Werner, R., Ch. 6 n. 14
Whatmough, J., Ch. 1 n. 9, n. 20
Whitehouse, R. D., Ch. 1 n. 10
Wickhoff, J., 28
Wilamowitz, U., Ch. 2 n. 25
Wilkins, J., Pl. 95 n.
Winckelmann, J. J., 25
Wolf, R. G., Ch. 11 n. 22
Woodhead, A. G., 297

Young, R. S., Ch. 2 n. 24

Zalesski, N. N., Ch. 3 n. 16, Ch. 4 n. 14, n. 23
Zambotti, P. Laviosa, Ch. 1 n. 8, n. 33
Zancani Montuoro, P., Ch. 8 n. 19
Zevi, F., Ch. 5 n. 6, Pl. 86 n.
Zielinski, T., Ch. 7 n. 18